LOCAL GOVERNMENT IN CANADA

Third Edition

LOCAL GOVERNMENT IN CANADA
Third Edition

C.R. Tindal

S. Nobes Tindal

McGraw-Hill Ryerson Limited

Toronto   Montreal   New York   Auckland   Bogotá   Caracas
Hamburg   Lisbon   London   Madrid   Mexico   Milan   New Delhi
Paris   San Juan   São Paulo   Singapore   Sydney   Tokyo

ISBN: 0-07-549726-3

1 2 3 4 5 6 7 8 9 0 W 9 8 7 6 5 4 3 2 1 0

Printed and bound in Canada

Care has been taken to trace ownership of copyright
material contained in this text. The publisher will gladly
take any information that will enable them to rectify any
reference or credit in subsequent editions.

Sponsoring Editor: Susan Erickson
Supervising Editor: Susan Calvert
Production Editor: Gail Marsden
Permissions Editor: Norma Christensen

Canadian Cataloguing in Publication Data

Tindal, C.R., date
    Local government in Canada

(McGraw-Hill Ryerson series in Canadian politics)
3rd ed.
Includes bibliographical references.
ISBN 0-07-549726-3

1. Local government – Canada.   2. Municipal government – Canada.   I. Tindal, S. Nobes, date.   II. Title.
III. Series.

JS1708.T55   1990   352.071   C90-093510-3

Table of Contents

Editor's Foreword

As metropolitan areas continue to grow rapidly and Canada becomes increasingly urbanized, the subject of local government acquires even greater significance than it has had in the past. In this century Canada has been transformed from a predominantly rural country to a highly urbanized polity. More than three-quarters of our population now live in urban areas of one kind or another. Since an increasing number of people depend on local governments for many vital services — such as fire and police protection, sanitation, education, welfare, and culture and recreation — and the demand for such services will likely grow with an aging population, local government has become not only more important to individuals but a big business as well. Total expenditures now run to something like fifty billion dollars a year.

For all these reasons books on local government are very pertinent and useful, especially when they are up-to-date, comprehensive, and analytical. The third edition of *Local Government in Canada* can claim all these qualifications. The Tindals have updated the contents of their very successful second edition, added new material, and rewritten some sections. They have added also several features that will be particularly helpful to students. Each chapter begins with a clear, brief statement of objectives and ends with a summary, and along the way boxed inserts have been added to highlight the contents.

The authors deal with both the history and process of local government in Canada. Part A traces the evolution of the institutions in the various provinces and recent relations with the federal government, while Part B explains the mechanics of governance and administration, describing structures, elections, policy-making, finances, personnel management, and citizen participation.

The book, however, is far from being merely descriptive. The Tindals analyze problems as they go and do not hesitate to state their opinions. Thus the new Chapter 7 that they have added is a ringing defence of politics at the local level. The authors also have some provocative things to say about the much-maligned property tax, which they do not believe is as regressive and outmoded as its critics allege.

The Tindals continue to be interesting and challenging in their final chapter. Summing up their views in "Retrospect and Prospect," they make a strong case for vigorous and forceful local governments. They believe that "municipalities need to be treated as a separate level of government, serving separate and legitimate purposes, not just as agents of the provincial government." Since decentralization is apt to increase, local governments will need to take greater control of their destinies. To do so, they will have to become more creative and aggressive, but that outcome will depend on a change in the attitude of the general public, which hitherto has been too apathetic. In the last analysis, therefore, responsibility lies with the citizens.

The Tindals cannot be accused of not doing their part. The third edition of *Local Government in Canada* lays out the framework of the matter clearly, analyzes it closely, and offers a number of challenging improvements.

Victoria College   Paul W. Fox
University of Toronto   General Editor
August, 1989.

Preface to the Third Edition

This edition retains its examination of the evolving structure of local government in Canada and expands its treatment of the political process through which that structure operates. The book is reorganized into two main sections, reflecting these twin themes.

Once again, we have benefited from a great deal of assistance and cooperation from academics in the field. Thanks are extended to Caroline Andrew of the University of Ottawa, Peter Boswell of Memorial University, Harley D'Entremont of the University of Moncton, Pat Jardine and Jack Novack of Dalhousie University, Harry Kitchen of Trent University, Warren Magnusson of University of Victoria, Andrew Sancton of the University of Western Ontario, David Siegel of Brock University, David Walker of the University of Winnipeg (and now the House of Commons), and Jean Wolfe of McGill University. The information and suggestions provided by George Betts of University of New Brunswick and Tom Plunkett of Queen's University are particularly appreciated.

Helpful information was also provided by Brian Walisser, Municipal Affairs Ministry of British Columbia, Reg Robson, Municipal Affairs Ministry of Manitoba, George Manios of the Ontario Ministry of Municipal Affairs, Daniel Ouimet, formerly of that Ministry and now C.A.O. of the City of Vanier, Shingai Nyajeski of the Department of Municipal Affairs in Nova Scotia, Gerald Hawkins of New Brunswick's Department of Municipal Affairs & Environment, and David Perry of the Canadian Tax Foundation.

We appreciate the assistance of Don Smeltzer of the Maritime Training Board and Michael Goldrick of York University for reviewing all or parts of the manuscript for the book and offering suggestions. As with both previous editions, Paul Fox read the entire manuscript and provided guidance and encouragement.

We are also indebted to the staff at McGraw-Hill Ryerson Limited, including Catherine O'Toole, Danelle D'Alvise, David Walker, Anne Ferguson, Clive Powell, Gail Marsden, Susan Calvert and especially Susan Erickson, for their cooperation and support.

Richard and Susan Tindal,
Inverary, Ontario
July, 1989

1 *Introduction*

Objectives:

1. To introduce the local government system in Canada, its fundamental representative and administrative roles, and the conflicting views about its effectiveness and value.
2. To outline the organization of the remainder of the text.

This book is concerned with the most prevalent, accessible level of government in Canada, arguably the most important level, and certainly the most neglected. Its prevalence is evident in the great number and variety of local governing bodies. There are over 4 000 incorporated municipalities in Canada, approximately half of these found in Ontario and Quebec. The specific classifications include cities, towns, villages, rural municipalities (also categorized as townships, parishes, and rural districts), counties (both single tier and upper tier), and regional and metropolitan municipalities.

In addition, there are various other local special purpose bodies that defy classification or even precise numbering. In Ontario alone, where the use of such local bodies has been most prevalent, it is estimated that there are at least 2 000 of these bodies of 70 different types. Common examples include police commissions, health units, conservation authorities, public utilities commissions, parks boards, and school boards.

The importance of local government stems, in part, from its role in the provision of services. While few people seem to be aware of it, a very wide range of services, programs, facilities, and regulations that largely shape our day to day lives are provided by local governments — albeit acting as a delivery agent for the provincial or federal government in a number of instances. To illustrate, consider the local government responsibilities identified in the 1977 Report of the Royal Commission on Metropolitan Toronto.

> Local governments provide roads, streetlights and sidewalks, and they operate buses, subways and streetcars. They regulate the taxi industry and control traffic movement and parking. Still in the field of transportation, they run airports and participate in the operation of port facilities.
>
> With respect to social services, local governments provide not only general welfare assistance but also day care centres, homes for the aged, counselling services, hostels and emergency shelters, and rent supplement programs. They also provide public housing, including rent-geared-to-income housing.

Local governments operate schools and libraries and provide or financially support art galleries, theatres, zoos, historic sites and museums. Parks are provided and facilities for such recreational activities as tennis, squash, track and field, swimming and golf.

Public health programs of local government have traditionally been concerned with the prevention and control of communicable diseases, the assurance of a safe water supply, and the maintenance of sanitary standards in such activities as the handling of food and private waste disposal. More recently there have been suggestions that public health activities will be broadened to deal with health problems caused by factors such as stress, drugs, poor nutrition, environmental hazards and the aging of the population.

Physical services provided by local governments include waterworks and sewer systems, land drainage and garbage collection and waste disposal. Planning policies and by-laws regulate how land may be developed. Industrial promotion and economic development activities are carried out, as are downtown revitalization programs. In addition to police and firefighters, the protective services of local government extend to ambulance service and an extensive use of municipal licensing powers.

Obviously, this wide range of services is not found in all localities of Canada but tends to be most prevalent in major urban centres. Nor is it suggested that provision of these services is problem-free. Indeed, questions are frequently asked about how efficiently local governments operate and, even more fundamentally, how they determine which services to provide.

BASIC ROLES LINKED:
PROVISION OF SERVICES
(ADMINISTRATIVE ROLE)
IN ACCORDANCE WITH
NEEDS AND WISHES OF LOCAL INHABITANTS
(REPRESENTATIVE ROLE)

This latter question, by directing attention to the way decisions are made, suggests a second sense in which local government is felt to be important. It is not just that local governments provide a wide range of services; they supposedly provide these services in accordance with the needs and preferences of their local inhabitants. Precisely because they are "local," local governments are familiar with local views and concerns, they are readily accessible, and they are sensitive and responsive to these concerns — or so this viewpoint suggests. The services that are provided are experienced directly by those living in the community, including the people making the decisions. Accordingly, they are well aware of the impact of these decisions, and are also readily available to any local inhabitants who might wish to express satisfaction or disapproval. For these reasons, it is argued, the various services provided by local government should be a reflection of the wishes of the local residents. In other words, local government is important because it is democratic in its operations.

Yet, dissatisfaction with the democratic role of local governments has been expressed almost since they were first established in Canada. In essence, local democracy was to be provided by concentrating the responsibilities of government in a council elected by the local inhabitants. In the ensuing years, however, and especially since the turn of the century, many responsibilities have been removed from council control and allocated to separate, appointed boards so as to "take the issue out of politics."

The apparent contradiction can be explained through a closer examination of what is meant by politics. In the broadest sense, politics might be defined as the process of attempting to influence the decisions of any authority entitled to make them. Seen in this light, the political process is evident in the activities of almost every decision-making organization, not just governments. However, particular concern is expressed about how these decisions are made by government because of their widespread public impact and because the nature of this decision-making process is supposedly an indication of how democratically the system operates.

For both of these reasons the political role of local governments should be especially important. As has been indicated, local governments provide a wide range of services that significantly influence the day to day life of the populace. They face conflicting demands for the allocation of their scarce resources. Because of the relatively small scale of operations of most municipalities, these allocation decisions are made in what has been termed a "goldfish-bowl" atmosphere — one supposedly highly sensitive to local views and concerns. Moreover, in the postwar period local governments have been called upon to deal with a growing number of controversial issues and to resolve these issues in the face of strongly expressed community concerns put forth by citizens and citizens' groups.

Yet the political role of local government has never been well defined or understood, is not especially well fulfilled, and has even been vigorously denounced as an inappropriate intrusion into the operations of local government! A major part of the problem is the fact that the terms *politics* and *political* are quite value-laden and are often given narrow, negative definition. To many people, local politics is undesirable because it is viewed as "a matter of unseemly and unprofitable squabbling, an opportunity for sectional interests to triumph over the public interest and, like all politics, become a dirty business."[1] Granted, such practices have been observed at the local level in Canada, but to abhor such practices should not be to deny the validity of a political role for local government.

This extreme response, however, was precisely what happened during the municipal reform era at the turn of the century. Advocating more efficient administration and the removal of all corruption, reformers called for the exclusion of politics from local government. Decisions should be made on objective, rational grounds. Municipal administrators should be free to provide services efficiently without political interference from the elected representatives — in part through the previously mentioned approach of transferring responsibilities from the elected council to an appointed board.

In attempting to eradicate the excesses of patronage and the pork barrel, the reformers were making a positive contribution. They were appalled by a situation in which the "public treasury was perceived as a basket of goodies, of uncertain origin, to be freely tapped by anyone who could and to the fullest extent possible."[2] But in denying any political role for local government, the reformers were misguided and harmful. Even if they perceived local government very narrowly as only concerned with service delivery, it is still necessary to decide "what services to deliver, in what quantities, and where, and such decisions cannot be made without some kind of political process."[3]

While this nonpolitical tradition of the reform era was never appropriate, it became particularly unacceptable in the postwar period. Many of the newer services provided by local governments were quite controversial, increasingly affecting the character of the neighbourhoods and the life style of the residents. The affected populace felt that their views and concerns were at least as important as the advice and recommendations that council might receive from their technical experts. The "best" decision was not pure and abstract, insulated from politics, but was a politi-

---

[1]   T.J. Plunkett and G.M. Betts, *The Management of Canadian Urban Government*, Kingston, Queen's University, 1978, p. 15.

[2]   Harold Kaplan, *Reform, Planning, and City Politics: Montreal, Winnipeg and Toronto*, Toronto, University of Toronto Press, 1982, p. 144.

[3]   Plunkett and Betts, *op. cit.*, p. 27.

cal decision based on a consideration of the views and concerns of the citizens involved.

However, even if this latter approach were recognized and attempted, a number of factors inhibit its prospects for success. Identifying local views and concerns is easier said than done. Local citizens' groups may or may not be representative of the views of the larger population. The majority of the residents of a municipality appear to pay very little attention to its activities, including at election time. There is a widespread feeling that voting isn't worth the effort, especially when municipal election campaigns are largely devoid of any discussion of specific local issues and alternatives, and when the voter must contend with multiple ballots (for head of council, for councillors, for school board trustees and, perhaps, for utility commissioners) that make an informed selection very difficult. In any event, how can concerned voters attempt to enforce accountability when no group within the municipal council is specifically responsible for providing leadership and initiating policies or for acting as an opposition and providing alternative suggestions — except in those few Canadian municipalities with some form of political party organization within council.

Structural limitations on public participation are also evident. Many municipalities have retained historical boundaries that bear little relation to the living patterns of today. Citizens are unlikely to take an active interest in the activities of their municipality if their normal circle of movement for work, shopping, and recreation embraces quite different — and usually larger — areas. Yet the consolidation of municipalities, which has taken place in many of the urban areas, and the expansion of professional staff, which has accompanied such "reforms", have produced large bureaucratic units of local government that also appear to discourage widespread public participation.

There is, of course, one other very important limitation on the ability of local governments to govern in accordance with the wishes of their local electorate. They also have a second major purpose that is, in K. G. Crawford's words, "to carry out the duties imposed upon local authorities by the provinces which have created them, and to which they are ultimately answerable."[4] Crawford went on to observe that while opinions differed as to which of these two purposes should be dominant, legally and constitutionally, if not politically, the latter must receive priority. Certainly it is impossible to understand the workings of local

---

[4] K. G. Crawford, *Canadian Municipal Government,* Toronto, University of Toronto Press, 1954, p. 3.

government today without reference to the complex network of inter-governmental relationships that exist, not only with provincial governments but also with the federal level. Indeed, one analysis of the state of municipal government concludes that various factors have caused local governments to adhere to their role as agents of the provincial government to the point where they are less and less able to fulfill their role as interpreters of the local scene. It offers the view that the two distinct purposes of local government specified by Crawford almost forty years ago have not survived intact — "what now exists may not be local government so much as a complex form of local administration."[5]

WHICH IS IT?
CONFLICTING VIEWS OF LOCAL GOVERNMENT

This assessment illustrates one of the many paradoxes surrounding the nature and operations of local government. It is praised as the foundation of democracy and yet dismissed as incapable of responding to local needs. Its services have been described as "the difference between savagery and civilization,"[6] and yet we hear constantly that our municipalities lack the resources to meet the challenges of urbanization, and the financial plight of local governments is likened to "Puppets on a Shoestring."[7]

Given these contradictions, how does one attempt a balanced assessment? This text will argue that the best approach is through an examination of the historical background and evolution of Canadian local government. How can one judge if modern municipal administrations are doing a particularly poor job of governing their cities and solving their policy problems except through historical comparisons?

A number of other important insights are provided by an historical perspective. It provides an awareness of the relevance and influence of urbanization from the very earliest beginnings of local government. Also prevalent from the beginning has been controversy and confusion about

---

[5] T.J. Plunkett and Katherine A. Graham, "Whither Municipal Government," in *Canadian Public Administration,* Winter 1982, p. 614.

[6] Quoted in Harold J. Laski, W. Ivor Jennings, and William Robson (eds.), *A Century of Municipal Progress, 1835–1935,* London, Allen and Unwin, 1935, p. 11.

[7] The title of a brief prepared by the Federation of Canadian Municipalities, April 28, 1976, in response to the findings of a Tri-Level Task Force Report on Public Finance in Canada.

the political role of local government and its appropriateness. Moreover, the organizational structure and governmental machinery found in most municipalities today still reflect historical developments. Many boundaries have not changed since their original delineation. Such internal governmental arrangements as the use of executive committees and chief administrative officers also derive from an earlier period. If one is to understand the present institutions of local government, therefore, it is necessary to appreciate how and why they arose and evolved.

An historical perspective is also helpful in any assessment of local government relationships with the senior levels of government. While the constitutional division of responsibilities merits much of the emphasis it receives, it is important to remind ourselves that many municipalities were incorporated before Confederation and had already experienced a period of considerable operating independence before becoming "creatures of the provinces." In addition to the formal legal arrangements, therefore, a number of other political and practical considerations have shaped the relationships that evolved between municipalities and the provincial level. These latter considerations are also evident in the development — in spite of the constitutional provisions — of federal-local and tri-level relationships.

In addition to the emphasis on the evolving *structure* of local government, however, this book is also very much concerned with the *process* of government. It is all very well to trace the evolution of the local government structure, but it is equally important to examine how it is being used, for what purposes, and with what effectiveness. Accordingly, a second major emphasis of this book concerns the political process within which the local government system operates and, more specifically, the way in which policy decisions are made and resources allocated.

Organization of the Text

All of the factors introduced above will be dealt with in this book. The material is organized into two sections. **Part A** traces the origins and evolution of the local government system. The historical foundations are traced in **Chapter 2**, and **Chapter 3** examines the turn of the century reform era and its contribution to the machinery and operating philosophy of local government. **Chapter 4** continues the chronological evolution through the twentieth century and gives particular attention to the impact of postwar urbanization. The various local government restructuring and reform programs introduced in response to the pressures of growth and change are examined in **Chapter 5**, which concludes with a summary of the present local government system and its predominant features. No examination of the local government system would be complete without some consideration of the senior levels of government with which municipalities have become increasingly intertwined. Therefore, **Chapter 6** examines both provincial-local and federal-local and tri-level relations. In addition to illustrating the intergovernmental context within which local governments must operate, the chapter attempts to demonstrate the importance of local government for the senior levels, and the interdependent nature of the present relationships among our levels of government.

In **Part B**, the focus moves inside the municipality to consider how we are governed. **Chapter 7**, which is new to this edition, serves as a bridge between the two sections of the book. It provides a considerably expanded treatment of the political role of local government, and touches on such aspects as the roles of councillors and staff, of interest groups, and of the media. It considers why there has been such an antipathy to politics at the local level and makes a case for political decisions, arguing that they are not only appropriate but highly desirable. **Chapter 8** outlines the basic municipal machinery — including reformed structures that have been introduced — and assesses their adequacy. Profiles of developments in four of Canada's largest urban centres provide the basis for the discussion in **Chapter 9** of the activities of citizens' groups and political parties at the local level, and of the links between local government and the property development industry.

Building on this foundation, the next three chapters explore the operations of municipalities in making and implementing policy decisions. **Chapter 10** begins with a somewhat idealized version of the policy-making process and then considers various constraints on policy making in practice. A number of suggestions are offered for improving the policy-making process. Financial management is examined in **Chapter 11**, with particular reference to the importance of a broadened budget process that gives more attention to the initial determination of priorities and the followthrough to measure results. **Chapter 12** notes the changing nature of municipal management and considers several aspects of personnel management. Staff training and development are singled out, and suggestions offered for improving performance appraisals. Overall, these latter chapters are intended to demonstrate how the structure and machinery of municipal government analyzed earlier in the text actually performs in the formulation and implementation of policies.

The concluding Chapter (13) of the text reinforces the evolutionary approach followed throughout by considering how Canadian local government is likely to respond to its future challenges in light of its past experience and present performance.

A
The Evolving Local Government Structure

2 *The Foundations of Local Government*

Objectives:

1. To trace the historical evolution of the municipal government system in the provinces and territories of Canada.
2. To identify the dominant influences in shaping the particular structures that evolved.
3. To describe the main features of the municipal systems originally established.

Introduction

How did our local governments evolve, and why in the particular form that we find in Canada? One answer — that is correct as far as it goes — is that they were shaped by decisions made by the provincial governments to which they owe their very existence (and by the federal government in the case of municipalities in the Yukon and Northwest Territories).

This explanation is based on the constitutional legal arrangements provided by the British North America Act (now the Constitution Act). While both the national and provincial levels of government were given separately defined spheres of operation within which each would act relatively autonomously, local governments were accorded no such status. Instead, local governments were only mentioned in the British North America Act as one of the responsibilities allocated to the provinces. It follows, therefore, that from a strict legal perspective, local governments only exist to the extent that the provincial governments have seen fit to provide for them. The types of municipality and their boundaries, responsibilities, and finances must be authorized through provincial legislation. But since provincial governments are responsible to their legislatures and their electorates, they are unlikely to create municipal institutions that are too out of step with public views and attitudes concerning local government. In any event, the basic features of Canadian local government evolved before Confederation, and the new provincial governments established in 1867 inherited existing municipal institutions and/or operating philosophies of how local governments ought to operate. We must, therefore, look beyond the legal explanation, important though it is.

EARLY INFLUENCES:
PROVINCIAL DECISIONS
SETTLEMENT PATTERNS
POLITICAL VALUES AND TRADITIONS OF SETTLERS

The earliest local governments in Canada evolved in response to the settlement of the country. As the population increased, and particularly as it became concentrated in the limited urban centres of the early years, it was necessary to administer a growing variety of programs and regulations. With pockets of population scattered in a vast area, and with very rudimentary forms of transportation and communication, the responsibilities could not be handled directly by a centralized colonial government.

While some form of local administration was, therefore, inevitable for quite practical reasons, the particular form that did evolve was strongly influenced by the political values and traditions of the settlers of this country and the beliefs that they held or developed about local government. In this connection, the extent to which this country was settled through immigration was a significant factor, especially because of the belief in local self-government held by many of the United Empire Loyalists who entered this country in the years during and after the American War of Independence.

These and other influences will be evident throughout this chapter as we trace the historical evolution of local government in each of the provinces. No standard time frame is employed; rather, developments in each province are described up to the point where the basic municipal structure was established. Chronological considerations are evident, however, in the sequence of provinces. We begin with Central Canada because a comprehensive system of municipal government was first established there — in Upper Canada (Ontario) — and this system influenced the municipal institutions subsequently created in a number of other provinces. The chapter then examines developments in the Atlantic Provinces, the Western Provinces and, finally, the Northern Territories.

Central Canada

Local government made its first, although somewhat brief, appearance in Canada under the French regime in the settlements of Montreal, Quebec, and Trois Rivières. As early as 1647 a mayor, councillors, and syndics d'habitations (who made representations on behalf of local residents to the provincial authorities) were elected in Quebec. This practice was strongly discouraged by the very authoritarian and centralized home government in France that felt that it was a dangerous innovation. In 1663 the mayor and aldermen of Quebec resigned. The whole issue of local self-government was allowed to lapse until 1760 and the advent of British rule.

After the British conquest, all government was vested in the military and subsequently in a governor and an appointed council. In 1763 a proclamation was issued that promised to introduce English law and the English system of freehold land grants in Quebec, in order to encourage English settlement. In the following year the Governor-General did establish the ancient English system of local justices of the peace meeting in the Courts of Quarter Sessions for the three districts around Montreal, Quebec, and Trois-Rivières for the trial of unimportant matters.

Despite the rule by British governors and the promise of the benefits of English law, little occurred to interrupt the traditional running of the affairs of Quebec. There was little interference with the Roman Catholic Church, the Court of Common Pleas continued to administer French civil law, and land was still granted through the feudal French system, "en fief et seigneurie." The Quebec Act, passed in 1774, formally recognized this situation and also extended the Quebec boundaries west to the Great Lakes and Mississippi River and north to Labrador.

The American Revolution broke out soon after and precipitated a flow of United Empire Loyalists to Nova Scotia and the western part of Quebec. The peak years of this immigration were 1782-1783 when approximately 10 000 arrived in the Saint John area of the Bay of Fundy, 25 000 arrived in Nova Scotia (doubling its previous population), and 20 000 arrived in the unsettled areas around Lake Ontario, particularly at Kingston, Toronto, and Niagara.[1]

LOYALIST INFLUX:
MAJOR IMPETUS FOR LOCAL GOVERNMENT
BROUGHT TRADITIONS OF LOCAL GOVERNMENT
INCREASED POPULATION AND SERVICE DEMANDS

These immigrants came chiefly from New York and the New England colonies where they had enjoyed a certain measure of local self-govern-

---

[1] K.G. Crawford, *Canadian Municipal Government,* Toronto, University of Toronto Press, 1954, p. 21.

ment. They brought with them the tradition of local government through the town meeting. Under this system, selectmen (councillors) were elected at the annual town meeting by the inhabitants residing within one-half mile of the meeting house. These selectmen were to oversee the affairs of the town between meetings. In theory their appointment and actions were to be approved by the governor, but in practice they operated independently of the central authorities.

Upper Canada (Ontario)

Needless to say, these Loyalists were unhappy under French civil law, especially the system of land grants under the seigneurial system, and the limited local autonomy. There soon were numerous petitions from the Loyalists around Lake Ontario for some form of local courts and adminstration, English civil law, and separation from that area of Quebec that was east of Montreal. Because of population growth pressures, but much against their better judgment, the British acquiesced. In 1787 they passed an ordinance dividing the western settlements, previously a part of the District of Montreal, into four new districts with various appointed officials including justices of the peace who constituted the Courts of Quarter Sessions. The Quarter Sessions assumed judicial, legislative, and administrative responsibilities including maintaining the peace, regulating domestic animals running at large, the conduct of licensed taverns, the appointment of minor officials, and the superintending of highways.[2] As new problems arose, the Quarter Sessions, which were the only official agency dealing with local matters, were simply given more powers to deal with them.

However, this new system proved to be unworkable under the French feudal laws and institutions that had been established with the Quebec Act, and pressure continued for a separate province with English civil law and an English system of land tenure. This continuing pressure finally culminated in the Constitutional Act of 1791 (also referred to as the Canada Act).

The main provisions of the act were:

1.   The creation, from the province of Quebec, of the provinces of Upper and Lower Canada, with the Ottawa River roughly as the dividing line.

---

2 *Ibid.*, p. 23.

2.   The provision of a government for each province consisting of a British Lieutenant-Governor, an appointed executive council, an appointed legislative council, and an elected legislative assembly.
3.   The use of English law and land tenure in Upper Canada.
4.   The allotment of land as clergy reserves for the support of the Protestant clergy.

Lord Dorchester, then Governor-General, was reluctant to approve the Constitutional Act because he felt that the Loyalists would be safer under French rather than British law since, in his view, too free an indulgence in British political institutions had led to the American Revolution. Therefore the act contained certain precautions against the rise of democratic institutions such as the establishment of an hereditary political aristocracy (through the appointed councils) and the establishment of an episcopal state church (clergy reserves).

Both Lord Dorchester and Lord Simcoe, the first Lieutenant-Governor of Upper Canada, strongly discouraged any form of local government. To this end surveys were to be of royal seigniories and not townships, and they were to be numbered and not named as was customary, to discourage any strong attachment to a particular place. However, the Loyalists had already set up town meetings and designated their settlements and townships named after King George and his family, even before the Constitutional Act was passed.

In 1792 Simcoe divided Upper Canada into counties for militia purposes and for the election of representatives to the newly created assembly. He was very keen to develop an aristocracy in an effort to reproduce the highly classed society found in England. From this privileged class he planned to appoint his executive council to oversee the actions of the assembly. He therefore promoted half-pay army officers as candidates in the first provincial election, most of whom were rejected by the voters in favour of men of lower classes. Instead of heeding this indication of popular thought and giving up his plans, Simcoe redoubled his efforts to eradicate all democratic tendencies. In time an aristocracy known as the Family Compact became organized around the executive branch of the provincial government. This group had developed both family and economic ties throughout the province.[3] Its members felt it was their duty to "guard the body politic from the corrupting influences

---

[3]   In Lower Canada the Family Compact had a counterpart known as the Chateau Clique with whom it also had family and economic ties. An elite group surrounding the Lieutenant-Governor, such as the Family Compact and Chateau Clique, was found in most of the provinces.

of republicanism" and fought all efforts at establishing any kind of responsible government at any level.[4]

On the other hand, the Loyalists, who constituted most of the population of the province, felt that they had proven their loyalty to the Crown by fleeing the rebellious colonies and therefore deserved to have local self-rule. Perhaps it is not surprising then that the first bill introduced in the first session of the legislative assembly of Upper Canada was "to authorize town meetings for the purpose of appointing divers parish officers." Although not passed in that session, it was passed in 1793 as the Parish and Town Officers Act. This act permitted annual town meetings[5] to appoint a town clerk, assessors, a tax collector, road overseers and fence viewers, a poundkeeper, and town wardens. The only legislative authority the town meeting had was to fix the height of fences and to regulate animals running at large. An assessment act was also passed in 1793 to provide for raising money to pay for the costs of court and jail houses, paying officers' fees, and building roads.

By the turn of the century, urban concerns of sanitation, streets, education, welfare, and local police were becoming sufficiently pressing that the powers of the justices of the peace had to be extended.

A severe fire in Kingston in 1812 persuaded central authorities that some action was needed, and in 1816 an act to regulate the police[6] was passed for Kingston. This act gave the magistrates the power to make and publish rules and regulations for the safety and convenience of the inhabitants and to finance local improvements through a special tax. By the end of the year, Kingston had fourteen rules that covered such areas as streets, slaughterhouses, weights and measures, and animals running at large.

Another potentially important event in 1816 was the passage of the first Public School Act. This act enabled local residents to meet together to elect three trustees who were to hire a teacher and authorize school textbooks. This was the first example of true local self-government, whereby local people could elect representatives to administer a local need. Unfortunately, this was not a successful attempt at local government because of the lack of funds and experienced trustees.

---

[4]   Adam Shortt, *Municipal Government in Ontario, An Historical Sketch*, University of Toronto studies, History and Economics, Vol. II, No. 2, p.8.

[5]   In Ontario, town meetings were actually township meetings.

[6]   Use of police in this sense meant regulation, discipline, and control of a community.

**WAR OF 1812
FOLLOWED BY WAVE OF URBANIZATION
INCREASED PRESSURE FOR LOCAL GOVERNMENT**

The end of the War of 1812 in North America and the Napoleonic Wars in Europe saw the beginning of a new wave of immigration from the British Isles. Between 1815 and 1850 approximately 800 000 came to British North America, the great bulk of whom settled in Upper Canada. This population growth magnified the already existing urban problems and petitioning continued for some form of municipal government. In 1828 Belleville applied to be incorporated as a town. The Legislative Council rejected this application saying that:

> Since men do not like to be forced, they are pretty certain to elect only such persons as will not make effective rules or adequately enforce them; hence in the interest of efficient administration, such innovations must be discouraged.[7]

Despite this setback for Belleville, in 1832 the legislature capitulated and created a distinct corporate body in the President and Board of Police of the town of Brockville. This body was, in essence, the first form of elected municipal council and it assumed responsibility for all of the local government functions previously undertaken by the Quarter Sessions, with the justices of the peace retaining only their judicial functions within Brockville. This movement to representative local government proved to be popular. In 1834 York was created the self-governing city of Toronto, and by 1838 there were eight police towns and two cities.

While the urban areas of Upper Canada were gaining more local self-government, the rural areas were still functioning under the Parish and Town Officers Act with the magistrates of the Quarter Sessions in almost total control of local affairs. Reform newspapers of the time often charged that many magistrates were unfit, intemperate, and ready to stir up the mob against reformers.[8] The magistrates decided which local works were to be carried out (often ignoring areas in which they had no personal interest) and how much tax revenue was to be raised. In 1835 the assembly came under the control of a reform group that produced a report stating that magistrates were half-pay officers and strangers who

---

[7] Shortt, *op. cit.,* p. 19.

[8] Fred Landon, *Western Ontario and the American Frontier,* Toronto, McClelland and Stewart Limited, 1967, p. 223.

often became members of the Family Compact.[9] Similar conditions existed in the other provinces and the unrest culminated in Upper and Lower Canada in the Rebellion of 1837.

After the Rebellion, the Earl of Durham was appointed to investigate the insurrection particularly and the general state of government in all of the provinces. Durham produced a comprehensive report dealing with the conditions in British North America, and of particular importance for our purposes are his recommendations dealing with local government. He wrote that "municipal institutions of local self-government ... are the foundations of Anglo-Saxon freedom and civilization."[10] Further he stated: "The latter want of municipal institutions giving the people any control over their local affairs, may indeed be considered as one of the main causes of the failure of representative government and of the bad administration of the country."[11] Durham recommended that the two Canadas be reunited and that local matters should be looked after by municipal bodies of a much smaller size than the province.

DURHAM REPORT:
EMPHASIZED IMPORTANCE OF LOCAL GOVERNMENTS
"FOUNDATIONS OF FREEDOM AND CIVILIZATION"

Governor-General Sydenham, who replaced Durham in 1840, recognized the importance of the recommendations in Durham's report and he wrote to the Colonial Secretary:

> Since I have been in these Provinces I have become more and more satisfied that the capital cause of the misgovernment of them is to be found in the absence of Local Government, and the consequent exercise by the assembly of powers wholly inappropriate to its functions.[12]

Sydenham also sent the Colonial Secretary a draft bill for union of the Canadas that incorporated Durham's recommendations. Unfortunately at this time Durham had fallen into personal unpopularity and the Colonial Office considered the Family Compact and the Chateau Clique as the

---

[9]   John M. McEvoy, *The Ontario Township*, University of Toronto studies, Politics, 1st series, No. 1, 1889, p. 22.

[10]   Gerald M. Craig, (ed.), *Lord Durham's Report*, Toronto, McClelland and Stewart Limited, 1963, p. 60.

[11]   *Ibid.*, p. 67.

[12]   Landon, *op. cit.*, p. 223.

loyal heart of the country.[13] The principle of responsible government and the clauses on local government were dropped from the Union Act introduced and passed by the English Parliament.

However, Lord Sydenham persisted. In 1841 he persuaded the new Canadian legislature to pass an act that established an elected district council to take over the administrative authority formerly exercised by the Courts of Quarter Sessions in rural areas. There were no drastic changes in the general way that local government was carried on; the annual town meeting still elected various officers and passed town laws. But it also elected one or two district councillors from each township. The head of the district council, the warden, was appointed by the Governor-General, although subsequently the councils were given the right to choose their own warden. The councils were given responsibility for roads, municipal officers, taxing, justice, education, and welfare. Their expenses could be met by tolls or taxes on real or personal property or both. The Governor-General could disallow any by-laws and could dissolve any or all of the district councils.

DISTRICT COUNCILS ACT:
COURTS OF QUARTER SESSIONS ABANDONED
50 YEARS EARLIER THAN IN ENGLAND

The District Councils Act is perhaps even more important than any succeeding act because it was the first real break with the system of local government by Courts of Quarter Sessions and it preceded by almost 50 years the abandonment of this system in England.[14] While it was too radical for conservative elements in the legislature and not radical enough for the reformers, it did provide for a transition period in the rural areas between no local self-government and full local self-government. The central authorities retained much power because it was genuinely felt that local people would not be able to manage their own affairs.

Despite initial fears, the first district councillors were apparently fairly capable people who were able to stimulate the development of their townships because of their knowledge of local needs. By far the most important functions were the construction and repair of roads and bridges and the laying out and creating of school districts. The councils

---

[13] Thomas H. Raddall, *The Path of Destiny*, Toronto, Doubleday and Company, Inc., 1957, p. 31.

[14] Crawford, *op. cit.*, p. 31.

were hampered however by problems with assessment, provincial control, and scarce finances; problems that persist to this day. It has been written of the revenues available to district councils that:

> These were paltry sums for the needs of large districts, and it is quite certain that the very light direct taxation on which Canadians long prided themselves was a rather important factor in the backward condition of the country for so many years.[15]

In 1843 the Baldwin or Municipal Act was introduced, although because of a rupture with the Governor-General it was not passed until 1849. A primary function of the act was the consolidation of all municipal legislation under one measure. It built upon the District Councils Act while extending certain powers. The Baldwin Act differed in two major respects: (1) the county rather than the district became the upper tier of municipal government, and (2) for the first time townships were recognized as a rural unit of municipal government. As well, the act established villages, towns, and cities as urban municipal units. Cities and separated towns were not a part of the county for municipal government purposes. This municipal system established in 1849 has endured to the present in many areas of Ontario and, as will be seen, even the reformed structures introduced in the past couple of decades are essentially modified county systems.

Lower Canada (Quebec)

It will be recalled that under the French regime the province of Quebec enjoyed little or no autonomy and the first attempts at local government were strongly discouraged. This was undoubtedly because of the extent of local control by central authorities and the lack of a French tradition of local self-rule. The British conquest and takeover in the 1760s made little impact on this situation, although by 1764 the Quebec grand jury petitioned for regulations regarding markets, schools, and poor houses. In 1777 an ordinance was passed to "empower the Commissioners of the Peace to regulate the Police of the Towns of Quebec and Montreal for a limited time."[16] But this must have proven inadequate since both Quebec

---

[15] Adam Shortt and Arthur G. Doughty (Gen. eds.), *Canada and Its Provinces, A History of the Canadian People and Their Institutions,* Toronto, Glasgow, Brook and Company, 1914, Vol. XVIII, p. 437.

[16] *Ibid.,* Vol. XV, p. 301.

and Montreal petitioned for incorporation because of the bad conditions existing in the towns. In 1799 districts were established under justices of the peace to supervise roads and bridges, and by 1807 a market was established in Montreal under the magistrates.

In Lower Canada, as in Upper Canada, government by the magistrates grew to be very unpopular. A citizen meeting in Montreal in 1828 expressed the need for an improved local administration

> ... to cope with police and financial problems of the prosperous town, the long neglected harbour, the insanitary conditions of surrounding swamps, and the lack of a general and effectually prosecuted plan of improvements.[17]

It was not until 1832 that Quebec and Montreal were granted charters that enabled the citizens to elect a mayor and two aldermen per ward. But these provisions expired in 1836 and were not renewed until after 1840 because of the political turmoil caused by the 1837 Rebellion.

PROGRESS TOWARD LOCAL GOVERNMENT MUCH SLOWER IN LOWER CANADA

Although Lower Canada was subject to almost the same urban pressures as Upper Canada, the first 80 years of British rule saw little progress in the establishment of local government. Lord Durham made the following observation on Lower Canada in 1839:

> In fact, beyond the walls of Quebec all regular administration of the country appeared to cease; and there literally was hardly a single public officer in the civil government except in Montreal and Three Rivers, to whom any order could be directed.[18]

Thus the need for some system of municipal government was apparent. In 1840, under the guidance of Lord Sydenham, an ordinance was passed providing for a system of local government that in many respects resembled the district councils established soon after in Upper Canada. Lower Canada was divided into districts that were to be governed by an elected council and an appointed warden. Another ordinance passed at the same time provided for the election of a clerk, assessors, tax collector, surveyors, overseers of roads and the poor,

---

[17] *Ibid.,* p. 304.
[18] *Ibid.,* p. 290.

fence viewers, drain inspectors, and poundkeepers. Townships and parishes with sufficient population were constituted corporate bodies and elected two councillors each to the district councils. Although the district councils were given the power of taxation, much of the real power remained with the governor.

Both of the 1840 ordinances proved to be unpopular in Lower Canada. The execution and deportation of rebels of the 1837 Rebellion caused resentment and mistrust, and the people were especially wary of Lord Sydenham and his motives. The Union Act itself was unpopular and local government was seen as another means of oppression. But perhaps the most unpalatable measure was the power of taxation that, except for customs duties, had previously been unknown in Lower Canada. Therefore, it is not surprising that in 1845 an act was passed that repealed both ordinances and constituted each township or parish a body corporate with an elected council with most of the duties of the district councils.

• TABLE 1 •
HISTORICAL HIGHLIGHTS: CENTRAL CANADA

Ontario

1763	British rule of Quebec begins
1774	Quebec Act
1782–83	United Empire Loyalists immigrate
1791	Constitutional Act
1793	Parish & Town Officers Act
1816	Passage of Public School Act
	Police regulations in Kingston
1832	Board of Police in Brockville
1837	Rebellion and Durham's Report
1840–41	District Councils Act
1849	Baldwin (Municipal) Act

Quebec

1777	Ordinance regulating the police of Quebec and Montreal
1832–36	Quebec City and Montreal granted charters of incorporation
1840	System similar to District Councils
1845	Townships and parishes incorporated
1847	Townships and parishes abolished in favour of county government
1855	Lower Canada Municipal & Road Act

In 1847 a county system roughly based on the district councils was established. This system lasted until 1855 when the Lower Canada Municipal and Road Act was passed and became the foundation of

Quebec municipal institutions. This act established parishes, townships, towns, and villages, while retaining the county level as an upper tier unit. The heads of the local councils sat on the county council and chose their own warden. Each level could appoint the officers it felt were necessary and could levy taxes. Cities continued to be provided for by special charters rather than being incorporated under the provisions of the general act. This system remained in effect with minor changes until the turn of the century.

Atlantic Provinces

The development of municipal institutions in the Atlantic provinces initially paralleled that in Ontario. In the early 1700s the area known as Acadia was ceded by France to Britain. The area soon became known as Nova Scotia and gradually people from New England spread north and settled in the new province. These settlers brought with them a tradition of local government through the town meeting, although officially local government was to be carried on by the Courts of Quarter Sessions and a grand jury.

After the American Revolution, a wave of Loyalists migrated to the area, this time less from New England than from New York, New Jersey, Pennsylvania, and the South. The Southern Loyalists brought with them a different tradition of local government based on the classed society of the American South in which the Courts of Quarter Sessions discharged local government functions and the governor appointed local officials. Because of anti-American feelings caused by the Revolution, the New England Loyalists were unsuccessful in promoting local self-rule. Despite dissatisfaction with corrupt practices of certain magistrates, the system of the Courts of Quarter Sessions was to prevail for over 100 years.

WHY SLOW EVOLUTION?
FEAR OF TAXATION
LESS NECESSARY IN COMPACT AREA
PUBLIC APATHY

At this point, developments in the Atlantic provinces proceeded on a different course from those in Ontario. Far from fighting for local municipal institutions, many Loyalists actively discouraged their development. Many reasons have been suggested for this attitude. They include the feeling that the town meeting had contributed to the revolutionary tendencies of the Americans, a fear of increased taxation, a concern that local officials would lose patronage, and public apathy. In addition, the compactness of the area and the availability of cheap water transportation rendered road construction, one of the major municipal functions, less important. The developments in each province will now be briefly examined.

Nova Scotia

Early local government in Nova Scotia was provided by Courts of Quarter Sessions established by the British authorities around 1750. A wave of immigration from New England at the beginning of the 1760s brought settlers accustomed to the town meeting form of local government. The colonial authorities were unwilling to consider such a democratic approach, especially after the American War of Independence. It wasn't until 1841 that the first municipal incorporation occurred, with the granting of a charter to Halifax.

However, after the introduction of responsible government in 1848 the authorities showed more willingness to allow local government. Legislation permitting the incorporation of counties was enacted in 1855, and the following year the incorporation of townships was authorized. Ironically, now that the right to local government was finally granted, Nova Scotians did not exercise it. According to Higgins, the early enthusiasm waned with the realization that incorporation would bring with it higher taxation.[19]

However, the provincial government was determined to shift some of the financial burden for local services on to local residents, and this led to the 1879 County Incorporation Act. The rural areas of the province were incorporated as counties or districts, single tier municipalities governed by a warden and an elected council. Urban areas were dealt with in the Towns Incorporation Act of 1888, which stipulated geographic and population requirements that would enable a town to apply for a charter of incorporation. (Eight such towns had already been incorporated by charter prior to the passage of the statute.) These provisions for separate rural and urban municipalities have remained the basis for the Nova Scotia system to this day.

---

[19] Donald J.H. Higgins, *Local and Urban Politics in Canada,* Toronto, Gage, 1986, pp. 39–40.

Prince Edward Island

In 1769 Prince Edward Island separated from Nova Scotia. Two years earlier the island had been divided into counties, parishes, and townships for judicial purposes and for the election of representatives to the provincial legislature, but these areas were never used as municipal units. Indeed, there wasn't any obvious need for municipal government, or even for a decentralization of the colonial administration, given the small size and tiny population of Prince Edward Island.

The first municipal government appeared in 1855 with the incorporation of Charlottetown as a city. In 1870 an act was passed that enabled the resident householders of a town or village to petition the provincial authorities to allow the election of three or more wardens who could appoint local officers and pass by-laws with regard to finance and police matters. Summerside was incorporated as a town in 1875 but, presumably because of the very small population of most settlements, only six more towns had been incorporated by the time the procedure fell into disuse, in 1919. It was abolished in 1950.

P.E.I. SYSTEM LIMITED:
COVERS ONLY HALF OF POPULATION
AND ONE-QUARTER OF AREA
PROVINCE PROVIDES
MANY LOCAL SERVICES

Limited as it is, that constitutes the basic municipal system in Prince Edward Island. Close to half of the province's population and about three-quarters of its area are not municipally organized, and the provincial government continues to provide many of the usual local government services for much of the province.[20] Granted, some 30 villages have been established since the passage of the Village Services Act of 1950, but these are not municipalities. Instead of elected councils they are governed by commissioners appointed by the provincial government. Given the compactness of the island and its still relatively small population (122 506 in 1981), no major changes are anticipated in what has been a very stable municipal structure.

---

[20] *Ibid.*, p. 43.

New Brunswick

Fifteen years after Prince Edward Island separated from Nova Scotia, New Brunswick followed suit — the break being precipitated by an influx of United Empire Loyalists. The following year, 1785, Saint John was incorporated as a city, preceding by almost fifty years the creation of cities in the rest of Canada. Elsewhere in the colony, however, local government was carried on by the Courts of Quarter Sessions and a grand jury. The local citizenry, according to Higgins, seems to have been largely indifferent to the idea of local self-government.[21] This attitude has been partly attributed to the smaller population of Loyalists who came from New England and had thus experienced local government. However, Whalen rejects this viewpoint, contending that only about 7% of the Loyalists came from the Southern Colonies with their system of Quarter Sessions and that, in any event, even the Loyalists from New England made little demand for more democracy at the local level.[22] Certainly the substantial French population of the province, with their tradition of centralism, did not push for local government.

> IMPETUS FROM CENTRE:
> LOCAL CITIZENS INDIFFERENT
> TO LOCAL GOVERNMENT
> CENTRAL AUTHORITIES
> WISHED TO AVOID LOCAL
> SQUABBLES AND TO
> SHIFT EXPENDITURES

Interestingly, much of the impetus for the incorporation of municipalities came from the central authorities who were concerned about "reducing the time consumed on endless debates and squabbles over parish and county issues in the legislature"[23] and anxious to shift a growing expenditure burden. Finally, in 1851 an act was passed for the incorporation of counties, but its provisions were permissive and only six counties were established over the next three decades. How-

[21] *Ibid.*, p. 40.
[22] H. J. Whalen, *The Development of Local Government in New Brunswick*, Fredericton, 1963, Chapter Two.
[23] *Ibid.*, p. 20.

ever, the Municipalities Act of 1877 made county incorporation mandatory, thus bringing the entire population and area of the province under municipal government. The county system was two-tiered like that in Ontario, but differed in that councillors from the rural areas were directly elected to county council while all urban areas, except Fredericton, were represented at the county level usually by ex-officio members.

During this period a number of urban communities sought corporate status. Fredericton had received its charter in 1848, over 60 years after the first urban incorporation in Saint John. By 1896 nine towns had been established by separate charter. In that year the Town Incorporation Act was passed providing for a uniform system for the creation of towns with an elected council consisting of a mayor and aldermen.

The basic municipal system of New Brunswick was established in this 1896 statute along with the 1877 Municipalities Act. Cities each have their own separate charters of incorporation and a 1920 act provided for the incorporation of villages. As discussed in Chapter 5, however, a major reorganization of local government in New Brunswick begun in 1967 resulted in the abolition of county governments and a number of other major changes.

Newfoundland

The development of municipal institutions in Newfoundland has been a slow and arduous process, attributed to several factors.[24] The settlements that developed in the early years were numerous but geographically isolated from each other, generally quite limited in population, and financially unable to support any form of local government. Moreover, since Newfoundlanders only gained the right to own property in 1824, they jealously guarded this right against the taxation that would inevitably come with local government.

WHY SLOW DEVELOPMENT?
STRONG OPPOSITION TO PROPERTY TAX
ISOLATION FROM DEVELOPMENTS ELSEWHERE
LITTLE APPARENT NEED

---

[24] Higgins, *op. cit.,* pp. 33–34.

Newfoundland, because of its geographic isolation, was not influenced by the development of municipal government elsewhere; nor did its early settlers have prior experience with such a system. In any event, there was little apparent need for municipal government in much of the province. Transportation needs were partly served by water and the central government provided services such as roads that were provided at the local level in other provinces.

• TABLE 2 •
HISTORICAL HIGHLIGHTS: ATLANTIC PROVINCES

General

1713	Nova Scotia granted to Britain
1765	Government by Quarter Sessions
1769	P.E.I. separated from Nova Scotia

New Brunswick

1784	New Brunswick separated from Nova Scotia
1785	Saint John incorporated as a city
1877	Municipalities Act
1896	Town Incorporation Act

Nova Scotia

1841	Halifax received charter
1879	General Municipal Act
1888	Town Incorporation Act

Newfoundland

1888	St. John's created a town
1949	Joined Confederation
	Passed general local government act

After some unsuccessful attempts, St. John's was created a town in 1888, but once again the impetus was not the demand for local democracy but the desire of the colonial authorities to shift some of their expenditure burden. As Higgins explains, municipal status for St. John's was imposed partly to facilitate costly improvements to the sewerage and street systems and partly to be a mechanism whereby the privately owned and heavily in debt St. John's Water Company would become the financial responsibility of the city — a Water Company in which the Premier of Newfoundland and other prominent government supporters and business people were shareholders![25]

No other municipalities were formed for fifty years. Acts were passed in 1933 and again in 1937 providing for the incorporation of municipalities. However, no community requested incorporation and the central authorities did not use their authority to impose such incorporations. Instead, a new approach was attempted that offered subsidies and provided a special act giving a municipality any taxation form it desired if it would incorporate. By 1948 twenty municipalities had been incorporated by special charter and only five of these imposed the real property tax.[26]

After Newfoundland joined Confederation in 1949, the provincial legislature passed a general local government act that bestowed municipal status by proclamation for areas with a population of at least 1 000, and also provided for rural districts. Since that time the number of municipalities has grown steadily as have such quasi-municipalities as local improvement districts and local government communities.

Western Provinces

The provinces of Manitoba, Saskatchewan, and Alberta were part of the original Hudson's Bay Company land grant and later of the Northwest Territories. For most of their early history these provinces were governed by the Company which had complete judicial, legislative, and administrative authority. In 1869 the Company's rights in Rupert's Land and the Northwest Territories were acquired by the newly created Dominion of Canada. It was not until late in the nineteenth century that a substantial amount of settlement occurred in the Prairie provinces. When population growth pressures finally necessitated the provision of local services and subsequently a local government system, it was only logical for these provinces to look to their nearest eastern neighbour, Ontario, for a model upon which to base their systems. Because of the different physical characteristics of the West, the Ontario model was somewhat modified to suit local needs.

---

[25] *Ibid.*, pp. 34–35.

[26] Crawford, *op. cit.*, p. 41.

Manitoba

In 1870 Manitoba was created a province separate from the Northwest Territories. The first provincial legislature provided for a system of local government by a grand jury and Courts of Sessions that were to administer a County Assessment Act and a Parish Assessment Act. As well, the judges of the Sessions selected local officers such as treasurers, assessors, highway surveyors, poundkeepers, and constables from lists presented by the grand jury.

The first municipality was established in 1873 with the incorporation of Winnipeg as a city — although not without a struggle. Apparently the Hudson's Bay Company and four other property owners, who together owned well over half of the assessable property in Winnipeg, had opposed the incorporation and the resultant taxation of that property.[27] In that same year, general municipal legislation was also passed that provided for the establishment of local municipalities upon petition of the freeholders within a district. Only six areas became incorporated during the decade that this act was in force.

**UNSUCCESSFUL TRANSPLANT:
ADAPTATION OF ONTARIO'S
TWO-TIER COUNTY SYSTEM
ABANDONED AFTER THREE YEARS**

This permissive approach was dropped in 1883 when the Manitoba government decided to introduce a municipal system for the whole province modelled on the two tier county system of Ontario. The new act established 26 counties with councils composed of the heads of both rural and urban local (lower tier) municipal councils. The county council elected a warden from among its own members. This Ontario county system proved to be ineffective, however, because of the large areas covered, the often sparse and scattered population, and the local objections to a two tier system. It was abandoned after only three years and the province was divided into smaller rural municipalities. In 1902 a general act established cities, towns, villages, and rural municipalities as the basic units of local government, although Winnipeg was given its

---

[27] Higgins, *op. cit.,* pp. 50–51.

own special charter. This system has continued to the present, except for major changes in the structure of government for the Winnipeg area as discussed in Chapter 5.

Saskatchewan

Like Manitoba, Saskatchewan had been part of the lands granted to the Hudson's Bay Company. It was taken over by the Canadian government in 1870 and administered essentially as a colony until it gained provincial status in 1905. The territorial council first provided for municipal government in 1883 by enacting a municipal ordinance that was patterned on the previously cited Manitoba legislation of that year, which, in turn, had been modelled on the 1849 Municipal Act of Ontario. The ordinance provided for either rural municipalities or towns, depending on area and population and if local citizens petitioned for municipal status. Regina received town status that very year and four rural municipalities were organized in 1884, but little initiative was evident thereafter. By 1897 only one additional town had been created and two rural municipalities had dropped their municipal status. One major problem was the vast area and small, scattered population that made it difficult to generate the financial base needed to support municipal government.

However, since some form of local organization was necessary to provide roads and protection against prairie and forest fires, an ordinance was passed allowing the creation of "statute labour and fire districts" in areas not organized as rural municipalities. By 1896 these local improvement districts, as they were now called, were made mandatory, and the following year legislation was passed that allowed for elected committees to administer the districts. In 1903 the districts were reorganized into larger units made up of four of the former districts, each with one elected councillor on a municipal district council. Meanwhile, a revision and consolidation of municipal ordinances in 1894 provided for the incorporation of cities, towns, and rural municipalities.

**IMMIGRATION SPURRED DEVELOPMENT
OF LOCAL GOVERNMENTS**

Throughout this period the federal government was strongly encouraging Western settlement and large numbers of settlers arrived from Europe and from Eastern Canada, the latter bringing previous experience with municipal government. The impetus that these developments gave to the creation of municipal institutions is evident from the fact that when Saskatchewan became a province in 1905 there were already four cities, 43 towns, 97 villages, two rural municipalities, and 359 of the local improvement districts.[28]

The new province appointed a commission to carry on with a study previously started by the assembly of the Northwest Territories, which was to consider all aspects of municipal government. In 1908 Saskatchewan adopted the commission's recommendation that a system of municipal units be established with a separate act covering each type of unit. Accordingly, the City Act, Town Act, and Village Act were passed in 1908 and the Rural Municipalities Act in the following year. One result was a very rapid increase in rural municipalities—to 200 by 1912. However, many rural residents opposed municipal organization, mainly because of a fear of increased taxes, and the provincial government had to force remaining local improvement districts to become rural municipalities.[29] This municipal structure has remained basically unchanged through to the present.

Alberta

Since Alberta was also part of the federally administered Northwest Territories from 1870 until 1905, its municipal background resembles that of Saskatchewan. The first municipal government was introduced in Calgary, which was incorporated as a town in 1884 under the previously described municipal ordinance of 1883. In what has by now become a familiar pattern, incorporation efforts were initially thwarted by large landowners, among them the CPR, opposed to the prospect of property taxes.[30] Two more urban municipalities were created over the next decade (Lethbridge and Edmonton in 1891 and 1892 respectively), but because of the very sparse, scattered rural population, there were no petitions for the creation of rural municipalities under the ordinance. As in the area that later became Saskatchewan, the main form of local government was the statute labour and fire district or local improvement district.

---

[28] Horace L. Brittain, *Local Government in Canada*, Toronto, Ryerson Press, 1951, p. 179.

[29] Higgins, *op. cit.*, p. 53.

[30] *Ibid.*, p. 54.

Toward the end of the century, however, the large influx of settlers began to stimulate the creation of local governments. When Alberta became a province in 1905 its population was about 170 000 (compared to 18 000 in 1881) and it had 2 cities, 15 towns and 30 villages. By 1912 a new municipal system was established with cities, towns, villages, and local improvement districts. The latter could be erected into rural municipalities upon reaching a specified population, but here again few incorporations were requested because of local fears about tax increases.

COUNTY REFORM:
SINGLE TIER COUNTIES
ESTABLISHED IN RURAL AREAS
RESPONSIBLE FOR EDUCATION

The organization of municipal government in rural Alberta has undergone considerable change over the years. Beginning in 1942 the provincial government began to reduce the number of local improvement districts (by now called municipal districts) through amalgamation. A much more radical change was introduced in 1950 with the creation of single tier county governments in the rural areas handling virtually all local government functions including education.[31]

British Columbia

The area of what is now British Columbia was also under the jurisdiction of the Hudson's Bay Company during its early years of settlement. In 1849 the British assumed responsibility for Vancouver Island. By this time there was a general movement of population to the west side of the continent because of the discovery of gold in California (in 1848). A significant influx of population to the mainland of British Columbia occurred with the discovery of gold on the Fraser River in 1858. That year the British also assumed control of the mainland from the Hudson's Bay Company. The mainland and Vancouver Island were administered as two separate colonies until 1866.

---

[31] See Eric J. Hanson, *Local Government in Alberta,* Toronto, McClelland and Stewart Limited, 1956 and Jack Masson, *Alberta's Local Governments and Their Politics,* Edmonton, University of Alberta Press, 1985, Chapter Four.

INFLUENCE OF TOPOGRAPHY:
MOUNTAINOUS TERRAIN
SCATTERED SETTLEMENTS
MOST AREAS WITHOUT MUNICIPAL ORGANIZATION

The physical characteristics of British Columbia played a significant role in the development of municipal institutions in the province. Because of the mountainous terrain, early settlements were scattered and isolated. Westminster, the capital of the mainland colony, became a municipality in 1860, and two years later Victoria, the capital of the Vancouver Island colony, was incorporated as a town. Shortly after gaining provincial status in 1871, British Columbia enacted the Consolidated Municipal Act providing for local petitions for municipal incorporation, but by the end of 1874 there were still only five municipalities in the province.

• TABLE 3 •
HISTORICAL HIGHLIGHTS: WESTERN PROVINCES

Manitoba

1870	Created a province
1873	General Municipal Act
1883	Municipal Act based on Baldwin Act
1902	General Municipal Act

Saskatchewan & Alberta

1872	Surveyed into townships
1883	Ordinance for creating municipal units
1897	Won right of responsible government
1905	Separate provinces created
1908	Saskatchewan passed City, Town & Village Acts
	Established first Municipal Affairs Department
1909	Saskatchewan passed Rural Municipalities Act
1912	Alberta appointed Municipal Affairs Minister
	Established general local government system

British Columbia

1871	Became a province
1872	Permissive municipal legislation
1886	Vancouver incorporated
1892	Municipal Clauses Act

In 1892 the Municipal Clauses Act was passed, governing all new municipalities formed and providing for a system similar to that in Ontario, but without a county level. Municipalities were either cities with a mayor and council or rural districts with a reeve and council. By 1900 there were some 52 of these municipalities. In 1920 a Village Municipalities Act was passed allowing for smaller urban areas to incorporate with limited powers.

The vast majority of the area of the province remained unorganized territory, however, with the British Columbia government directly responsible for the provision of all necessary services. Under this centralized administration, a government agent received local revenues and supervised public expenditures, and often was stipendiary magistrate, gold commissioner, mining recorder, water commissioner, issuer of marriage licenses, assessor, tax collector, and policeman.[32] As described in Chapter 5, a municipal response to the governing of the vast rural areas was introduced beginning in 1965 with the creation of regional districts.

Northern Territories

The area of the Yukon and Northwest Territories was controlled by the Hudson's Bay Company until acquired by the federal government in 1870.[33] Its territory was reduced that year by the establishment of Manitoba as a separate province. Further reductions occurred in 1905 when Alberta and Saskatchewan became provinces, and in 1912 when the northern boundaries of Ontario, Quebec, and Manitoba were extended north to their present positions. The discovery of gold in the Klondike in 1896 sparked a rapid increase in the population of the Yukon, and in 1898 it was established as a separate territory.

Dawson City was incorporated as the first municipality in 1901, but its charter was revoked in 1904 and the provision of local services reverted to the territorial administration for a number of years. Also in 1901, a provision was made for the establishment of unincorporated towns upon petition. These units were not full municipal governments, however, since residents could only elect one official and only a very

---

[32] Shortt and Doughty, *op. cit.,* Vol. XXII, p. 355.

[33] The description in this section is partly based on Higgins, *op. cit.,* pp. 59–60.

limited range of services could be provided. In any event, the one unincorporated town created was disbanded when its population subsequently declined.

> **MUNICIPAL BARRIERS:**
> **SCATTERED SETTLEMENTS,**
> **OFTEN TEMPORARY**
> **POWER CENTRED IN OTTAWA**
> **UNTIL RECENTLY**

This often temporary nature of northern settlements has added to the problems caused by the extremely small, scattered population. Therefore, while both the Yukon and Northwest Territories have municipal ordinances authorizing the establishment of municipal governments, relatively few units were created until the past couple of decades.

Prior to 1960, virtually all real government within the Northern Territories came from Ottawa. With the re-location of the Territorial Council from Ottawa to Yellowknife in 1967, however, new municipal structures were introduced that allowed for more decision making at the local level.[34] The category of city was introduced in 1969, with Yellowknife becoming the first city.

There has been increasing emphasis on the passing of authority down from the Territorial government to local governments, along with an attempt to strengthen the political role of the municipalities. One government study claimed that "[In] the NWT the importance of the local level of government is of particular magnitude because of the cultural diversity and the vast distances between communities."[35]

While only a very small portion of the vast area of the Northern Territories is organized municipally, the organized portion contains three-quarters of the population. The few cities, towns and villages, which contain the bulk of the population, are basically modelled upon the structure of municipal government found in Southern Ontario.

---

[34] This discussion is based on Government of the Northwest Territories in conjunction with the Association of Municipal Clerks and Treasurers of Ontario, *Municipal Administration Program,* 1984, Unit 1, Lesson Two.

[35] *Constitutional Development in the Northwest Territories,* Report of the Special Representative (Drury Report), Ottawa, 1980, quoted in *ibid.,* p. 33.

Summary

By the beginning of the twentieth century, most provinces had in place, or were about to establish, a system of municipalities. All of the systems were fairly similar, in large part because of the influence of the Ontario model established in 1849. The systems generally consisted of cities, towns, and villages as urban units, a rural unit variously known as a township, municipal district, or rural municipality, and in some cases an upper tier county unit. Councils were for the most part directly elected, with the notable exception of the county level in Ontario, Quebec, and to some degree New Brunswick. Generally, an Assessment Act was also passed that provided municipalities with their main source of revenue.

FEATURES OF ORIGINAL SYSTEMS:
URBAN-RURAL SEPARATION
LIMITED RESPONSIBILITIES
RELIANCE ON PROPERTY TAX

These municipal systems were quite appropriate for the conditions of the time. They were generally based on a distinction between urban and rural classifications of municipality, on an expectation that municipalities would provide a quite limited range of services, primarily services to property, and on an assumption that the property tax would be both appropriate and adequate to finance the cost of these limited services. However, the primarily agricultural and rural nature of the economy and society in which these municipal systems were established, was to undergo a fundamental change over the next 50 to 100 years. As Chapter 4 makes clear, this change rendered the traditional municipal systems increasingly inadequate.

THE ORIGIN OF THE "SPECIES":
ROMANTIC MYTH
LESS STIRRING REALITY

But, what of the circumstances surrounding the introduction of municipal institutions in each province, and the expectations held out for the new level of government? Over the years a romantic notion has developed concerning the long, bitter struggle waged by our forefathers to wrest local self-government from an unsympathetic and paternalistic regime both in the colonies and in Britain. This vision is used to defend the status quo whenever change threatens "historic" boundaries.

Yet the true record is considerably less stirring. While something approaching this chain of events did take place in Ontario, municipal government was less warmly received in Quebec where it was viewed as simply another means of oppression because of the power of taxation. In the Atlantic provinces, this fear of the property tax prompted strong opposition to the introduction of municipal government. An editorial in the *New Brunswick Courier* in 1843 about a proposed municipal bill stated that had the bill been passed, "it would have cut loose that many-headed monster, Direct Taxation and its Myrmidon, the Tax-Gatherer, into the happy home of every poor man throughout the land."[36] Indeed, the history of municipal government in Newfoundland, far from being a tale of local agitation and central government resistance, was instead a case of central government overtures complete with financial incentives, all of which were largely ignored by the local people.

It is also noteworthy that where the provincial authorities did encourage or ultimately impose municipal governments on their populace, it was not because of any apparent belief in the values of local democracy — rather it was motivated by a desire on the part of the provincial administrations to shift at least some of the growing burden of expenditures to the local level. This pattern is evident in the historical developments in a number of the Atlantic and Western provinces — and one could draw some fascinating parallels with developments today.

Because of the later settlement of the West, however, there was fairly general acceptance of the logic and desirability of having municipal government. Usually one of the first actions of the new Western provincial governments was to establish a municipal system. This was due in part to the fact that many of the settlers arriving in the new provinces had come from areas where they had enjoyed municipal government, and in part to the fact that, with the greatly increased population, it was more efficient to provide certain services at the local level.

From the historical developments in the various provinces it is clear that municipal governments were mainly established in response to population growth and consequent service demands. Even in On-

---

[36] Quoted in Whelan, *op. cit.*, pp. 20–21.

tario, where pressure for local self-government was most pronounced, an important factor in the creation of municipal institutions was the inability of the Courts of Quarter Sessions to deal with growing urban problems. The preoccupation with local government as a provider of services has remained a central feature of the system to the present day.

HISTORICAL ROLES:
SERVICE DELIVERY ROLE OF LOCAL
GOVERNMENT ROOTED IN HISTORY
OTHER CONFLICTING ROLES ALSO EVIDENT

Kaplan suggests that there were a number of conflicting views and motivations influencing the establishment of our original municipal institutions and that these contradictions continue to affect local governments.[37] He notes that while reformers pushed for the democratic virtues of local government, the image of local officials as magistrates — arising from the operation of the justices of the peace and the Courts of Quarter Sessions — was too firmly established to be completely erased. Landowners liked this latter image that appeared to provide some assurance that the new municipal institutions wouldn't embark on costly local improvements. "Rather than seek out local problems and needs and then devise suitable governmental solutions, the municipal officials would wait until individual complaints were brought before them and then would resolve only the case at hand."[38]

In addition to these perspectives, a third view saw local government as a public corporation, drawing its life from a Crown-issued charter, and exercising only those powers assigned to it in the charter. These three premises were obviously inconsistent. As Kaplan points out:

> One cannot model local government on both a judicial tribunal and a business corporation. Local government cannot be both an experiment in mass participatory democracy and a corporation created by and for property owners.[39]

---

[37] Harold Kaplan, *Reform, Planning and City Politics: Montreal, Winnipeg, Toronto*, Toronto, University of Toronto Press, 1982.

[38] *Ibid.*, p. 61.

[39] *Ibid.*, p. 63.

The democratic image emphasized that local government was another level of government but "far more democratic and more intimately linked to the average citizen than were the 'remote' senior levels." According to the other two images, local government was "an arbiter of individual complaints or a dispenser of limited assistance to property owners but not ... a general purpose government."[40]

Further confusion about the appropriate role of local government occurred during the turn of the century reform era with its strong emphasis on removing politics from the local level. These developments, whose influence on both operating philosophy and governmental machinery is still felt today, are examined in the next chapter.

---

[40] *Ibid.*

3   *Turn of the Century Reform Era*

Objectives:

1. To describe the forces and influences that formed part of the turn of the century reform movement in Canada and the U.S.
2. To describe the main changes in municipal machinery that were introduced as part of the reform movement.
3. To assess the influence of the reform movement on the structure and operating philosophy of municipal government today.

Introduction

With the onset of the twentieth century Canada was at the end of 25 years of industrialization and in the midst of large-scale immigration. During this period of unprecedented economic and population growth, Canadians developed a "boom" mentality and municipal councils were no exception. They began to compete with each other for the location of industry, population growth, and new residential and commercial construction. An indication of the extent of this growth is the fact that the number of real estate agents in Halifax, Saint John, Montreal, Ottawa, Toronto, London, Winnipeg, Regina, Calgary, Edmonton, Vancouver, and Victoria increased from 506 in 1901 to 4 250 in 1913.[1] This surge of development brought with it not only prosperity but also new servicing demands and problems. In this chapter we will examine the impact that this growth had on Canadian municipal institutions.

Urban Problems Develop

Between 1901 and 1911 Canada led the Western world in population growth. Much of this growth was due to immigration, with the foreign-born population of Canada increasing by over 2 000 000. While many of these immigrants were in Canada as temporary labour, a significant

---

[1]   John C. Weaver, *Shaping the Canadian City: Essays on Urban Politics and Policy 1890–1920,* Toronto, Institute of Public Administration, Monographs on Canadian Urban Government, No. 1, 1977, p. 12. This monograph provides an excellent examination of the reform era and is used as a partial basis for this chapter.

number were permanent arrivals seeking employment in urban centres. For example, Calgary and Edmonton multiplied their populations forty times and changed almost overnight from villages to cluttered cities. Winnipeg, which had already shown an impressive increase in population from 1 800 to 40 000 between 1874 and 1899, surged to 150 000 by 1913. The bulk of this increase came from immigration, and by 1911 no other city in Canada had as high a proportion of European-born residents. The problems of assimilation that resulted led to what Artibise called a "Divided City".[2]

Even without these ethnic and cultural strains, however, the sheer numbers involved generated greatly increased service demands. The years 1900-1913 saw a tremendous jump in urban land values that was accompanied by extensive land speculation. In 1913 an English traveller wrote of the Victoria land boom that in two and one half years values increased 900 per cent.[3] The increase in land values precipitated a change in downtown land use from that of a mix of small businesses and residential housing to high rise office towers. This change in land use and higher real estate prices also served to push the working class out to the suburbs. Despite a building boom accompanied by large scale land assemblies and suburban development, the supply of housing could not keep up with the demand. Soon all major Canadian cities were faced with a serious housing shortage and the subsequent development of ghettos and slums.

> **URBAN PROBLEMS:**
> **REAL ESTATE INFLATION**
> **SCARCITY OF HOUSING**
> **WATER POLLUTION**
> **HEALTH HAZARDS**
> **TRAFFIC CONGESTION**

Besides a scarcity of housing, Canadian cities were confronted with other new servicing problems. In order to accommodate immigrant workers, inferior housing units were hastily built, often without sanitary conveniences. Families frequently shared accommodation and over-

---

[2] Alan F. Artibise, "Divided City: The Immigrant in Winnipeg Society, 1874–1921," in Gilbert A. Stelter and Alan F. Artibise (eds.), *The Canadian City: Essays in Urban History,* Toronto, McClelland and Stewart, 1977.

[3] John Bensely Thornhill, *British Columbia in the Making,* London, Constable and Company, 1913, pp. 126–127, as quoted in Weaver, *op. cit.,* p. 13.

crowding became a strain on already overworked municipal water and sewer systems. In 1910 in Canada, 57 systems of inland water were receiving raw sewage from 159 municipalities, and 111 water supply systems were obtaining their water from bodies of water into which raw sewage had been discharged. The combination of these factors produced a serious health hazard that became only too apparent in the early 1900s with an alarming increase in the number of epidemics. During this period, one of every three deaths was caused by tuberculosis, and typhoid and flu epidemics produced more casualties than World War One.[4]

Other major problem areas were transportation and the provision of utilities. The overcrowding of the downtown district plus the increased numbers commuting from the suburbs created the need for new modes of transportation or, at the very least, the construction of more roads and sidewalks. By 1913 most cities had electrified streetcar systems, which were often privately owned monopolies. At the same time municipalities were being pressured into providing municipal electric power plants. The mayor of Medicine Hat proclaimed "Municipal ownership (of utilities) and industrial progress go hand in hand."[5]

These new and expanded services in turn meant increased costs and therefore higher municipal taxes. Morley Wickett, an academic, businessman, and Toronto alderman, pointed out in 1907 that:

> The annual expenditure of Winnipeg clearly exceeds that of Manitoba; Montreal's that of the province of Quebec; and until the present year Toronto's that of the province of Ontario.[6]

These growth pressures resulted in the development of various reform movements throughout Canadian society, which were also part of a larger international movement common to most industrialized nations. At this time groups such as the Women's Christian Temperance Union, YMCA, YWCA, Salvation Army, and White Cross Army were founded to

---

[4] The above figures on the pollution and health problems are from Alan H. Armstrong, "Thomas Adams and the Commission on Conservation," in L.A. Gertler (ed.), *Planning the Canadian Environment*, Montreal, Harvest House, 1968, pp. 20–22.

[5] Mayor Foster, "Development of Natural Resources Under Municipal Ownership," *Canadian Municipal Journal*, II, April 1906, p. 133, as quoted in Weaver, *op. cit.*, p. 38. See Weaver's monograph, pp. 37–39 for a detailed discussion of public ownership of utilities.

[6] As quoted in Paul Rutherford, "Tomorrow's Metropolis: The Urban Reform Movement in Canada, 1880–1920," in Stelter and Artibise, *op. cit.*, p. 376.

help stamp out crime, vice, and poverty, evils associated with the emergence of the wicked city. In response to the servicing and financial pressures facing municipal governments, groups were formed such as the Civic Art Guild of Toronto, City Improvement League of Montreal, Union of Canadian Municipalities, Good Roads Association, and the Civic Improvement League of Canada. The goals of these various groups included social justice, a healthy and beautiful city, regulation of utilities and the restructuring of municipal government. Two movements that had a significant impact on local government were those that encouraged town planning and the reform of municipal government.

From City Beautiful to City Healthy: Prelude to Planning

There were three main forces that affected the development of municipal planning. The first to emerge was the civic enhancement or "city beautiful" movement that was often embraced by civic boosters. While city beautiful had supporters who wanted to improve the city for its own sake, councillors and businesspeople frequently regarded it as simply another means of attracting industry and growth. This often manifested itself in the desire for new public buildings. In Calgary, the ugly appearance of billboards advertising vacant lots for sale resulted in council hiring a consultant to prepare a master plan. But council also felt that the plan would prove to be of "great value from a publicity standpoint," and indeed sent a copy to every prominent news publication.[7]

THREE INFLUENCES:
CITY BEAUTIFUL MOVEMENT
CITY HEALTHY MOVEMENT
CITY EFFICIENT MOVEMENT

A second force that influenced planning resulted from the deteriorating health conditions in urban areas. For example, Fort William tripled its population between 1896 and 1905 as the result of railroad expansion. In the winter of 1905-1906 a sewer that emptied into the city's water supply caused approximately 800 cases of typhoid.[8] This and other similar situations gave rise to what might be called the "city healthy" movement.

---

[7]   Weaver, *op. cit.*, p. 33.

[8]   *Ibid.*, p. 28.

People were becoming convinced that housing conditions were related to public health. Toronto's Medical Officer of Health described slums as "cancerous sores on the body politic, sources of bacteria spreading disease, crime, and discontent throughout the city.[9] The middle and upper classes, mindful of the fact that disease did not respect social standing, pressed for measures that expanded the powers of health and building inspectors and legislated housing standards. J.J. Kelso, an Ontario lobbyist for children's aid, advocated a form of urban renewal:

> Rear houses and those built in the notorious alleys and lanes of the city should be pulled down. There should be a by-law that every dwelling must front on a forty or sixty foot street and that only one dwelling should be created to each 20 by 100 foot lot.[10]

Unfortunately, because many dwellings were subsequently condemned, these measures only served to make the existing housing shortage worse.

These reform themes, those of city beautiful and city healthy, were brought together with the creation of a federal Commission for the Conservation of Natural Resources. Dr. Charles Hodgetts, Advisor to the Commission on Public Health, in summing up the purpose of the commission stated that housing and town planning involved two important factors, the physical and the vital:

> The former relates to the protecting of our land, our forests, our minerals, our water, our sunlight, our fresh air; the latter, to the prevention of diseases, to health, and the prolongation of life.[11]

Thomas Adams was appointed Advisor on Town Planning to the Commission in 1914. Adams, a native of Scotland, had studied law and then been attracted to the Garden City Movement. He had served on the board that administered the British Town Planning and Housing Act. When he arrived in Canada Adams already had a reputation as "an eloquent author and speaker on the Garden City Movement, on agricultural land use and on town planning and housing as aspects of local government."[12] Adams proceeded to draft local plans and model provincial town planning acts based on the British Act. By 1916 only British Columbia and Prince Edward Island did not have a planning statute of Adams'

---

[9]   Rutherford, *op. cit.*, p. 375.

[10] *Labour Gazette*, July 1910, p. 128, as quoted in Weaver, *op. cit.*, p. 33.

[11] Armstrong, *op. cit.*, p. 21.

[12] *Ibid.*, p. 28.

making in force. His model created a separate honorary planning board, influenced by American prototypes, with the mayor as the only elected representative. Adams also assisted many Canadian municipalities in the preliminary stages of local planning and promoted the creation of provincial departments of municipal affairs in Ontario and Quebec.

> **THOMAS ADAMS**
> **DOMINANT PLAYER IN EARLY MUNICIPAL PLANNING**
> **INFLUENCED CREATION OF SEPARATE PLANNING BOARDS**

A third force, and one which also influenced municipal structural reforms, was the "city efficient" movement. In this movement the goals of city beautiful and city healthy — that is beauty, order, convenience, and health — were interpreted as economy and efficiency. Planning became a rational scientific process in which experts would provide technical solutions. As one spokesman explained, "if all the facts can be collected ... then a solution of any town planning problem becomes comparatively simple."[13]

Although most reformers claimed that they were working to improve the plight of the slum dwellers, a certain amount of self-interest can be detected in reforms actually implemented. Zoning by-laws were often passed to protect middle and upper class property values and neighbourhoods since, according to one of the supporters of the Manitoba Tenement Act of 1909, tenement houses "may ... to a large extent spoil the appearance of a neighbourhood."[14]

From City Corrupt to City Efficient: The Business Way

By 1900 urban reformers were advocating changes in the structure of local government as a means of eliminating corruption and improving efficiency. Structural reforms had first been popularized by newspapers covering the corruption of the Tammany Society in New York City and

---

[13] Gilbert Stelter and Alan Artibise, "Urban History Comes of Age: A Review of Current Research," *City Magazine,* vol. 3 no. 1, September/October 1977, p. 31.

[14] John C. Weaver, " 'Tomorrow's Metropolis' Revisited: A Critical Assessment of Urban Reform in Canada, 1890–1920," in Gilbert A. Stelter and Alan F. J. Artibise (eds.), *The Canadian City: Essays in Urban History,* p. 407. Tenement houses were built as multiple dwellings to accommodate the sudden population increase at the turn of the century.

subsequent American efforts at municipal reform. In fact, much as American immigrants had influenced the original developments of Canadian municipal government, Americans also exerted a strong influence on Canadian reforms at the turn of the century. But while the corruption of municipal government had reached crisis proportions in the United States, the situation in Canada was somewhat less severe.

This is not to say that Canadian municipal politicians were immune to the opportunities presented by the sudden urban growth and get-rich mentality of the times. In Toronto, corporations bidding on contracts and franchises complained that aldermen were "shaking them down." This allegation precipitated an inquiry in which only a few were found guilty but the whole council was tarnished by association. Soon after it was also discovered that the Montreal Police Commission was running a protection racket, the Toronto zoo keeper was stocking his own kitchen with food meant for the animals, and Regina city councillors were being given unusually low assessments and utility bills.[15] These revelations and others left the public with a rather low opinion of municipal government and calls for some kind of action were soon heard.

In the forefront of the municipal reform movement were middle-class merchants and businessmen, many of whom had little sympathy for the democratic aspects of local government. They were mainly concerned with expanding local services in order to attract more growth (often on land they owned), which in turn would expand the local tax base to help pay for new services. Bryce M. Stewart wrote in 1913 in *The Housing of Our Immigrant Workers:*

> There have been many unholy unions of city and industry. Anxious to be the Mother of many people, the city forgets herself and begs the industry to come.

But as Stewart went on to point out, the growth mentality only exacerbated already existing problems facing the city:

> She gives all she can — bonuses, free sites, exemption from taxation— and then finds herself alone and unprepared for the sheltering and training of a larger family of ignorant children.[16]

Businessmen were not prepared to accept any responsibility for the problems caused by urban expansion, since this growth was perceived

---

[15] Weaver, *Shaping the Canadian City, op. cit.,* pp. 56–59.

[16] Bryce M. Stewart, "The Housing of Our Immigrant Workers," quoted in Paul Rutherford (ed.), *Saving the Canadian City: The First Phase 1880–1920,* Toronto, University of Toronto Press, 1974, p. 152.

as only allowing nature to follow its own course. Instead they blamed corrupt local politicians and inefficient municipal governments for the situation. While the initial purpose of municipal reforms was to eliminate corruption, a second important purpose was to improve efficiency. The obvious solution, to the business community at any rate, was to take the politics out of municipal government and to run it on business principles. In Hamilton, reform mayor Captain McLaren ran on the slogan that "civic business is not politics."[17]

BUSINESS BIAS:
WIDESPREAD PERCEPTION OF MUNICIPAL GOVERNMENT AS A
BUSINESS TO BE RUN ON BUSINESS PRINCIPLES

The business community was not alone in its perception of municipal government as simply a business venture that should be run on business principles. Many contemporary newspapers felt this way and frequently carried editorials promoting municipal reforms. Typical of this view is the following opinion that compares municipal government to a joint stock company:

> If we would only manage our business as private corporations manage
> theirs we certainly would not have such a queer lot of directors —
> aldermen we call them — or make presidents — mayors as we call
> them — out of men who have never proven themselves as good busi-
> nessmen....[18]

Businessmen were also concerned about the power and narrow focus of ward-based politicians who failed to understand the importance of municipal reforms and hindered their implementation. In many cities these ward politicians were elected from areas where foreigners constituted most of the electorate. As Winnipeg's Mayor Sharpe stated: "The city's many foreigners could not comprehend civic issues and hence the role of the wards which gave them a degree of influence should be reduced in any new system.[19]

Much of the reform fervor was also due to a certain amount of enlightened self-interest as many businessmen stood to gain financially through municipal actions. Winnipeg's Mayor Sharpe was a wealthy contractor who specialized in sidewalks; in Regina the reform candidate was known

---

[17] Weaver, "Tomorrow's Metropolis Revisited," p. 42.

[18] *Saturday Night,* 1899, as quoted in Weaver, *Shaping the Canadian City,* p. 41.

[19] *Ibid.,* p. 62.

as "the Merchant Prince" who claimed that he paid $3 out of every $100 of local taxes. In Montreal the leaders of the business community, including the president of the Street Railway Company, privately financed a plebiscite on structural reforms.[20]

The reforms advocated by the business community really only served to give businessmen a greater hand in municipal affairs. Those in the business community had ambitions to have certain public works undertaken, but they found that in city politics they were only one of many competing interests. Since they were "unwilling to fully accept the realities of political pluralism they worked to scupper the rules of the game."[21] What follows is a discussion of how, specifically, the rules were changed.

The Reforms

The American schemes of municipal reform that were to influence Canadian reformers had two main thrusts: first, to give more power to the mayor and, second, generally to separate legislative and executive powers. Reforms actually implemented in Canada seemed to have been tempered by British traditions. The main concession made toward obtaining a strong mayor was the move to "at large" elections for the head of council. But there was a greater acceptance of the need to remove certain responsibilities from the control of council and in effect create separate executive and administrative bodies.

ELECTIONS:
AT LARGE ELECTIONS ADVOCATED FOR ALL
HEAD OF COUNCIL NOT CHOSEN BY COUNCILLORS

One of the structures most under attack was the council-committee system that seemed to allow ward aldermen a great deal of power in specific areas and thus "opened the door to corruption." In a move to reduce this power reformers called for the complete abolition of the ward system in favour of "at large" elections for all of council. One of the more convincing arguments for abolishing wards was that they fostered a parochial view of municipal issues instead of a broader city-wide view

---

[20] *Ibid.*, pp. 62–63.

[21] *Ibid.*, p. 64.

of city-wide concerns. This situation frequently resulted in "back scratching" and "log rolling," or "I'll give you what you want in your ward if you'll give me what I want in mine." An editorial in the *Financial Post* in 1912 stated that the ward system was one of the dominant evils of municipal life and that "all aldermen should hold their seats by the vote of all the electors and should represent all the city at all times."[22] Of course, at large elections, plus a concurrent move to raise the property qualification for voters, would reduce the influence of foreign born and slum residents. As early as 1857 Montreal changed from aldermen choosing their mayor to the mayor being elected at large, and in 1873 Toronto followed suit. In 1891 Toronto reduced the number of wards, and in 1894 Saint John and Fredericton abolished wards completely. In Toronto and Montreal an unsuccessful attempt was made to extend the franchise to companies.

Another reform, which was directed at strengthening the executive at the expense of council, was the introduction of the board of control. The board of control made its initial appearance in Toronto in 1896 in response to a water and sewer crisis. It was influenced by local business models and by the commission system popular in the United States. Only one Canadian city, Saint John, New Brunswick, specifically adopted the commission system. In 1912 they abolished their council and elected at large a five man commission with provision for democratic control through public recall, initiative, and referendum. One of the concepts behind this scheme of government was that each commissioner would become responsible for overseeing a particular field or department and would therefore become an expert in that area.

BOARD OF CONTROL:
INFLUENCED BY LOCAL BUSINESS MODELS
AN EXECUTIVE COMMITTEE OF COUNCIL
2/3 VOTE TO OVERTURN ITS DECISIONS

The Canadian board of control differed significantly from the American commissioner system in that it retained a council. Initially the members of the board of control were chosen by the councillors from among themselves, but subsequently they were elected at large. The purpose of the board of control was to take important executive func-

---

[22] *Financial Post*, February 10, 1912, as quoted in Weaver, *Shaping the Canadian City*, p. 67.

tions out of the control of council by allowing the board to prepare the budget, appoint and dismiss department heads, and award all contracts. Board decisions could only be overturned by a two-thirds vote of council that was difficult to accomplish since council included the board of control members. This form of executive committee proved to be popular in Ontario where it became mandatory for municipalities of a certain size. It also spread to other provinces and in 1906 was adopted by Winnipeg, in 1908 by Calgary where it was called a commission, and in 1910 by Montreal. The Montreal board of control, which was actually part of a more comprehensive reform that also cut the size of council in half, was seen as a managing commission whose powers were subject to the majority approval of council.

Proponents of the board of control often drew an analogy between the board and the provincial or federal cabinets. Yet the most important element of a cabinet was missing because there was no party loyalty and the controllers were not responsible to the rest of council, but instead to their own electorate. Unfortunately the board of control did not live up to reformers' expectations because the same people were still in the executive and administrative positions and the committee structure was usually retained. Friction often arose between the board of control and the committees because of overlapping jurisdiction. It was also far too easy to pass the buck and postpone decisions when contentious issues arose. As one contemporary observer noted:

> Our councillors have long ago discovered the truth of the maxim that there is safety in numbers. When any ticklish matter comes up, the board of control passes it on to the council; council refers it back to the board.[23]

According to this observer, after everyone has had a say it is customary to ask some senior staff member for a full report and "when that long-suffering individual, after much waste of valuable time, has prepared his report no one any longer has interest enough to read it."[24]

In Western Canada most politicians were reluctant to adopt the extreme measures of the American commission system or even the somewhat more democratic board of control. Western cities adopted a system of appointed commissioners. Instead of electing commissioners who would specialize in specific fields these cities retained their

---

[23] Frank H. Underhill, "Commission Government in Cities (1911)," in Paul Rutherford (ed.), *Shaping the Canadian City*, p. 327.

[24] *Ibid.*

councils and appointed experts to be administrators without any formal role in policy making. Edmonton was the first city to implement this system in 1904; Regina, Saskatoon, and Prince Albert followed in 1911-1912.

**MANAGER SYSTEM:
COMPLETE SEPARATION OF POLICY (COUNCIL)
AND ADMINISTRATION (MANAGER)**

Another American reform adopted by many Canadian municipalities was the city manager system. This was especially popular in Quebec after 1920. The system entailed the appointment of a chief administrator who was to coordinate and supervise all of the departments and affairs of the municipality. The system was based on the assumption that policy making, which was to be the exclusive concern of a small elected council, could be completely separated from policy implementation. It was an extremely popular reform in the United States where it was expected to solve the problem of coordinating the various people who had been given bits and pieces of power, by centralizing authority in one person. Despite the somewhat different conditions in Canada, the city manager system was appealing to reformers because it appeared to be one step closer to the corporate model. In 1919 Guelph, Ontario adopted the system and their city clerk described the organization as similar to a joint stock company with the aldermen as directors and the mayor as president. According to him:

> The city manager through his different departments, plans the work, submits same to council for their approval. When approved, it is up to the city manager to carry it out in a businesslike manner, without interference from the aldermen.[25]

In some cities it was even suggested that the elected council should be abolished and local affairs should be managed by an appointed executive. In London, Ontario, it was proposed that this appointed executive should be composed of representatives of special interest groups such as Rotary clubs, ratepayers associations, and the Board of Trade. In Montreal it was intended to retain the council with the mayor, two members elected by council, one by the Board of Trade, and one by the

---

[25]　*Ibid.*, p. 68.

Chambre de Commerce as the executive committee.[26] While these proposals were not adopted for councils, the idea of special interest group representation became a popular plan when establishing special purpose bodies.

BOARDS AND COMMISSIONS:
TAKE ISSUE OUT OF POLITICS
PROVIDE EXPERTISE
BUT, INCREASED FRAGMENTATION

In a further effort to reduce council's control, reformers advocated the creation of various boards and commissions that would oversee activity in a specific area and thus remove it from the political arena. Although these special purpose bodies were not a new phenomenon, Ontario having had police commissions as early as 1856, they flourished between 1890 and 1920. To some extent this is understandable. The pressures of urban growth and new technological developments made municipal government more complex. Municipalities were now faced with decisions in areas relating to sewers, pumping stations, streetcars, power systems, street and sidewalk paving, building codes, assessments, department budgets, tenders, debentures, and sinking funds.

Goldwin Smith, a member of a Toronto municipal reform group, summed up the general attitude in 1890 when he said that in the past city government was a proper setting for debates on principles, but now "a city is simply a densely peopled district in need of a specially skilled administration."[27] The age of the experts or the professionals had arrived and their coming was seen as the panacea for urban problems. The creation of a committee of experts was that much better.

Another argument in favour of creating special purpose bodies was that "a commission could attract 'the services of bright, able men who have not the time to serve in the council.'"[28] What this also meant was that businesspeople were more likely to serve in an appointed position

---

[26] In fact, in the 1940s Montreal did have a council consisting of a mayor and 99 councillors of whom 66 were elected, and 33 were appointed by public associations. For full details of Montreal's evolving structure see Paul Hickey, *Decision Making Processes in Ontario's Local Governments,* Toronto, Ministry of Treasury, Economics and Intergovernmental Affairs, 1973, p. 203.

[27] Weaver, *Shaping the Canadian City,* p. 72.

[28] Mayor Bethune, Vancouver (1907), as quoted in *ibid.,* p. 70.

than they were to endure an election. And so the lobbying for appointed commissions increased; in Toronto for a parks commission, fire commission, hydroelectric commission, and transportation commission; in Montreal for a parks commission; and in Vancouver for a water works commission. As previously discussed, the impetus for town planning also included the creation of a separate planning board or commission. As well, when municipalities took over the operations of street railway systems in the name of efficiency, they usually established a separate body to oversee the administration of this very important function.

By 1917 the proliferation of special purpose bodies was causing concern over the amount of dencentralization and fragmentation that had resulted. The October issue of *Municipal World* that year carried an article with the following statement:

> Decentralization has been carried too far. Town Planning Commissions, Suburban Road Commissions, Railway Commissions, Police Commissions, Boards of Education, Hospital Trusts, Utilities Commissions have usurped Council powers. The Council today is little more than a tax-levying body with little or no control.[29]

Summary: The Legacy of the Reform Era

Each of the reform movements had its own vision of what tomorrow's city should be like: a city beautiful, filled with parks, trees, boulevards, and stately buildings; a nation full of Garden Cities in which development was controlled to ensure all the basic amenities of life; the Canadian city converted into a Christian community where poverty, crime and vice were eliminated; or an orderly community with a municipal government run on principles of economy and efficiency.[30] While many of the reformers undoubtedly were sincere in their efforts, others had less noble motives behind their reform proposals. C. S. Clarke, an opinionated Torontonian, denounced those crusaders who wanted to purify city life as "a small group of pious fanatics who bothered the respectable and terrorized the weak".[31] In only slightly more generous terms, Kaplan states that "the reform doctrine was self-congratulatory, contemptuous

---

29 S. M. Baker, "Municipal Government Reform," *Municipal World,* Vol. 27, October 1917, p. 154, as quoted in Weaver, " 'Tomorrow's Metropolis' Revisited," p. 411.

30 Rutherford, *Saving the Canadian City,* p. xvii.

31 Rutherford, "Tomorrow's Metropolis," p. 371.

of outsiders, and thus highly vulnerable to charges of hypocrisy,"[32] especially since, as indicated above, its main advocates were prominent businesspeople seeking to expand their influence.

The reforms pertaining to municipal government were meant to eliminate corruption and to improve efficiency. The primary method of achieving this was to remove powers from council control by decreasing the number and importance of ward politicians, by increasing the power of a small executive through the board of control, by increasing the powers of the administration through the commissioner and city manager systems, and finally by creating separate special purpose bodies to take over completely certain important functions that could not be entrusted to politicians. Local government was regarded less as a level of government and more as a business. In discussing the municipal franchise, Goldwin Smith asked:

> What is the power which we now exercise, and which is largely illusory so far as the mass of us are concerned, compared with our health, our convenience, and the rescue of our property from the tax-gatherer?[33]

The net result of the reforms was a more complex, less accountable local government, more responsible to economy and efficiency than to the voters. Yet even in these former respects the success of the new municipal organizations was questionable. As early as 1899 there was some recognition in Toronto that structural reforms had not eliminated waste and corruption. A Toronto Star editorial claimed that council and the board of control were playing "a game of shuttlecock and battledore."[34] In 1909 the Fort William-Port Arthur Utilities Commission had to admit that service was poor. In 1913 Calgary's commissioners bought a $5 000 car with special paint and a special siren horn for their use,[35] perhaps not the most efficient use of public funds. The problem, of course, was that even businessmen and experts were as prone to self-interest and corruption as those municipal officials they had previously chastised. In 1895 the Telegram had written that "the fault is not with the system but with the people."[36]

---

[32] Harold Kaplan, *Reform, Planning and City Politics: Montreal, Winnipeg, Toronto,* Toronto, University of Toronto Press, 1982, p. 173.

[33] Weaver, *Shaping the Canadian City,* pp. 45–46.

[34] *Ibid.,* p. 72.

[35] *Ibid.,* pp. 72–73.

[36] *Ibid.,* p. 48.

It is ironic that while many of these turn of the century reforms were prompted by the excesses of party politics and the "spoils" system in American local government, they were adopted by Canadian municipalites that, for the most part, were not organized on party lines. A number of indigenous factors have been suggested to explain this different pattern of development in Canada.[37] Because urbanization came later to Canada, Canadian cities were smaller and more homogeneous and lacked the patronage potential found in American cities with a heavily immigrant population. In addition, since provincial governments controlled their local governments more than state governments did, "the sandbox politics of City Hall offered little incentive for organized partisan activity or division."[38]

These indigenous factors changed with the passage of time, of course, and reference has previously been made, for example, to the extensive immigrant population in Winnipeg by the first decade of the twentieth century and the "Divided City" that resulted. But as Anderson has noted:

> By the time Canadian cities reached the size and complexity sufficient to make them attractive to political parties, the reform ideology and the accompanying structural innovations imported from the U.S. had become firmly established, and provided an effective barrier to the entry of parties.[39]

The legacy of the reform era is evident in the continued existence of many of the structural reforms of the early 1900s and in the continued denial of the relevance of politics at the local level. Yet, as discussed in the next chapter, these nonpolitical traditions became increasingly inappropriate as the twentieth century advanced, as did the historical boundaries, revenue sources, and allocation of responsibilities.

---

[37] See J.D. Anderson, "Nonpartisan Urban Politics in Canadian Cities" in Jack K. Masson and J. D. Anderson (ed.), *Emerging Party Politics in Urban Canada,* Toronto, McClelland and Stewart, 1972.

[38] James Lightbody, "The Rise of Party Politics in Canadian Local Elections," in Masson and Anderson, p. 196.

[39] Anderson, *op. cit.,* p. 12.

4 Cracks in the Foundation: The Pressures of Growth and Change

Objectives:

1. To assess the impact of urbanization in the mid-twentieth century, with particular reference to its effect on local government.
2. To describe the inadequacies of the traditional local government system that resulted.

Introduction

As the twentieth century advanced, the local government system and operating values came under increasing pressure. These pressures were not new, of course, and the preceding chapters have indicated that pressures of change, including urbanization, have been affecting Canadian local government from its very beginnings. What was different was the magnitude of these pressures, particularly arising from the extent of urbanization in the "baby boom" years following World War Two. By this time, the basic structure of local government was between 50 and 100 years old in most of the provinces and was facing greatly changed conditions. To understand the significance of these changes, let us first examine the urbanization that occurred and its consequences.

Increased Urbanization

Canada's urbanization has to be considered in the context of the changes in the overall population of the country. As previously discussed, the early years of the twentieth century saw rapid population growth, almost half of it caused by immigration. The rate of increase in population then slowed during each successive decade reaching a low of only 10.9% during the intercensal decade of 1931 to 1941, because of reduced birth rates, negligible immigration, and substantial emigration. After 1941, population growth again accelerated to a near-record expansion rate of 30.2% between 1951 and 1961. In subsequent periods the rate of increase has steadily declined, largely because of the reduction in birth rates.

PACE OF URBANIZATION:
FASTEST URBANIZING WESTERN
NATION AFTER WWII
75.5% URBAN BY 1976
3/4 OF POPULATION ON LESS
THAN 1% OF LAND AREA

Of particular interest is the classification of the population as between urban and rural. The Census of Canada defines as urban all persons living in an area having a population concentration of 1 000 or more and a population density of at least 386 per square kilometre. On this basis, Canada's population was classified as 75.5% urban in the 1976 Census. Indeed, at this point Canada's urban growth since the end of World War Two had exceeded that of any Western industrial nation and three-quarters of the nation's population was concentrated on less than one per cent of its land area.[1]

GROWING URBAN CONCENTRATION:
MUNICIPALITIES OVER 10 000
9 IN 1871
246 IN 1971
300 IN 1976
CENSUS METROPOLITAN AREAS
19 IN 1971
23 IN 1976, CONTAINING 55.7%
OF POPULATION

More significant than this general shift from rural to urban has been the concentration of that urban population. In 1871 only nine municipalities had populations of over 10 000, but by 1971 there were 246 such municipalities, and although representing only 5.7% of all municipalities, they contained 62% of the Canadian population.[2] By 1976 the number of municipalities with populations of over 10 000 had risen to 300, with 75 of these having populations of over 50 000 and 30 over 100 000.[3] By 1981, 118 municipalities had populations of over 50 000.

---

[1]   Len Gertler and Don Crowley, *Changing Canadian Cities: The Next 25 Years,* Toronto, McClelland and Stewart, 1977, p. 41.

[2]   Institute of Local Government, *Urban Population Growth and Municipal Organization,* Kingston, Queen's University, 1973, p. i.

[3]   Statistics Canada, *Canada Year Book,* 1980–81.

Even greater concentration is evident from the fact that in 1971 more than 50% of the population was centred in 19 census metropolitan areas (census areas comprised of at least two adjacent municipal entities, each at least partly urban, with an urbanized core of 100 000 or more). In fact, of the 1 500 000 added to the Canadian population between 1966 and 1971, almost two-thirds were located in the nine centres with populations of 400 000 or more, and more than 40% were located in the metropolitan areas of Toronto, Montreal, and Vancouver. By the 1976 Census, the number of metropolitan areas had increased to 23, containing 55.7% of Canada's population. In 1978, 30% of the population of Canada was found in the three census metropolitan areas of Toronto, Montreal, and Vancouver. By the 1981 Census there were 24 census metropolitan areas and the proportion of the Canadian population within Toronto, Montreal and Vancouver was up to 35.4%. The number of census metropolitan areas had increased to 25 by 1986, with these areas growing by 5.9% between 1981 and 1986, almost 50% faster than the national average.

Compounding this growth and its attendant pressures has been the "mushrooming growth in a few metropolitan agglomerations: the 'Lower Mainland' in British Columbia; the Calgary-Edmonton 'Transportation Corridor' in Alberta; the 'Golden Horseshoe' in Southwestern Ontario; the 'Golden Triangle' in Southern Quebec and the 'Central Corridor' in the Maritimes."[4]

This chapter examines the impact of urbanization — particularly the rapid urbanization that Canada experienced in the first couple of decades after World War II — on the local government system.

Impact of Urbanization

Urbanization involves much more than the concentration of population. It arises from, and gives rise to, fundamental changes in the nature of our economy and society. It was industrialization, and especially the development of mass production, that encouraged the concentration of population in cities. The transformation was described by the Economic Council of Canada in its *Fourth Annual Review,* a document that helped to focus attention on the problems of urbanization.

> ...economic change in Canada has thus been marked by a relative shift in the focus of employment and output from the on-site exploitation of the natural resource base to the processing of materials, to manufacturing

---

[4] Gertler and Crowley, *op. cit.,* p. 5.

and advanced fabrication, and to the provision of a rapidly widening range of modern private and public services. Inevitably this change has implied a shift in the location of economic activity away from the rural area and its small service centres towards the larger urban centre.[5]

With this shift in population, other changes occurred. The movement from farm to factory created growing numbers of workers who were dependent upon industrial employment and its attendant uncertainties, instead of being relatively self-sufficient by living off the land. They increasingly turned to government to provide them with some protection and security. Gradually the "positive state" evolved with its elaborate range of services and programs designed to ensure all citizens a minimum standard of living conditions. All levels of government were affected by this development, and the resultant increase in services demanded of local government represented a heavy burden for most municipalities.

"POSITIVE STATE"
RESULTED FROM DECLINE IN SELF-SUFFICIENCY
GOVERNMENT COMMITMENT TO MINIMUM LIVING STANDARDS
INCREASED SERVICE DEMANDS ALSO FELT AT LOCAL LEVEL

The shortage, expense, and inadequacy of urban housing brought greater government involvement by all levels. The concentration of low income families in inner city neighbourhoods strained the social service system. The loss of spacious country living led to growing demands for parks and recreational facilities. The higher living standards and leisure time of a technological society accentuated this demand. Transportation and traffic movement required increasing government attention, as did the provision of an adequate supply of water and the disposal of domestic and industrial waste. Governments had to deal with air pollution concerns, in large part because of the exhaust from the concentration of motor vehicles. New problems of subdivision control and urban renewal and redevelopment also claimed the attention of the urban municipality. Population sprawl caused the conversion of land from agricultural production to urban uses and government action was needed to protect against developments that had an undesirable impact on the natural environment.

---

[5] Economic Council of Canada, *Fourth Annual Review,* September 1967, p. 181. Quoted with permission from the Economic Council of Canada.

It should be noted that rural municipalities also experienced new servicing pressures, largely because of the influx of the nonfarm rural population. Improved road maintenance and fire protection were demanded and such urban amenities as sidewalks and streetlights were expected in many hamlets. New recreational facilities were requested. Extensive cottage development on scenic lakes and rivers and excessive residential development on unsuitable soil often caused pollution problems requiring government action. Where these problems arose in a concentrated area, the municipality often faced the very heavy financial burden of a water supply and sewage treatment system. Residential development and farming activities proved an uneasy mix and the resulting friction provided one more example of the need for land use planning policies and controls in rural areas.

While the list of problems requiring government solution seems almost endless, especially in large urban areas, Harvey Lithwick contends that we must recognize and deal with those problems that are inherent in the process of urbanization, as opposed to the myriad of other so-called urban problems that happen to be conspicuous in our cities. As he sees the situation:

> Urban poverty in backward regions is a reflection of regional underdevelopment rather than some unique urban phenomenon. Pollution in a one-industry town is essentially an industrial problem rather than an urban one. Unemployment and inflation, although obvious in urban areas, are not genuine urban problems.[6]

According to Lithwick, the distinctive feature to be noted is that the growth of cities produces "competing demands for the one common feature of all cities, scarce urban space, driving core prices upward and households outward." He suggests that transportation, pollution, and poverty problems flow from this. Moreover, he argues that because of these interdependencies efforts to deal with each problem in isolation have inevitably failed.

**URBAN PROBLEMS INHERENT IN PROCESS OF URBANIZATION:
SCARCE URBAN SPACE DRIVES PRICES UP AND HOUSES OUTWARD
TRANSPORTATION, POLLUTION & POVERTY PROBLEMS FOLLOW**

Housing policy has added to the stock of urban accommodations, but has led to urban sprawl and fiscal squeeze for the municipalities.

---

[6]   N.H. Lithwick, *Urban Canada: Problems and Prospects,* Ottawa, Central Mortgage and Housing Corporation, 1970, pp. 14–15.

Transport policies have moved people faster initially, but have led to further sprawl, downtown congestion, pollution, and rapid core deterioration.[7]

In response to this situation, Lithwick called for a comprehensive approach to urban problems and one that coordinated the efforts of all three levels of government. As will be seen, however, his plea for " a new kind of vertical integration within the hierarchy of government" has proven to be an elusive goal.

Other writers and analysts have called for even more fundamental changes in order to deal effectively with the problems caused by urbanization. They see the issue in the wider context of the economic development patterns within Canada and the impact of private decision making on land and its uses. Lorimer, for example, contends that "most of the development of Canadian cities in the three boom decades from the Forties to the Seventies was a direct consequence of the economic development strategy chosen by Ottawa for Canada."[8] In his view, this strategy had two principal components — exploitation of natural resources for use mainly by the major metropolitan economies, and expansion of a branch-plant secondary manufacturing industry in Southern Ontario.

Lorimer goes on to suggest that this American boom is over for Canada. He contends that the less dominant position of developers in our cities is mainly because of the slower growth of recent years rather than any significant breakthrough by citizens' groups that had fought for the preservation of neighbourhoods and a more moderate approach to growth and development. Developments in recent years offer some support for this viewpoint, in that developers have once again come to the forefront with the upsurge in growth and development in some centres, notably Toronto, as discussed in Chapter 9.

**RESPONSES TO URBANIZATION PROBLEMS:
MORE GOVERNMENT INTERVENTION?
FUNDAMENTAL REDISTRIBUTION OF ECONOMIC POWER?**

---

[7] *Ibid.,* p. 15.

[8] James Lorimer, "The post-developer era for Canada's cities begins," in *City Magazine Annual 1981,* Toronto, James Lorimer and Company, 1981, p. 7.

According to Richardson, the problems of urbanization can only be resolved through greater government intervention into what has hitherto been the private domain. As he expresses the general issue:

> We will never be able to build the institutions needed to keep the pressures of urbanization under control if we do not accept the fact that the basic problem is to redistribute wealth, equalize opportunity and extend the areas in which the public interest has priority over the private.[9]

Those who hold to this viewpoint have numerous examples to support their contention. Perhaps the most blatant example is the land speculation in and around our cities. The extension of services, at public expense, often brings windfall profits to the private speculator who purchased and held land against such an eventuality. Another example has been the widespread disruption (some would say destruction) of the city to meet the needs of the private use of automobiles without anything like this degree of support for public transit. Indeed, public transit services have been struggling to maintain ridership, hesitating to increase fares that would likely lose more riders, yet faced with growing deficits and, traditionally, very little financial support from the senior levels of government. According to the Science Council of Canada's Report on *Cities for Tomorrow,* "it appears that barely one-half of the cost incurred by the automobile is returned to different levels of government in gasoline taxes and license fees."[10] Not only do public transit services face unfair competition because of this subsidy, but too little consideration is given to the broad social benefits that they bring — and the social costs of our devotion to the automobile. As Richardson notes, economists can be quite explicit about such factors as time saved for truckers or the cost of congestion for businesspeople, but they seem unable to estimate "the cost of isolation for 200 000 old people; or of congestion, pollution, noise, and a general shattering of the urban environment for the entire population."[11]

Private enterprise has also been deficient in providing adequate and appropriate housing for the varied needs of the Canadian population. Here again, the forces of urbanization have played a part by making land

---

[9] Boyce Richardson, *The Future of Canadian Cities,* Toronto, New Press, 1972, p. 51.

[10] Quoted in *ibid.,* p. 130.

[11] *Ibid.,* p. 139.

very scarce and therefore very valuable. As land prices increase it becomes necessary to have buildings that will generate a large income for the landowner.

> ...poor houses inhabited by poor people must be swept away, their occupants with them; new places go up, let at high rents; young men and women, married couples, or the rich, move in where poor people lived before; the poor people just "disappear" — most of the time we don't even take the trouble to find out where they go to live. [12]

Ironically, government programs have, in the past, done little to help this situation and, indeed, the traditional urban renewal initiatives of the federal government often served to increase the housing shortage — especially low cost housing that the poor in the population could afford. "Traditionally in North America, rehabilitation has meant upgrading the quality of an area so that it could be handed over to middle class citizens, whose housing needs are already being met by the private enterprise system."[13]

While Richardson's analysis of the shortcomings of private decision making and traditional government policies may seem quite critical, to some it is far too tame. Roussopoulos, for example, argues that while Richardson analyzes the problems radically, his solutions are short term and realizable within the system. It is the power of the private property industry that is particularly of concern and Roussopoulos contends that:

> Any urban liberation movement that does not present a revolutionary critique of contemporary society and does not make clear that the "urban crisis" is not separate from the "crisis of capitalism" and more important does not demand and work for the revolutionary transformation of existing social relations, amounts to reaction in disguise....[14]

At the other extreme is the conservative viewpoint, as expressed by Banfield in *The Unheavenly City*. He contends that the urban problems have been exaggerated and are largely inherent in the nature and temperament of the lower class. He also argues that while urban conditions are improving in absolute terms, we tend to view them from a changing, ever more demanding perspective.

---

[12] *Ibid.*, pp. 155–156.

[13] *Ibid.*, p. 199.

[14] Dimitrios Roussopoulos, "Understanding the City and Radical Social Change," in Dimitrios Roussopoulos (ed.), *The City and Radical Social Change*, Montreal, Black Rose Books Ltd., 1982, p. 61.

It is because the process of "middle-classification" has given great
numbers of people higher perspectives and standards that dissatisfaction with the city is so widespread. The city that was thought pleasant
when most people were working class is thought repellant now that most
are middle class, and it will be thought abhorrent when, before long,
most are upper middle class.[15]

Banfield suggests that the urban reformer "wants to improve the situation of the poor, the black, the slum dweller, and so on, not so much to
make them better off materially as to make himself and the whole society better off morally" — rather like the attitude of the English Puritans
toward bear-baiting: "that they opposed it not for the suffering that it
caused the bear but for the pleasure that it gave the spectators".[16] He
provides considerable evidence to support his assertion that well-inten-
tioned but misguided reform initiatives have usually done more harm
than good. He then offers a number of proposals that he believes would
be more effective — such as shortening the number of years of compulsory education — and then explains how each would be vigorously opposed by organized interests — in this case, teachers' federations.[17]
Given that his solutions would be unacceptable, Banfield argues against
government intervention on any major scale, concluding that "Hard as it
may be for a nation of inveterate problem-solvers to believe, social problems sometimes disappear in the normal course of events." [18]

Inadequacies of the Traditional System

Regardless of how one perceives the situation, several conclusions
seem inescapable. The increasing concentration of population in our
cities call for a growing variety of responses from government. Differing views exist about the nature of the urban problems, their underlying causes, and the most appropriate solutions. The urbanization that
has been experienced is largely the result of the actions (and inaction)
of the senior levels of government, and yet the resulting urban problems
have been primarily the responsibility of the local level of government.

---

[15] Edward C. Banfield, *The Unheavenly City,* Boston, Little, Brown and Company, 1968, pp. 65–66.

[16] *Ibid.,* p. 251.

[17] See *ibid.,* Chapter Seven.

[18] *Ibid.,* p. 257.

A primary concern of this chapter is to determine how well equipped to handle these problems the local government system was in the early postwar period.

Structural Limitations

One fundamental weakness was that most municipal institutions had originated in the previous century and had been designed only "to carry out the public functions and to operate within the restricted area boundaries considered appropriate for that time." Yet, the pace of change had brought about "a complex transformation in functions of municipal government and the complete obliteration of many previously significant territorial boundaries."[19] Consider, for example, the 18 metropolitan areas or large city complexes of 100 000 people and over identified in the 1961 Census. Within these 18 areas "there were some 260 separate municipal government jursidictions, together with an additional unknown number of semi-independent single purpose special authorities such as school boards, water boards, transit and utility commissions, and sewerage districts."[20] Obviously with such a fragmented structure, concerted action to deal with urban problems was both difficult and unlikely.

> **STRUCTURAL WEAKNESS:**
> **OUTDATED BOUNDARIES, ESPECIALLY IN URBAN AREAS**
> **TOO MANY SEPARATE BOARDS AS WELL AS MUNICIPALITIES**

Functional Fragmentation

In addition to this structural fragmentation, functional fragmentation also inhibited and complicated the ability of municipal government to respond to urban problems. A number of traditionally local responsibilities "outgrew" the local level in terms of their significance, importance, and impact. The result, in fields such as health, education and welfare, has been a gradual shift of responsibility to the senior levels of government and an increasing sharing of responsibilities between two or more levels of government.

---

[19] Economic Council of Canada, *op. cit.,* pp. 209–210.

[20] *Ibid.,* p. 210.

FUNCTIONAL:
SHIFT OF FUNCTIONS UPWARD
INTERTWINING AND MUTUAL INTERDEPENDENCE

At the same time, a parallel but reverse trend was underway in which senior governments launched new initiatives but delegated responsibility to the local level for at least some aspects of program delivery. This pattern was evident in such areas as housing, urban renewal, and environmental protection. The combined result was that the operations of local government became increasingly intertwined with those of the senior governments.

> In many traditional areas of local competence, provincial supervision, regulation or outright control have been deemed the acceptable solutions....Their overall effect has incorporated municipal affairs more completely in the broader contexts of provincial and federal public administration. Indeed, local autonomy in all but a few ... areas is extinct.[21]

Thus, not only were municipal governments facing the pressures of an urbanizing trend largely shaped by the policies of the senior levels of government, but they were also constrained in responding to these pressures by the extent to which their responsibilities were entangled with those senior governments. A number of provinces had established departments of municipal affairs around the turn of the century, but these departments — and often municipal boards as well — really came to the fore during the depression of the 1930s. In the years that followed, their supervision and control of local governments increased steadily. These intergovernmental developments and the experience with federal-local and tri-level relations are examined in Chapter 6.

Financial Constraints

In addition to its structural and functional shortcomings, the traditional local government system also faced increasing financial problems. When local governments were first established, it was expected that they would meet their revenue needs through the real property tax. This tax could be administered effectively on a local basis and it appeared

---

[21] H. J. Whalen, *The Development of Local Government in New Brunswick*, Fredericton, 1963, p. 90.

adequate to finance the limited servicing requirements of the day, mainly related to education, local roads, and the care of the poor. The tax seemed appropriate since property was the main form of wealth in the early days, and it wasn't considered particularly burdensome since the local taxpayer was not subject to the income tax and other forms of direct and indirect taxation that subsequently made their appearance. [22]

However, as the twentieth century advanced, a number of the traditional responsibilities of local government became much more significant and costly — including the above-mentioned examples of education, roads, and welfare. A growing number of new service demands also arose, largely because of urbanization, as has been amply illustrated in the preceding discussions. Yet the real property tax remained the primary source of muncipal revenues.

FINANCIAL:
PROPERTY TAX NO LONGER ADEQUATE OR AS APPROPRIATE
BACKLOG OF EXPENDITURES FROM DEPRESSION & WAR
SHORTFALL FILLED BY GRANTS, MOST CONDITIONAL

The inadequacy of this financial base became all too evident during the 1930s, when the entire burden for unemployment relief assistance was initially considered to be within the scope of municipal responsibility for poor relief. Even when the federal and provincial levels had assumed 80% of the costs, municipalities still had difficulty financing their share for the substantial unemployed population of the urban industrial centres. They cut back on services and postponed expenditures for maintenance and new construction. Further postponements occurred with the diversion of resources for the Second World War.

Thus, an enormous backlog of expenditures had already built up even before the municipalities faced the greatly increased demands of the postwar urbanization. The challenge that this posed is well described by Goldenberg:

> They (the municipalities) faced the problem of financing not only the expenditures which had been deferred during fifteen years of depression

---

[22] T.J. Plunkett, *The Financial Structure and the Decision Making Process of Canadian Municipal Government,* Ottawa, Canada Mortgage and Housing Corporation, 1972, p. 21.

and war, but also vast new expenditures on works and services required to meet an unprecedented growth in population and economic activity.[23]

The resultant upsurge in municipal spending in the immediate post-war years is vividly illustrated by the fact that total urban municipal expenditures increased by 131% over the eight-year period from 1945 to 1953, compared to an increase of only 13% during the fifteen-year period 1930 to 1945. [24]

Not surprisingly, the real property tax couldn't generate sufficient revenues to meet this explosion of municipal expenditures. While this tax was still providing over 80% of municipal revenues in 1930, the proportion had fallen to 53% by 1953 and to 47% by 1963.[25] By 1974-75, the proportion had declined to below 40% according to the Report of the Tri-Level Task Force on Public Finance in 1976. As will be seen in Chapter 6, contributions from the property tax and other local revenue sources have stabilized and even increased somewhat in recent years because of reductions in the level of transfer payments from the senior levels.

The growing shortfall in municipal revenue needs in the postwar period was remedied almost entirely by grants from the senior levels of government.[26] By the beginning of the 1970s, this assistance accounted for over 40% of gross general revenues of Canadian local governments. While these transfer payments allowed municipalities to meet their expenditure obligations, they were a mixed blessing. The municipal submission to the first national tri-level conference in 1972 noted that approximately 90% of this financial assistance was in the form of conditional grants that reflected the priorities of the senior levels of government and threatened to turn local governments into "hollow receptacles into which the values of the federal and provincial governments are poured."[27]

---

[23] H. Carl Goldenberg, "Municipal Finance and Taxation: Problems and Prospects," in *Forecast of Urban Growth Problems and Requirements 1956–1980*, Montreal, Canadian Federation of Mayors and Municipalities, 1955.

[24] Plunkett, *op. cit.*, p. 33.

[25] Economic Council of Canada, *op. cit.*, p. 219.

[26] More recent developments, including provincial-municipal revenue-sharing agreements, are discussed in Chapter 6.

[27] Municipal Submission to the first National Tri-Level Conference, *Policies, Programs and Finance*, Ottawa, 1972, p. 20.

In fairness, one can find considerable justification for a number of the provincial conditional grant programs. Many traditional local government responsibilities are now recognized as having much wider than local significance and it has become necessary to find some means of ensuring that these responsibilities are exercised to at least a minimum standard across the province. Given a multiplicity of municipal jurisdictions with widely varying financial capacities, the most effective means of ensuring these standards has been through the grant structure. Whatever the rationale, it seems clear that this process has been carried too far. A basic difficulty is that "there is a rapidly diminishing relationship between the taxes paid to any one level of government and the services rendered by it."[28] The most fundamental problem with such arrangements, which apply to the federal-provincial relationship as much as to the provincial-local, is well expressed in a pamphlet by the Ontario Economic Council:

> Through the development of a complex transfer system, each level of government can influence the nature and scope of the services provided, take a share in the political rewards, maintain the fiction of autonomy, and have a convenient excuse for avoiding any criticism for inadequate services. The only drawback is that the public never knows who is responsible for what or how much the services provided really cost.[29]

Unfulfilled Political Role

This lack of a clear focus of accountability and responsibility relates to one of the most important inadequacies of local government to be highlighted by the pressures of postwar urbanization. The traditional system was quite ineffective in fulfilling its political role — that is, in representing the views of the local inhabitants, choosing between alternative courses of action, setting priorities for the allocation of scarce resources, and then answering for these decisions to the local electorate.

POLITICAL:
CONFLICTING VALUES UNDERLYING POSTWAR ISSUES
RESPONSIVENESS AND ACCOUNTABILITY DEMANDED
NOT READILY APPARENT IN TRADITIONAL STRUCTURE
AND NONPOLITICAL EMPHASIS

---

[28] Ontario Economic Council, *Government Reform in Ontario*, Toronto, 1969, p. viii.

[29] *Ibid.*, p. 19.

As we have seen, the turn of the century reformers vigorously denied the relevance of a political role for local government. They viewed this role much too narrowly — equating politics with excessive divisiveness and abuse of power through patronage and the pork barrel. In addition, many of the reformers who purported to want politics removed from local government actually wanted to impose their own notion of what the local priorities should be. Whatever their motivations, however, the reformers bequeathed us a deeply ingrained notion of municipal government as administrative and not political in nature, with the council performing a caretaker or custodial role and preoccupied with considerations of efficiency. Also from this reform period came the belief that servicing questions were best resolved by the application of technical expertise, with "politics" being kept entirely out of the picture if possible.

Given the growth pressures and challenges of the postwar period, this concept of municipal government became increasingly unworkable. The issues that now demanded the attention of local governments involved widespread controversy about the best course of action. Concern about the quality of life and the preservation of established neighbourhoods increased as rapid development threatened the fabric of the city. The traditional reliance on technical expertise was found unacceptable and the public demanded that decision makers show a greater awareness of social and environmental considerations. For example, meeting transportation needs through expressways or public transit has been an ongoing dispute, with the much publicized Spadina expressway controversy providing a good illustration, along with similar disputes in Vancouver and Edmonton.[30] The fondness for single family dwellings, supported by the lending policies of the Central (now Canada) Mortgage and Housing Corporation, has had to be reconciled with the cost and space demands of such housing compared with the economics of higher density construction. Urban renewal projects have aroused strong opposition from neighbourhoods where residents wanted rehabilitation rather than the traditional response of tearing down and building anew.

Nor were the tensions confined to urban areas. Rural residents also debated the desirability of growth and the validity of new service demands. There has been a growing concern about the loss of farmland and, paradoxically, about controls intended to protect the farmland but which were felt to be too restrictive. Conflicting views about both the

---

[30] See Christopher Leo, *The Politics of Urban Development: Canadian Urban Expressway Disputes,* Monographs on Canadian Urban Development, No. 3, Toronto, Institute of Public Administration, 1977.

style and substance of municipal government were presented by the nonfarm rural dweller and the farmer, the new resident and the long time settler, the seasonal population and the permanent inhabitants.

Given these developments, the caretaker or custodial role of local government became less and less appropriate, as did the notion of periodic voting as the primary method of citizen involvement. Instead, citizens and citizen groups increasingly questioned the actions of their municipal councils and demanded a more open, consultative decision-making process that considered their views at least as much as the technical advice provided by staff. An even more direct response was evident in some cities where reform candidates and local parties ran for municipal office. These developments, which are examined in Chapter 9, were not new. Indeed, Kaplan provides numerous examples of both citizen group and party activity in the early years of local government in our major cities and notes that "a culture that ascribed a high mission to local government and forbade all forms of 'politics' co-existed alongside an intensive, undignified scramble for specific facilities." [31]

However, the upsurge in this activity in the postwar period reflected a growing public conviction that local governments must demonstrate responsiveness and accountability in the discharge of their responsibilities. But, here again the traditional system was inadequate in several respects. The fragmentation of the structure made it very difficult to assign responsibility for action (or inaction). Not only was power divided among the council and varying numbers of local special purpose bodies, but in addition responsibilities were shared between the local and senior levels of government, and an extensive network of conditional grant payments further blurred the focus of responsibility.

Nor was accountability any clearer within the council of most municipalities. All councillors were collectively responsible, and yet none were specifically responsible for anything! Except in the few instances where organized political parties operated, councils were made up of a group of individuals with potentially different interests and concerns and no sense of cohesion or collective purpose. There wasn't any particular governing group responsible for taking the initiative in dealing with the problems facing the municipality. Nor was there any group responsible for scrutinizing and criticizing the initiatives taken to ensure that they were in the best interests of the public. It was almost impossible for citi-

---

[31] Harold Kaplan, *Reform, Planning and City Politics: Montreal, Winnipeg, and Toronto,* Toronto, University of Toronto Press, 1982, p. 146.

zens to know where to direct criticism or praise. Any particular council-lor could claim that he or she was for (or against) the matter at issue but was outvoted by the other councillors. The chances for buck-passing in this system were endless.

Even if councils wanted to be accountable and responsive, previously mentioned legal and financial limitations acted as severe constraints. Often councils couldn't do what their local citizens wanted them to because they lacked the authority, or had failed to receive provincial approval, or felt unable to finance the expenditures involved. These limitations are well summarized by Plunkett and Graham in their exami-nation of "Whither Municipal Government."

> When many of the apparent characteristics of contemporary urban local government in Canada are taken into account (the tendency to adhere to a purely service role, increased dependence on conditional provincial grants, fragmentation of responsibilities, intergovernmental linkages based on professional and functional ties rather than on broad policy issues, lack of policy direction and the failure to furnish an indentifiable government), we have to conclude that local governments are adhering to their role as agents of provincial interest to the detriment of their role as interpretors of the local scene.[32]

Summary

By the middle of the twentieth century, approximately 100 years after the establishment of local government in Canada — if the Baldwin Act of Ontario is used as a major starting point — the local government system had become increasingly inadequate, largely because of the pressures of urbanization. To review, this chapter has discerned a number of cracks in the foundation, including:

1. Inappropriate municipal boundaries arising from an excessive number of small municipalities and from the fragmented municipal structure found in most urban centres.
2. An erosion of the powers of the municipality to separate boards and commissions and to the senior levels of government.
3. Insufficient municipal revenue sources and an increasing de-pendence upon provincial grants, heavily conditional in nature.
4. An incompatibility between the nonpolitical tradition inher-ited from the turn of the century reform era and the increasingly

---

[32] T. J. Plunkett and Katherine A. Graham, "Whither Municipal Government," in *Canadian Public Administration*, Winter 1982, p. 614.

controversial issues and value judgments facing municipal governments, especially in urban Canada.
5.   Municipal governing bodies that were ineffective in providing
leadership, coordination, and a clear focus of accountability and
responsibility.

As these problems intensified, various adaptations and modifications
occurred, culminating in major local government reform initiatives in a
number of the provinces. However, as will be seen, rather than building
new foundations for a modern system of local government based equally
on considerations of effective representation and efficient service delivery, most of these reforms did little more than patch up the cracks in the
traditional foundation, leaving the structure over-balanced in favour of
the service delivery function.

5   *Local Government Reform*

Objectives:

1.   To describe the main local government reforms introduced in the various provinces in the post World War Two period.
2.   To examine the strengths and weaknesses of these reform initiatives.
3.   To assess the overall impact of these reforms on the shortcomings in the traditional system of local government described in the preceding chapter.

Introduction

The present local government system in Canada is the product of extensive reform efforts in a number of the provinces, especially in the first couple of decades following World War Two. A major purpose of this chapter is to examine these reforms and the resulting local government system in relation to the inadequacies identified in the previous chapter.

In addition to the breadth of this topic, a further difficulty is determining the beginning of the reform period since, as has already been demonstrated, the system of local government has undergone considerable adaptation since its establishment. Examples include the shift of functions upward to more senior levels of government, the establishment of intermunicipal special purpose bodies, intermunicipal servicing agreements, boundary extensions through annexations and amalgamations, and increased financial assistance from the senior levels of government.

As early as the 1930s and 1940s the Alberta government was involved in consolidating not only rural municipal districts but also school districts. A further consolidation of rural educational and municipal administrative units into one tier county governments was begun in 1950. Over the next decade we witnessed a period of what might be termed *ad hoc metropolitan reform,* commencing with the establishment of Metropolitan Toronto in 1953 and extending to Montreal and Winnipeg by the beginning of the 1960s. These reforms were ad hoc in the sense that they represented unique responses to serious servicing problems in the three urban areas involved, rather than arising from any comprehensive study of local government in the particular province.

In contrast, the decade of the 1960s can be distinguished by not only a great increase in reform activities but also much more comprehensive approaches in several of the provinces. For example, fundamental

77

examinations of the provincial-local relationship were carried out in New Brunswick in 1963 and in Manitoba in 1964, although only the New Brunswick recommendations were acted upon. Reform initiatives were introduced in British Columbia and Quebec in 1965 with particular emphasis on the creation of upper tier governments for the urban areas and, in the case of Quebec, voluntary amalgamations of small municipalities. The establishment of regional governments was the central feature of Ontario's local government reform efforts during this period.

REFORM PERIODS:
1950s — AD HOC REFORMS
1960s — MORE COMPREHENSIVE APPROACHES
1970s — REFORM MOMENTUM ABATED

The reform momentum has abated markedly since the beginning of the 1970s, with the only major structural changes being the creation of Winnipeg Unicity in 1972 and the introduction of regional county municipalities (RCMs) in Quebec in 1979. Major local government studies in both Nova Scotia and Newfoundland were completed in 1974, but were not acted upon except for some gradual changes in recent years. Instead, there appears to be a movement back to a more ad hoc approach such as characterized the 1950s. Grand designs for the local government system of a whole province have been abandoned. (Perhaps they were simply too "grand" — the monumental Graham Commission on Nova Scotia comprised some 7 000 pages!) Specific urban areas are being dealt with individually again, although there have been more studies than actual reforms. Examples include St. John's, Halifax, various regional government areas in Ontario, and Edmonton. In this latter instance, a major annexation battle preceded the expansion of Edmonton's boundaries.

Since a strict chronological presentation would necessitate returning to certain provinces on two or more separate occasions, the complete reform experience of each province will be examined even though this approach will obviously range back and forth chronologically. For a listing of the main reform initiatives in sequence, consult Table 4 in the summary section of this chapter.

Ontario

Since the pressures of change, which rendered the traditional local government system increasingly inadequate, have been previously described as arising because of urbanization, it is not surprising that the first major structural reform in Ontario was introduced in the Toronto area. A brief examination of the background to, and nature of, this reform is useful in assessing subsequent reforms.

Metropolitan Toronto

With the postwar "population explosion," the rapid growth of a number of the municipalities surrounding the city of Toronto produced serious servicing difficulties. Most pressing were the problems of water supply and sewage treatment facilities arising from the fact that only six of the thirteen municipalities involved had direct physical access to Lake Ontario. Arterial road development could not keep pace with the rapidly increasing volume of traffic. Public transportation and the existing highway network were poorly integrated. There was a desperate need for new schools. Many of the outlying municipalities were particulary ill-equipped to finance these service demands since, as dormitory suburbs, they lacked industrial assessment to help relieve the tax burden of the residential taxpayer.

The city of Toronto also faced serious economic and social problems, with a large backlog of public works because of the disruption of the depression and war years, and a greatly increased demand for welfare services. There was growing traffic congestion because of the extent of commuter population, and urban renewal and redevelopment needs were increasingly obvious. With each municipality seeking capital funds on its own credit, borrowing by the burgeoning suburbs became more and more difficult as interest rates rose.

METROPOLITAN TORONTO:
ESTABLISHED JAN. 1, 1953
TWO TIERS, WITH POWERS SHIFTED TO UPPER TIER
INDIRECT ELECTION OF METRO COUNCIL
BECAME UNOFFICIAL "MODEL" FOR REGIONAL GOVERNMENTS

By the beginning of the 1950s it was evident that a radical solution was required to meet existing servicing crises and ensure orderly future growth. The need for intermunicipal cooperation had already prompted innumerable joint agreements between two or more municipalities and a number of proposals for annexations and amalgamations. Indeed, it was the presentation of three such separate applications to the Ontario Municipal Board in 1950 that brought the matter to a head and led to the recommendations that created Metropolitan Toronto.

This reform, which was radical and yet simple, established a federated form of government embracing the city of Toronto and the 12 surrounding municipalities. As the lower tier in a two tier structure, these 13 municipalities retained their existing boundaries and continued to exercise a wide range of responsibilities. In addition, an upper tier unit, the municipality of Metropolitan Toronto, was established with the responsibility for such major functions as assessment, debenture borrowing, water supply and trunk mains, sewage treatment works and trunk sewers, and designated metropolitan roads. A number of responsibilities were also to be shared between the two levels of government. The fact that the metropolitan council was indirectly elected, that is composed of individuals elected in the first instance to designated positions on the lower tier councils, made the new structure similar to the century old county system in Ontario. The major differences, of course, were the inclusion of the city in the metropolitan system and the much stronger powers given to the upper tier council.

In its early years, Metropolitan Toronto was substantially successful in combating the servicing problems facing the member municipalities, particularly as regards sewers, water supply, education, and general financial stability. To a considerable extent, these early successes have been attributed to the forceful, skilled leadership of the first chairman of the metropolitan council, Frederick Gardiner, who held this position from 1953 to 1961. Gardiner's personal philosophy was clearly consistent with the founding objectives of the new metropolitan system — to develop the servicing infrastructure needed to accommodate the growth pressures. As Timothy Colton observes, Metropolitan Toronto was invented to promote what was presumed to be a common and profound interest in rapid urban growth.[1]

While Gardiner was quite successful in meeting these initial objectives, Colton notes that doubts were growing even before his retirement.[2] Yes, there was a massive expansion of housing, but primarily in the form of high rise apartment construction that was accompanied by an increasing concentration of power in the development industry. Public transit was upgraded and expanded, but the construction of ex-

---

[1] Timothy J. Colton, *Big Daddy,* Toronto, University of Toronto Press, 1980, p. 175.

[2] *Ibid.,* pp. 177–178.

pressways prompted a growing anti-expressway sentiment, culminating in the Stop-Spadina movement. Toronto enjoyed a boom in downtown development, but fears mounted about an excessive growth mentality and the disruption of established neighbourhoods — as reflected in the activism of citizens and citizen groups in the 1960s.

Quite apart from these changing public attitudes, Kaplan offers some interesting explanations for the decline in Metropolitan Toronto's momentum after the first few years.[3] He emphasizes the significance of the indirect election of metropolitan councillors, noting that they stood, succeeded, or failed largely on the basis of their records in their local (lower tier) council. The councillors only referred to Metro when it was politically expedient to blame it for not delivering enough for the local municipality in question. Ironically, according to Kaplan it was this very parochialism of councillors that helped to explain Metropolitan Toronto's initiatives and successes in the early years. Gardiner astutely avoided issues that would threaten local municipalities, and councillors were largely indifferent to everything else and prepared to accept Gardiner's persuasive leadership. However, when Metro turned to the more complex issues of the 1960s, especially under the less forceful chairmen who succeeded Gardiner, the limitations of this passive support became increasingly apparent. Noting that Metropolitan Toronto's main achievements were between 1953 and 1957, Kaplan contends that "in retrospect, the early burst of activity was the aberration and the subsequent prolonged retreat a more accurate expression of the system's character."[4]

Some problems and limitations were documented by the Royal Commission on Metropolitan Toronto, established in 1963 to examine the first decade of operation. However, the Commission's 1965 Report endorsed continuation of the two tier system.[5] The main change, introduced effective January 1st, 1967, was a consolidation of the original 13 municipalities at the lower tier into six. In addition, the metropolitan council was increased to 32 members, with the city retaining its 12 representatives but the five suburban municipalities now sending 20 in recognition of their much greater population growth since the original establishment of Metro. A few responsibilities, notably waste disposal

---

[3] Harold Kaplan, *Reform, Planning, and City Politics: Montreal, Winnipeg, Toronto,* Toronto, University of Toronto Press, 1982, pp. 685–690.

[4] *Ibid.,* p. 694.

[5] *Report of the Royal Commission on Metropolitan Toronto* (H. Carl Goldenberg, Commissioner), Toronto, Queen's Printer, 1965.

and social assistance, were transferred from the lower tier municipalities to Metropolitan Toronto, continuing a trend that had become evident throughout the 1950s.

As Kaplan observes, there was little in these reforms to revive Metro.[6] While the suburban municipalities now enjoyed a majority position, they had no regional aspirations on which to use their power. They had received the necessary expansion of their basic services during the first decade. Now it was the City of Toronto that needed Metro more — to help finance the renewal of aging facilities. But Kaplan concludes that with a complacent suburban majority Metropolitan Toronto was even less inclined to blaze new trails.

In 1974 another Royal Commission was appointed to review the Metropolitan Toronto system.[7] It recommended retention of the existing structure, including the six lower tier municipalities, with some boundary modifications. Partly in recognition of some of the problems previously discussed, it did recommend changes relating to such matters as the election of the metropolitan council and the division of governmental responsibilities.

Its recommendations were not acted upon, however, and it appeared that the commitment to reform in the Metropolitan Toronto area was languishing just as were the growth pressures that originally launched the metropolitan system. Metropolitan Toronto is now "hemmed in" on all sides by regional governments (and Lake Ontario), it is largely developed, and its growth has been slowing even before the economic downturn at the end of the 1970s. While its population increased by 45% from 1951 to 1961 and by 29% from 1961 to 1971, the increase from 1971 to 1976 was only 2%, and the population is expected to decline by 10% between 1976 and 1991.[8]

THIRD TIME LUCKY?
THIRD MAJOR STUDY OF METRO, IN 1986
SOME CHANGES INTRODUCED FOR 1988 ELECTIONS

Some limited, but important, changes to Metropolitan Toronto's governing system did finally occur — as the result of yet another major study completed in 1986.[9] Effective at the time of the 1988 municipal election, the composition of Metro's council was changed to 34 members,

---

[6] Kaplan, *op. cit.*, p. 697.

[7] *Report of the Royal Commission on Metropolitan Toronto* (Honourable John P. Robarts, Chairman), Toronto, Queen's Printer, 1977.

[8] Colton, *op. cit.*, p. 180.

the mayors of the six lower tier municipalities as before, and 28 directly elected members — who do not hold any seats on the lower tier. Provision was also made for the Chairman of Metro to be chosen by the metropolitan council from among the 28 directly elected members. These changes appear to reflect a belated concern by the Ontario government for the representative role of local government and its accountability and responsiveness — a point returned to at the conclusion of this chapter.

The importance of the Metropolitan Toronto experience lies not only in what was done there, but on the extensive influence that this model wielded on the reforms elsewhere in the province, as described below.

Regional Government: What's in a Name?

A more comprehensive approach to local government reform in Ontario was introduced toward the end of the 1960s, although, as will be seen, the actual reforms introduced were considerably more limited than the reform policy. Indeed, the process began well before any governmental policy statement with the appointment of local government studies in several, mostly heavily urbanized, areas — beginning with Ottawa-Carleton in 1964. At this time, significantly, the Metropolitan Toronto system was still in its initial, conspicuously successful phase, and the model was to influence greatly all subsequent reforms. The actual local government reform policy set out in Design for Development, Phase Two at the end of 1968 was potentially quite broad and imaginative, largely because of guidelines and a philosophical base taken from the Report of the Ontario Committee on Taxation the previous year. The policy recognized the need to provide not only efficient delivery of services but also adequate access and effective representation of local views and concerns. It called for regional governments based on such criteria as community of interest, an adequate financial base, and sufficient size to generate economies of scale.[10] The policy also proposed varied structural approaches including both two tier and one tier governments and the direct election of upper tier councillors in the former instance.

---

[9]   Report by the Task Force on Representation and Accountability in Metropolitan Toronto, *Analysis and Options for the Government of Metropolitan Toronto*, November 1986.

[10] See the Honourable John Robarts and Darcy McKeough, *Design for Development: Phase Two*, Statements to the Legislature of Ontario, November 28th and December 2nd, 1968, and *The Ontario Committee on Taxation, Volume Two*, Toronto, Queen's Printer, 1967, Chapter 23.

REGISTER —

REGIONAL GOVERNMENTS:
IMAGINATIVE POLICY IN DESIGN FOR DEVELOPMENT: II
BUT IN PRACTICE, JUST MODIFIED COUNTY SYSTEMS

In practice, the reforms introduced were all regional governments closely resembling Metropolitan Toronto. As such, they can best be described as a modification of the traditional county system in Ontario. The reformed structures have all contained two tiers with the upper tier closely paralleling the boundaries of one or more counties in most cases. All or major municipal responsibility for such functions as welfare, parks, roads, water supply, sewage disposal, planning, and capital borrowing have been vested in this upper tier. The lower tier units in the structure have been formed by a consolidation of constituent municipalities and have included any cities and separated towns, previously separate under the county system. With minor exceptions and recent changes, election to the upper tier closely resembles the indirect election of county councillors, and the costs of regional services are apportioned to lower tier municipalities in accordance with their assessment in essentially the same manner as under the county system.

In the decade from the commissioning of the first local government reform study (of Ottawa-Carleton) in May 1964 to the coming into operation of the Regional Municipality of Haldimand-Norfolk in April 1974, 11 regional governments were established,[11] covering over one-third of the population of Ontario. However, well before this time, the regional government program was losing momentum. Indeed, most local government reform studies were undertaken before the government announced its policy on the subject in the aforementioned Design for Development statement. As the unpopularity and political cost of the reforms became apparent, the government increasingly disavowed any intention of introducing new regional government initiatives.

Instead a County Restructuring Program was announced in February 1974. Under this program, the Ontario government indicated its willingness to participate jointly with counties in local government studies and to share equally the costs of such studies under certain specified condi-

---

[11]　These were Ottawa-Carleton, Niagara, York, Waterloo, Sudbury, Peel, Halton, Hamilton-Wentworth, Durham, Haldimand-Norfolk, and Muskoka, with the latter being known as a District Municipality. If we add the prototype, Metropolitan Toronto, and the subsequently established Restructured County of Oxford (described below), there are thirteen regional governments in Ontario, containing two-thirds of its population.

tions. On the surface this new policy appeared to involve a significant shift toward local initiative in reform. However, the policy went on to identify certain conditions that would have to be met for a county to qualify as a restructured county and thereby be eligible for the additional powers and grants being given to the regional governments. These specified conditions were essentially the basic features of the regional governments already established, and the only restructured county to date (Oxford) has adopted a two tier system basically the same as the regional governments. Therefore, one can reasonably wonder whether the County Restructuring Program was intended as anything more than a change in name and shift in emphasis from provincial to local initiative with the same reform objectives in mind.

**COUNTY RESTRUCTURING:
REGIONAL GOVERNMENT BY ANOTHER NAME?
TRUE OF OXFORD COUNTY, BUT NONE SINCE**

The question may be academic since very little action was taken on the studies carried out under this program, and the prolonged period of minority government in Ontario in the latter part of the 1970s forestalled any new initiatives. Indeed, the provincial government even appeared unwilling to modify existing reformed structures if there were local objections. The previously-cited Robarts Royal Commission on Metropolitan Toronto was but one of several reviews appointed in the mid-1970s to examine established regional governments.[12] In spite of a wide variety of recommendations, however, only minor changes were introduced, notably the creation of the City of Kanata and the elevation of Nepean to city status, both in the Regional Municipality of Ottawa-Carleton.

Instead, Ontario appeared to return to a traditional method of adapting local government to growth pressures — annexation and amalgamation. The Municipal Boundary Negotiations Act enacted at the end of 1981 outlines a new approach to boundary adjustments with procedures somewhat similar to the negotiation process found within collective bargaining. Since its introduction, this process has been used to bring about boundary adjustments in a number of urban areas in Ontario.

---

[12] See also William Archer's *Report of the Niagara Region Study Review Commission,* 1977; Henry Mayo's *Report of the Ottawa-Carleton Review Commission,* 1976; Henry Stewart's *Report of the Hamilton-Wentworth Review Commission,* 1978; and William Palmer's *Report of the Waterloo Region Review Commission,* 1979.

Further evidence of a return to traditional practices was found in the major revision of The Planning Act enacted in 1983. By providing for the delegation of planning responsibilities to county governments under certain conditions, the government appeared to be accepting (and, in fact, reinforcing) the continuation of this long established system.

The momentum for reform revived somewhat toward the end of the 1980s however, fueled by the completion of yet another round of regional government reviews.[13] About every ten years one can count on a series of these "regional recycles" to bring the topic of reform back to the fore. Given the Ontario government's action on introducing some of the changes recommended by the Task Force on Metropolitan Toronto, it may be that these latest regional reviews will bring about change, unlike their predecessors in the mid-1970s.

The county restructuring initiatives of the early 1970s may also be undergoing a revival — as a result of an Advisory Committee Report on County Government.[14] The Ontario government is considering a wide range of recommendations that include the possibility of counties assuming a number of additional responsibilities and that also suggest improvements in the representative nature of the county system.

FOCUS OF REFORMS
IMPROVING EFFICIENCY AND SERVICE DELIVERY
REPRESENTATIVE ASPECTS LARGELY IGNORED

Even if no further major changes are made in Ontario, it is striking to note that, as a result of the reform initiatives that have been introduced, two-thirds of the population of Ontario is under regional governments (including Metropolitan Toronto), so it is important to consider the nature of these reforms. Clearly, they were preoccupied with structural changes designed to improve administrative efficiency and the provision of services. (This emphasis was also evident in the parallel reform in educational administration culminating in the still very controversial county and district boards of education established in 1969.) Service

---

[13] These include reviews of Ottawa-Carleton, Niagara, and Haldimand-Norfolk, in addition to the previously cited Task Force Report on Metropolitan Toronto.

[14] Report of the Advisory Committee on County Government, *Patterns for the Future*, Toronto, Ontario Government Bookstore, November 1987. See also Report of the Consultation Committee to the Minister of Municipal Affairs, *County Government in Ontario*, Toronto, January 1989.

standards have doubtless improved, although some would dispute this, and the division of responsibilities between the upper and lower tiers has caused friction and inhibited coordination.

Moreover, the reforms have been quite narrow in focus. Until recently, the representative role of local government has been largely ignored and little attention has been given to ways of making local governments more responsible and accountable to their inhabitants. The consolidation of lower tier municipalities reduced the number of elected councils and, with the enlarged areas, many citizens felt that their municipal government was less accessible and less sensitive to their particular needs. The feeling of alienation was even stronger with respect to the regional councils, which not only appeared remote but also had taken over a number of responsibilities previously exercised at the lower tier. The increase in regional staff made the system seem increasingly bureaucratic and the essentially indirect election of regional councillors did little to generate public involvement in, and support for, the regional system.

One analysis of the reformed structures in Ontario discerns a change in the balance of power at the local level and describes "a major increase in the influence of public servants, especially regional ones, at the expense of local elected officials and residents."[15] Because of the municipal consolidations there are fewer elected representatives and their role has changed. Rather than being closely involved in the operations of the municipality (perhaps too closely at times), councillors appear relegated to a role of responding to policy proposals put forward by the bureaucracy, especially at the regional level.

This analysis further notes that with fewer councils and councillors and more formal, streamlined procedures for handling business, the nature of citizen participation in local government has also changed. "The emphasis now was on scheduling an appointment before a council and presenting a brief outlining one's arguments...instead of a spontaneous appearance and an informal discussion...." The result was a reallocation of power among citizens since "the new technical rules of citizen participation not surprisingly favour those with formal argumentative skills or those who can afford to hire people with these skills."[16]

---

[15] Henry J. Jacek, "Regional Government and Development: Administrative Efficiency versus Local Democracy," in Donald C. MacDonald (ed.), *The Government and Politics of Ontario,* Toronto, Nelson, 1985, p. 111.

[16] *Ibid.,* p. 112.

Recent reforms in the composition of the council of Metropolitan Toronto and in the selection of the Metro Chairman have already been noted — and are discussed further in Chapter 8. The previously cited Advisory Committee Report on County Government also gave considerable attention to the composition of county councils and the need for more equitable representation of lower tier municipalities. It may be, therefore, that the long-neglected representative role of local government will receive greater attention in any future reform initiatives in Ontario. As will be seen, however, the relative neglect of this role has characterized reform efforts in most of the provinces.

Manitoba

Local government reform activities in Manitoba have been concentrated on Winnipeg which, as the provincial capital and the centre for over half of the population of the province, understandably dominates the local government scene.[17] However, the opportunity for a more comprehensive reform affecting the overall system of local government was presented by a major Royal Commission study in the early 1960s.

Missed Opportunities in Manitoba

In 1963 the Manitoba government appointed a commission:

> to inquire into all aspects of the powers, responsibilities and organization of local government in Manitoba, its financial structure and resources, and in particular to examine the division of responsibilities between the municipalities and the Provincial Government.[18]

The Manitoba Royal Commission's 1964 Report attempted a new delineation of provincial and municipal responsibilities. While similar to the services to people versus services to property distinction employed

---

[17] Indeed, by 1971 — the year the present Winnipeg Unicity structure was introduced — the city accounted for over 65% of the province's labour force, 70% of its personal income, 80% of its industrial production, 62% of its retail sales, fully 95% of its wholesale sales, and nearly 70% of total provincial tax revenue. See Mathew J. Kiernan and David C. Walker, "Winnipeg" in Warren Magnusson and Andrew Sancton (eds.), *City Politics in Canada,* Toronto, University of Toronto Press, 1983, p. 225.

[18] *Report of the Manitoba Royal Commission on Local Government Organization and Finance* — popularly known as the Michener Report, after its chairman, Roland Michener — Winnipeg, Queen's Printer, 1964.

by the Byrne Commission in New Brunswick (as described later in this chapter), the Manitoba breakdown was more refined and included a category of services best provided through cooperation among the municipalities, school divisions, and provincial agencies. To administer these joint municipal services, provincial services, and revenue collection, the report called for the division of Manitoba into 11 administrative regions.

Each region was to have a regional council composed of elected representatives from municipalities within the region. However, these regional councils were not to constitute another level of government, as do the county councils in Ontario for example, but were to serve as a forum for developing and carrying out joint works of the municipalities. Executive authority and the responsibility for formulating policy and imposing taxes would remain with the individual municipal councils. The municipalities themselves would be considerably changed, however, with the report recommending that the existing 106 municipalities in Manitoba be amalgamated to form 40 or 50 units. Whatever its merits, this major study was largely ignored but, in the meantime, the first of two structural reforms in the Winnipeg area had been introduced.

Metropolitan Winnipeg

The factors leading to this reform were quite similar to those leading to the establishment of Metropolitan Toronto. The population growth following World War Two brought the by now familiar urban problems. Expenditures soared, notably in education, while the revenues were distributed unevenly and there were wide variations in property assessment. There was inadequate sewage disposal for the area and water rationing became common. A considerable number of intermunicipal special purpose bodies operated in the Greater Winnipeg area and, while they enjoyed some success, their very existence pointed to the need for some form of area-wide government. In fact, it has been suggested that the Metro Planning Commission established in 1943 helped to shape thinking about wider planning issues and thus to create the more unified outlook that was needed for subsequent reforms.[19]

A Greater Winnipeg Investigating Commission was established in 1955. In 1959 it reported with recommendations for the establishment of a two tier system of metropolitan government in the area. Apparently the

---

[19] Kaplan, *op. cit.*, pp. 501–504.

commission was strongly influenced by the newly created system of Metropolitan Toronto and frequent consultations were held with its chairman, Fred Gardiner. [20]

METROPOLITAN WINNIPEG:
ESTABLISHED IN 1960
TWO TIER SYSTEM, INFLUENCED BY METRO TORONTO
DIRECTLY ELECTED UPPER TIER COUNCIL

The reform introduced by the Manitoba government in 1960 was more modest than the commission's recommendations and it also differed from Metropolitan Toronto in certain significant respects. A two tier system of municipal government was established with ten municipalities completely within Metro's jurisdiction and nine more partly in the Metro area and partly in the outlying "additional zone" where Metro had planning authority. The metropolitan government was given full authority over all planning, zoning, and issuing of permits as well as such operating functions as assessment, civil defence, flood protection, sewage disposal (but not collection), and water (excluding local distribution). Many responsibilities that had previously been exercised by separate special purpose bodies were vested directly in the metropolitan council and no new boards were established — in marked contrast to the Metropolitan Toronto system in which the numerous separate boards were retained.

In a notable departure from the Toronto approach, the ten members of the metropolitan council were directly elected from special pie-shaped districts including both central and suburban areas. Moreover, metropolitan councillors could not also hold local office. It was hoped that this type of district and method of representation would encourage area-wide thinking. This it did do, but almost too successfully! The metropolitan council contained a strong core of Metro supporters and with more specific, parochial demands being directed at lower tier councils, they were able to take the broader view. However, in their enthusiasm they were rather aggressive in their initiatives and insufficiently sensitive to the concerns of the local councils. Municipalities that questioned whether they were receiving a share of Metro expenditures

---

[20] T. Axworthy, "Winnipeg Unicity," in Advisory Committee on Intergovernmental Relations, *A Look to the North: Canadian Regional Experience*, Washington, D.C., 1974, p. 90.

commensurate with their financial contribution were informed that decisions were made objectively, in the public interest, not on the basis of the pork barrel.

This approach certainly contrasts with Gardiner's skilful balancing of city and suburban benefits in the Metropolitan Toronto system. As Kaplan points out, if Metropolitan Toronto had insufficiently strong boundaries between it and its lower tier and could not avoid being exploited and manipulated by the municipal governments (especially after Gardiner), "Metro Winnipeg's problem was that it forged impermeable boundaries between it and the municipalities and thus remained singularly obtuse about the wishes of those municipalities."[21] Adding to the problems was the extent of the opposition to the new metropolitan system. Some negative reaction had been expected since the suburbs had wanted the status quo and the City of Winnipeg had wanted complete amalgamation.

> What occurred instead was a virtual municipal insurrection, an assault on metro far exceeding anyone's expectations. During its ten year history, but especially in 1961–65, metro lived under a state of siege.[22]

In the face of these attacks, "metro became even more insular and self-righteous.[23]

The attack on the metropolitan system was led by Stephen Juba, the long time mayor of the City of Winnipeg, "conducted without restraint or let-up in the mayor's characteristically strident, affectively charged, assaultive style."[24] The criticisms were kept up partly because of the provincial government's lukewarm support for its creation. Premier Roblin had stated that there wouldn't be any review of the new system until 1965, but in the face of mounting criticism of the system he appointed a review commission in 1962. The Commission's Report in 1964 reaffirmed the basic system, although some changes were made in the status of municipalities partly in and partly without Metro's jurisdiction.

Attacks on the system subsided somewhat after 1965, with Premier Roblin's assertion of stronger support. Instead, attention increasingly shifted to the possibility of amalgamation of the municipalities within the system. The 1969 election of an NDP government suddenly made such a change quite probable because of the NDP's long time support for an

---

[21] Kaplan, *op. cit.*, p. 684.

[22] *Ibid.*, p. 554.

[23] *Ibid.*, p. 556.

[24] *Ibid.*, p. 562.

amalgamated approach. Indeed, even though a Local Boundaries Commission appointed by the previous government was still continuing its studies, the new provincial government commenced preparation of a White Paper "Proposals for Urban Reorganization," released December 22, 1970. From this initiative came the establishment of the Winnipeg Unicity structure, effective January 1st, 1972.

Winnipeg Unicity

As its name implies, Unicity replaced the two tier metropolitan system with one enlarged city government. Much more than amalgamation of municipalities was involved, however, and the administrative centralization for efficiency in service delivery was to be offset by a number of provisions for political decentralization. To understand the new structure, it is important to bear in mind the philosophy and objectives of local government on which the reform was based.

Of particular note was the emphasis on the representative role of local government and the importance of citizen access and participation. In part, this was reflected in the provision for an unusually large council of fifty members, each elected from a separate ward. In addition, the Unicity legislation established thirteen community committees, each covering a number of wards and consisting of the councillors from these wards. These committees were originally seen as providing a forum for public involvement and for the political decentralization of certain functions. They were to maintain close two-way communication between Unicity and its residents concerning present and potential policies, programs, and budgets. Each committee was also to be responsible for preparing its own budget for services with a local orientation that were assigned to it, a provision that suggested the possibility of some variation in local services. To advise and assist each committee, the legislation also provided for the election of a residents advisory group (RAG).

WINNIPEG UNICITY:
ESTABLISHED IN 1972
ONE TIER GOVERNMENT
EMPHASIS ON PARLIAMENTARY MODEL
ELABORATE STRUCTURE FOR MANAGEMENT

A second significant feature of the new system was the attempt to build in the elements of the parliamentary model of government, particularly in terms of a separate executive responsible for providing leadership and answering to the elected council. A key provision of this model, which was proposed in the White Paper but deleted from the legislation, was the stipulation that the mayor be chosen by and from the elected members of council. Through this process, the mayor could provide leadership on council since he or she had majority support and, at the same time, the mayor would only remain in this position so long as he or she retained the confidence of the councillors. It was envisaged that the members of the executive committee would be chosen in the same way and, with the mayor chairing them, this body would be akin to the cabinet in the parliamentary system. An important element, of course, was the existence of organized political parties. As discussed in Chapter 9, some form of political party activity has been evident in Winnipeg since 1919, but it was hoped that a more formalized party system would evolve to complement the new government structure.

INTERNAL STRUCTURE:
EXECUTIVE POLICY COMMITTEE
THREE STANDING COMMITTEES
BOARD OF COMMISSIONERS
CHIEF COMMISSIONER AND THREE OTHER COMMISSIONERS

A third distinctive feature of Unicity was the amount of emphasis given to the internal organization of the municipality. It is clear that an attempt was made to concentrate council's role on representation and policy making, while delegating much of the executive power of council to committees and staff and endeavouring to ensure coordination of the administrative activities of the municipality. To this end, a fairly elaborate structure was established. Starting at the bottom, departments were grouped under three commissioners of works and operations, environment, and finance. The commissioners were responsible for coordinating the activities of the departments under their jurisdiction and also met with a chief commissioner as a board of commissioners on which the mayor was the fifth member ex officio. This board had overall responsibility for administrative operations and the implementation of council decisions. The council itself was organized into three standing committees with both policy and administrative responsibilities and with terms of reference identical to that of the three commissioners. In addition, there was the previously mentioned executive policy committee chaired by the mayor and including the heads of the three standing committees. The board of commissioners, backed by a newly established budget bureau, reported to this executive policy committee, but individual commissioners also reported to their appropriate standing committee.

Unfortunately, the actual performance of Unicity has received mixed reviews, with some of the disappointment probably stemming from the innovative, ambitious objectives that had been initially set for the system. Perhaps the most positive achievement is the fact that the principle of unification under a one tier government is apparently well accepted — according to a Committee of Review appointed in 1975.[25] The committee also noted that greater equity in distributing the burden of taxation had resulted from the establishment of a single tax rate throughout the urban area, and that disparities in the level of services provided in the former separate municipal jurisdictions had been considerably reduced. On the other hand, Axworthy claims that capital works expenditures between suburbs and inner city ran as high as 7-1 in favour of the suburban areas. [26]

A number of the primary objectives of the new structure have not been realized. The Committee of Review laid much of the blame for Unicity's shortcomings on the fact that the mayor was directly elected rather than chosen from council, thereby removing the focus of leadership and accountability central to the parliamentary model. This lack of strong political leadership was especially significant given the large size of the council and the potentially fragmented outlook inherent in election by ward. Indeed, there is considerable evidence to suggest that traditional attitudes, outlooks, and practices continued to prevail within the council in spite of the changes in approach envisaged in the legislation.[27] Parochialism remained, and considerable attention was directed to the securing of public services for particular wards — often taking the form of a city-"suburbs" division — rather than the establish-

---

[25] *Report and Recommendations, Committee of Review, City of Winnipeg Act,* Winnipeg, Queen's Printer, October 1976.

[26] Lloyd Axworthy, "The Best Laid Plans Oft Go Astray: The Case of Winnipeg," in M. O. Dickerson, S. Drabek, and J. T. Woods (ed.), *Problems of Change in Urban Government,* Waterloo, Wilfred Laurier Press, 1980, p. 114.

[27] This observation is made by P. H. Wichern, Jr., *Winnipeg's Unicity After Two Years; Evaluation of an Experiment in Urban Government,* a paper prepared for the 46th annual meeting of the Canadian Political Science Association, Toronto, June 3–6, 1975, and a similar assessment is found in the Report of the Committee of Review.

ment of overall policies for the Unicity area. After a major study of the new system, Plunkett and Brownstone conclude that "city policy making has not been altered drastically, and that it has only been improved slightly from what it seems likely to have been if the former structure had remained unchanged."[28]

**MECHANISMS FOR PARTICIPATION:
COMMUNITY COMMITTEES
RESIDENT ADVISORY GROUPS (RAGS)
VAGUE MANDATE AND LITTLE INFLUENCE
EARLY ENTHUSIASM FADED QUICKLY**

Another major issue of concern has been the effectiveness of the new structure in facilitating citizen involvement, expecially through the community committees and the resident advisory groups. The roles of these bodies were insufficiently clear from the outset, although the Unicity legislation certainly gave them less power than had been envisaged by the White Paper. The community committees were not lawmaking bodies and they had no taxing powers. While there were suggestions that they would in some respects fulfil the role of the former lower tier municipalities, Higgins provides a more accurate description in calling them "sub-committees of the city council."[29]

Even less specific was the mandate of the resident advisory groups — to advise and assist the community councils! As Higgins outlines, the initial response from local citizens was strong, with almost 500 advisors elected at the first meetings of the resident advisory groups.[30] Disillusionment set in, however, with the realization that these groups had little influence and that even if their particular community committee was responsive to their views, the committee only comprised from three to six of the fifty-one members of council.

Other analysts haven't even been as positive as Higgins. Axworthy, for example, feels that the consultative mechanisms made very little impact and notes that in a 1973 survey "less than 5% of citizens recalled ever

---

[28] Meyer Brownstone and T. J. Plunkett, *Metropolitan Winnipeg: Politics and Reform of Local Government,* Berkeley, University of California Press, 1983, p. 173.

[29] Donald J. H. Higgins, *Urban Canada: Its Government and Politics,* Toronto, Macmillan, 1977, p. 150.

[30] *Ibid.,* p. 203.

having contact with the RAG's or Community Committees."[31] He also describes an increasingly centralized system characterized by bureaucratic "stonewalling." According to Axworthy, "Civic administrators became notorious for not divulging information, for controlling the activity of the junior members of departments in their public dealings, and for refusing public access to information."[32] Another study notes that in 1976 the Unicity Council prohibited the Community Committees from continuing with the allocation of modest sums to various community cultural and recreational groups. This action also blocked the limited financial support that had existed for the RAGs, and in 1981 — 10 years after the creation of these much-heralded instruments of citizen participation — council was allocating RAGs on average $400 each![33]

In June 1977 the Manitoba government adopted a number of amendments to the Unicity structure. However, ironically, these changes did little to resolve the weaknesses identified and, in some cases, have intensified them. In several respects, the amendments undermined the recommendations of the Committee of Review just as the original Unicity legislation had weakened the approach of the White Paper. The Committee of Review had recommended that the mayor be elected from within the council and that he or she appoint those chairing the standing committees. Those chairing and certain other specified members would constitute the executive and would be given the powers necessary to function as a cabinet. The committee had further recommended that the mayor and executive committee should be confirmed or replaced in their positions annually by a vote of council and that a chief critic should also be elected annually by those councillors not voting for the mayor. While it could not legislate a party system, the committee expressed the hope and conviction that such a system would evolve "under the influence of the parliamentary characteristics of our model."

Instead, however, the revised legislation removed the mayor from the board of commissioners and replaced the mayor on the executive policy committee by a council-elected chair. These changes, together with the continuation of direct election of the mayor seem intended to reduce the position to the largely ceremonial role found in most Canadian municipalities. A further change saw the reduction in the size of council from 50 to 29. The number of community committees (12 since 1974) was

---

[31] Axworthy, "The Best Laid Plans," *op. cit.*, p. 117.

[32] *Ibid.*, p. 116.

[33] Kiernan and Walker, *op. cit.*, pp. 236–7.

reduced to six and their vague and limited powers were further reduced. They now exercise discretion only with respect to libraries, parks and recreation, and some planning functions, a reflection of the growing trend toward centralization in program design and service delivery.[34] Moreover, with greatly increased areas and populations of approximately 100 000, the community councils and RAGs lost the close contact and familiarity with local issues that had been their main (and just about only) strength.

In June 1984, the Manitoba government appointed a committee to review the Unicity legislation and governing system. The committee's 1986 report found a lack of identifiable and consistent leadership within the Unicity Council, as well as confused roles and relationships among the various elements of the city governing machinery.[35] The committee recommended that significant powers of the city be delegated to an executive committee composed of six councillors and chaired by the mayor. These members would be nominated by the mayor and elected by council. The mayor would also appoint a deputy mayor from the members of the executive committee and would appoint, with the approval of the executive committee, all members of its sub-committees, which would replace the existing standing committees.

REFORMS ON HORIZON?
1986 REPORT OF REVIEW COMMITTEE
PROPOSALS TO STRENGTHEN LEADERSHIP
AND CITIZEN INVOLVEMENT
1987 WHITE PAPER — WATERED-DOWN RESPONSE
NO ACTION YET

The review committee also recommended that the community committees be given greater powers concerning the initiation, preparation, and approval of local plans and zoning. It further recommended that these bodies be allocated financial resources for expenditures on local services, programs, and facilities according to their individual priorities and needs.

---

[34] Lionel G. Feldman Consulting Ltd. and Institute of Local Government, Queen's University, *Evaluation of Alternative Structures and A Proposal for Local Governance in the Edmonton Region,* January 1980, p. 67.

[35] Ministry of Urban Affairs, *Discussion Paper,* "Strengthening Local Government in Winnipeg: Proposals for Changes to The City of Winnipeg Act," Winnipeg, February 27, 1987, p. 10. The summary of recommendations which follows is based on this Discussion Paper.

The government's response, in a 1987 White Paper,[36] was mixed. It rejected any change that would eliminate the standing committee system. While it agreed with the mayor chairing the executive committee, the government proposed that this committee consist of 12 members not six, with the additional members being councillors from each of the community committees as elected by those committees. Once again, therefore, the government's approach — if implemented — seems designed to prevent the mayor from exercising the kind of strong leadership intended. There is no reason why these additional six members of the executive committee would necessarily follow the mayor's direction. The government agreed with increasing the planning powers of the community committees, but without any increase in financial resources to these committees — here again limiting the potential of the change.

With the defeat of the NDP government and the election of a minority Conservative government at the end of the 1980s, any further reform of Unicity has been pushed into the background. Whatever the future brings, however, Unicity remains one of the most innovative approaches to local government reform and one of the few that accorded the representative role of local government at least as much attention as the service delivery role. As such, it will continue to generate attention and analysis. It seems clear, however, that much of its great potential has not been realized — in large part because of deficiencies in the original and amended legislation. Its shortcomings also reflect the limitations of structural reforms and the extent to which political traditions and practices continue to prevail — a fact that casts doubt on the potential of structural reform alone.[37]

New Brunswick

The first province to undertake comprehensive local government reform initiatives in the 1960s was New Brunswick, and it did so by appointing a Royal Commission on Finance and Municipal Taxation. The emphasis on fiscal matters implicit in the title reflected the difficulties facing local government in New Brunswick at the time. The level of municipal services compared unfavourably with other provinces and there were wide variations in the standard of service within New Brunswick, notably in

---

[36] *Ibid.*

[37] Kiernan and Walker, *op. cit.*, pp. 245–6.

education. A multitude of assessment and tax acts resulted in a variety of taxes, again differing from one municipality to the next. There were marked inequities in municipal taxation and high tax arrears. Moreover, municipalities faced increasing difficulties financing their servicing demands and by the 1960s three of the single tier rural counties were virtually bankrupt.

To its credit, the Byrne Commission, as it came to be known, did contend that the problems facing local government in New Brunswick were not just a matter of allocation of tax fields but also involved government organization and structure. In its 1963 report it made a commendable attempt to distinguish between services appropriate for the provincial level and for the local level. On this basis it recommended the transfer of a number of functions to the provincial level and called for the New Brunswick government to provide services directly for rural areas, hitherto governed by the counties. Recommendations such as these caused some observers to conclude that the commission's preoccupation with finances had led it to overemphasize efficiency and administrative rather than representative considerations.[38]

Major Reforms Carried Out

Following extensive public discussions the government of New Brunswick launched a Program for Equal Opportunity in 1967 under which the main recommendations of the Byrne Commission were implemented. The province took over responsibility for the administration of justice, welfare, and public health, and also financial responsibility for the provision of education with the number of school districts reduced from 422 to 33. All types of municipal taxation except the real property tax were abolished, and assessment — now to be at market value — and tax collection became provincial responsibilities. The 15 single tier rural counties were abolished and, in partial compensation, some 90 new villages were created. Nonincorporated local service districts were also created, as administrative units for the province to provide services that had been provided by the now-abolished county councils. Provision was

---

[38] Indeed, T. J. Plunkett in his "Criticism of Byrne Report" in Donald C. Rowat, *The Canadian Municipal System,* Toronto, McClelland and Stewart Limited, 1969, p. 180, charged that the Commission's proposed solutions "make the continuance of municipal government in New Brunswick of doubtful value". Plunkett repeated this criticism in an assessment carried out with W. Hooson, "Municipal Structure and Services: Graham Commission", *Canadian Public Policy,* Summer 1975.

made for the establishment of advisory local service district committees, if a sufficient number of local inhabitants actively participated in forming them.[39] To meet their expanded responsibility, the province established a number of field offices in rural areas.

Notwithstanding the apparent neglect of the representative dimension of local government, the reforms were beneficial in several respects. There was a substantial improvement in the quality of such services as education, justice, health and welfare. Moreover, the Byrne Commission's weakness in not recommending boundary changes needed in the urban areas was partly corrected by subsequent reforms, prompted by a number of other studies.[40] The boundaries of Saint John were extended to include the built-up areas of two adjacent municipalities, a number of other urban areas have been studied, and similar boundary adjustments have been made in the Moncton and Fredericton areas.

Governing Rural New Brunswick

One major problem not resolved, however, concerned the approximately 250 000 people (one-third of the population of New Brunswick) left without any form of local government.[41] These people looked to nearby villages and towns for some local services. They demanded some form of local government and, at the same time, the incorporated municipalities complained that these residents of nonincorporated areas were not paying fully for some local services they received.

In response to this situation, a Task Force on Nonincorporated Areas was established in June 1975. The resultant report[42] found not only the predictable concern about the lack of elected councils to represent the people but also inequities in the financing of services. It noted that many services underwritten by property taxation in the incorporated municipalities were, in the case of the unincorporated areas, provided by the

---

[39] Edwin G. Allen, *Municipal Organization in New Brunswick,* Ministry of Municipal Affairs, Fredericton, 1968, p. 12.

[40] Notably *Report of the Royal Commission on Metropolitan Saint John* (H. Carl Goldenberg, Chairman), Fredericton, 1963.

[41] See Harley d'Entremont and Patrick Robardet, "More Reform in New Brunswick: Rural Municipalities," *Canadian Public Administration,* Fall 1977.

[42] *Report of the Task Force on Nonincorporated Areas in New Brunswick,* Fredericton, Queen's Printer, 1976.

New Brunswick government without the imposition of any property taxation. Moreover, the report stated that some of the services provided by the provincial government, notably community planning, could not be implemented effectively by that level of government and that more opportunity for local citizen input was necessary. As a result of these and other considerations, the report recommended that all existing legislation pertaining to local service districts be repealed and that 11 new municipalities with the status of "rural municipalities" be incorporated. No action was taken on this recommendation, and one analysis concluded that the report was a piecemeal response to the problems facing the New Brunswick municipal system, handicapped by narrow — and narrowly interpreted — terms of reference. [43]

In the years since, however, there have been some changes in the arrangements for providing services to the population in the unincorporated rural part of New Brunswick. The area now includes some 325 Local Service Districts, within which "local" services are provided by the Department of Municipal Affairs and Environment.[44] In recent years, municipalities and Local Service Districts have discovered the advantages of combining to provide some services on a wider area. Regional ventures for the delivery of services have been organized in fields such as police protection, ambulance, solid waste management, and library services. The arrangements have usually involved the creation of commissions or regional boards with representation from the municipalities and Local Service Districts involved.

Because of the ad hoc nature of these arrangements, the Ministry of Municipal Affairs is currently undertaking a study that will propose "a legislative, policy and financial framework ... to accommodate and guide the creation and operation of regional services ventures."[45] However, this study will not examine the creation of other forms of local government; it will deal only with the provision of services within the current structure. A more comprehensive municipal review would seem appropriate (and has been demanded by municipalities and their associations) since the reformed structure has now been in existence for over two decades.

---

[43] D'Entremont and Robardet, *op. cit.,* p. 480.

[44] Letter from Gerald Hawkins, Ministry of Municipal Affairs and Environment, April 4, 1989. The summary of the current situation in rural New Brunswick that follows is based on this correspondence.

[45] *Ibid.*

British Columbia

In contrast to the comprehensive studies carried out in Manitoba and New Brunswick, British Columbia's approach to local government reform has been very pragmatic and directed to specific problems as perceived by the provincial government. To a large extent these problems were related to the absence of a municipal structure over much of the province. In 1966 only 2 870 square miles out of the 266 000 square miles in British Columbia were within organized municipalities.[46] The remainder of the province, containing one-sixth of B.C.'s population, received services directly from the provincial government, although much of the affected populace resented paying taxes without some form of local government. The provincial administration was felt to be too small to deal with the vast territory involved, particularly when people moved into this unorganized area to avoid municipal taxes and then expected municipal services.

> **PROBLEMS WITH LOCAL GOVERNMENT:**
> **ONLY .5% OF AREA OF B.C. INCORPORATED MUNICIPALLY**
> **1/6 OF POPULATION IN REMAINING AREA,**
> **RECEIVING SERVICES FROM PROVINCE**
> **PROLIFERATION OF BOARDS IN MAJOR URBAN CENTRES**

The organized municipalities also faced problems, with small, financially weak areas finding it difficult to provide necessary services. Some municipalities suffered from sprawl and poor land use. The need for a joint approach to the provision of services in the Greater Vancouver area had already prompted the establishment of a number of regional special purpose agencies — the Greater Vancouver Sewerage and Drainage District (1914), the Greater Vancouver Water District (1926), four area health boards (established between 1936 and 1948), the Lower Mainland Regional Planning Board (1948), the Greater Vancouver Parks District (1966), and the Greater Vancouver Hospital District (1967). A form of metropolitan government for the Greater Vancouver area had been recommended in 1960, but the government had taken no action on this proposal.

---

[46] The figures are from D. W. Barnes, "The System of Regional Districts in British Columbia," in Advisory Commission on Intergovernmental Relations, *op. cit.,* p. 110.

Strategy of Gentle Imposition

Instead, the British Columbia government provided for the creation of regional districts to administer certain functions over wide areas. The specific objectives of this reform were not made clear by the government. However, this may well have been deliberate since one analysis[47] contends that the provincial government was especially interested in the potential of these regional districts in the two major urban centres of Vancouver and Victoria. It argues that the government used a strategy of gentle imposition to implement potentially significant regional governments, particularly for Greater Vancouver.

Whatever the government's motives, since the enabling legislation was passed in 1965, 28 regional districts have been established covering all of British Columbia except the northwest corner. Each district is governed by a regional board of directors comprising representatives from incorporated municipalities within the regional district and from the population of the unorganized territory.

> REGIONAL DISTRICTS:
> 28 ESTABLISHED
> COVER MUNICIPALITIES AND UNORGANIZED AREAS
> REGIONAL FUNCTIONS VARY — GREATEST
> IN VICTORIA AND GREATER VANCOUVER

Because of the previously referred to strategy of gentle imposition, the regional districts originally did not have any assigned responsibilities. Instead it was left to the board of directors of each district to decide on the responsibilities they wished to assume. Individual municipalities or unorganized electoral areas were free to opt in or opt out of any of the servicing arrangements at their own discretion. Gradually, however, this discretion was reduced with certain responsibilities becoming mandatory and the opting out provision being removed. Thus, all regional districts became responsible for the adoption of an official plan, for the development of community planning services in their constituent electoral areas, for building inspection, and for certain "local works and services." In addition, individual districts voluntarily adopted a variety

---

[47] Paul Tennant and David Zirnhelt, "Metropolitan Government in Vancouver: the strategy of gentle imposition," in *Canadian Public Administration*, Spring 1973, pp. 124–138.

of other responsibilities including ambulance service, pest control, recreation facilities, refuse disposal, sewers, and water.[48] The end result is that regional districts are hybrids, delivering a mixture of upper tier and lower tier services.[49]

The overall impact of the British Columbia reforms is difficult to assess. There was some feeling that the regional districts would be a transitional stage toward a strong regional government system in which the existing municipalities would be amalgamated. There is no indication, however, that this was the provincial government's intention and, except for the Greater Vancouver and Victoria (Capital) areas, the regional districts have not developed into an important level of government. But if, as previously mentioned, the government's main purpose was to strengthen local government in these two metropolitan areas, it may feel that this objective has been largely met.

The regional districts have proven to be a flexible structure for dealing with a variety of considerations. They have assumed direct responsibility for the provision of municipal services to the population in unorganized areas. They have also acted as the administrative agency for certain functions or projects that some of their member municipalities wished to pursue jointly. In addition, they have assumed responsibility for various functions delegated to them by their constituent municipalities and they can acquire functions through the affirmative vote of two-thirds of the directors of the regional district having among them at least two-thirds of the votes of the board.

One analysis of the regional district scheme cites several positive features.[50] Existing municipal units are allowed to continue under this structure thereby contributing to the preservation of an existing sense of community, allowing for diversity within the regional area, and helping to ensure accessibility and responsiveness in the municipal system. At the same time, the services provided by the regional districts have promoted the common interests of area municipalities, and the fact that these regional services have been assigned by the area municipalities means that they are determining their common interests themselves rather than having this definition imposed from above.

[48]   Barnes, *op. cit.*, p. 116.

[49]   Brian Walisser, *Understanding Regional District Planning: A Primer*, Ministry of Municipal Affairs, June 1987, unpaginated.

[50]   Feldman Consulting Limited and Queen's University, *op. cit.*, especially pp. 37–42.

However, this analysis also identified certain problems or issues of concern. Because of the structure of the regional districts, notably the indirect election of members to the regional board, there appears to be little public discussion of board activities and decision making appears very insulated. The one exception to this pattern has been in the field of planning and development. Both the Capital and Greater Vancouver Regional Districts have undertaken regional planning exercises accompanied, in the latter case, by an elaborate public participation program. However, the results have been controversial in that future development has been restricted beyond the core municipalities and suburban areas have complained about undue limits on their rights of self-determination.

> **PROBLEMS:**
> **REGIONAL DISTRICTS APPEAR REMOTE**
> **BECAUSE OF INDIRECT ELECTION**
> **DEALING WITH BOTH MUNICIPALITIES AND UNORGANIZED AREAS**
> **ROLE UNCLEAR; DIFFICULT RELATIONS WITH PROVINCE**

Some difficulties have also been noted with respect to coordination and information exchanges between the staffs of the regional district and its member municipalities. There have been complaints by incorporated municipal members that the regional boards spend too much time on the administration of the unorganized areas and that some of the overhead costs of this administration are borne by the incorporated municipalities. Finally, where a regional district is responsible for provision of a particular service over only part of its area, as in the Capital Regional District, there have been complaints that the committees of the regional district board that deal with these partial functions are not limited to representation by board members from only those affected areas.

A Regional District Review Committee was set up by the government in 1977. Its report, the following year, identified several problems.[51] The relationship between the public and the regional district was found to be negative, with the public feeling that the district was inaccessible, dictatorial, and a secretive organization. The committee felt that the regional districts needed to do more to explain their responsibilities and to encourage public involvement. The Review Committee Report also described problems in the provincial-local relationship,

---

[51] Regional District Review Committee, *Report of the Committee*, Victoria, Ministry of Municipal Affairs and Housing, 1978.

stemming from the heavy-handed way in which the provincial level, and particularly the Ministry of Municipal Affairs and Housing, dealt with the regional districts.

Feldman and Graham concluded that the regional districts were "basically a low-profile nonthreatening system of area-wide responsibility for the delivery of certain local government services.[52] They correctly pointed out, however, that because of the limited scope of the regional district reforms and the reluctance of the provincial government to introduce more major changes, the issues arising from urban growth pressures, especially in the Vancouver and Victoria areas, had not been resolved.

The provincial government showed more inclination to act in the 1980s, although not in ways that the regional districts would have wished. Patrick Smith illustrates the changed situation by describing "regional structures under attack."[53] He examines two provincial initiatives that have limited the regional districts — the 1983 legislation declaring null and void all regional plans and removing the right of regional districts to plan for their regions as a whole, and the 1985 legislation centralizing the transit function at the provincial level. In spite of these developments, Smith argues that the need for regional institutions is evident. He notes that the number of functions that have been assumed by the regional districts indicates that they fill an important gap. He also points out that bilateral arrangements in planning are still permitted, and the fact that, for example, 14 of the 15 municipalities in the Greater Vancouver area participate voluntarily in such arrangements shows the necessity for the broader perspective brought by the regional districts.[54]

Another Review Committee was appointed in 1983, and reported in November 1986.[55] This committee reiterated the concern about lack of public understanding about the roles of regional districts. It observed that the provincial level had reduced its support for the regional districts over the years and was sending out very mixed signals

[52] Lionel D. Feldman and Katherine A. Graham, "Local Government Reform in Canada," in Arthur B. Gunlicks (ed.), *Local Government Reform and Reorganization: An International Perspective*, London, Kennikat Press, 1981, p. 156.

[53] Patrick J. Smith, "Regional Governance in British Columbia," in *Planning and Administration*, 13, 1986, pp. 7–20.

[54] *Ibid.*, p. 14.

[55] Regional District Survey Committee, *Summary Report of the Regional District Survey Committee*, Victoria, Queen's Printer, 1986.

about the future of these organizations (as described by Smith above). The committee called for, among other matters, closer liaison between the regional districts and the Ministry of Municipal Affairs and clear and consistent statements of public policy with respect to the regional districts.

British Columbia introduced draft legislation (Bill 60) on the regional districts in 1989. For the first time, it is proposed to give regional districts a full set of standard service powers, to be exercised by by-law. There are provisions to allow the regional districts to function more autonomously and with more flexibility. In addition, Bill 60 provides simplified procedures for the establishment of "local communities," designed to offer an opportunity for self-government in rural areas. One observer concludes that the goals of the legislation are not very ambitious, but that its very existence affirms "that regional districts are here to stay."[56]

Quebec

By the 1960s, the local government system in Quebec had evolved, after more than a century of existence, into a very fragmented system, characterized by an excessive number of very small municipalities. Over 90% of the more than 1 600 municipalities had less than 5 000 population and nearly 50% had less than 1 000 population. At the same time, problems of urban concentration and sprawl were evident, with the cities of Montreal, Quebec, and Hull (Outaouais) containing 30% of the population.[57]

After the election of the Liberal government in 1960, a "Quiet Revolution" brought a variety of reforms at the local level. As Sancton outlines, this led to:

> the replacement of classical colleges by public colleges for general and professional education (CEGEPS), the consolidation of school boards into regional units, and the establishment of a completely new network of health and social service institutions to replace hospitals and agencies which had previously been controlled by the church or private charities.[58]

---

[56] Walisser, *op. cit.*

[57] These figures are from Jean Godin, "Local Government Reform in the Province of Quebec," in Advisory Commission on Intergovernmental Relations, *op. cit.*, p. 50.

[58] Andrew Sancton, "The Impact of Language Differences on Metropolitan Reform in Montreal," in Lionel D. Feldman (ed.), *Politics and Government of Urban Canada*, Toronto, Methuen, 1981, p. 369.

Dealing more specifically with municipal government, the major Liberal response was the Voluntary Amalgamation Act of 1965 that allowed two or more municipalities to amalgamate following a council's resolution to that effect. Not surprisingly, however, this voluntary approach was ineffective, with fewer than 100 municipalities abolished between 1965 and 1971, hardly enough to reduce the badly fragmented municipal structure in Quebec. While new legislation in 1971 gave the Minister of Municipal Affairs more power to force amalgamations where he felt that it was desirable, this power was little used because of opposition and because (as will be seen) the government was by then preoccupied with metropolitan reforms. According to Higgins,[59] new government efforts did result in the reduction of some 80 municipal units to about 20 between late 1975 and early 1976.

The other major reform initiative involved the creation of upper tier governments (urban communities) for the Montreal, Quebec, Hull, and (subsequently) Chicoutimi areas. Understandably, because of its population, the Montreal area was of particular concern and it was also the subject of a number of earlier structural adjustments. Accordingly, this background is briefly reviewed before consideration of the present reforms.

Metropolitan Government for Montreal

Traditionally, problems of urban sprawl in the Montreal area were handled through annexation. Indeed, beginning as early as 1883, Montreal proceeded to annex 33 municipalities in roughly as many years. By 1920 this policy had halted, but the provincial government wanted the city to annex four island municipalities recently declared bankrupt. Instead, a regional agency was established — the Montreal Metropolitan Commission — that was to have the authority to approve or veto all local decisions on borrowing and capital expenditures of Montreal and 14 island municipalities. Under pressure from Montreal, however, the province amended the legislation to remove the commission's authority over the city's financial decisions. The commission was governed by a sixteen-member board, eight named by Montreal, seven by the suburbs and one by the provincial government.

With its limited jurisdiction, the Montreal Metropolitan Commission was never a very significant body and by the 1950s two studies had

---

[59] Higgins, *op. cit.*, p. 137.

confirmed that it was not settling basic intermunicipal problems and that its existence was no more than a makeshift solution to a financial dilemma.

In 1959 the commission was replaced by the Montreal Metropolitan Corporation. At the outset the new body appeared to represent much more than a change in name. It was authorized to exercise a number of important functions including sewers, water distribution, arterial roads, planning, mass transit, major parks and all other services considered as intermunicipal by agreement among the municipalities or by decision of the corporation. Moreover, its jurisdiction extended to the City of Montreal as well as to the 14 island municipalities that had come under its predecessor.

REGIONAL AGENCIES NOT NEW:
1920 — MONTREAL METROPOLITAN COMMISSION
1959 — MONTREAL METROPOLITAN CORPORATION
1970 — MONTREAL URBAN COMMUNITY

The governing body comprised 14 representatives from the city, 14 from the suburbs, and a chairperson appointed by the province. This balancing of city and suburbs ensured the vigorous opposition of Montreal's Mayor Drapeau, who was like most central city mayors in resisting any form of metropolitan government that he could not control.[60] As Sancton points out, another and unique reason for Montreal's opposition was the concern that any metropolitan government, by extending to the suburbs and their higher proportions of English-speaking citizens, would decrease the influence of the French.[61] In any event, Montreal's refusal to cooperate effectively sabotaged the new Metropolitan Corporation, which was never a major innovation in spite of its greatly expanded terms of reference.

As an alternative approach, Drapeau and his chief lieutenant, Lucien Saulnier, pursued annexation with a view to establishing one city covering the entire island. The provincial government, not surprisingly, had no desire to see Montreal grow so large as to rival the importance of the province itself, and the city only managed the annexation of three virtually bankrupt suburbs in 1963, 1964 and 1968 respectively.

---

[60] Sancton, *op. cit.,* p. 372. Note the similar response by Winnipeg's Mayor Juba, discussed earlier in the chapter.
[61] *Ibid.*

In the meantime, the Liberal government had been defeated (in 1966) without acting upon the recommendations of a study committee on the future government of the Montreal metropolitan area (Blier Commission). The Union Nationale government apparently had little interest in urban reform and left the matter with the civil servants in the Municipal Affairs Department. They were impressed with structural reforms introduced in France in the form of "communautés urbaines," upper tier, indirectly elected governments established for several metropolitan areas. In June of 1969 the Minister of Municipal Affairs tabled plans for the creation of communautés urbaines in Montreal and Quebec City and a communauté regionale around Hull. Strong negative reactions, especially from Montreal, caused the minister to announce postponement of the plan for one year.

Montreal Urban Community

Ironically, just three months later, January 1, 1970, the Montreal Urban Community (MUC) came into existence. The governing council consisted of the mayor and councillors of the city of Montreal and one delegate from each of the other 29 municipalities under its jurisdiction, with the city having seven of the twelve members on the powerful executive committee and providing the first chairman in the person of Lucien Saulnier.

The new structure owed little to the prior recommendations of the Quebec civil service; instead it was a hastily implemented response to the devastating effect of a police strike that hit Montreal on October 7th, 1969. A prompt end to the strike was engineered by none other than Lucien Saulnier, whose strategy was "in essence, to promise to pay the police what they wanted and then to force the suburbs and the provincial government to finance the increases."[62] The vehicle for this redistribution of funding was the new MUC, "organized such that in many ways it was a mere extension of the City of Montreal."[63] Contrast the background to the establishment of Metropolitan Toronto, with Frederick Gardiner having several months to acquire staff and organize his approach even before the new structure came into effect. As Sancton observes, the way in which the MUC came into existence without planning or any administrative structure "is a vivid illustration of the fact that its

---

[62] *Ibid.,* p. 376.

[63] *Ibid.*

original purpose was to act as a conduit of funds rather then as an important force in the management of Montreal's urban development."[64]

By January 1, 1972 all of the police forces on the island had been unified into the MUC Police Department, but controversy over this decision and related policing issues dragged on for a number of years. It is important to realize, however, that while public security still accounts for almost half of the annual budget of the MUC, the new upper tier government has also become involved in several other areas of activity. In financial terms, the major initiatives have been with respect to subways and sewers, although these projects have come under considerable provincial influence because of the extent of provincial funding. The provincial government has also been extending its influence with respect to regional planning issues. In part, this may reflect the more interventionist philosophy of the Parti Quebecois, in power from 1976 until the mid-1980s. To a large extent, however, it results from the failure of the MUC to take initiative in this area, largely because of a city-suburb split and the effectiveness of the suburban veto.[65]

WHY MUC INEFFECTIVE:
CITY-SUBURB SPLIT
LACK OF INTERNAL BOUNDARY CHANGES
PROVINCIAL DOMINANCE

A recent analysis by Sancton concludes that the original hopes that the MUC would evolve into a genuine metropolitan government have never been realized.[66] He notes that suspicion between the City of Montreal and the suburbs has paralyzed the structure from the beginning. While the original legislation contemplated that internal boundary adjustments would be made, any such changes would have involved some merging of French-speaking and English-speaking populations — a task no politician wanted to tackle. Without significant boundary changes, Sancton observes, it was only possible "to tinker with the Community's clumsy institutions."[67] The principle that a double majority (city and

---

[64] *Ibid.*

[65] While the City of Montreal has a majority of the votes on the MUC, reflecting its population dominance, a motion cannot pass unless supported by at least half of the suburban delegates present.

[66] Andrew Sancton, "Montreal's Metropolitan Government," Hanover, *Quebec Studies,* No. 6, 1988, p. 23.

[67] *Ibid.*

suburb) was needed before action could be taken meant that often no decision was made. As a result, the provincial government, which held most of the financial power anyway, seized most of the initiative. Instead of being a counterweight to provincial influence, the MUC "passively accepts provincial funds and implements provincial decisions."[68]

Other Urban Communities

The December 1969 legislation that created the MUC also provided for an urban community for Quebec City and for a similarly constituted regional government for Hull and environs known as the Regional Community of Outaouais. The latter municipality has been hampered by municipal opposition based on a feeling that the reform was introduced without sufficient prior consultation. A primary motivation for its establishment was apparently the perceived need to provide a counterweight to the adjoining Regional Municipality of Ottawa-Carleton in Ontario, and to represent the area's interests to the National Capital Commission. A somewhat more positive attitude was evident in the Quebec Urban Community where more advance consultation with local leaders occurred.

In all instances, however, the regional level has failed to attract much feeling of loyalty. Instead, there has been some movement for municipalities to consider amalgamation to better defend their interests against the new regional units. Indeed, the number of lower tier municipalities within Quebec and Outaouais has been reduced from 26 to 13 and from 32 to 11 respectively — a consolidation that is even more striking when compared with the total absence of any such change in the Montreal Urban Community.

OTHER REFORMS:
FISCAL REFORMS TO IMPROVE MUNICIPAL FINANCIAL BASE
FORMATION OF REGIONAL COUNTY
MUNICIPALITIES, REPLACING COUNTIES

A number of significant local government reforms were introduced in 1979. As discussed in more detail in Chapter 6, Bill 57 transferred the basic cost of education to the provincial level, as part of a major fiscal

---

[68] *Ibid.*, p. 24.

reform. The year 1979 also saw legislation concerning land use planning (Bill 125), which led to the establishment of 95 regional county municipalities (RCMs) that replaced all the former county municipalities. The latter consisted entirely of rural municipalities and exercised very limited responsibilities.

Municipalities were grouped together to form these RCMs on the basis of "affinity" — a criterion that was very similar to the community of interest concept specified (but almost never applied) in Ontario's regional government program. Each RCM is governed by a council composed of the head of council (or representative) of each member municipality. The regional councillors elected one of their members as warden for a two-year term. The RCMs exercise all of the powers of the county governments that they have replaced. In addition, they have specific, mandatory responsibilities with respect to the preparation of a development plan. There is a requirement that the planning policies of member municipalities must be in conformity with the regional plan within two years of its adoption.

The RCMs have largely completed their primary task of drawing up regional master plans to guide future growth and development. They will now be vested with the power and responsibility of implementing the regional plans.[69] However, they are not likely to become significantly stronger according to the viewpoints expressed in a major local government study commissioned by the Union of Quebec municipalities.[70] The Parizeau Report (named after its chairman, Jacques Parizeau) and the ensuing recommendations from the Union envisage that the powers of these regional bodies will be limited, "for the simple reason that the democratic mandate is given at the local level, not at the regional level."[71]

One other noteworthy proposal of the Parizeau Report calls for the creation of a new urban community, regrouping the Towns of Gatineau, Hull, and Aylmer, with all of the other member municipalities of the Outaouais regional community to become a new regional county municipality (RCM).

---

[69] Notes for an address by Jean Pelletier, President of the Union of Quebec Municipalities, at the Association of Municipalities of Ontario Annual Convention, August 1987, p. 6.

[70] *Report of the Municipal Study Commission* (Parizeau Report), Montreal, Union of Quebec Municipalities, December 1986.

[71] *Ibid.,* p. 13.

Nova Scotia

June 1974 saw the release of the massive Report of the Royal Commission on Education, Public Services, and Provincial-Municipal Relations in the Province of Nova Scotia. Established in March 1971 under the chairmanship of Professor John F. Graham, this study dealt with not only local government organization but also with the reorganization of provincial departments and agencies, although the latter proposals are of less relevance for our purposes.[72]

As with the previously discussed Byrne Commission in New Brunswick a decade earlier, the Graham Report examined the most appropriate distribution of provincial and local responsibilities. The report concluded that local government should be relieved of such "general services" as education, health, social services, housing, and administration of justice. It also called for the Nova Scotia government to provide such "support services" to the local governments as capital borrowing, assessment, tax billing and collection, water and sewer user billing and collection, and the administration of municipal staff pension funds.

In relation to the municipal structure, the Graham Report recommended that 11 one tier counties be established throughout Nova Scotia replacing the existing rural municipalities, towns, and cities. Three of these counties with large urban cores would be called metropolitan counties. Existing towns and some villages, with their elected councils, would remain in the nonmetropolitan counties to allow citizen input, provide county services under contract and, where desired locally, provide such services as recreation, culture, and local beautification. In addition, the report called for the establishment of community associations supported by county council staff in areas with common interests as another means of facilitating citizen participation. The concern about citizen access and involvement was also evident in the recommendation that the Nova Scotia government decentralize the administration of the general services it was to assume. Specifically, it was proposed that these services be administered over 11 regions coinciding with the new county boundaries under the jurisdiction of regional boards of local citizens including county council appointees.

---

[72] For a useful summary of the main recommendations of the Graham Commission, see the Appendix prepared by W. Hooson in Tindal, "Structural Changes in Local Government," Toronto, Institute of Public Administration, 1977, on which this section is partially based.

The Graham Report devoted considerable attention to the internal organization of the new county system. It emphasized the need for councillors to concentrate their attention on matters of broad policy. In the words of the report:

> Their deliberations ... should not be frustrated or cluttered by trivia and day to day administrative detail. We have sought to simplify and rationalize council procedures, to reduce the proliferation of committees, subcommittees, boards, commissions, and joint bodies.[73]

For each of the 11 new counties proposed for Nova Scotia, the Graham Commission recommended a council of 12 members, each elected from a separate ward for a three-year term. The mayor would be elected from among these councillors for a three-year term but could be replaced at any time through a nonconfidence vote endorsed by eight members. A maximum of three standing committees was recommended, an executive and planning committee, and two others dealing essentially with hard services and soft services. The mayor would chair the executive committee, would appoint those chairing the other two committees who would also be members of the executive committee, and would recommend to council the remaining appointments. As proposed by the Graham Commission, council could not approve recommendations from the other two committees until they had been reviewed by the executive committee, although the latter body was not to have a veto power. To coordinate the administration, the commission called for the establishment of a chief administrative officer system.

Overall, the proposed arrangements appeared to provide the opportunity for both political leadership and administrative coordination. The lack of action on the recommendations has been attributed, in one analysis, to "the degree of detail, the vast and comprehensive nature of the recommendations, the lack of detailed argumentation of alternatives...."[74] Instead, informal discussions involving representatives from the Union of Nova Scotia Municipalities and the Department of Municipal Affairs evolved into what became known as the Task Force on Municipal Reform.[75] Their deliberations culminated in a departmental White Paper in February 1978 titled "New Directions in Municipal Government in Nova Scotia."

---

[73] Quoted in Hooson, *ibid.*, p. 52.

[74] Feldman and Graham, *op. cit.*, p. 164.

[75] See Donald J. H. Higgins, "Nova Scotia's 'New Directions in Municipal Government'" in *Urban Focus,* Institute of Local Government, Queen's University, March-April 1979.

The main emphasis of the White Paper was on the reform of some aspects of provincial-municipal financial relations, although not in relation to the most expensive local services such as education, health and social services, housing, and justice. Proposals included an unconditional general grant, provincial grants in lieu of taxes, road user charges, and a revenue guarantee. Strong emphasis was given to the expansion of user-related charges, such as in relation to water and sanitary sewerage. While the proposals were relatively modest, their positive reception is a tribute to the consultative process that was followed.

In the intervening years, most of the major proposals of the 1978 White Paper have been implemented.[76] These include the development of an unconditional municipal operating and capital grant program and a restructuring of educational administration that saw the municipal school districts consolidated into 21 district school boards comprised of one-third municipally appointed, one-third provincially appointed, and one-third elected representatives.

REFORMS GRADUAL AND PIECEMEAL
MASSIVE GRAHAM REPORT NOT ADOPTED
GRADUAL REFORMS IN GRANTS AND IN
SCHOOL DISTRICT CONSOLIDATION
INTER-MUNICIPAL AGREEMENTS
IN HALIFAX-DARTMOUTH AREA

One other noteworthy change, over the past couple of decades, relates to developments in the Halifax-Dartmouth urban area. Initially, there was an expansion, through annexation, of the cities of Halifax and Dartmouth. In 1961 Dartmouth annexed portions of adjacent Halifax County, increasing its population by 90% and increasing its area by nine times. A 1969 annexation by the City of Halifax nearly quadrupled its area and increased its population by a third.[77]

Two studies in the early 1970s recommended forms of metropolitan government for the Halifax-Dartmouth area, but no action had been taken by the time the previously described Graham Commission commenced its study. The commission, in turn, proposed a "metropolitan county," a single tier municipality encompassing the urbanized areas of

---

[76] Correspondence from Shingai Nyajeka, Nova Scotia Department of Municipal Affairs, April 17, 1989, on which this section is based.

[77] These figures are from David M. Cameron and Peter Aucoin, "Halifax," in Magnusson and Sancton, *op. cit.,* p. 183.

the two cities and the county and additional area from the county for future growth. Again, no action was taken. However, the increasingly close cooperation between Halifax and Dartmouth led to the establishment of a number of intermunicipal bodies that may yet provide the foundation for a form of metropolitan government.

Of particular potential is the "Metropolitan Authority," originally established to operate a regional jail but also responsible for a regional transit system and a regional sanitary land-fill operation.[78] In 1986 Bedford became the fourth member of this Metropolitan Authority, joining Halifax, Dartmouth, and the County of Halifax. The authority is governed by a 12 member Board of Directors comprised of elected representatives appointed from the councils of each of the four member municipalities. If a metropolitan government is to appear in Nova Scotia, it seems likely to evolve gradually from this type of intermunicipal arrangement.

Newfoundland

A Royal Commission study completed in 1974[79] recommended the gradual creation of as many as 20 regional governments envisaged as two tier structures with the upper tier units similar to, but much stronger than, British Columbia's previously described regional districts.[80] It also recommended a tightening up of incorporation procedures and some modifications in municipal classifications, as well as the introduction of the real property tax because of the poor financial conditions in most municipalities.

Initially, no major changes were introduced, but considerable attention was directed to the St. John's area which was excluded from the Royal Commission study but has been the subject of four other studies and reports. The St. John's metropolitan area is comprised of the central city of St. John's and about 20 smaller surrounding municipalities that are largely dependent on the central city for employment and retail services.[81] The initial study of the metropolitan area in 1957 led to one

---

[78] *Ibid.,* p. 185.

[79] *Report of the Royal Commission on Municipal Government in Newfoundland and Labrador* (H. J. Whalen, Commissioner), St. John's, Queen's Printer, 1974.

[80] Higgins, *op. cit.,* p. 127–128.

[81] See Peter G. Boswell, "Regional Government for St. John's?" in *Urban Focus,* Institute of Local Government, Queen's University, January–February 1979, on which this section is based.

change — the creation in 1963 of the the St. John's Metropolitan Area Board. The Board, which does not have any directly elected members, has served primarily as a means of administering unincorporated areas in the region, although the subsequent creation of new municipalities has removed extensive territory from its jurisdiction. A second study in 1971 offered three alternative reforms for the area. This prompted the government to appoint a commission to conduct hearings and make specific recommendations concerning an appropriate governmental structure for the metropolitan area.

The Henley Commission, as it came to be known, recommended that a two tiered structure of regional government be established along with an expanded city of St. John's. While this approach was not new, the proposed membership was quite distinctive — a chairperson and four members appointed by the provincial government, six members appointed by the enlarged city of St. John's council, and four members to be chosen from four clusters of second tier municipalities and unincorporated communities. Also unusual was the recommended term of office, five years for the person chairing and the four government-appointed members, and three years for the rest.

The release of the Henley Commission's recommendations in January 1977 generated considerable controversy. Draft legislation was introduced twice, with the Henley recommendations substantially incorporated except for the lack of a provision for the enlargement of St. John's. Following the defeat of the second bill, the regional government concept appeared to be dropped. However, the Municipalities Act of 1979-1980 includes enabling legislation for the establishment of regional governments anywhere in the province without further legislative approval.

October 1987 saw the report of yet another study (Commission of Inquiry) into the St. John's metropolitan area.[82] Known as the Fagan Commission, it recommended that the existing Metropolitan Board should be disbanded and replaced with a regional authority that would have responsibility for regional water supply and, perhaps in the future, other common services. This new authority would have representation from the municipalities in the area, but its exact structure has not been decided. However, the new authority will apparently not have taxing power, nor did the commission consider that it would be a regional government. No action had been taken on this recommendation at the time of the spring 1989 provincial election in Newfoundland.

---

[82] This section is based on correspondence from Peter Boswell, February 11, 1989.

Notwithstanding the lack of action on regional governments, The Municipalities Act did follow the Whalen Commission recommendations concerning the real property tax, municipal incorporation, and classification changes. Generally, the impact of the reforms should be to give municipalities somewhat more autonomy and fiscal responsibility, thus reducing provincial "tutelage" — although it will take some time for the old attitudes on the part of elected and appointed personnel at both the provincial and local levels to change.[83]

Alberta

As mentioned earlier, Alberta embarked on a program of consolidating rural units of both municipal and educational administration that culminated in the County Act of 1950. Under this act, the educational and municipal units were combined, initially on a voluntary basis, to form one tier county governments that now cover the majority of the populated rural area of the province.

No such comprehensive restructuring was introduced in urban areas, although the population increase that accompanied the development of the petroleum industry strained the existing municipal organization, especially in the Calgary and Edmonton areas. The result was the frequent annexation of adjacent territory — some 19 separate annexations involving Edmonton between 1947 and 1980 — usually at the initiative of landowners and developers wishing an extension of services. However, this piecemeal approach frustrated both Calgary and Edmonton. Further concern arose when the Alberta government, between 1974 and 1976, unilaterally imposed restricted development areas around both cities. While intended as utilities and transportation corridors, these RDAs were also seen as potential barriers to future expansion.

PIECEMEAL URBAN REFORM:
NO COMPREHENSIVE STUDY
FREQUENT ANNEXATIONS BY CALGARY AND EDMONTON

Edmonton's response was a March 1979 application to the Local Authorities Board for a massive annexation, including the City of St. Albert and the entire county of Strathcona (an application that would add over 467 000 acres to the city's existing 80 000). The subsequent

---

[83] Correspondence from Peter Boswell, August 30, 1983.

Board hearings extended from September 1979 to the end of June 1980, comprising 106 days of testimony, the hearing of about 200 witnesses, the examination of 299 official exhibits and the generation of 12 235 pages of transcript — at a cost of over $6 million! After all of that, the outcome was a compromise solution. While the Local Authorities Board approved a very large expansion of Edmonton's boundaries in December 1980, the Cabinet issued a revised order in June 1981, awarding the city some 86 000 acres of land but not its dormitory suburbs. As Feldman observes, there weren't really any winners or losers and none of the protagonists was severely harmed.

> Edmonton got land on which to expand, possibly not the lands and assessment it really wanted. St. Albert ... lost no territory. Strathcona saw 54,000 acres ... go to Edmonton.[84]

Quite apart from the great cost involved, this approach to developing reformed structures for Alberta's major urban areas is not very satisfactory. It is at best a piecemeal, fragmented approach that does not consider the overall needs of the entire urban area, but instead focuses on particular territories affected by proposed annexation, and does so in an inevitably confrontational atmosphere. Especially with the pronounced growth pressures that have been experienced in Western Canada in recent decades, and the especially rapid growth of the Edmonton and Calgary area, a specific provincial policy on urban governance would appear increasingly necessary.

Summary

In the almost four decades since Metropolitan Toronto launched the modern era of local government reform in Canada, there have been extensive changes in a number of the provinces — Prince Edward Island and Saskatchewan being the only real exceptions. The main developments are summarized in Table 4 below. The resultant classifications of municipality vary somewhat in the different provinces. Essentially, however, there are urban units known as cities, towns, and villages, and rural units known as districts, parishes, townships, and counties. There are also upper tier municipalities with wider jurisdiction known variously as county, regional, metropolitan and district municipalities, and urban communities.

---

[84] Lionel Feldman, "Tribunals, Politics and the Public Interest: The Edmonton Annexation Case — A Response," in *Canadian Public Policy,* Summer 1982, p. 371.

• TABLE 4 •
LANDMARKS IN LOCAL GOVERNMENT REFORM

1953	Metropolitan Toronto
1959	Montreal Metropolitan Corporation
1960	Metropolitan Winnipeg
1963	Byrne Commission on New Brunswick
1964	Michener Commission on Manitoba
1965	Regional Districts in B.C.
1967	Equal Opportunity Program — New Brunswick
1968	Regional Government Policy — Ontario
1969	Urban Communities for Montreal, Quebec, Hull
1972	Winnipeg Unicity
1974	County Restructuring Program in Ontario
	Graham Commission on Nova Scotia
	Whalen Commission on Newfoundland
1979	Regional County Municipalities — Quebec
1981	Edmonton Annexation Decision
1986	Parizeau Report on Quebec Municipalities

Of particular interest is the extent to which the reformed structures and organization of local government in Canada have overcome the weaknesses identified in Chapter 4. Judged on this basis, the reforms must be considered a disappointment.

> **WEAKNESSES OF REFORMS:**
> **PREOCCUPIED WITH EFFICIENCY**
> **LITTLE IMPROVEMENT IN DISTRIBUTION OF POWERS**
> **LITTLE IMPROVEMENT IN LOCAL GOVERNMENT REVENUES**
> **LITTLE ATTENTION TO INTERNAL ORGANIZATION**
> **NEEDED FOR LEADERSHIP, COORDINATION**
> **AND EFFECTIVE REPRESENTATION**

With notable exceptions, the reforms have been preoccupied with improving the efficiency of local government, especially in relation to urban service demands. The emphasis on urban areas is understandable since it has been the pressures of urbanization that have undermined the traditional local government system with its distinct urban and rural classification of municipality, its multiplicity of small units, and its continuing reliance on the real property tax as the principal source of municipal revenue. The emphasis on service delivery is also understandable since, from the origins of municipal institutions through the turn of the century reform era to the present, provision of services has been seen as the most important role of local government. The result of this reform focus has been a considerable improvement in the boundaries of local government, especially in the major urban areas of Canada, and some reduction in fragmentation through municipal consolidations.

At the same time, however, this urban service emphasis made the reforms regrettably narrow in scope. There has been little improvement in the fragmentation of responsibilities among municipalities, separate boards, and the senior levels of government. While the present distribution of governmental responsibilities has evolved over a long period and not always according to some rational plan, efforts to delineate a new and more appropriate division of provincial and local responsibilities have been mainly limited to the Byrne Commission in New Brunswick, the Michener Commission in Manitoba, and the Graham Commission in Nova Scotia. Only in the first instance did reforms result. Moreover, in that instance (New Brunswick) the result was to reduce dramatically the responsibilities left to the local level. Yet if the local government system is to be strengthened it needs not only new and more appropriate boundaries but also a respectable range of responsibilities and some freedom to exercise them.

A strong local level of government also needs an improved revenue position, and here again the reforms were for the most part deficient. Where previously local responsibilities have been transferred to the provincial level, notably in New Brunswick (and Quebec in the case of education), the financial burden has been reduced but at a considerable cost to the importance of local government. There have also been some reforms related to property assessment and grants, but the inadequacy of municipal revenue sources has been relatively unchanged. The only modest improvement, as outlined in Chapter 6, has been the introduction of revenue-sharing arrangements in several of the provinces, although these changes relate to all municipalities and are not confined to specific local government reforms.

Finally, and perhaps most serious of all, the local government reform efforts have been deficient in another respect. Only in the reports concerning Winnipeg Unicity and the Graham Commission on Nova Scotia (and, belatedly, in some of the more recent regional government reviews in Ontario) were there serious considerations given to the most suitable internal organization of municipal government from the point of view of *effective leadership* and *coordination,* and *representation of the local citizenry.* The weaknesses of the system in these latter respects will become more apparent from the examination of the internal organization and functioning of local government in Part B of the text.

6   *Intergovernmental Relations*

Objectives:

1.   To trace the evolving pattern of provincial-local relations in Canada.
2.   To examine the provincial-local financial relationship and the prospects for municipal fiscal autonomy.
3.   To assess the real property tax and to demonstrate that it is the subject of unfair criticism.
4.   To explain the reasons for federal-local and tri-level relations and to describe Canada's experiences to date in formalizing such relationships.

Introduction

The examination of the local government system that is the focus of Part A of this text would not be complete without some reference to the senior levels of government with which local governments have become increasingly intertwined.

Any discussion of intergovernmental relations usually begins by emphasizing the subordinate constitutional position of municipal governments. As noted in Chapter 2, the basic point is that municipalities, unlike the provincial and federal levels of government, do not have any guaranteed right to exist under the constitution. From a strict legal viewpoint, therefore, they only exist and take such form as their respective provincial governments see fit to provide.[1]

This aspect of the provincial-local relationship should not be overemphasized, however. There are other considerations, both practical and political, that also affect the relationship. It is noteworthy that the basic structure of municipal government was already in place in some provinces before the provincial governments came into existence. To that extent, provincial governments did not really have a choice of whether or not to establish municipal institutions. Rather, the question was how the provinces would deal with the municipal system that

---

[1]   For an outline of the provincial jurisdiction with respect to municipal institutions, see Jacques L'Heureux, "Municipalities and the Division of Powers," in Richard Simeon (Research Coordinator), *Intergovernmental Relations,* Royal Commission on the Economic Union and Development Prospects for Canada, Vol. 63, Toronto, University of Toronto Press, 1985.

they had inherited, especially as demands on government increased with fundamental changes in the nature of the Canadian economy and society.

In other provinces where there wasn't already a municipal system in existence, the provincial governments were often the main protagonists in the establishment of such a system — to relieve their administrative burdens and/or to shift some of the expenditure burden to the local level. As noted in Chapter 2, this was the case, for example, in several of the Western provinces and in Newfoundland. Indeed, as the demand for services grew, all provincial governments came to regard a network of local governments as not just administratively convenient but almost essential. Without such local governments, the provincial authorities would face an overwhelming administrative burden. They would also be deluged by a myriad of local grievances and concerns that would compete with broader provincial issues for their attention.

BASIS OF RELATIONSHIP:
NOT JUST CONSTITUTIONAL
ALSO PRACTICAL AND POLITICAL CONSIDERATIONS
INCREASING STATE OF INTERDEPENDENCE

In addition to these practical considerations, of course, there was also a recognition of the political reality that local governments could not be dealt with in too heavy-handed or arbitrary a manner without adverse public reaction. Even in provinces where the populace was at first reluctant to have municipal institutions, once they were in place they developed a legitimacy of their own in the eyes of the local inhabitants, and a resulting security of status that belied their subordinate constitutional position. Dramatic evidence of just how deep rooted this public feeling became over the years is provided by the strong opposition to local government reform efforts in the postwar period that sought to consolidate municipalities or even alter existing boundaries. David Cameron suggests that "the political process has bequeathed a de facto security to municipalities" and that they "may be said to occupy a quasi-constitutional position vis-a-vis the provinces."[2]

Further evidence that the constitutional, legal aspect is only one element of intergovernmental relations is found in the development,

---

[2]   David M. Cameron, "Provincial Responsibilities for Municipal Government," in *Canadian Public Administration*, Summer 1980, p. 234.

primarily in the postwar period, of federal-local and tri-level relationships — contrary to the constitution! Here again, it is practical considerations that have prevailed. As will be outlined below, federal government programs and policies have long had an impact on the operations of local government, especially in such areas as housing, transportation, and social services. It also became apparent, however, that municipalities could, by their actions or inaction, have a significant impact on matters that concerned the senior governments as well. Indeed, it was federal concern about the ability of local governments to deal with the consequences of the rapid urbanization of Canada in the postwar period that provided a major impetus to federal-local relations. It seems clear that we have reached the point in Canada where some form of tri-level relationship is inevitable — nothwithstanding the constitution — simply because of the interdependence of the programs and policies of all three levels of government. As O'Brien points out, the various functions of government are interrelated in ways that would require intergovernmental activity even if they were all parcelled out in separate pieces to one level only — which they aren't and can't be.

> The line between health and welfare is not always easy to find. Welfare and social housing are part of one policy. Housing density depends on transit or the automobile. The latter affects the environment and depends on energy policy. Add the need for planning and financing and there is no escaping the fact that governance in our society requires a lot of communication among governments at various levels.[3]

By its very nature, we can only provide a general examination of this complex topic. The provincial-municipal relationship will be considered first, including particular emphasis on the financial aspect of that relationship, followed by an outline and assessment of federal-local and tri-level relations.

Provincial-Municipal Relations

The evolution of provincial-municipal relations in Canada has involved, for the most part, a pattern of increasing provincial supervision, influence, and control. In the early years of their existence, municipalities often had considerable operating freedom, especially where their

---

[3]   Allan O'Brien, "A Look at the Provincial-Municipal Relationship," in Donald C. MacDonald (ed.), *Government and Politics of Ontario,* Toronto, Van Nostrand Reinhold, 1980, p. 167.

provincial governments were still in their infancy. As Crawford describes the considerable local autonomy enjoyed by Ontario municipalities following the 1849 Baldwin Act:

> Within the scope allowed, and the scope was extensive, the municipalities had gained the right to local self-government with a minimum of parliamentary or executive control, the elected representatives being answerable in matters of policy to their electors and in matters of law to the courts.[4]

Before long, however, provincial governments began to exercise a growing supervisory role. Departments of municipal affairs were established by the turn of the century in a number of the provinces, "to give leadership and guidance in municipal development and to provide for the continuous study of the problems of the municipalities."[5] This need was first evident in the Western provinces where a rapid development of local government institutions was made necessary by a sudden expansion of population. Manitoba established a Department of Municipal Commissioner as early as 1886, with Saskatchewan following suit in 1908 and Alberta in 1911. British Columbia appointed an Inspector of Municipalities in 1914, but a full department was not created until 1934. Ontario's experience was somewhat similar, with an office of Provincial-Municipal Auditor as early as 1897 and a Bureau of Municipal Affairs from 1917, but no department until 1935. That same year Nova Scotia created a Department of Municipal Affairs and in 1936 New Brunswick established a Department of Education, Federal, and Municipal Relations.

The common factor here, of course, was the Depression of the 1930s and attendant municipal defaulting on financial obligations. In response, provincial governments established or expanded not only municipal departments but also boards with a variety of administrative and quasi-judicial responsibilities relating to local government. A number of these bodies had originally been formed to regulate public utilities and their relations with municipal authorities. As a result of the financial difficulties of the 1930s, many of these bodies were assigned responsibility for controlling municipal financing as well as jurisdiction in other areas such as zoning and assessment. As an example, the Ontario Railway and

---

[4]   K. G. Crawford, *Canadian Municipal Government,* Toronto, University of Toronto Press, 1954, p. 32.

[5]   *Ibid.,* p. 345. Chapter 17 of Crawford, on which this section is based, provides a good description of the historical evolution of provincial-local relations.

Municipal Board, created in 1906 primarily to deal with railway matters, was reconstituted as the Ontario Municipal Board in 1932. That same year, the Municipal and Public Utility Board of Manitoba, which had been established in 1926, was given the responsibility for approving debenture issues and the Quebec Municipal Corporation was established.

**TREND IN RELATIONSHIP:
TOWARD PROVINCIAL CONTROL
INFLUENCE OF DEPRESSION AND FINANCIAL CRISIS
PRESSURES OF POSTWAR URBANIZATION**

By the mid-1930s, all but one of the then provinces[6] provided extensive supervision and control over municipalities through a department and, in most cases, a board. In several instances this control was quite sweeping. Nova Scotia provided that every municipal by-law was subject to the Minister of Municipal Affairs, and the Lieutenant-Governor-in-Council in Quebec was empowered to disallow any municipal by-law. All of the provinces except Prince Edward Island required approval of by-laws to incur debt. Other types of by-laws, such as those relating to public health, traffic, and zoning, were also made subject to approval by the appropriate provincial departments and boards. In many cases, municipalities were authorized to exercise specific powers only subject to review or control by some provincial authority. Provincial control was also gradually extended over personnel and the conditions of employment of municipal staff. This included provincial standards of qualification for appointees and the limitation of the right of councils to dismiss employees without provincial approval. In addition, provision was made for the inspection or investigation of the affairs of a municipality both on a regular basis and as a special inquiry at the request of council or citizens or on the initiative of the province.

The postwar period brought a further increase in provincial supervision and control, largely because of the growing service demands on local government arising from the extensive urbanization of the time. As the revenues from the real property tax became less and less adequate

---

[6] The exception was Prince Edward Island, no doubt because of the very few incorporated municipalities, as described in Chapter 2. A similar situation existed in Newfoundland, which still had only 27 incorporated municipalities in 1951, two years after joining Canada. A Director of Local Government was appointed in 1944 but less to supervise municipalities than to encourage their incorporation.

to finance the growing expenditures of local government, the provinces increased their financial assistance. Most of this increased assistance, however, was in the form of conditional grants, as described below. By attaching conditions, provinces were attempting to ensure that certain services were provided to at least a minimum standard regardless of the varying financial capacities of their individual municipalities. But as municipalities participated in more and more of these conditional grant and shared cost programs, their local expenditures increasingly reflected provincial priorities.

In some instances, provincial intervention was even more direct, with the provincial government taking over all or partial responsibility for functions traditionally exercised by the local level on the grounds, often quite valid, that the function had outgrown local government — or at least its limited boundaries — and now had much wider implications. This pattern of responsibilities shifting upward to more senior levels occurred with respect to such matters as roads, assessment, the administration of justice, education, public health, and social services. A related development in some of the provinces saw the establishment or enlargement of a number of intermunicipal special purpose bodies that were ostensibly part of the local government structure and yet came under increasing provincial influence and control. Here again there was a valid concern on the part of the province about minimum standards in such areas as health and education, but the end result was a further weakening of municipal government in relation to the provincial level. As one analyst saw the situation:

> The succession of efforts to enlarge local administrative structures in education, public health, welfare, and toward regional municipalities has simply reduced the number of units confronting the provincial administrator at any one time .... The taxpayer's dollar has been the fulcrum of power for the bureaucrat to use in organizing things, ostensibly for the citizen's benefit but inevitably for the bureaucrat's benefit as well.[7]

By the 1960s then, local governments had been subjected to three decades of developments that undermined their operating independence and brought them increasingly into the orbit of the senior levels of government. As a result of the Depression of the 1930s, municipalities experienced increased provincial surveillance over their financial activities and they lost their historical place in the social services field to the

---

[7] Vernon Lang, *The Service State Emerges in Ontario*, Toronto, Ontario Economic Council, 1974, p. 61.

senior governments, increasingly the federal government. They were confined to their historical dependence upon the real property tax as a result of the centralization of government and tax-rental and tax-sharing agreements brought on by the Second World War. The greatly increased demands of the postwar period resulted in further provincial and federal encroachment on the operations of local government. Consider the following observation concerning New Brunswick:

> In many traditional areas of local competence, provincial supervision, regulation or outright control have been deemed the acceptable solutions.... Their overall effect has incorporated municipal affairs more completely in the broader contexts of provincial and federal public administration. Indeed, local autonomy in all but a few...areas is extinct.[8]

By this time, provincial intervention had taken an even more direct form with local government reform initiatives being undertaken in a number of provinces. Since these reforms were concerned with modernizing and strengthening the local government systems, one might have expected the end result to be a reduction in provincial supervision and control. To the extent that provincial controls had developed because local governments were unable or unwilling to exercise the necessary responsibilities, such intervention should presumably not be needed with the reformed systems. As discussed in Chapter 5, however, such was not the result.

EFFECT OF REFORMS:
FAILED TO STRENGTHEN LOCAL GOVERNMENTS MUCH
PROVINCIAL CONTROL STILL WIDESPREAD

One major problem was that the reforms did not really strengthen local government very much. While the reform policies were sometimes quite imaginative, resistance to change was widespread. As a result, boundaries, internal machinery and operating procedures, and distribution of responsibilities still reflected historical patterns in many cases. The reforms also suffered from a lack of balance, being over-preoccupied with improving service delivery and, in most instances, missing the opportunity to strengthen the political and representative dimensions of local government. With some important exceptions noted below, the reforms also failed to resolve the financial dilemma posed by local

---

[8]   H.J. Whalen, *The Development of Local Government in New Brunswick,* Fredericton, 1963, p. 90.

government's overwhelming dependence upon the property tax. To the contrary, as previously outlined, a number of the local government reform studies exhibited a rather narrow viewpoint of the role of local government because of their attempt to define its operations in relation to services to property.

Whatever the reasons, the reformed local government structures cannot be said to enjoy significantly greater operating freedom than those that have not been reformed. There has been no dramatic breakthrough in terms of a reduction in the provincial encroachment on the operations of local government. Perhaps the best example of this fact is found in the operations of the Municipality of Metropolitan Toronto, the largest and oldest of the reformed systems in Canada and one which, therefore, we would expect to exhibit some independence. According to the 1977 Royal Commission on Metropolitan Toronto:

> In a comprehensive review of all local services provided in Metropolitan Toronto and prescribed by statute, it was found that only in one-fifth of these areas do municipalities exercise relative autonomy. For the overwhelming majority of services, the scope of municipal policy discretion is limited severely by provincial standards and regulations, or by provincially designated special purpose authorities.[9]

The extent of provincial supervision and control is evident if one examines the two key areas of finance and planning. With minor variations, all provinces and the territorial governments exercise approval power over municipal long term borrowing and municipal planning.[10] In fact, it is in the area of finance that provincial-municipal relations have usually been most difficult and unsatisfactory (from the point of view of municipalities).

---

[9]   *Report of the Royal Commission on Metropolitan Toronto,* Toronto, Queen's Printer, 1977, Vol. 1, p. 35. These findings were the result of a background study for the Commission, "Local Decision-Making and Administration," by Karl D. Jaffary and Stanley M. Makuch.

[10]   Based on information contained in *Provincial and Municipal Finances 1987,* Toronto, Canadian Tax Foundation, 1988, pp. 2:1 to 2:20. The variations included some provision for local approval of long term borrowing and some instances where borrowing can proceed within specified limits. In the case of planning, regional authorities with plans in place sometimes exercise the approval power of the province.

Provincial-Local Finances

The fundamental problem facing local government finances is that the revenue sources under the control of the municipalities have been increasingly inadequate in meeting their greatly expanded expenditures, largely caused by the extensive urbanization of the postwar period. The provincial and federal governments have also faced greatly increased expenditures but they have been able to impose a variety of new taxes to finance their needs. While the federal government has unlimited taxing powers under the constitution and the provincial governments can levy any form of direct tax, municipalities are restricted to those tax sources that their provincial governments have seen fit to delegate to them. A number of different taxes have been available to municipalities over the years, but most of these have since disappeared or been reclaimed by the senior levels of government as part of the centralization of finances referred to above. The mainstay of municipal revenues has always been the tax on real property, supplemented in some provinces by an additional tax on business at a rate on a stipulated percentage of the assessed value of the property.[11]

Real Property Tax

As has been indicated, the real property tax became increasingly inadequate and was also felt to be less appropriate because of the growth of the tenant population and the expansion of services to people rather than services to property. It is also criticized on a number of other grounds. The property tax is considered regressive in nature in that, since it is not based on people's income but on the assessed value of their properties, it does not reflect ability to pay. To illustrate, consider two identically assessed houses, each paying taxes of $1 000. To the first owner whose annual income is $20 000, this represents a tax burden of 5%, but for the second owner who is retired on an income of $10 000, the tax burden is 10%. The real property tax is also criticized as a slow growth tax because its base does not change in proportion to changes in the general level of economic activity. In fact, it is necessary to undertake property reassessment at regular intervals

---

[11] For a detailed, up-to-date outline of municipal revenues see *Provincial and Municipal Finances,* a biennial publication of the Canadian Tax Foundation, Toronto.

if property values and therefore municipal tax yields are to reflect actual conditions. In the absence of such reassessments, properties are underassessed to varying degrees both within and between municipalities, causing a further criticism of the inequities resulting with the people owning properties that are most underassessed not paying their proper share of the tax burden.

CRITICISMS OF PROPERTY TAX:
INAPPROPRIATE & INADEQUATE
REGRESSIVE & INEQUITABLE
SLOW GROWTH TAX

These latter criticisms, of course, are really directed to the system of assessment not the property tax per se. If there was a very efficient system of reassessment that kept property values in line with changing economic conditions, the property tax would not be a slow growth tax. Indeed, one study estimated that over the period 1937-1961 market property values in Ontario grew faster than personal income, even though assessed values grew more slowly.[12] As a result, a property tax on true market values might have produced faster growing revenues than an income tax. In addition, it is reasonable to assume that an efficient system of reassessment would remove most of the inequities that presently exist.

While progress has been slow in some instances, the desire for an improved system of assessment was a factor in the provincial assumption of responsibility for this function in a number of the provinces. Assessment remains a completely local responsibility only in Alberta and Quebec. It is all, or primarily, a provincial responsibility in the remaining provinces and is a territorial responsibility in the case of the Northern Territories.[13] In addition to efforts to introduce market value assessment, provincial reforms have been concerned with such aspects as the categories of tax-exempt property, the treatment of farmland, and the provincial payments-in-lieu on provincial tax-exempt properties.

---

[12] Frank A. Clayton, "Revenue Productivity of the Real Property Tax (Ontario)," in John R. Allan and Irving J. Goffman (eds.), *Papers in Taxation and Public Finance*, Toronto, Canadian Tax Foundation, 1966, pp. 129–161.

[13] Based on information in *Provincial and Municipal Finances, 1987*.

CASE FOR PROPERTY TAX:
PROPER ASSESSMENTS WOULD OVERCOME SLOW GROWTH
AND INEQUITABLE FEATURES
TAX CREDITS AND REBATES REDUCE REGRESSIVENESS
NOT ESPECIALLY BURDENSOME
UNFAIRLY CRITICIZED

Provincial governments have also introduced a variety of payments to ease the tax burden on those with lower income levels, thereby offsetting much of the regressiveness of the property tax. Finnis notes that "the most popular forms of direct provincial relief to individual taxpayers are home owner grants, rebates, or credits against the property tax practised in varying degrees in Quebec, Ontario, Manitoba, Saskatchewan, Alberta and British Columbia."[14] Largely because of these rebates and credits, most analysts now disagree with the criticism that the property tax is regressive. An Ontario study in 1978 concluded that while increases in property taxes may in some instances be regressive in their impact on some people, the property tax is not significantly regressive. It noted that Ontario's tax credit system "is quite successful in providing relief to those most in need," although it argues that "most citizens do not, in fact, 'need' such relief from what is, in the final analysis, not such a bad tax at all."[15]

Further evidence that the property tax has not been especially burdensome is provided by Kitchen who compares the utilization of this tax with that of the personal income tax.[16] He finds that the utilization of the personal income tax field increased in every province from 1968 to 1979, but that only two provinces — Newfoundland and Manitoba — increased their use of property taxes. Kitchen calculates that if

---

[14] Frederic Finnis, *Property Assessment in Canada,* Toronto, Canadian Tax Foundation, 1979, pp. 1–2. See also Harry Kitchen, *Local Government Finance in Canada,* Toronto, Canadian Tax Foundation, 1984, 206–208.

[15] R. M. Bird and N. E. Slack, *Residential Property Tax Relief in Ontario,* Toronto, Ontario Economic Council and University of Toronto Press, 1978, pp. 114 and 7. For a discussion of the possible regressivity of the property tax and various methods of property tax relief provided by provincial governments, see Robin W. Boadway and Harry M. Kitchen, *Canadian Tax Policy,* Toronto, Canadian Tax Foundation, 1980, Chapter Four. See also Ronald Meng and W. Irwin Gillespie, "The Regressivity of Property Taxes in Canada: Another Look," in *Canadian Tax Journal,* 34, November-December 1986, pp. 1417–1430.

[16] Kitchen, *op. cit.,* Chapter Fifteen.

the reliance on property taxes in 1980 had corresponded to that in 1968 or 1970, total tax revenues would have been between $2.1 and $3.3 billion more than was actually collected.

Why then, has the real property tax become so widely criticized and unpopular? A major cause is likely the fact that the property tax is so conspicuous and identifiable. Most of us rarely think about the tax portion of the price of gasoline, cigarettes, or alcohol, for example, and we have gradually become numbed to the inclusion of a retail sales tax in the price of many of our daily purchases. Consider, as well, the quietly efficient operation of the income tax system that, in most instances, removes its revenues throughout the year before we even see our pay cheques. In contrast, increases in the property tax are announced annually with maximum local media coverage. The tax appears more substantial when introduced in this fashion, especially if payment is requested in one lump sum or even a few installments.

Moreover, the accessibility of local government encourages strong public reaction to the property tax. How many citizens take the trouble to enclose a letter with their income tax statement outlining deficiencies in the performance of the senior levels of government? Yet, these citizens do not hesitate to pass on criticisms at the local level, especially when taxes are paid in person across the counter as is still the case in many of the smaller municipalities particularly. It is almost as if people vent their general dislike of all taxes (and all governments) by criticizing the taxing authority that is handiest. Regrettably, too many municipal politicians have simply accepted such criticisms and offered unrealistic promises to "hold the line" on tax increases, rather than educating the public as to the financial implications of their servicing demands. Media coverage, as outlined in Chapter 7, has also been less than responsible, with any increase in mill rates given exaggerated attention without regard to overall policy and financial considerations.

Miscellaneous Local Revenue Sources

While the real property tax has received all of the attention, municipalities also generate revenues from such sources as licenses, fees, permits, fines and penalties, user charges, and developer charges. Historically, these sources of revenue were quite minor for municipalities in most provinces, but they have been expanding significantly in the past couple of decades. Given not only the political limits (however self-imposed) on property tax increases but also the decline in the rate of transfer payments (discussed below), the miscellaneous local revenue sources appear to represent the best opportunity for municipalities to generate the additional revenues that they need.

> **MISCELLANEOUS LOCAL REVENUES:**
> **SHOWING MAJOR INCREASE**
> **ESPECIALLY USER FEES**

Ridler indicates that this response has, indeed, been occurring, particularly in relation to an expansion of user fees.[17] Examining the period between 1973 and 1982, he notes that transfer payments as a share of gross municipal revenues remained relatively stable, as did the yield from the property tax. In contrast, the share from user fees increased from 5.4% to 9.2% during this period.[18] This expansion occurred particularly in recreational services, but was also evident in areas such as waste removal and police control. Ridler cites a number of potential advantages of the increased application of user fees,[19] and concludes that their expanded use resulted in a slight reduction in fiscal imbalance for municipalities (the difference between expenditures and revenues from own sources) in 1982 as compared to 1973.

The increased reliance on miscellaneous local revenues has continued in the intervening years. For example, 22% of the revenues of British Columbia municipalities came from this category in 1986.[20] Approximately 25% of the revenues of Ontario municipalities are derived from this category,[21] particularly from the growth of user fees, the expanded use of developer charges and lot levies, and the return on investment derived from improved techniques of short term money

---

[17] Neil B. Ridler, "Fiscal Constraints and the Growth of User Fees among Canadian Municipalities," in *Canadian Public Administration*, Fall 1984, pp. 429-436.

[18] *Ibid.*, p. 434.

[19] *Ibid.*, pp. 435–436.

[20] Report prepared by the British Columbia Ministry of Municipal Affairs, Recreation and Culture and the Union of B.C. Municipalities, *Financing Local Government*, September 21, 1988, p. 3.

[21] C. Richard Tindal, *Municipal Councillor's Course*, Kingston, St. Lawrence College, 1989, Lesson Five, p. 5.

management. Particularly striking is the situation in Metropolitan Toronto, where user fees account for 34% of municipal revenues, almost as significant as property taxes (35%) and more important than transfer payments (31%).[22]

Transfer Payments from the Senior Levels

The third main source of local government revenues, of course, is transfer payments from the senior levels of government. These payments are primarily from the provincial level and are mostly conditional grants that have the effect of limiting the spending discretion of the municipalitities. Since a number of these conditional grants are paid directly to separate special purpose bodies, they also serve to "reduce their budgetary and policy accountability to locally elected councils."[23] Other serious deficiencies from the municipal viewpoint include the uncertainty of provincial funding and the complexity of the process, with virtually every provincial ministry offering a variety of grants.

Revenue-Sharing Arrangements   One change that appeared to offer the possibility of overcoming at least some of the above-noted difficulties was provincial-municipal revenue sharing that, as outlined below, has been introduced in a number of the provinces. However, some of the early promise of this concept has not been realized, and provincial financial support generally has been increasingly adversely affected by the preoccupation of both the federal and provincial levels with their budget deficits.

Ontario was the first province to introduce revenue sharing, although its experience has been less than encouraging. Known as the Edmonton Commitment because it was first announced at the national tri-level conference in Edmonton in October 1973, the revenue-sharing policy was officially introduced in the 1974 Ontario Budget. The Ontario government pledged that it would increase its transfers to local governments and agencies at the rate of growth of total provincial revenues. This appeared to guarantee the municipalities at least a minimum level of provincial financial support while introducing a greater degree of certainty and stability.

---

[22] Municipality of Metropolitan Toronto, *The Crumbling Financial Partnership*, Toronto, March 1989, p. 37.

[23] Dale E. Richmond, "Provincial-Municipal Transfer Systems," in *Canadian Public Administration*, Summer 1980, p. 260.

Unfortunately, the implementation of this revenue-sharing scheme was plagued by problems of interpretation and growing controversy. The final straw from the municipal viewpoint was a provincial redefinition of the Edmonton Commitment to include certain existing assistance programs of direct financial benefit to local government such as the Teachers' Superannuation Fund, payments in lieu of taxes, and farm tax rebates. Whether or not this redefinition was valid, municipalities resented the fact that it was imposed without consultation and they saw it as an attempt to reduce the province's financial support for local government. The *Municipal World* editorialized that the Edmonton Commitment had been brutalized, depleted and changed almost beyond recognition before being laid to rest.[24]

In the ensuing years a variety of new financial arrangements have been suggested, but none have been agreed upon. Provincial transfers have reverted to an ad hoc basis. Regardless of the level of the financial support from the province, local governments are back in the familiar position of having to wait each year for provincial announcements before they know what their financial situation will be. They also receive the bulk of this provincial assistance in conditional form, 75% in the case of municipalities alone, and 88% if transfers to school boards are included.[25]

Matters came to a head in early 1989 after the province introduced a freeze on both the Municipal Unconditional Grants Program and the Municipal Roads Subsidy Program. The result was an emergency session of the Association of Municipalities of Ontario at which concern was expressed about not only the reduction in financial support but also the province's activities in shifting a number of responsibilities and expenditure burdens to the local level. One of the outcomes of the meeting was a call, as yet ignored by the province, for a provincial/municipal review of local government finance.

Manitoba enacted a Provincial-Municipal Tax Sharing Act in 1976 that provides municipalities with specified portions of the yield from personal income taxes and corporation taxes. At present the act assigns 2.2 percentage points of personal income tax and 1 percentage point of corporation tax to local governments in the form of per capita payments that vary with the size and type of municipality. The Manitoba government also introduced a new unconditional grant — the

[24] *Municipal World*, St. Thomas, October 1977, p. 255.

[25] *Municipal Councillor's Course*, Lesson Five, p. 3.

Local Government General Support Grant — for 1983, calculated as 1.65% of each local government's net payroll costs in 1982.[26]

British Columbia has had a Revenue Sharing Act since 1977, providing both conditional and (mostly) unconditional grants based on 1 percentage point of personal income tax, 1 percentage point of corporation tax, and 6 percentage points of revenue from other revenue sources. The amount of assistance for each municipality is based on population, total expenditure, and relative assessment deficiency.[27] In addition, British Columbia has permissive legislation under The British Columbia Transit Authority Act concerning municipal gasoline taxes to finance urban transportation. Such a tax is currently levied in the greater Vancouver area.[28]

Provincial restraint measures have also had an impact in British Columbia, with municipalities expressing concern about the resulting decline in the level of financial support for the local level. According to one study, while revenue-sharing grants made up 19% of local government budgets in 1981, this figure had declined to 12% in 1982 and 10% in 1986.[29]

Saskatchewan began a revenue-sharing program in 1978. In the first year a base amount was determined that was equivalent to the amount of certain conditional grants that were being eliminated. Since then, the transfer has grown at the same rate as the bases of specified provincial taxes — originally four of them, now three.[30] This financial assistance is distributed to municipalities in both conditional and unconditional fashion.[31]

Quebec introduced a major change in the Municipal Finance Act of 1979, which came into effect January 1, 1980. Acknowledging that the real property tax couldn't finance both municipal and school needs, the provincial government handed over the property tax exclusively to municipalities. This was accomplished, however, by removing education from the local level in a move somewhat reminiscent of New Brunswick's

---

[26]   Ministry of Municipal Affairs, *Background,* March 7, 1983.

[27]   David Siegel, "Provincial-Municipal Relations in Canada: An Overview," in *Canadian Public Administration,* Summer 1980, p. 312.

[28]   Municipality of Metropolitan Toronto, *The Crumbling Financial Partnership,* March 1989, p. 49.

[29]   *Financing Local Government,* p. 28.

[30]   *Provincial and Municipal Finances, 1987,* p. 13:21.

[31]   Siegel, *op. cit.,* p. 311.

reforms in the late 1960s. Related reforms included an increase in payments in lieu of taxes and modifications to the business tax. As a result of the reforms, provincial aid to municipalities was substantially reduced, but the net financial position of municipalities was still significantly improved because of the removal of the educational burden.[32]

Nova Scotia introduced a new unconditional grant program in 1980, as a result of the deliberations of a Joint Union of Nova Scotia Municipalities-Department of Municipal Affairs Task Force. Calculated by taking as a base the payments that were made under certain previous grant formulas and increasing this figure by the percentage increase in gross provincial revenues, this form of indexing is to continue annually.[33]

New Brunswick made a number of changes to strengthen the financial position of its municipalities, particularly as a result of the Equal Opportunity Program introduced in 1967 following the Byrne Commission. Municipal expenditure pressures were relieved by the transfer of a number of responsibilities to the provincial level — a mixed blessing as discussed in Chapter 5. In addition, a new unconditional grant program was introduced, its grant formula largely derived from a Task Force Report on Municipal Structure and Financing (the Allen Report). The amount of the grant was calculated as a percentage of municipal expenditure (net of non-tax revenue), with grant increases annually in line with the growth of net provincial revenues.[34]

While New Brunswick was the only province during the 1970s in which unconditional grants were a more significant revenue source for municipalities than conditional grants, the proportion of conditional grants began to increase by the end of the decade.[35] In 1983 the province announced that it was freezing the 1984 unconditional grant at the 1983 level as part of a series of restraint measures.[36] Growing municipal concern about the grant prompted a provincial review that reported in 1986. A new unconditional grant formula was introduced the following year, and was supposed to increase at the rate of 4% per year. However, the

---

[32] For an examination of the Quebec reforms see Jean-Louis Lapointe, "La Reforme de la Fiscalité Municipal au Québec," in *Canadian Public Administration,* Summer 1980, pp. 269–280.

[33] Siegel, *op. cit.,* p. 309.

[34] *Ibid.,* p. 310.

[35] *Ibid.,* p. 303.

[36] Department of Municipal Affairs and Environment, *Review of New Brunswick's Unconditional Grant to Municipalities,* February 1986, p. 41.

province announced a freeze for 1989, prompting municipal demands for a royal commission. According to the municipalities, unconditional grants as a percentage of gross budgets in New Brunswick cities have declined from 49.8% in 1974 to 34.9% in 1988.[37]

Summary

Even this brief outline provides a number of insights into revenue sharing and the provincial-municipal relationship generally. At the outset, one is struck by the potential complexity of the concept of revenue sharing. Among the variables are the way in which transfers are indexed or increased annually, the base to which such an index is applied, the way in which the transfers are distributed to municipalities, and the method of determining which municipalities are most in need of such transfers.

While the concept of revenue sharing is welcome, its significance should not be exaggerated. The basic financial problem of municipal governments remains — their expenditures far exceed the revenue sources directly available to them. Accordingly, they must obtain a major portion of their funding in the form of financial assistance from the provincial level. While the basis of this funding and its continuance *can* be made more clear and secure in a number of provinces with revenue-sharing arrangements, the fact remains that the bulk of the transfer payments are still conditional.

> **MUNICIPAL FINANCIAL POSITION:**
> **RELIANT ON OUTSIDE SOURCES**
> **MOSTLY CONDITIONAL SUPPORT**
> **NO GUARANTEE OF STABILITY EVEN WITH REVENUE SHARING**
> **VULNERABLE TO PROVINCIAL RESTRAINT ACTIVITIES**

Recent reductions and transfer payment freezes have done nothing to alter Richmond's critical assessment of the provincial-municipal financial relationship and the changes that have been made to it. He compares the approach used quite unfavourably with that of the provincial and federal levels in resolving their problems of fiscal imbalance.[38] Gen-

---

[37] Brief to the Policy and Priorities Committee of the Government of New Brunswick, *Re The Unconditional Grant to Municipalities and Related Matters*, Provincial-Municipal Council, Inc., October 11, 1988, p. 3–3.

[38] Richmond, *op. cit.*, pp. 252–255.

erally, Richmond finds that greater centralization and control by the provinces over local governments has been the result and notes that:

> In contrast to the federal-provincial response, the provincial-municipal mechanism for dealing with financial dilemmas was generally characterized by unilaterally determined transfer mechanisms, a proliferation of conditional grants, an irrational equalization system and a large number of special purpose bodies.[39]

He also points to the harmful effects of the financial restraint experienced by provincial governments and observes that some provinces such as Ontario and British Columbia have frozen their contribution to shared cost programs and "left the municipal sector out on a limb when attempting to budget for an ongoing responsibility."[40] Two examples involving Ontario illustrate the difficulty.[41] In 1971 the provincial government increased its support for the capital costs of public transit systems from 25% to 75% and, in addition, agreed to pay 50% of the operating deficit of transit systems — changes that prompted some municipalities to expand their transit facilities. But, in 1975 the province imposed a ceiling on the amount it would contribute to operating deficits and the following year it limited its contribution to a 5% increase from the previous year, at a time when operating costs were increasing much more rapidly. Similarly, municipalities greatly expanded their day care facilities when the province funded 80% of the costs. Here again, 1976 saw the province limit funds for this service to a 5.5% increase, with municipalities locked into more rapidly expanding expenditures over which they had little control.

Much more recently, reference has already been made to declining provincial financial support in provinces such as British Columbia, Ontario, and New Brunswick, with freezes in the latter two provinces leading to municipal demands for a complete study of the provincial-local relationship. Significant improvements in provincial support are unlikely, however, at a time when the provinces are having their own difficulties in maintaining existing levels of financial support from the federal level. This fact is but one illustration of the effect that federal actions have on municipalities and of the federal-local relationship that exists in Canada — in spite of the constitutional division of powers.

---

[39] *Ibid.*, p. 253.

[40] *Ibid.*, pp. 258–259.

[41] Kitchen, *op. cit.*, pp. 384–385.

Federal-Local and Tri-Level Relations

In addition to their involvement with provincial governments, municipalities have also been increasingly affected by federal programs and policies. Since the Dominion Housing Act of 1935 and especially since the establishment of the Central (now Canada) Mortgage and Housing Corporation (CMHC) in 1946, federal financial assistance for single family dwellings has reinforced low density sprawl with all of its implications for the local level. The actions of CMHC also contributed to neighbourhood dislocations and attendant problems because of what has been described as a bulldozer approach to urban renewal.[42] More positively, Chapter 9 notes experiences in both Vancouver and Toronto where the federal government responded to local concerns about proposed urban renewal schemes, in Strathcona and Treffan Court respectively, by threatening to withhold funds until the affected residents were brought into the planning process.

Decisions by the Department of Transport concerning rail services have had a critical impact on the economic vitality of communities[43] as have various industrial incentive and other programs offered by the Department of Regional Economic Expansion. Federal loans for sewage disposal facilities have been very helpful to municipalities while reflecting the national concern about water pollution. Altogether, by the late 1960s, "more than 117 distinct programs administered by 27 departments in Ottawa influenced metropolitan development plans."[44]

In almost every case, however, the federal programs were introduced without regard for their possible impact on the local level, and municipalities had no opportuntity for advance consultation and little hope of obtaining adjustments after the fact. Indeed, in many cases, the varied federal initiatives were not even coordinated with each other. For example, during the 1960s the CMHC financed extensive residential construction in the vicinity of the Malton Airport near Toronto. When the

---

[42] For a description of the role of the CMHC and of the background to tri-level relations see Donald J. H. Higgins, *Urban Canada: Its Government and Politics,* Toronto, Macmillan, 1977, pp. 76–90.

[43] It is hard to imagine a more dramatic impact on Canadian communities than the threatened cutbacks to passenger rail service in Canada that loom at the end of the 1980s.

[44] Elliot J. Feldman and Jerome Milch, "Coordination or Control? The Life and Death of the Ministry of Urban Affairs," in Lionel D. Feldman (ed.), *Politics and Government of Urban Canada,* Toronto, Methuen, 1981, p. 250.

Ministry of Transport sought to expand the airport in 1968 it found that an entire residential community had been constructed on what had been uninhabited farmland, and it turned its attention to seeking a new site.[45]

> **IMPETUS FOR TRI-LEVEL RELATIONS:**
> **MUNICIPALITIES SEEKING FEDERAL FUNDS**
> **FEDERAL LEVEL CONCERNED ABOUT GOVERNING OF CITIES**

By this time, however, developments were underway that appeared to offer the possibility of a much more coordinated approach to the handling of federal activities that affected urban Canada. Two major factors were combining to produce strong pressure for a closer and more formalized federal-local relationship. First, there was a growing municipal interest in the possibility of increased federal funds being made available to deal with major service demands, especially in urban areas. Doubtless this interest was stimulated by the fact that requests to the provincial governments for more financial assistance were constantly rebuffed on the grounds that the provinces were short of funds because of federal dominance of the main revenue fields. As the only national municipal body, the Canadian Federation of Mayors and Municipalities (now the Federation of Canadian Municipalities) took the initiative in espousing the municipal cause, especially after discussions on constitutional reform commenced in 1967. A joint Municipal Committee on Intergovernmental Relations was established and prepared an excellent paper on "The Municipality in the Canadian Federation" for presentation to the annual conference of provincial ministers of municipal affairs in Winnipeg in August 1970.

In the meantime, the second factor encouraging a federal-local relationship was developing with the growing federal appreciation that because of the large number of Canadians living in urban areas the ability of municipal governments to meet their needs was of more than local, or even provincial, interest. In this connection, December 1967 saw a Federal-Provincial Conference on Housing and Urban Development, and this was followed by a conference of civil servants in April 1968 at which the federal government outlined a number of specific shared-cost program proposals. Within a few months a Federal Task Force on Housing and Urban Development was appointed and its January 1969 Report called for a greatly expanded federal role. Headed by the then Minister

---

[45] *Ibid.*, p. 251.

of Transport, Paul Hellyer, the Task Force did not hesitate to make a number of recommendations involving matters within the jurisdiction of the provincial and municipal governments and appeared to incorporate a number of the proposals that had been made by federal officials at the above-noted April 1968 conference of federal and provincial civil servants.

Thus, for example, the Task Force recommended that the federal government make direct loans to municipalities to assist them in assembling and servicing land for urban growth, acquiring dispersed existing housing for use by low income groups, and developing urban transit systems. Noting that urban planning must be undertaken on a regional basis to be effective, the report called on the provinces to establish a system of regional governments for each major area. In addition, it recommended that the federal government establish a Department of Housing and Urban Affairs. The Task Force envisaged that the CMHC would retain its role as administrator and implementor of federal housing policy, while the new department would concentrate on advising on policy and coordinating research activities, at least at the federal level and possibly with other governments and agencies as well.

Initially, the federal cabinet appeared not ready to accept such an enlarged role, and within a few months Hellyer resigned as Minister of Transport, expressing dissatisfaction with the lack of government action on housing and urban questions generally. He later claimed that he was sabotaged by senior civil servants opposed to his recommendations.[46] While there was undoubtedly some truth to this charge, David Cameron notes that by using "outsiders" on his Task Force Hellyer was bound to create opposition from the bureaucracy, especially when the tight schedule for preparation of the report left insufficient time for the accommodation of views. Moreover, by making himself chairman, Hellyer "forged an identity between the results of the policy recommendations and his own political future."[47]

Ironically, within a year of his resignation Hellyer's successor, Robert Andras, was designated Minister of State for Urban Affairs, and the establishment of a Ministry of Urban Affairs was announced. This reversal of position was unquestionably influenced by a report by Harvey Lithwick, commissioned by Andras while he was minister without portfolio, which strongly criticized the federal government's failure to integrate and

---

[46] See Hellyer's comments in *City Magazine,* Toronto, December 1977.

[47] David M. Cameron, "Urban Policy," in G. Bruce Doern and V. Seymour Wilson (eds.), *Issues in Canadian Public Policy,* Toronto, Macmillan, 1974, p. 231.

coordinate policy decisions having urban ramifications.[48] As recommended by the Hellyer Task Force, the new ministry was not to be a traditional operating department but was to concentrate on policy development and on coordinating the projects of other departments. Also emphasized was the need to increase consultation and coordination among all three levels of government in dealing with the challenges of urbanization. Here again, the influence of the Lithwick Report was apparent; it had called for "a new kind of vertical integration within the hierarchy of government."[49]

MSUA:
TO DEVELOP URBAN POLICY
TO COORDINATE FEDERAL ACTIVITIES IN URBAN CANADA
TO INCREASE TRI-LEVEL CONSULTATION & COORDINATION

The new ministry began with ambitious objectives considering "the absence of any authority with which to control the legislative or spending proposals of other agencies."[50] One analysis observed that "it was created as a new David without a sling; the new ministry of state could fulfil its mission only with mutual trust and goodwill."[51] These commodities turned out to be in short supply and none of the approaches attempted by the ministry had much success.

Initially, in an attempt to gain credibility, "MSUA offered to represent the interests of municipalities and provincial governments in discussions with other federal agencies."[52] But this approach brought it into direct confrontation with other federal agencies and little was accomplished. By 1972 MSUA had adopted a new stategy — it would promote coordination by arranging meetings among representatives of all three levels of government and the various federal ministries whose programs affected urban areas. This approach had already been advocated by the Canadian Federation of Mayors and Municipalities and partly through the efforts of the Federation the first ever national tri-level conference was held in Toronto in November of 1972. The fact that the municipal

---

[48] Higgins, *op. cit.,* p. 83.

[49] N. H. Lithwick, *Urban Canada, Problems and Prospects,* Ottawa, Canada Mortgage and Housing Corporation, 1970, p. 178.

[50] Cameron in Doern and Wilson, *op. cit.,* p. 245.

[51] Feldman and Milch in Feldman, *op. cit.,* p. 254.

[52] *Ibid.,* p. 255.

level was represented in its own right was in itself a breakthrough, but the extent to which the conference might be considered a success depends upon the expectations of those participating in it. A Joint Municipal Committee on Intergovernmental Affairs presented several well researched papers, but little progress was made because of the uncompromising attitude of the provinces, particularly Ontario.[53]

A second national tri-level conference was held in Edmonton in October 1973. It was decided to undertake a study of public finance with particular reference to the adequacy of municipal revenue sources, a development seen optimistically as "the first important piece of firm evidence of the success of the tri-level process."[54] But difficulties and delays were encountered in launching the Tri-Level Task Force on Public Finance and the third national tri-level conference was accordingly postponed, indefinitely as it turned out.

In the meantime, however, agreement had been reached to hold tri-level meetings at the provincial and city level. A regional tri-level meeting was held, for example, in Peterborough, Ontario in May of 1973, and at the city level a number of tri-level meetings have been held in such places as Halifax, Quebec, Calgary, Fredericton, Montreal, Saint John, Regina, Toronto, Winnipeg, and Vancouver. Developments in the latter city illustrate the useful role of such meetings. The Ministry of Transport's plans for the expansion of Vancouver Airport were strongly opposed at the local level. Through the mediation efforts of the MSUA at a tri-level meeting in March of 1973, Transport agreed to establish an Airport Planning Committee, although they refused to let MSUA chair it.[55] These types of tri-level meeting continued for a while even after the demise of MSUA,[56] a reflection of the need for a more coordinated approach to urban issues.

With the national tri-level conferences stalled by provincial intransigence, MSUA adopted another strategy. It attempted to move from persuasion to power — which it sought through the CMHC, which

---

[53] For a thoughtful assessment of this first conference see *Urban Focus*, Vol. 1, No. 2, "The Tri-Level Conference — The Morning After," Queen's University, Institute of Local Government and Intergovernmental Relations, January-February 1973.

[54] *Urban Focus*, Vol. 2, No. 1, November-December 1973.

[55] Feldman and Milch in Feldman, *op. cit.*, p. 256.

[56] See J. M. Brodie, "Tri-Level Meeting — The Windsor Experience," in *Urban Focus*, Vol. 10, No. 2, November-December 1981.

controlled major expenditures.[57] Here again, however, successes were limited and by 1975 there was "a state of open warfare between MSUA and CMHC."[58] To resolve this conflict, William Teron was brought in as both Secretary of MSUA and Chairman of the Board of the CMHC. Within 18 months the number of MSUA personnel had been slashed by 40%. It adopted yet another approach at this point, whereby it didn't initiate, but would organize meetings if requested. "MSUA thus evolved from an agency that had flirted with the imposition of policy to an urban consultant active only on invitation."[59] This final phase of MSUA activity was received more favourably, but this was largely because of its much more modest mission, not because of any real support. By the spring of 1979 it had fallen victim to the politics of austerity. "Total savings would be less than $4 million (and perhaps closer to $500,000), but the public would be impressed by a government prepared to abolish a whole ministry in the name of fiscal responsibility."[60]

While the reasons for the failure of MSUA are fairly obvious for the most part,[61] viewpoints vary on its original appropriateness or the consequences of its demise. While conceding that "responsibility for urban policy — as policy for cities — must rest with the provinces," Cameron concludes that there still could be an important role for a federal body like MSUA "to concentrate on analyzing the impact of federal activities on cities and in turn interpreting provincial and municipal urban policy to federal agencies."[62] What is clear is that because of the failure of MSUA we continue to have federal policies enacted without regard to their urban impact. "Federal initiatives in the cities have been not only incoherent and irrational, often they have been inconsistent and unequal."[63]

In spite of the experience of MSUA, we will continue to have some form of tri-level relations in Canada. Such a relationship is unavoidable given the interdependence of programs and policies at all three levels of

---

[57] *Ibid.,* pp. 257–258.

[58] *Ibid.*, p. 258.

[59] *Ibid.*

[60] *Ibid.,* p. 260.

[61] In addition to the frequently cited article by Feldman and Milch, see Cameron in Doern and Wilson, *op. cit.,* and Allan O'Brien, "The Ministry of State for Urban Affairs: A Municipal Perspective," in *The Canadian Journal of Regional Science,* Halifax, Spring 1982.

[62] Cameron in Doern and Wilson, *op. cit.,* p. 249.

[63] Feldman and Milch in Feldman, *op. cit.,* p. 263.

government. The end of the 1980s has seen repeated calls by municipalities and some provincial governments for a tri-level approach to
the funding of infrastructure investment in Canadian cities. Without
such support, it is alleged, many basic municipal services that provide
the foundation for growth and development will begin to crumble. One
is reminded of the situation just two decades earlier, when municipal concerns about the high costs of such items as urban transportation systems helped to precipitate the previously described period of
formal tri-level relations. The difference is that in that earlier period
the federal government was actively interested in pursuing a more formal tri-level relationship; today, no such interest is apparent, especially
with the federal government trying to reduce its financial commitments
wherever possible.

> **TRI-LEVEL RELATIONS INEVITABLE:**
> **IN SPITE OF MSUA'S DEMISE**
> **BECAUSE OF INTERDEPENDENCE OF ALL THREE LEVELS**
> **EXAMPLE OF FUNDING OF INFRASTRUCTURE**
> **EXAMPLE OF REVENUE SQUEEZE PASSED DOWN**
> **THROUGH SUCCESSIVE LEVELS**

The federal government's actions in attempting to put its own financial house in order provide an excellent illustration of the way in which
federal initiatives can impact on the local level and of the interdependence of all three levels of government. By the mid-1970s, continued large
budget deficits prompted the federal government to review its transfer
payments to the provinces in those areas under provincial jurisdiction.
In the 1977-1982 federal-provincial fiscal arrangements, for example, the
federal government moved away from its policy of providing financial
assistance on a cost-shared basis. Instead, it initiated Established Program Financing (EPF), covering areas primarily of provincial jurisdiction
including hospital insurance, medicare, and post-secondary education.[64] It offered the provinces greater program flexibility through block
funding by tying its own contributions to the rate of growth in the national economy rather than to growth in provincial expenditures. This
policy has had a detrimental financial impact on the provinces because
their expenditures have increased faster than the growth in the national
economy. Further reductions in federal transfers to the provinces were

---

[64] Municipality of Metropolitan Toronto, *op. cit.*, pp. 16–17.

evident in the 1982-1987 federal-provincial fiscal arrangements. The tightening up has continued since the re-election of the Conservative government in 1988 and its commitment to reduce the federal deficit. If each level of government attempts to solve its financial problems by reducing its transfers to the next lowest level, it is obvious where that leaves local governments as the final recipients of such cut-backs.

Given the interdependence of the three levels of government, the real question is what type of new formal relationships, if any, will develop, and especially what recognition the views and concerns of the municipal level will receive. While much depends on the attitudes and willingness of the senior governments, local governments must also make every effort to articulate their views in a forceful, consistent fashion. As indicated below, such has often not been the case.

Municipal Consultations with the Senior Levels

Discussions of intergovernmental relations affecting municipalities tend to portray the municipal level as a passive observer — it is dictated to by the province or adversely affected by thoughtless federal action. Such a focus is much too narrow. It ignores the important role played by local government and the extent to which all levels of government have now become dependent upon each other. It overlooks the extent to which local governments can take the initiative in pressing their viewpoint upon the senior levels and attempting to obtain concessions from them. Accordingly, this closing section will briefly consider the consultative mechanisms available to municipalities and the apparent effectiveness of their consultative efforts.

The one national association of municipalities is the Federation of Canadian Municipalities, founded in 1937. Mention has already been made of its influential role in connection with the short-lived national tri-level conferences. However, the Federation has had continuing problems maintaining a strong membership and many municipalities prefer to deal directly with the federal government. At the beginning of the 1980s, it only represented about 300 of the over 4 000 municipalities in Canada, although they contained about 50% of the nation's population.[65] By the end of the 1980s, membership had increased to over 500

---

[65] George M. Betts, "Puppets on a Shoestring Revisited: The Municipalities and the Constitutional Struggle," a paper presented at the Municipal Finance Officers Association Conference, Halifax, October 1982, p. 15.

municipalities, containing two-thirds of the Canadian population, according to information provided by FCM. Its membership also extends to 15 associations of municipalities from across Canada.

The Federation has suffered from some internal squabbling about urban versus rural considerations, and its need to find a middle ground has forced it to espouse generalized positions that reflect the lowest common denominator at times. The Federation's position may also be weakened by the existence of a number of very active provincial associations of municipalities, and there have been recurring suggestions that it become a federation of these bodies.[66] However, its championing of the need for infrastructure renewal seems to have given FCM a strong focus as the 1990s begin.

Most provinces have a number of municipal associations representing both staff and councillors, although it is the political associations that are critical to the consultations with the senior governments. Some provinces have several of these associations while others have only one. Obviously, one large association representing all municipalities has the potential to speak with a more powerful voice. This potential may not be realized, however, since the attempt to represent a variety of municipal viewpoints may cause internal strife and foster excessive compromising that pleases no one.

**ONTARIO EXPERIENCE:
FORMAL CONSULTATIVE MACHINERY BROKE DOWN
NEW UMBRELLA MUNICIPAL ORGANIZATION FORMED (AMO)**

Ontario's experience is interesting in this regard, and it also illustrates the workings of a formalized municipal-provincial consultative process.[67] In 1969 a Municipal Liaison Committee (MLC) was established to provide more coordinated activity on the part of the four political associations then in existence. A series of joint meetings were held between a committee of cabinet ministers and the MLC, and by 1972 these sessions had become regular monthly meetings of what became known as the Provincial-Municipal Liaison Committee (PMLC).

---

[66] Siegel, *op. cit.,* p. 314.

[67] The analysis that follows is partly based on Sheila Gordon, *Intergovernmental Relations,* a paper presented to the Ontario Conference on Local Government Seminar, September 26, 1978.

During 1973 the PMLC was involved in discussions leading up to the previously described revenue-sharing arrangement known as the Edmonton Commitment. Other important issues included a proposal to move toward a system of unconditional grants. The consultation mechanism appeared to be working and municipalities were encouraged. However, the provincial government appeared less and less responsive with the financial restraint and minority government position of the second half of the 1970s. Some ministers tended to consult with the MLC only when it was in their interests to do so, and one analysis suggests that the MLC was occasionally used as a scapegoat to cover up for provincial mistakes or to shift the blame for unpopular policies.[68]

The MLC itself was hampered by limited staff and financial resources. It also had difficulty deciding on its proper role. If the MLC was essentially a federation and a policy-presenting body rather than one that made policy, then its members had to reconcile their desire to reach a consensus with their responsibility to represent the potentially diverse views of their respective associations. Making this reconciliation even more difficult was the fact that the associations tended to compete with one another for profile and recognition.[69] In late 1979 the largest political association withdrew from the PMLC and within a short time the regular monthly meetings had ceased.

By June of 1980, however, a new umbrella municipal organization had been recommended, and the founding convention of the new Association of Municipalities of Ontario (AMO) was held in October 1981. The new structure attempts to combine for strength while still preserving the diversity of viewpoints that often arise on municipal issues. Thus, it contains within it five sections: Large Urban, Small Urban, County and Regional, Rural, and Northern Ontario. Its principle of operation is that all viewpoints will be forwarded on any issue that comes to it for comment. While this new organization appears to be functioning successfully, formal, regular municipal-provincial consultations have not yet been reinstated. In the absence of such regular consultative mechanisms, AMO's response to growing financial concerns in 1989 was to call an emergency meeting and to pass a resolution demanding a joint review of local finances.

New Brunswick has a body similar to Ontario's PMLC, the New Brunswick Provincial-Municipal Council. It is composed of fifteen members,

---

[68] T. J. Plunkett and G. M. Betts, *The Management of Canadian Urban Government,* Kingston, Institute of Local Government, Queen's University, 1978, p. 90.

[69] Gordon, *op. cit.,* p. 14.

four from each of the three municipal associations in the province and three from the provincial cabinet. They meet on a monthly basis to discuss items of mutual concern.[70] It is this Provincial-Municipal Council that demanded a royal commission after the New Brunswick government froze the 1989 unconditional grant program, as discussed above. It remains to be seen what effect there will be from the formation in early 1989 of a new fourth municipal association — for francophone municipalities. Generally speaking, the more separate associations there are, the more difficult it is for municipalities to take a common stand and to maximize their pressure on the provincial level.

To take one more example, Alberta's most prominent municipal association is the Alberta Urban Municipalities Association (AUMA). But Masson has noted that even though this association's membership consisted of 100% of the province's cities and towns and 94% of its villages, it has been limited in its influence because of internal tensions.[71] He describes a picture very reminiscent of Ontario's experiences, explaining that in many policy areas small towns and villages have had much different concerns than large cities, and that these differences have made it very difficult for AUMA to take a firm position.

Notwithstanding the activities of the various municipal associations, Feldman and Graham suggest that since these associations are not accountable to the public and are "somewhat immune to public opinion," their use for the conduct of important intergovernmental affairs may have stifled the emergence of much public concern about important municipal (intergovernmental) issues.[72] They question whether or not an association can represent adequately an individual municipality's specific concerns, arguing that associations generally represent "the lowest common denominator" of opinion among their members, thereby blurring the interests of individual municipalities. They raise a concern that municipal associations partially financed by the provincial level may be unduly influenced accordingly. They also point out that provincial governments can sometimes subvert the focus of a municipal association so that it becomes a vehicle for disseminating information about provincial policy, rather than for expressing municipal views and concerns. In this situation, Feldman and Graham conclude, "municipal rep-

---

[70] Siegel, *op. cit.*, p. 316.

[71] Jack Masson, *Alberta's Local Governments and Their Politics*, Edmonton, University of Alberta Press, 1985, p. 201.

[72] Lionel D. Feldman and Katherine A. Graham, *Bargaining for Cities*, Toronto, Butterworth and Company, 1979, pp. 21–27.

resentatives tend to be thought of at best as glorified office boys and at worst as whipping boys." In their view, intergovernmental concerns should be addressed by individual municipalities, particularly in the case of Canada's larger municipalities.

PROBLEMS OF MUNICIPAL ASSOCIATIONS:
FORCED TO COMPROMISE
CAN'T REPRESENT INDIVIDUAL MUNICIPALITIES
MAY BE INFLUENCED BY PROVINCIAL FUNDING
NOT ACCOUNTABLE

Lightbody illustrates what can be done by an individual municipality pursuing an aggressive strategy in his case study of Edmonton's successful effort to gain a larger share of long distance tolls for its municipally owned telephone company from the provincial monopoly. He describes a situation in which "the accepted rules for central-local relations were tested, breached and the established order of intergovernmental relations was directly confronted."[73] He also cites two other examples that suggest "the evolutionary changes which are emerging in city-provincial relations."[74] The first was the one-day police strike in Montreal in October 1969 that, as discussed in Chapter 5, gave Mayor Drapeau a situation in which he could lever the Montreal Urban Community reorganization through a cautious Union Nationale government. The second, also described in Chapter 5, was the prolonged attack on the Metropolitan Winnipeg structure led by Stephen Juba throughout the 1960s, which helped to discredit that institution and pave the way for the Unicity reform that followed the NDP provincial election victory in 1969.

Summary

This chapter began by tracing the general pattern of provincial-municipal relations in Canada. This pattern has been one of gradually increasing provincial supervision and control over local governments, an increase given particular impetus by the combined impact of the financial pressures of the Great Depression, the centralization of government

---

[73] James Lightbody, "With Whom The Tolls Dwell: The Great Edmonton Telephone Dispute, 1984–1987," in *Canadian Public Administration*, Spring 1989, pp. 42–62.

[74] *Ibid.*, pp. 53–54.

during World War Two, and the upsurge in service demands because of rapid postwar urbanization. The local government reforms that were introduced in various provinces did little to arrest this trend.

The generally unsatisfactory nature of the provincial-local relationship is also evident in the field of finances. The traditional mainstay of municipal revenues, the real property tax, was providing less than 50% of these revenues by the 1960s and only about one-third by the 1980s. Municipalities were able to generate additional revenues through a substantial increase in the yield from their miscellaneous local revenue, particularly user charges. For the most part, however, the shortfall in the real property tax yield was made up by transfer payments from the senior levels. The overwhelmingly conditional nature of these payments (about 90%) raised concerns about the survival of municipal autonomy.

Improvements brought about by the introduction of revenue-sharing agreements in a number of the provinces have proven to be somewhat illusory. Even with these agreements, municipalities have still found themselves vulnerable to unilateral provincial freezes or reductions of transfers to meet provincial restraint objectives.

In fact, municipalities in some provinces have been experiencing what they see as a double or triple revenue squeeze. In addition to the reduction in the rate of increase of transfer payments, municipalities claim that there has also been an attempt by their provincial government to solve their own financial problems by shifting certain responsibilities and expenditure burdens to the local level. Third, they charge that the province has extended existing programs or imposed new ones without providing corresponding funding support. The Association of Municipalities of Ontario, for example, has identified some 22 examples of these latter two developments, which provided much of the focus for its early 1989 emergency meeting, already discussed.

INTERGOVERNMENTAL ISSUES:
INCREASING PROVINCIAL SUPERVISION & CONTROL
MUNICIPAL REVENUE SQUEEZE
LIMITED FORMAL CONSULTATIVE MACHINERY
UNIFIED MUNICIPAL VOICE DIFFICULT

The provincial restraint that has prompted this revenue squeeze on municipalities is itself being caused, at least in part, by actions of the federal government motivated by its desire to bring its own financial house in order. This is but one example of the many ways in which federal action (or inaction) can significantly affect the operations of local government. For a few years in the 1970s, it appeared that formal tri-level consultative machinery might develop, largely through the initiative of the federal Ministry of State for Urban Affairs. MSUA was short-lived, but there remains a clear need for some mechanism through which municipalities can have a voice in the many senior level decisions that affect them.

Whatever consultative mechanisms might be established, however, a continuing problem has been the determination of who speaks for Canada's 4 500 municipalities. There are numerous municipal associations within the provinces, some organized into a provincial-municipal consultative structure. There is also one national body, the Federation of Canadian Municipalities, which has attempted to represent municipal concerns to the federal level. It has been shown, however, that many of the larger municipalities prefer to deal with intergovernmental problems by acting on their own, and some reservations have been expressed about the suitability of municipal associations for dealing with intergovernmental issues. Yet, only a few of the largest municipalities can be expected to have much success attempting to deal with the provincial or federal levels on their own. For the vast majority of Canadian municipalities, then, an attempt must be made to organize and put forth a united position on the issues that concern them. Ironically, efforts to develop this united position and to bargain from strength are undermined to the extent that large and potentially influential municipalities are inclined to act on their own.

There may be one blessing, albeit a mixed one, arising from the difficult intergovernmental relationships that municipalities have been experiencing in recent years. It has been noted that one consequence of the federal and provincial preoccupation with fiscal restraint has been a tendency to cut transfers and/or shift expenditures to the next lowest level. For the local level, this means that a larger proportion of funding must now be found from local revenue sources — the real property tax and miscellaneous local revenues — and this shift has already begun. Preliminary figures for 1988[75] indicate that 53% of gross general revenues of local governments was derived from the real property tax and related taxes and miscellaneous local revenues, with transfer payments making up the remaining 47%.

---

[75] From *Provincial and Municipal Finances, 1989,* Toronto, Canadian Tax Foundation, 1990, Chapter 3 (forthcoming).

These figures represent a modest improvement in the fiscal autonomy of the local level. In other words, a slightly larger portion of municipal expenditures is being financed by municipal revenue sources. To that extent, municipalities have potentially greater independence and flexibility in their operations. Perhaps this is nothing more than "making a virtue of necessity," but if it is the new reality, then municipalities will have to make the best of it.

A SILVER LINING?
MUNICIPAL PORTION OF FUNDING ON INCREASE
POTENTIALLY GREATER OPERATING AUTONOMY
REQUIRES IMPROVED PRIORITY SETTING, FINANCIAL
AND PERSONNEL MANAGEMENT

To do so, municipalities will have to continue to expand their use of miscellaneous local revenue sources. They will also have to be prepared to increase the property tax as necessary — and to defend this tax when it is subjected to the inevitable criticisms that follow. More importantly, municipalities will have to become more proactive in dealing with the issues and challenges that face them, and more focused on the selection of limited priorities among many conflicting demands on their resources. Innovative approaches to management will also be needed, and efforts to increase the motivation and productivity of local employees. All of this will require changes in the municipality's approach to policy making, financial management, and personnel management. These topics are among the matters to be explored in Part B, as the focus of this text shifts from the structure of local government to its internal organization and processes.

B *The Local Governing Process*

7 *From Structure to Process: Politics at the Local Level*

Objectives

1. To examine the nature of the local political process and differing views as to its primary features.
2. To outline the key players in the local political process, both official and unofficial.
3. To explore and reject the lingering notion that politics has no place in local government.

Introduction

So far in this book, the primary emphasis has been structural. The system of local government in Canada has been traced from its historical origins, through various pressures of change and reform programs, to the present arrangements. In the second half of the text, the emphasis shifts to process — to the way in which local governments operate, make decisions, determine priorities, and allocate resources. These actions of local governments largely determine the character of their communities and the quality of life of their inhabitants.

Officially, local decisions are made by representatives elected by, and responsible to, the local electorate. These representatives are advised by staff who provide expertise and continuity. It has already been noted, however, that local decisions are often made subject to provincial approval, or under constraints or conditions imposed by the province. In addition, these decisions are not made "in a vacuum," but in an environment in which various external forces (such as citizens' groups and business interests) seek to exert their influence.

The Local Political Process

The local political process is concerned with the interaction of governing institutions, municipal elected and appointed personnel and external influences, and the resultant decisions that are made. Assessments of the local political process, however, inevitably reflect the biases and value judgments of the observers. As a result, the process is both praised as the fundamental basis for democracy and condemned for serving the interests of the property industry above all else.

The Nature of the Local Political Process

Various writers from de Tocqueville and John Stewart Mill to K. G. Crawford[1] have emphasized the democratic features of local government. To some, such as Mill, local government constituted a training ground for democracy, wherein elected representatives would "learn the ropes" before going on to service at a more senior level, and local citizens would learn about exercising their democratic rights in the context of issues that were relatively simple and understandable. Others, such as de Tocqueville, with his oft-quoted statement that "municipal institutions constitute the strength of free nations," saw local government's democratic role in a much more direct, fundamental light.

> **DEMOCRATIC VIEW:**
> **TRAINING GROUND**
> **FOUNDATION FOR DEMOCRACY**
> **LEVEL AT WHICH DEMOCRATIC IDEAL MOST FULFILLED**

Indeed, far from just being a training ground, Crawford saw local government as the level at which the democratic ideal was most likely to be fulfilled. The citizen is more likely to understand the issues under consideration locally than the increasingly complex, technical matters that predominate at the senior levels of government. Moreover, because the results of local decisions (or indecision) are readily apparent in the local community, citizens should be able to evaluate the effectiveness of their municipal government and the degree to which elected representatives have fulfilled their campaign pledges.

A contrasting viewpoint is provided by Langrod who viewed local government as "but a technical arrangement within the mechanisms of the administrative system, a structural and functional detail...."[2] Langrod not only rejected the assumption that local government is vital to democracy, he also contended that local government could be contrary to the democratic process.

---

[1]   See Alexis de Tocqueville's *Democracy in America*, J. S. Mill's *Considerations on Representative Government* and *On Liberty,* and *Canadian Municipal Government* by Crawford.

[2]   Georges Langrod, "Local Government and Democracy," in *Public Administration,* Vol. XXXI, Spring 1953, pp. 25–33. The Langrod and Panter-Brick exchanges on the subject of local government and democracy are reprinted in Lionel D. Feldman (ed.), *Politics and Government of Urban Canada,* Toronto, Methuen, 1981, Section A.

In some countries local government, with its structural anachronisms, the high degree of its internal functionalisation, the preponderance in practice of the permanent official over the elected and temporary councillor, its methods of work and its obstinate opposition to all modernization, can ... act as a brake on the process of democratisation.[3]

ECONOMIC VIEW 1:
PUBLIC CHOICE PERSPECTIVE
PROVISION OF PUBLIC GOODS
MULTIPLE JURISDICTIONS PREFERABLE
FOR COMPETITION IN PROVISION OF SUCH GOODS

Still other viewpoints about the nature of local government derive from a political economy perspective. For example, public choice (neo-classical) analysts have developed certain views about local government based on individuals and their preference for goods and services.[4] It is assumed that arrangements will provide for a free market in "private" goods and services — that is, items that are divisible and packageable so that their provision and acquisition can be left to individual initiative. "Public" goods, on the other hand, cannot be provided in this manner. They are distinguished by being enjoyed or consumed by all members of a community. As such, they cannot be provided on any stable, long term basis through private initiatives.

If payments were purely voluntary, each citizen would find it in his own interest to withhold payment so long as enough others paid to keep the benefits flowing. The result of many individuals withholding payment would be inadequate provision of public goods and services. Resolution of this dilemma is usually sought through some form of governmental organization.[5]

The result is a natural division in the economy between a private sector that produces marketable goods and services and a public sector in which governments provide public goods and services.

Public choice analysis assumes that the private economy is more responsive to individual preferences than the public. In the private

---

[3]   *Ibid.,* pp. 5–6.

[4]   The outline that follows is based on Warren Magnusson, "The Local State in Canada: Theoretical Perspectives," in *Canadian Public Administration,* Vol. 28, No. 4, Winter 1985, pp. 575–599.

[5]   Robert L. Bish and Vincent Ostrom, *Understanding Urban Government: Metropolitan Reform Reconsidered,* Washington, American Enterprise Institute for Public Policy Research, 1973, p. 9.

economy, individuals with sufficient funds can order and get exactly what they want, since the goods and services are packageable and divisible. In the public sector, where goods are enjoyed in common, everyone must compromise and be satisfied with what the majority want. Little attention can be given to variations in individual preferences. Given this situation, the introduction of any competitive features within the public economy is seen as desirable. Such competition can occur when "people seek recourse by electing different officials, voting with their feet, using private alternatives or through other levels of government."[6]

Because of this desire for competition, public choice analysts favour the fragmented, multiple-jurisdiction local government structures that have usually been the target of reform efforts. They claim that the complex governmental system found in many metropolitan areas is not dysfunctional but is "an essential prerequisite for an efficient and responsive performance in the public sector."[7]

Some criticisms of public choice relate particularly to its conclusions about the value of fragmented government. Such critics contend that fragmentation inhibits government from responding to the wider public good, and that it tends to reinforce existing inequities.[8] The more fundamental criticism of public choice is that it is too narrowly focused, that it reduces society to a set of relations between individuals in a market. A municipality must have a purpose beyond the economically-motivated purposes of the individuals within it.

**ECONOMIC VIEW 2:
NEO-MARXIST PERSPECTIVE
PROVISION OF COLLECTIVE CONSUMPTION GOODS
MADE NECESSARY BY MONOPOLY CAPITALISM**

A similar criticism can be made of the neo-Marxist views of the nature of local government. These views stem from the two Marxist notions that the state belongs to capitalists and that it develops in accordance with capitalism. Another important concept is that of collective consumption, which seems to include "everything provided for consumption by the

---

[6]   *Ibid.,* p. 31.

[7]   *Ibid.,* p. 24.

[8]   See, for example,Richard C. Hill, "Separate and Unequal: Government Inequality in the Metropolis," *American Political Science Review,* 68, 1974, pp. 1557–68.

state in its widest sense, and not just public goods, in the sense used by the public choice analysts."[9] In Marxist theory, collective consumption has developed in conjunction with the rise of monopoly capitalism.

> The need for reliable, energetic and skilled workers became more apparent; the workers themselves demanded better conditions; and everyone found that many of the goods and services workers demanded could be provided more economically on a collective basis. Hence, the development of capitalism as a system of production involved considerable socialization of consumption, in the form of health, education and welfare services, cultural and recreational facilities, public housing and so on.[10]

Much of the responsibility for providing these collective consumption goods fell to local governing bodies and, it is claimed, gave local politics its particular character.

Magnusson comments on the similarity between the neo-Marxist and public choice viewpoints. Both see local authorities as agencies for collective consumption. Both reduce the local community to "a set of economic relations between individuals or a struggle between classes formed by the mode of production.[11]

If one is to examine the nature of local government from an economic perspective, Magnusson questions why so much emphasis has been placed on "consumption" rather than "production." He notes that municipalities were primarily established as organizations for regulating the local economy and promoting its development. As discussed in Chapter 9 of this text, the possibility of local governments becoming involved in the provision of a wide range of services financed by a variety of sources was largely undermined by the impact of the Depression, World War II, and rapid postwar growth. A more diversified role for local government has also been constrained by the extensive central government controls over such areas as health, education, and social services generally.

ECONOMIC VIEW 3:
MORE "PRODUCTION" THAN "CONSUMPTION"
REGULATING AND DEVELOPING THE LOCAL ECONOMY
"SERVING" THE PROPERTY DEVELOPMENT INDUSTRY

---

[9] Magnusson, *op. cit.*, p. 594.

[10] *Ibid.*

[11] *Ibid.*, p. 595.

Of all of the economic perspectives on the nature of local government, then, the one which seems to most closely approximate reality is that which sees local government's primary role as providing the physical services needed to support growth and development. Such a role not only largely determines the nature of the local community that results, but it also has a considerable impact on the broader regional and even national economy. James Lorimer has written extensively on this subject, charging that local governments have become the servants of the development industry that they were supposed to regulate.[12] To some extent, the Lorimer viewpoint can be seen as a variation of the Marxist perspective, with the dominant socio-economic elite locally being the property industry and related business interests.

The Players in the Local Political Process

Any examination of the local political process must also take into account the key players and how they participate in the process. For our purposes, these players will be grouped into these categories: (1) municipal councillors (2) municipal staff (3) the electorate (4) local groups (5) political parties and (6) the media. Each of these players is examined briefly below.

Municipal Councillors

Canadian local governments comprise not only municipalities but also a variety of special purpose bodies. The governing bodies of the latter are made up of citizen appointees for the most part, and these people should really be included in a discussion of those who govern locally. The primary local governing body is the municipality, however, and elected municipal councillors are singled out for examination as the first key players in the local political process. The powers given to any incorporated municipality are exercised, on behalf of the inhabitants, by the elected councillors — making them the most important players officially (if not always in practice).

What kind of people are these elected councillors? The short answer is that they are more varied and less "typical" than they were two or

---

[12] See, for example, *The Real World of City Politics,* Toronto, James Lewis and Samuel, 1970; *A Citizen's Guide to City Politics,* Toronto, James Lewis and Samuel, 1972; *The Developers,* Toronto, James Lorimer, 1978; and *After the Developers* (with Carolyn MacGregor), Toronto, James Lorimer, 1981.

three decades ago. A Bureau of Municipal Research study in the early 1960s, for example, found that the typical candidate in local elections was male, about 50 years of age, married with two or three children, a homeowner, long-time resident of the community, self-employed, of better than average education and income, active in organizations and a member of a political party.[13] One of the effects of the "citizens' movement" of the 1960s and 1970s, however, was to change the make-up of our municipal councils, especially in a number of major urban areas. In particular, the types of professionals who run for local office and get elected have broadened beyond those connected with the development industry and now include people involved in social work, teachers in public schools, and university and college professors.[14]

Managers and owners of small businesses, especially of the small independent variety, have remained a strong force on elected councils.[15] The previously cited Bureau of Municipal Research study found that owners and managers of businesses accounted for 34% of the seats in Metropolitan Toronto in 1962, and constituted the single largest occupational category. People with this background made up 30% of the councillors in Metropolitan Toronto at the time of the Robarts Royal Commission some 14 years later. Such people held some 19 of the 55 seats on Montreal City Council in 1980.

Another fairly constant factor in the make-up of councils has been the relative domination by men. This pattern has long been observed at the federal and provincial level, and has been very slow to change. Higgins notes that women held only 15% of the seats on the municipal councils of 56 major municipalities across Canada in 1984, and occupied the mayor's chair in only seven of these municipalities.[16]

Of particular interest is the way in which municipal councillors perceive and carry out their roles, especially in relation to local issues. It is commonplace to speak of a **representative** role for local councillors. This role stems from the expectation that elected local governments exist to represent the views of the public and to provide services in accordance with their needs and wants. It assumes that government

---

[13] Bureau of Municipal Research, *The Metro Politician: A Profile,* Toronto, June 1963, as summarized in Donald J. H. Higgins, *Local and Urban Politics in Canada,* Toronto, Gage, 1986, p. 368.

[14] Higgins, *op. cit.,* p. 363.

[15] The discussion of this point is based on *ibid.,* p. 362.

[16] *Ibid.,* p. 364. Calculated from S. Bracken (ed.), *Canadian Almanac and Directory, 1984,* Toronto, Copp Clark Pitman, 1984.

decisions are made for the benefit of the public. It further assumes that decisions will be made only after some degree of public consultation and participation. It is with respect to these latter considerations, however, that considerable differences of opinion exist about the nature of the representative role.

THREE VIEWS OF REPRESENTATIVE ROLE OF COUNCILLOR:
TRUSTEE — EXERCISE OWN JUDGMENT
DELEGATE — FOLLOW LOCAL VIEWS AND WISHES
POLITICO — DEPENDS ON THE ISSUE

In somewhat oversimplified terms, there are two quite contrasting views of the appropriate representative behaviour for the councillor. Those who see their roles as *trustees* believe that they have been elected to exercise their own judgment on the issues that require their decision. They don't feel that it is necessary to seek out the views of their constituents, or to be bound by such views should they be offered. In contrast, those who see themselves as *delegates* believe that they must act in accordance with the perceived wishes of the local electors, faithfully reflecting the apparent local views in their decisions. There is also a third type, known as *politicos* — politicians who vary their behaviour depending on the nature of the issue.[17]

However the local politicians see their representative roles, a distinctive feature of the local level (as contrasted with the provincial and federal) is the absence of predictable voting blocks. As discussed in Chapter 9, organized political parties have made very few inroads at the local level in Canada. Local political parties or coalitions of like-minded candidates have been a feature of a number of our largest city councils over a number of decades. Studies of voting patterns, however, indicate that the cohesion of such voting blocks or caucuses is much weaker than at the senior levels of government where disciplined political parties prevail.[18]

---

[17] For a discussion of these types, see H. Eulau, "The Legislator as Representative: Representative Roles," in J. Wahlke et al (eds.), *The Legislative System*, New York, John Wiley and Sons, 1962.

[18] See Higgins, *op. cit.*, pp. 375–378 for a summary of several of these studies including Paul Tennant, "Vancouver City Council Roll-Call Analysis," Comments for the annual meeting of the Canadian Political Science Association, 1975; J. K. Masson, "Decision-Making Patterns and Floating Coalitions in an Urban City Council," in *Canadian Journal of Political Science*, Vol. VIII, No. 1,

In an effort to ensure that councillors' decisions are "in the public interest," and not motivated by self-interest or by favouritism toward any particular organization or economic interest, there has been a gradual expansion of legislation dealing with conflict of interest and with the financing of election campaigns — both matters that have also long been a concern at the provincial and federal levels. While only three provinces have enacted separate legislation on conflict of interest, all others have dealt with this matter, more or less thoroughly, in their general municipal legislation. The basic principle at issue is that those elected to govern should be free from having a direct personal involvement or pecuniary interest in any matter on which they are called up to vote. At the local level, this principle has reflected itself in concerns about "any circumstances where the personal interest of the council member in any matter before council may prevent him, or appear to prevent him, from giving an unbiased decision with respect to such a matter."[19] While the objective of avoiding such conflicts is obviously commendable, its achievement through legislation has not been easy, and there is ample case law to illustrate the problems that have arisen because of unclear or poorly worded legislative provisions.[20]

LEGISLATION GOVERNING COUNCILLORS:
CONFLICT OF INTEREST
CAMPAIGN FINANCING

March 1975; J. E. Rae, *Parties and Power: An Analysis of Winnipeg City Council, 1919-1975,* Appendix IV of the Report of the Manitoba Committee of Review of the City of Winnipeg Act, 1976; P. H. Wichern Jr., "Winnipeg's Unicity After Two Years: Evaluation of an Experiment in Urban Government," paper presented at the annual meeting of the Canadian Political Science Association, Toronto, 1974; and B. J. Kay, "Voting Patterns in a Non-partisan Legislature: A Study of Toronto City Council," in *Canadian Journal of Political Science,* Vol. IV, No. 2, June 1971 and "Urban Decision-Making and the Legislative Environment: Toronto Council Re-examined," in *Canadian Journal of Political Science,* Vol. 15, No. 3, September 1982.

[19] Ian MacF. Rogers, "Conflict of Interest — A Trap for Unwary Politicians," in *Municipal World,* St. Thomas, May 1974, p. 115.

[20] See Michael J. Smither, *Municipal Conflict of Interest,* St. Thomas, Municipal World Inc., 1983. While this book focuses particularly on the Ontario experience, it does make reference to judicial rulings in other provinces.

Legislation dealing with election financing is much more recent and rare. Until 1988, only Quebec had enacted such legislation, and the Quebec law applies only to municipalities over 20 000.[21] It requires disclosure of campaign contributions and expenditures, and places limits on election expenses. There is also a limit on individual contributions, to an aggregate total of $500 per year. The legislation also provides for the municipality to reimburse a candidate, out of its own funds, for an amount equal to 50 per cent of the election expenses, if the candidate is elected or obtains at least 20 per cent of the votes cast for the office. Provision is also made for an audit of the candidate's campaign contributions and expenditures and there are severe penalties for contraventions.

The Ontario government enacted amendments to The Municipal Elections Act governing election financing just prior to the 1988 municipal elections.[22] Under the legislation, campaign expenditures are limited, as are campaign contributions — to a maximum of $750 per contributor. Municipalities, school boards, and public utilities commissions are permitted to establish an optional campaign contribution rebate system, with the rebate — a percentage of the contribution up to a maximum of $350 — funded by the jurisdictions that adopt the system. Candidates are required to disclose campaign contributions and spending. This disclosure takes the form of an audited statement for any candidate in a jurisdiction that has adopted a contribution rebate system, or for any candidate who raises or spends more than $10 000. An unaudited statement or a statutory declaration are required from those spending specified lesser amounts.

The Ontario and Quebec provisions are similar in nature, and both incorporate many of the features long established in legislation dealing with federal and provincial election campaigns. It is likely that such legislative provisions will gradually be extended to municipalities in other provinces as another means of attempting to ensure the impartiality and integrity of municipal elected representatives.

---

[21] See "An Act Respecting Elections and Referendums in Municipalities," Bill 100, 1987, Chapter 57. The brief summary that follows is based on the Report of the Advisory Committee on Municipal Elections to the Minister of Municipal Affairs, *Issues and Options: An Interim Report on Municipal Elections in Ontario,* 1986, pp. 5.6–5.7.

[22] The following summary is based on Ministry of Municipal Affairs, *Background,* April 11, 1988.

Municipal Staff

While municipal councillors constitute the official decision-making body at the local level, municipal staff are considered by many to be at least as important players in that decision-making process.

First and foremost, senior staff provide technical expertise, research and analytical capability, and policy advice. Since councillors serve, in most instances, on only a part-time basis, they come to rely very heavily on the recommendations given by their staff. Indeed, there is a widespread concern — also felt at the provincial and federal levels — that senior staff are too dominant in the policy process, with elected bodies being reduced to rubber-stamping decisions that are essentially made by appointed personnel.

Second, municipal staff are key players in the local political process because they often have their own objectives and priorities that they want to see achieved. In other words, far from playing an essentially passive role responding to policy initiatives of councillors, municipal staff may attempt to control the policy agenda themselves — determining what gets attention and (equally important from their view) what doesn't get attention.

STAFF ROLES:
NOT ONLY ADVISE ON POLICY, BUT ALSO:
INFLUENCE POLICY AGENDA
ACT AS ARBITERS OF CONFLICTING INTERESTS
IMPLEMENT DECISIONS

Municipal staff are also key players because of the extent to which they are in contact with the local public. As much or more than councillors, they are likely to be aware of the public view on a variety of local issues — especially concerning existing policies and programs. Increasingly, staff find themselves acting as brokers or arbiters of conflicting local interests, seeking to find common ground and to build a basis for action. Staff with good negotiating and human relations skills can make a major contribution in this area, but in so doing they are also helping to define the issue and to determine the limits of possible action on the issue — critical elements of the local political process.

A fourth and final example concerns the role of staff in implementing council decisions. As will be discussed in Chapter 10, this implementation stage can be far from smooth, and staff actions can be the major determinant of how effectively or ineffectively the objectives of a policy decision are realized.

The Electorate

The local electors *ought to be* key players in the local political process — if our earlier comments about local government as the foundation of democracy are to have any meaning. The decisions that are made are supposed to reflect the views and concerns of the local citizens. By what means is this achieved? In theory, at least, this desirable objective is achieved by allowing the public to vote for the candidates of their choice at regularly scheduled elections.

The first problem with this concept is that a disappointingly low proportion of voters take advantage of their democratic opportunities every municipal election year. While the approximately two-thirds voting turnout in federal and provincial elections is not great, it certainly contrasts with the 40% who vote at the municipal level.[23]

FACTORS AFFECTING VOTING TURNOUT:
SIZE OF MUNICIPALITY
WARD OR GENERAL VOTE
SOCIO-ECONOMIC VARIABLES
EXTENT OF COMPETITION
"QUESTIONS" ON BALLOT
COMPLEXITY OF CHOICES

A number of factors are commonly cited as influencing the municipal vote. Studies of voter turnout lend some support to the notion that the turnout is higher in smaller municipalities than in larger ones.[24] The same type of population-to-turnout relationship helps explain why the voting turnout in populous municipalities tends to be higher with a ward system than with elections at large. Socio-economic factors such as the educational level of the electorate and the proportion of homeowners

---

[23] For more detailed statistics, see Higgins, *op. cit.*, pp. 311–313.

[24] See, for example, J. M. Mackenzie, *Ontario Municipal Elections: An Overview (Or Who Cares Anyway?)*, Kingston, Institute of Local Government, Queen's University, undated.

versus tenants also have an influence.[25] Voting turnout is also affected by the extent of competition for the seats available. Acclamations for the head of council position usually result in a reduced turnout, while a close race for that position can have a very positive impact on turnout. A higher voting turnout is also common when there are "questions" on the ballot in the form of plebiscites or referendums.[26] Indeed, there is an old saying that the most effective way to increase voter interest is to add a liquor licensing question to the ballot.

It is widely held that a major negative influence on voting turnout is the complicated nature of the municipal election process. At the provincial and federal levels, voters are accustomed to selecting one name from three or four, all of them normally identified by a party label. In contrast, the municipal voter must make choices within several different categories (or from multiple ballots) from among many dozens of names — none of them identified with any party label.

> In the 1984 civic elections in Vancouver, for example, each voter had to choose one of five candidates for mayor, ten of twenty-seven candidates for aldermen, nine of twenty-seven for school board seats, and seven of twenty-nine candidates for the parks board.[27]

The rather daunting task facing each Vancouver voter, therefore, was to choose a total of 27 from a list of 88 names, while also answering "yes" or "no" to a plebiscite on the question on the testing of the cruise missile in Canada.

In addition to the problem of low voting turnout, there is a second, and more fundamental, problem with the concept that regular elections help to ensure that municipal decisions reflect the views and concerns of the local citizens. The reality is that voters are not able to enforce any sort of accountability for actions through the mechanism of periodic elections. How can accountability be allocated, and criticism or praise handed out where warranted? The fact is that there is no clear focus of accountability and responsibility within virtually any of our municipal councils. Without organized political parties, there is no "Government" and no "Official Opposition." Everyone is responsible for everything, which also means that no one is really responsible for anything.

---

[25] R. Vaison and P. Aucoin, "Class and Voting in Recent Halifax Mayoralty Elections," in L. D. Feldman and M. D. Goldrick (eds.), *Politics and Government of Urban Canada: Selected Readings*, Toronto, Methuen, 1976, pp. 200–219.

[26] For a discussion of these forms of "direct democracy" that are relatively common at the municipal level, see Patrick Boyer, *Lawmaking by the People: Referendums and Plebiscites in Canada*, Toronto, Butterworths, 1982.

[27] Higgins, *op. cit.*, p. 315.

Local Groups

For the minority who do exercise their franchise, voting in municipal elections is, at best, an infrequent and rather passive activity. Many citizens want more continuous, direct involvement. They want the opportunity to participate in the process of making decisions, not just to pass judgment "after-the-fact" by voting for or against certain councillors. For such citizens, the normal recourse has been to form or join local citizens' groups.

Such groups are not new, of course, and Chapter 3 described a number of local groups that spearheaded the turn of the century reform movement. Also of long standing were various residents' and ratepayers' associations established to protect the interests of the property owner as principal taxpayer. Groups representing the business community and the middle class have also been prominent in a number of cities for more than half a century, often promoting the election of like-minded councillors and attempting to prevent the election of candidates representing labour or socialist viewpoints.

What was different about many of the citizens' groups that formed in the 1960s and 1970s is that they often represented groups and neighbourhoods that had not previously been active or influential in public affairs. In addition, a number of these groups attempted to broaden their concerns beyond one specific issue (although it may have caused their initial formation) and sought to change the municipal decision-making process by building in a consultative element. If there was one common feature of most of these groups over the years, it was their attitude toward growth and development, as will be seen from the examples provided in Chapter 9. Just as many of the earlier groups, especially those representing the business community, were pro-growth, so many of the more recent groups, representing neighbourhoods, were concerned with stability and the preservation of existing lifestyles.

> **BUSINESS GROUPS:**
> **GREATER RESOURCES THAN CITIZENS' GROUPS**
> **SHARE COMMON BACKGROUNDS WITH MANY COUNCILLORS**
> **ALSO EXERT INFLUENCE THROUGH THEIR ASSOCIATIONS**

Groups representing the business community merit separate mention. They offer quite a contrast to most citizens' groups that rely heavily on volunteers, lack funds, have difficulty getting access to information, and often face an unsympathetic city hall. By comparison, business groups usually have a solid financial base, full time staff to provide continuity, and ready access to information. In addition, "there tends to be an affinity between the interests of the corporate sector and the business or professional background and perspectives of a large proportion of local elected officials."[28]

Higgins suggests that the elements of the corporate sector with the greatest interest in municipal operations include real estate agencies, construction companies (and unions), and their associated contractors in areas such as electrical and plumbing work, property development companies, and firms of architects and engineering consultants.[29] Among their associations, he cites the Canadian Real Estate Association, the Canadian Construction Association, and the Canadian Home Builders Association (formerly the Housing and Urban Development Institute of Canada). He also points to the influence of some of the very large property development companies such as Olympia and York and Trizec.[30]

Political Parties

On the surface, organized political parties have not been major players in the local political process — primarily because they have established their presence in only a few major urban centres. As discussed in Chapter 9, there appears to be a strong voter antipathy toward candidates who run as official representatives of any of our national parties. As a result, only the NDP has been active in municipal elections, with the other two major parties more inclined to throw their support behind like-minded candidates running as independents or as members of some sort of local coalition — ostensibly opposed to party politics, but in reality opposed to the philosophical stance of the NDP.

These local coalitions vary considerably in their structure and cohesion, but a number have shown sufficient durability to be considered a form of local party, usually called a "civic" party. Over the years, these civic parties have appeared in most of Canada's major

---

[28] *Ibid.*, p. 291.

[29] *Ibid.*, pp. 291–292.

[30] See *ibid.*, pp. 290–299 for a discussion of the influence of the private corporate sector, and of property development associations and individual companies.

centres. Indeed, 24 of 28 cities examined in 1969 had at least one such party.[31] Experiences with several of these civic parties are outlined in Chapter 9.

> **PARTIES:**
> **NATIONAL PARTIES HAVE HAD**
> **LIMITED *DIRECT* INVOLVEMENT**
> **BUT MANY LOCAL PARTIES, COALITIONS**
> **OF CANDIDATES OVER THE YEARS**

Political parties can be significant players in the local political process in Canada's major centres, therefore, to the extent that these local coalitions of councillors are considered parties. In addition, the national parties may be important players in municipal activities in centres both large and small. But they exercise their influence for the most part covertly, by supporting like-minded candidates, or by using their links with council to push for decisions consistent with their viewpoints.

The Mass Media

The mass media are key players in the local political process in a number of ways. The most direct and obvious way is through the coverage that they give (or don't give) to local government activities and issues. In addition, however, they are also influential because of the sheer size of some of the major corporations in the media field. Media outlets representing the Thomson and Irving empires or Power Corporation are part of major, diversified business interests that have considerable economic influence in their own right.

Local issues usually receive very little coverage in the national electronic media. Yet studies suggest that the general public is particularly interested in local and regional news,[32] and it is coverage of these issues that is most pertinent from the point of view of local governments. The adequacy of local news coverage depends on the local radio

---

[31]   J. G. Joyce and H. A. Hosse, *Civic Parties in Canada,* Ottawa, Canadian Federation of Mayors and Municipalities, 1970.

[32]   See Canada, Royal Commission on Newspapers, *Report* and *Research Studies,* Ottawa, Supply and Services, 1981, and P. Audley, *Canada's Cultural Industries,* Toronto, James Lorimer and the Canadian Institute for Economic Policy, 1983. These studies are briefly discussed in Higgins, *op. cit.,* p. 300.

and television stations (where they exist) and on local newspapers — with the latter being regarded by most citizens as their primary source of information.

It can be argued, however, that the media have contributed to the limited public participation in local government by their generally poor performance in providing information about, and promoting understanding of, local government. News stories tend to concentrate on the supposedly more important and glamorous activities of the senior levels of government. The municipal beat is often assigned to junior reporters and is seen as an unavoidable stepping stone to bigger and better things. Moreover, while local weekly newspapers may devote considerable space to municipal coverage, even printing the council minutes, the dailies are much more limited and selective in their coverage. As with all news items, there is a tendency to emphasize controversial or sensational matters. The bulk of the council's deliberations is regarded as routine, preoccupied with administrative details and not especially newsworthy. While there may be some truth in this assessment, the fact remains that without some media coverage of these ongoing municipal activities the public is ill-informed and often lacks the background necessary to the understanding of local issues. In addition, municipal councils and staff often become disillusioned with the media because occasional controversies are highlighted while the vast majority of municipal government activities appear to be largely ignored.

One conspicuous example of media influence relates to the coverage of municipal tax increases. Such increases receive very prominent, and negative, attention in the media. Paradoxically, while the media may criticize inadequate municipal services throughout the year, at budget time councils are somehow expected to hold the line on taxes. As discussed in Chapter 11, council budget deliberations conducted in this atmosphere focus almost entirely on mill rate considerations and ignore the basic priority setting exercise that should be undertaken.

The influence of the media is also felt in the positions they take on local issues and the editorial views presented. It is probably fair to say that the growth mentality that infected most municipalities, at least until recent years, has been encouraged or reinforced by the media. Lightbody, for example, describes the *Edmonton Journal* as "unashamedly a booster press," and notes that it normally endorsed the Citizens' Committee or its civic government successors, and the business pro-growth interests that they represented. He observes that "While the evidence is insufficient to 'prove' that the Journal was able to structure electoral choice, judging by results we can conclude with some certainty that the environment was scarcely conducive to the emergence of an effective challenge to the Citizens' Committee."[33]

MEDIA CONCERNS:
LOCAL COVERAGE NEGLECTED
CERTAIN VIEWS "PUSHED" — SUCH AS PRO-GROWTH
AND ANTI-PROPERTY TAX
CAN INFLUENCE ITEMS ON THE LOCAL AGENDA
CONCENTRATION OF OWNERSHIP IN MEDIA —
PART OF CORPORATE SECTOR

A Bureau of Municipal Research study documented several instances where press coverage appeared to have an influence on the outcome of issues.[34] One analyst suggested that the media influence was even greater — actually setting the agenda of public discussion. After studying three small Ontario cities, he concluded that there was a fairly close parallel between the ranking of items in the agendas of the press and of the local political community, and that the daily newspapers had influenced politicians to make particular policy decisions that they might not otherwise have made if left on their own.[35]

Dealing still with newspapers, the degree of concentration of ownership is seen by many as a concern. One worry is that newspapers may be hesitant to provide news coverage and editorial comment that appears critical of any of the varied business interests of their corporate owners. There is also a fear that newspapers will be similarly constrained from critical commentary that might offend major advertisers, notably the property industry.

Whatever their faults, it must be acknowledged that the media often receive very little support from municipalities in attempting to carry out their responsibilities. There are too many examples of local governments that at best exhibit no concern for public relations and at worst maintain as much secrecy as possible about their deliberations. Makuch has observed that except for certain limited common law rights, the right to information and to attend meetings at the local level is solely

---

[33] James Lightbody, "Edmonton," in Warren Magnusson and Andrew Sancton (eds.), *City Politics in Canada,* Toronto, University of Toronto Press, 1983, p. 266.

[34] Bureau of Municipal Research, "The News Media and Local Government," in *Civic Affairs,* Toronto, August 1976.

[35] E. R. Black, *Politics and the News: The Political Functions of the Mass Media,* Toronto, Butterworths, 1982.

determined by statute, and he finds the statutory provisions inadequate.[36] He notes that typically legislation requires only that formal municipal council meetings be open to the public, with the result that key discussions can (and often do) occur in meetings of committees and subcommittees without public access. Similarly, Makuch explains that the public's right to information is limited by a broad exception such as the Ontario provision that excludes "interdepartmental correspondence and reports of officials of any department or of solicitors for the corporation made to council, board of control or any committee of council."[37]

> **PUBLIC'S RIGHT TO KNOW:**
> **LIMITED STATUTORY GUARANTEE IN THE PAST**
> **RECENT ACTS IN SEVERAL PROVINCES — FREEDOM OF**
> **INFORMATION *AND* RIGHT TO PRIVACY**

Increased concern about the public's "right to know," however, has been prompting legislative changes intended to ensure greater public access to government documents, while at the same time providing more security concerning the release or use of personal information. For example, the Province of Quebec passed a 1982 Act concerning access to documents and the protection of personal information that applies to all of its municipalities. Manitoba legislation on this subject came into effect in September 1988. Ontario's local governments will come under such legislation effective January 1, 1991. Originally, they were to be governed by a statute initially drafted only for the provincial level and then extended to the local level. After strong criticism,[38] a new Municipal Freedom of Information and Protection of Privacy Act was introduced — specifically for the local level.

The Place of 'Politics' in the Local Political Process

Given all that has been outlined concerning the local political process and its principal players, how does one explain the still common exhortation to "keep politics out of local government?" Some examination of this phenomenon is in order before concluding this chapter.

---

[36] Stanley M. Makuch, *Canadian Municipal and Planning Law*, Toronto, Carswell, 1983, pp. 269–280.

[37] *Ibid.,* p. 275.

[38] See, for example, "Editorial," in *Municipal World,* St. Thomas, January 1989.

As discussed in Chapter 3, part of the legacy of the turn of the century reform movement has been this lingering notion that politics is somehow inappropriate at the local level. People who make this charge may mean a variety of things, given how value-laden the terms 'politics' and 'political' have become. To those who mean that political corruption has no place at the local level, there is no dispute. To those who mean that organized political parties have no place at the local level, a number of arguments can be offered on both sides of this issue as discussed in Chapter 9. Of particular concern are those who reject as political any decisions that they don't happen to like.

**POLITICAL DECISIONS:
TERM WRONGLY APPLIED TO
DECISIONS ONE DOESN'T LIKE**

This practice is far too common. For example, when city hall agrees with the concerns of a citizens' group, the decision is heralded as a victory for democracy. However, almost any time a council decides in favour of a development proposal then it is a 'political' (meaning unwise and probably unsavoury) decision. The situation is rarely that clear and simple. Citizens' groups may operate very much on the basis of enlightened self-interest, being more concerned about preserving certain features of their neighbourhoods than about the needs of the overall community. At the same time, development proposals may be well planned and beneficial for the community. Even if one believes that both of these instances are rare, it serves little purpose to label as political any decisions one does not like.

To take another example, when city council decides contrary to the advice given by its staff, then it is frequently criticized for making a 'political' decision. Even some councillors will dismiss decisions with which they disagree on the grounds that the decisions were political. The constant use of this term to describe anything with which one does not happen to agree has seriously distorted its meaning and has unfortunately undermined the vital importance of council's political role.

Most frustrating of all has been the fact that so many councillors disavow their political role and, indeed, behave in such a manner as to make it largely invisible. One of the most important roles that a municipal council can play is to act as a public forum for the discussion of issues of community concern. In so doing, councillors can help to educate the public about local issues, to stimulate public responses, and then to make decisions about these matters. Instead, however, councils often attempt to avoid airing controversial matters in public. This attitude appears to be especially prevalent in small municipalities where the scale of operations and small council almost seem to encourage the belief that it is unmannerly or improper to show disagreement or division in public.

It is appreciated that there may be a genuine concern on the part of some councillors that public arguments and disagreements might strain working relationships and harm the future effectiveness of the council. What councillors don't seem to understand, however, is that by denying the public the opportunity to witness lively debates, to observe that their councillors do care passionately about important local issues, they rob municipal government of much of its vitality and relevance. Only if municipal councils are seen to be discussing matters of topical local importance can they expect to attract and hold the attention of their local citizenry.

The Case for 'Politics' at the Local Level

It is contended that a meaningful role for municipal governments in Canada is only possible if it is accepted that councils make (and should make) political decisions. Within the limits of the authority delegated by the provincial government, municipal councils are expected to make policy decisions in the interest of the health, welfare, and safety of the residents of the communities they serve.[39] Makuch argues that municipalities must have a wide policy-making role in the delivery of services so that they can make local decisions respecting local political matters.[40] He acknowledges the need for some province-wide or nation-wide standards to protect minority groups and to ensure that all citizens have certain minimum rights, but feels that this must be balanced against the desirability of local political control.[41]

Gyford notes that much of the literature about local government has lacked any political dimension, but that in the past couple of decades the public has shown "an increasing awareness that the decisions which issue from their local council are not immaculately conceived."[42] He goes on to explain that it is as true locally as it is nationally that "politics

---

[39] T. J. Plunkett, *Urban Canada and its Government,* Toronto, Macmillan, 1968, p. 7.

[40] Makuch, *op. cit.,* p. 5.

[41] *Ibid.,* p. 6.

[42] John Gyford, *Local Politics in Britain,* London, Croom Helm Ltd., 1976, p. 9.

arises in the first instance when one realizes that there is no such thing as the people — that no single decision can please all people. There are only peoples, with contradictory and conflicting ideas and interests."[43] Higgins makes much the same point when he refers to politics as "competition among diverse interests to achieve goals that may not all be mutually compatible. According to that conception, it is impossible to have government without politics."[44]

COUNCILLORS ARE SUPPOSED TO MAKE *POLITICAL* DECISIONS

Councils resolve the issues they face by making political decisions. This means that they do not necessarily make the decision that was recommended by their staff — and their failure to follow the staff recommendation is not automatically a cause for criticism. As Goldsmith points out, "the extent to which much of what local government does is actually technical, neutral, value-free and requires expert skills may be very much open to debate."[45] Besides, it is a delusion to think that the advice given by staff is somehow more objective and value-free than the considerations entertained by politicians.

Higgins states that there are choices or options available for a broad range of local issues and problems, and that "the identification of the 'right' or 'best' one is not always obvious and should not always be left to administrative-professional personnel."[46] In any event, it is arguable that there even is one 'right' decision, or that one could be sure of identifying it by persevering long enough. Rather, there are a number of plausible or workable decisions, and it is council's task to seek out one of these to resolve the problem at hand.

Nor should councillors necessarily do what local citizens' groups might want them to do. Such groups may or may not be representative of the views of the larger population. It is very difficult to determine whether one has heard from only the "vocal minority" and what might be the concerns of the "silent majority." While public opinion is

---

[43] *Ibid.*, p. 11, quoting D. Bell and V. Held, "The Community Revolution," in *Public Interest*, No. 16, 1969, p. 177.

[44] Higgins, *op. cit.*, p. 254.

[45] Michael Goldsmith, *Politics, Planning and the City*, London, Hutchinson, 1980, p. 104.

[46] Higgins, *op. cit.*, p. 125.

obviously important on any issue, councillors are not in office simply to reflect whatever may be the currently popular view (something our provincial and federal politicians accomplish far too well thanks to their ever present public opinion surveys). As one notable observer of politicians has stated, "a leader must be more than a seismograph merely recording each subterranean movement of public opinion."[47]

Summary

This chapter has described some of the main players, both official and unofficial, in the local political process. It has offered several quite differing viewpoints about the nature of the local political process. Local governments have been described as both a training ground and foundation for democracy *and* a "brake on the process of democratisation." The primary purpose of local government has been stated as both the provision of public goods and collective consumption goods *and* the regulation and development of the local economy. The latter activity, it was concluded, is the one that seems to most closely approximate reality.

The chapter has also given particular attention to the emotional feelings that still attach to the concept of politics at the local level, and has attempted to demonstrate the validity of this concept — and, indeed, its essential nature for the operation of local government.

Further insights into a number of the issues raised herein will be provided in the next three chapters. Chapter 8 notes that several of the reforms in internal municipal machinery were preoccupied with efficiency and service delivery to the exclusion of any balanced consideration of their impact on the political role of local government. In Chapter 9, most of the discussion will focus on political activity at the local level as highlighted by profiles of four large Canadian cities. Throughout this chapter there is evidence of politics decried and denied — whether by citizens' groups labelling council decisions with which they disagreed, or local business groups/parties organizing to ensure their continued domination of their municipal councils in the name of keeping out politics. Finally, Chapter 10 provides yet another perspective of this topic by contrasting the rational model of policy making with the reality of policy making in practice — a reality that very much includes the political dimension.

---

[47] Theodore Sorenson, *Leadership in Transition*, undated address.

8 The Governing Machinery

Objectives:

1. To examine the weaknesses in the traditional internal machinery of municipal government.
2. To describe and assess the various forms of chief administrative officer system established to provide administrative leadership.
3. To describe and assess the various forms of executive committee system established to provide political leadership.
4. To identify the potential strengths and limitations of the reforms introduced.

Introduction and Overview

Most of the chapters in the first half of this book have examined the general structure of local government and how it has responded and adapted to the pressures of change. Chapter 7 began the shift of focus from the external structure to the internal governing process. This chapter continues that shift by examining the internal organization and functioning of municipal governments. Here again, one finds a pattern of adaptation to pressures, and this chapter will highlight both the shortcomings in the internal machinery of municipal government and the main reforms that have been introduced.

MUNICIPAL MACHINERY:
COUNCIL AND STAFF
STANDING COMMITTEES (OFTEN)
CAOS (INCREASINGLY)
EXECUTIVE COMMITTEES (LESS COMMON)

The basic machinery of municipal government is quite simple to outline. It consists, first and foremost, of the council as the governing body. The second component comprises the municipal staff, organized into a number of functionally specialized departments depending on the size of the municipality. A third component has often been a standing committee system providing a link between the councillors and staff. It is now increasingly common to find a Chief Administrative Officer heading up the municipal staff. Executive committees may be found at the council level, although much less frequently. While these latter two components first appeared as early as the beginning of the twentieth century, they have become more prominent in the past couple of decades.

What follows is a description of the traditional municipal machinery, then an analysis of its limitations, and finally an examination of the modifications to the machinery that have occurred and how well they have overcome the limitations.

A: Traditional Machinery

The Municipal Council

All municipalities in Canada are corporate bodies and as such exercise, and are limited to, the powers granted by their creators, the provincial governments. These powers are provided in various types of provincial legislation. Some provinces, notably Ontario and to a lesser extent Manitoba, have attempted to provide for all classes of municipality in a general act, while most other provinces have passed a separate act for each of the various classes of municipality. Quebec has had two main statutes, one dealing with cities and towns and the other applying to all other categories. These two statutes are being merged to produce one municipal act for all Quebec municipalities.

Whatever the arrangements, however, the general legislation has usually been supplemented by special acts dealing with large cities and with individual reformed areas such as the metropolitan and regional governments discussed earlier. In addition, a number of other acts deal with subjects of great importance to the municipality such as legislation on assessment, planning, parks and recreation, and roads. There are also private acts that apply only to individual municipalities and permit some deviation from the general municipal law.

> **COUNCIL:**
> **EXERCISES POWERS OF MUNICIPAL**
> **CORPORATION AS PROVINCIALLY AUTHORIZED**
> **COMBINES LEGISLATIVE AND**
> **EXECUTIVE RESPONSIBILITIES**

Whatever the legislative source, the powers of the municipal corporation are exercised on behalf of the inhabitants by an elected council. Indeed, the provincial legislation provides for the form of council that generally relates to the type of municipality in question. Municipal councils in Canada consist of a head (known as warden or chairman in counties and other upper tier governments, as mayor in cities and towns, and as reeve, chairman, or overseer in villages and townships) and a widely varying number of other councillors. While the total membership varies greatly, there has been a tendency to have small councils of from five to fifteen members, largely on the grounds that a small group is less unwieldy and more efficient in making decisions. In the past couple of decades, however, there has been some reawakening of interest in the representative and political role of local government and, as a result, some movement toward larger councils. This tendency is best exemplified in the establishment of a 50 member council for Winnipeg Unicity although, as has been outlined, in 1977 that body was reduced in size to 29 members. Montreal also stands out with its council of 58 members.

Perhaps the most distinctive feature of the council as a governing body is that it combines both executive and legislative responsibilities. As an executive body it initiates proposals for municipal action, makes a myriad of specific decisions — such as hiring a particular employee — and supervises the administration of the policies and programs of the municipality. As a legislative body, it makes by-laws that are the laws governing its citizens. At the senior levels of government, these functions are the responsibility of two separate branches: the Cabinet and the Legislative Assembly (House of Commons). The fact that these functions are combined in the council means, among other things, that the line between making policy and administering policy is often quite blurred at the local level. The combination of diverse responsibilities may also help to explain why there has often appeared to be a preoccupation with specific servicing considerations to the neglect of the other roles of municipal government.

Method of Election

The head of council is elected by a general vote of the entire municipality except in cases such as the head of a Nova Scotia, Quebec, or Ontario county where he or she is chosen by council from among its members. However, the other members of council may be elected either by general vote or on the basis of a ward system. In the latter instance, the municipality is divided into wards with a number of members (usually an equal number) to be elected from each of these geographic areas. Candidates don't campaign over the whole municipality but only in "their" ward, and the voters are limited to choosing from among the candidates in their particular ward. Whether election is by general vote or ward may be dictated by statute; it may be at the discretion of the local council; or it may be decided by council subject to the approval of the municipal electors.

Ward Versus General Vote   Both methods of election have their proponents and their alleged advantages and disadvantages. Supporters of the ward system argue that under this approach the voters are much more likely to be familiar with the limited range of candidates from whom they must choose and the candidates will be more aware of the particular needs and interests of their constituents. It is also contended that ward elections ensure that all areas of the municipality will be represented on council, that they mean less expensive campaign costs, and that they bring a higher voting turnout, an assertion that appears to have some validity.

WARD SYSTEM:
VOTERS KNOW CANDIDATES
CANDIDATES KNOW CONCERNS OF THE VOTERS
ALL AREAS REPRESENTED
HIGHER VOTING TURNOUT

On the other hand, those supporting election by general vote claim that ward elections tend to perpetuate and even accentuate differences and divisions within the municipality. It is argued that a ward council is very parochial in outlook with councillors worrying about their individual bailiwicks wherein they must seek reelection rather than being concerned about the good of the whole municipality. It is also contended that some representatives get elected on a ward basis who would not have been chosen if they were running over the entire municipality. Election by general vote is therefore felt to result in stronger, better qualified candidates since they must have support throughout the municipality. It also avoids the apparently unfair situation in which one candidate receives, as an example, 2 000 votes in a ward but finishes out of the running, while another candidate receives 1 800 votes and tops the polls in a different ward. While such situations will inevitably arise since the populations of all wards do not stay equal even with periodic attempts at redistribution, they add to the feeling that the "best" person may not be elected under a ward system. Finally, proponents of a general vote assert that it results in a council more capable of taking a broad view of the overall needs of the municipality.

> **GENERAL VOTE:**
> **STRONGER, MORE BROADLY-BASED CANDIDATES**
> **LESS PAROCHIAL OUTLOOK**
> **CONCERNED WITH OVERALL NEEDS OF MUNICIPALITY**

Whatever the respective merits of the two methods of election, it might be assumed that beyond a certain size of population (which is difficult to specify precisely) election by ward becomes almost inevitable, so that the citizen will have some prospect of knowing the candidates and so that the candidates will not be faced with the financial and time demands of canvassing an excessively large population. While this relationship between the population of a municipality and the method of election holds generally true, there are exceptions, the most notable being election at large in the City of Vancouver. The ward system in this city was abolished before the 1936 municipal election and has not been reinstated in spite of several local initiatives over the years.

> **WARD DESIGN:**
> **CAN HAVE MAJOR IMPACT**
> **"STRIP" VERSUS "BLOCK" WARDS**

Moreover, even where a municipality utilizes a ward system, there are wide variations in how effectively it achieves its alleged advantages. Particularly since the turn of the century reform era, those opposed to the notion of "politics" in local government have sought to eliminate wards or reduce their influence in representing the diverse interests of the municipality. For example, in 1891 the size of Toronto's city council was reduced from 40 to 25 and the existing wards were replaced with six elongated "strips" running north from the lake — supposedly to enlarge the political vision of the aldermen.[1] Almost 70 years later strip wards were still being used in Toronto, but a proposal to extend this pattern in 1969 at the time of an expansion from nine to eleven wards provoked a strong opposition from local citizen groups. Of particular concern was the fact that the heterogeneous areas embraced by these elongated strips militated against the representation of the varied local concerns

---

[1]   Warren Magnusson, "Toronto," in Warren Magnusson and Andrew Sancton (eds.), *City Politics in Canada*, Toronto, University of Toronto Press, 1983, p. 100.

and, instead, ensured that the upper middle class neighbourhoods prevailed at the expense of the lower class areas.[2] The Ontario Municipal Board, which had the responsibility for approving changes in ward boundaries, rejected the city's strip plan in favour of a block plan.

Efforts to design wards in which it is difficult to represent specific neighbourhoods or communities of interest have been fairly widespread. One is reminded, for example, of the special pie-shaped districts created for the election of members to the Metropolitan Winnipeg government created in 1960, districts whose combination of central and suburban areas was supposed to engender area-wide thinking. Edmonton's experience is also instructive.[3] Following a positive plebiscite on this issue, the city moved to develop a ward system for the 1971 elections. As with Lorimer's description of the Toronto experience, Edmonton's new wards were designed by a municipal employee who "certainly had a strong sense of political reality and knew that he was not being asked to prepare a map which would make the task of re-election for the sitting aldermen any more difficult than necessary".[4] He proposed the establishment of four strip wards running the length of the city and completely ignoring community, economic, and ethnic differences. As one observer described the change: "By establishing four wards completely heterogeneous in terms of socioeconomic composition, the council in effect provided four at-large elections at every municipal election"[5] — but at a quarter of the cost. Unlike the Toronto experience, local opposition did not materialize to block the new ward boundaries for Edmonton. However, revisions at the 1980 election did provide for six new wards having more of a block nature, and Lightbody speculates that "a local community attachment will play an increasing role in successful candidatures."[6] As these examples illustrate, it is necessary to look at the specific system in place, not just whether it is election by general vote or ward, in order to judge its likely impact on the municipal operations.

---

[2] See James Lorimer, *The Real World of City Politics,* Toronto, James Lewis and Samuel, 1970, Chapter Two.

[3] See James Lightbody, "Edmonton," in Magnusson and Sancton, *op. cit.,* pp. 272–273.

[4] Lorimer, *op. cit.,* p. 38.

[5] Jack K. Masson, "Decision-Making Patterns and Floating Coalitions in an Urban City Council," *Canadian Journal of Political Science,* March 1975, p. 128.

[6] Lightbody, *op. cit.,* p. 273.

Term of Office Another variation in municipal elections concerns the term of office, which has ranged from one to four years. Those favouring the short term argue that it is more democratic because the electorate can retain closer control over the elected representatives. Since an ineffective council can be turned out of office quite promptly it is felt that councillors elected for a short term are more sensitive to public views and concerns. On the other hand, it is argued that too much of the time of a short term is used learning the job and gearing up for re-election. The lack of long term planning exhibited by most councils may be caused, at least in part, by frequent elections. According to Munro, the historical Canadian one year term was influenced by the American practice prevalent in the nineteenth century but subsequently abandoned as unworkable.[7] Brittain makes the same observation and goes on to argue that:

> This one year term is probably the most effective method ever devised for preventing the adoption of bad measures, but it is equally effective in preventing or delaying good measures.[8]

In his view the one year term grew out of a lack of faith in representatives and electors and should be abandoned.

**LONGER TERM:
BETTER FOR FORWARD PLANNING
AND FOLLOW THROUGH
MOSTLY 3 YEAR TERM NOW**

In recent decades, the term of office has gradually been extended in most provinces. Three year terms are now in effect for all or some classifications of municipalities in eight of the provinces and in the Northwest Territories and the Yukon. Four year terms are found in the remaining two provinces, Newfoundland, and Quebec. Most local government reform studies have reflected this trend to a longer term, usually because of their preoccupation with improving the service delivery role of local government.

---

[7]   W. B. Munro, *American Influences on Canadian Government*, Toronto, Macmillan, 1929.

[8]   H. L. Brittain, in the annual report of the Bureau of Municipal Research, 1945, quoted in K. G. Crawford, *Canadian Municipal Government*, Toronto, University of Toronto Press, 1954, p. 82.

Direct or Indirect Election   A third variation in the method of election, and one which has been the subject of increasing debate in recent years, is whether it is considered to be direct or indirect. In most cases, election is direct in that the voters chose a candidate for a particular position and none other. Examples of indirect election are found with respect to the upper tier county councils in Ontario and Quebec (the latter were replaced by regional county municipalities or "municipalites regional de comte" (MRCs) in 1980). The councils are considered to be indirectly elected because they are composed of members who were directly elected to the constituent lower tier municipalities and as a result automatically became county councillors.

In Ontario, for example, all townships, villages, and towns are lower tier units in the two tier county system of government. Each of their councils includes a reeve and also, if they are entitled by the number of electors, a deputy reeve. Informed voters know when they are voting for reeve and deputy reeve that the successful candidates will not only take office locally but will become that municipality's representatives on county council. In that sense they are indirectly elected to county council.[9]

This form of indirect election has often been criticized, particularly on the grounds that it results in a parochial council with representatives feeling loyalty to their own municipality and no one taking a broader view of matters — essentially the same criticism as that which is made against election by ward. However, the traditional defence of the arrangement is that it provides valuable liaison between the two levels of government since the reeve and deputy reeve "wear two hats" and can represent the concerns of each level of municipal government to the other.

It is noteworthy that this concept of indirect election has been used, in whole or in part, for most of the strengthened upper tier governments created as a result of the local government reform efforts in the various provinces. This is true of Quebec's urban communities, the regional districts in British Columbia, and Ontario's regional governments. Where

---

[9]   A number of changes in the composition of Ontario county councils are recommended in the Report of the Advisory Committee on County Government, *Patterns for the Future,* Toronto, Ministry of Municipal Affairs, 1987 and in the report of the Consultative Committee to the Minister of Municipal Affairs, *County Government in Ontario,* Toronto, Ministry of Municipal Affairs, January 1989.

members are being elected in a lower tier municipality to serve on a regional council, however, the ballot specifies both offices — unlike the situation with respect to county council — so the term "double direct" or "joint seat" is sometimes used instead of indirect to describe the method of electing these regional councillors in Ontario. In any event, as was noted in Chapter 5, this method of election appears to have contributed to a feeling of alienation towards these upper tier governments and reinforced their image as bureaucratic, unresponsive regimes. In addition, councillors elected on this basis have little incentive to identify and deal with regional concerns since their re-election depends on satisfying much more specific, localized concerns.

> **INDIRECT ELECTION:**
> **COMMON IN UPPER TIER**
> **MUNICIPAL GOVERNMENTS**
> **FREQUENT CRITICISMS**
> **MOVE TO MORE DIRECTLY ELECTED**
> **UPPER TIER COUNCILLORS IN ONTARIO**

Perhaps partly in response to these criticisms, a number of recent local government reviews in Ontario have given particular attention to questions of representation and accountability and their implications for the method of electing upper tier councillors.[10] As a result, there has been increased emphasis on the potential benefits of direct election of upper tier councillors. Indeed, a major change was introduced for the Metropolitan Toronto council at the time of the 1988 municipal election. It is now composed of 34 members, 28 directly elected by wards, and the mayors of the six lower tier units comprising Metro. A similar combination of directly elected regional councillors and mayors of lower tier municipalities ex officio (indirect) has been proposed for Ottawa-Carleton, and the Niagara Review has reaffirmed the positive benefits of this existing arrangement on the Niagara Regional Council.

---

[10] See, for example, Brian Koscak and David Siegel, *Accountability and Representation,* Background Study, Niagara Falls, Niagara Region Review Commission, September 1988; Task Force on Representation and Accountability in Metropolitan Toronto, *Analysis and Options for the Government of Metropolitan Toronto,* Toronto, Ontario Government Bookstore, November 1986; and Ottawa-Carleton Regional Review, *Accountability and Representation, Phase 1 Report,* Toronto, Ministry of Municipal Affairs, December 1987.

Election of Head of Council   One other form of indirect election occurs in connection with the selection of the head of council in some instances. For example, the warden of the county in Nova Scotia and Ontario and the MRC in Quebec is chosen by and from the council membership. This selection process was adopted for the various regional governments in Ontario except in the first instance when the chairman, as the head is called, was appointed by the Ontario Cabinet. A similar approach was adopted for the selection of the head of the Montreal Urban Community.

This practice of indirectly electing heads of council has been strongly criticized as undemocratic in that it does not give the electorate an opportunity to choose directly the occupant of the most important municipal office. On the other hand, the practice has been persuasively defended in a number of local government studies[11] as being a central feature of a more effective organization of the municipality modelled upon the parliamentary system. It is argued that heads of council chosen by their fellow councillors have, in effect, been given an indication of majority support for their leadership, whereas this situation may not apply at all when the heads are directly elected. Moreover, having given their support, council can also take it away again in a vote of nonconfidence by not reappointing the particular head of council, thereby adding an important element of accountability. Dennis Flynn's unsuccessful attempt to obtain reappointment as Chairman of Metropolitan Toronto after the 1988 election can be seen as an illustration of this point.

Especially controversial has been the provision in Ontario's regional governments that the chairman need not have — and cannot retain — a seat on a lower tier council. As a result, the electorate may not even have indirectly chosen the executive head of their regional council. This has been the case with several long-serving chairmen of Metropolitan Toronto, such as Paul Godfrey, who were appointed to several terms by the metropolitan council without holding an elected office within the system or having any form of accountability to the electorate. This issue has also come under close scrutiny in the recent local government reviews previously cited. Changes in the composition of the Metropolitan Toronto council introduced at the time of the 1988 municipal election also extend to the method of selecting a chairman. Only the directly

---

[11] Notably the *Report and Recommendations, Committee of Review, City of Winnipeg Act,* Winnipeg, Queen's Printer, 1976, and the *Report of the Royal Commission on Education, Public Services, and Provincial-Municipal Relations in Nova Scotia,* Halifax, Queen's Printer, 1974.

elected members of council are now eligible. Someone who is not on council cannot be chosen. Nor can the metro councillors who are there by virtue of being heads of local municipalities — on the grounds that serving as the head of two councils could create situations in which there would appear to be a conflict of interest.[12] Also changed for the 1988 election was the method of choosing the chairman in Regional Hamilton-Wentworth; for the first time in Ontario provision has been made for direct election to this position.

Underlying Conflict about Roles   The differing viewpoints about the three aspects of election just discussed reflect the underlying conflict between the two fundamental roles of local government — representative and administrative or service delivery. Those who emphasize the representative role and who recognize the political nature of local government tend to favour election by ward, while supporters of at large elections show their concern for service delivery when they emphasize the prospect of a stronger caliber of candidate capable of taking a broad overview of the municipality's needs. Similarly, those who argue for a short term of office are emphasizing the representative role, but proponents of a longer term are concerned about the increasingly complex demands requiring attention. Finally, direct election of councillors is seen as more democratic, and is therefore favoured by those who emphasize the representative role. However, those concerned with the need for strong leadership and improved priority setting in the face of growing local responsibilities are drawn to the concept of a head of council chosen by, supported by, and responsible to council.

**REPRESENTATIVE EMPHASIS:
FAVOURS WARD SYSTEM, DIRECT ELECTION
AND SHORT TERM OF OFFICE
ADMINISTRATIVE EMPHASIS:
FAVOURS GENERAL VOTE, INDIRECT ELECTION
AND LONG TERM OF OFFICE**

The Municipal Administrative Structure

In addition to the council, the government of the municipality includes the appointed staff who are responsible for administering the programs

---

[12] Koscak and Siegel, *op. cit.*, p. 9.

and policies of council and for assisting council in making decisions by providing expert advice. Because they may be in frequent contact with the public, the staff are also potential public relations ambassadors for the municipality. Some staff have the responsibility for supervising a number of subordinates and demonstrating managerial skill and, as described below, some have a special role as a coordinating officer.

There is, of course, a tremendous variation in the number and organization of staff depending on the population of the municipality and the range of functions. At one extreme, and still found in some Canadian municipalities, is the staff of one, perhaps part-time at that. This individual may act as clerk, treasurer, tax collector, by-law enforcement officer, dog catcher, and building inspector while performing a variety of other duties and all without any formal job description whatsoever.

At the other extreme is the staff of thousands, grouped into twenty-odd functionally specialized departments, with detailed job descriptions and operating manuals and an elaborate hierarchy. In this latter instance, the municipality obviously has much greater staff resources and expertise available, but as with all larger organizations, it may have difficulty drawing these resources together into a coordinated operation. Probably the most common approach traditionally used to oversee administrative operations was the establishment of standing committees, although, as discussed below, these have often been modified or abandoned in recent years because they were perceived as contributing to the problems of fragmentation and lack of coordination.

Standing Committee System

Standing committees normally exercise both executive and legislative responsibilities. They provide a general oversight of the operations of one or more municipal departments and they also make reports and recommendations as requested by council. In large municipalities the committees may be policy-advisory only, without any responsibility for supervising the departments. Standing committees are composed of councillors, sometimes with citizen members as well, and the extent of their use depends upon the size of the council, the volume of business, and local customs and administrative arrangements. (For a typical structure, see Chart 1.)

Advantages: The use of a standing committee system is held to be advantageous because it speeds up work in council since the committee sifts through the details of an issue and presents a positive recommendation to council. It also allows councillors to specialize in the fields of administration under the jurisdiction of their standing committees rather than to attempt to be knowledgeable in all fields. It is also alleged that the informal atmosphere of a committee meeting encourages more "give and take" in debate, facilitates participation by municipal officials, and also provides a good opportunity for interested groups or individuals to be heard. In this latter connection, it is argued that the delay built in when matters are referred to committee gives public opinion a chance to develop and be heard and guards against overly precipitous action.

ADVANTAGES:
SPEEDIER
SPECIALIZED
INFORMAL
FACILITATES PUBLIC INPUT

• CHART 1 •
STANDING COMMITTEE SYSTEM

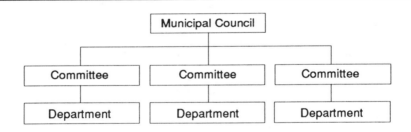

Disadvantages: However, there are also a significant number of alleged disadvantages of the standing committee system. While some delay in decision making may be regarded as beneficial, referrals from council to committee to another committee and back to council can create a very slow process and some opportunity for buck passing. If committee discussions are duplicated in the council chamber, much time is wasted and the value of the committee's specialized scrutiny is lost. There are often too many committees and one result is that a councillor's already limited time is seriously overburdened. An associated problem in many smaller municipalities is the tendency to establish standing committees when they are not necessary given the volume of work. Often such committees have no terms of reference, no regular schedule of meetings, and no systematic procedure of reporting to council. As a result, they are not an effective addition to the management of the municipality.

DISADVANTAGES:
TOO MANY
TOO INFORMAL
TOO FRAGMENTED
TOO INVOLVED IN ADMINISTRATION

Another criticism, and one of particular relevance for the ensuing discussion, is that standing committees tend to reinforce the departmentalism inherent in the municipal organization and contribute to a fragmented outlook. This is because members of a committee may put the interests of their particular department or departments first, an attitude that is hardly conducive to a coordinated approach or to a broad view of the municipality's needs. Often difficulties arise in this respect because the committee system has simply expanded with the increase in municipal departments. Yet, the departments themselves may have grown without sufficient forethought and if this structure is poorly organized for coordination then what can one expect from a committee system similarly designed. Finally, it is argued that committee members tend to become overly preoccupied with matters of administrative detail and internal management of the departments under their jurisdiction. This is a criticism of councils generally, but it is felt to be accentuated by the greater contact and familiarity with administration that the specialized scrutiny of the committee system permits.

B: Shortcomings — Traditional Machinery

Just as the pressures of growth and change undermined the traditional boundaries, responsibilities, and revenues of municipal government as discussed in Chapter 4, so these pressures increasingly called into question the traditional internal organization and operation of the municipality. In particular, there were growing problems related to leadership, planning and priority setting, accountability, and coordination.

Problems of Political Leadership

These weaknesses were focused at the top, in the limited powers given to the head of council. To illustrate, let us consider the Ontario legislation concerning the head of council and then note any significant variations. Perhaps the most striking feature of the Ontario Municipal Act's section on heads of council is that it is identical to the statement in the

Act of 1877.[13] As a result, it is hopelessly out-of-date, deals mostly with matters of administration, and does not recognize that the important duties of heads of council are "to lead, to initiate, and to coordinate the efforts of the councillors, the officers, and the many groups in the local communities that work for the betterment and the enrichment of the local citizens."[14] Briefly, the Ontario legislation requires the head of council to preside at council meetings, cause the municipal laws to be executed and obeyed, oversee the conduct of the officers, cause negligence, carelessness, and violation of duty by officers to be prosecuted and punished, and make recommendations to the council to improve the finances, health, security, cleanliness, comfort, and ornament of the municipality.

SHORTCOMING 1:
MOST HEADS OF COUNCIL HAVE VERY
VAGUE DUTIES, LITTLE REAL POWER

While many provinces have comparable provisions, some of the legislation gives the head of council other duties that strengthen his or her role as leader of the council. For example, the legislation in Manitoba, British Columbia, and Quebec provides a limited form of veto by authorizing the head of council to return any matter to the council for its reconsideration. The latter two provinces and Saskatchewan grant the head of council the power to suspend any officer or employee, subject to subsequent confirmation by council. In no instances, however, do the heads of council possess significant executive powers. While they are not limited to the largely ceremonial role of their British counterparts, neither are they comparable to the American "strong mayor" who has extensive authority in connection with the preparation of current and capital budgets, planning, hiring, and firing. Heads of council in Canada must rely heavily on their personality and persuasive skills and attempt to enlist council's cooperation. However, as indicated below, the council itself has serious limitations as a governing body.

Except in those few instances where organized political parties operate, the council is made up of a group of individuals with potentially

---

[13] According to Paul Hickey, *Decision-Making Processes in Ontario's Local Governments,* Toronto, Ministry of Treasury, Economics and Intergovernmental Affairs, 1973 — and there has been no significant change since this report.

[14] *Ibid.,* p. 62.

different interests and concerns and no sense of cohesion or collective will. This situation is accentuated when councillors are elected on a ward basis and parochial views are allowed to predominate over any concept of the good of the municipality. As a result, support for a particular measure is often arranged on the basis of trade-offs. This "log-rolling and back scratching" makes voting patterns even more unpredictable and further complicates the efforts of the head of council to develop a consensus for action. On the other hand, election by general vote, as espoused by the turn of the century reformers, has been increasingly criticized as providing insufficient representation of the diverse interests and needs of many municipalities today.

SHORTCOMING 2:
COUNCIL LACKS COHESION
PLANNING, PRIORITY SETTING INHIBITED BY
PROVINCIAL CONTROLS AND CONDITIONS
LACK OF ACCOUNTABILITY

Efforts to get councils to undertake long term planning or even to take the long view on a particular issue have been hampered by the relatively short term of office, although, as described above, this term has been extended in a number of provinces in recent years. Planning and priority setting have also been hampered by the limited control actually exercised by council over its activities and finances. Because of the dependence on conditional grants from the senior levels of government, municipal decisions often reflect the priorities of these governments rather than local priorities. The municipal council's control over its expenditures has also been eroded by the financial demands of various special purpose bodies, particularly the school boards as they operate in most provinces. Technical resources to undertake research, analysis, and long term planning have not been widely available to municipalities.

Because of the lack of cohesion on council, coordination of the activities of the municipality is difficult. This is particularly the case as the range of responsibilities increases and a large number of functionally specialized departments are established. At the provincial and federal levels, each government department is headed by a minister, an elected representative, and all ministers belong to the cabinet where the twin forces of party loyalty and cabinet solidarity serve to facilitate coordination. At the local level, however, there is no comparable arrangement. Perhaps the closest approximation is the establishment of standing committees of councillors to supervise each of the municipal departments, as described above. But it is generally agreed that these committees tend to perpetuate a fragmented outlook on municipal operations by being overly preoccupied with their particular department(s).

There is also a serious lack of accountability within most municipal councils. Granted, all members are normally elected and must regularly seek re-election. But who is responsible for taking the initiative in dealing with the problems facing the municipality? Who is responsible for scrutinizing and criticizing the initiatives taken to ensure that they are in the best interest of the public? Unlike the senior levels, there is no "government" or "official opposition" at the municipal level. Because these matters are the responsibility of everybody on council and yet of nobody, it is almost impossible for citizens to know where to direct criticism or praise. Councillors can claim that they attempted to represent a citizen concern but were outvoted by other councillors. In this situation, the opportunities for evading responsibility are all too evident.

Problems Caused by Boards

Problems of accountability are also caused by the existence of special purpose boards and commissions at the local level. As with so many features of local government, we are indebted(?) to the turn of the century reformers who urged the creation of boards as a way of insulating responsibilities from the control of councils and hence from politics and as a means of obtaining expert assistance. Some boards came even earlier of course — notably the school board dating from the early 1800s and preceding the creation of municipalites — and some came later, particularly in the form of intermunicipal bodies designed to help overcome the fragmented municipal structure in Canada's urban areas. The existence of these separate boards is most prevalent in Ontario, less so in the Atlantic and Western provinces, and least so in Quebec.

SHORTCOMING 3:
MANY SEPARATE BOARDS
LACK OF COORDINATION
LACK OF ACCOUNTABILITY

Almost all of these bodies are appointed rather than elected, many operate quite independently of council, and collectively they provide a wide range of services that ought to be, but often are not, closely integrated with the services provided by the municipality. It is hoped that the classic example of the street being paved by the council and then being torn up by the utility commission for sewer work is seldom in evidence. But there are many other, more subtle examples of lack of coordination or insufficient liaison between boards and council. School board decisions concerning the location of new schools or the closing of existing ones have an important bearing on the pattern of growth within a municipality. Municipal planning efforts may also be affected by decisions made by such bodies as utility commissions, park boards, conservation authorities, industrial commissions, and planning boards. A coordinated approach to social services administration by the municipality may be complicated by the fact that relevant programs are under the jurisdiction of such separate bodies as children's aid societies, health units, housing authorities, and library boards.

Quite apart from the problems of fragmentation, these boards increase the problem of accountability since most are not responsible to council or to the electorate in any very direct or effective mannner. As has been noted, the rationale behind the establishment of some of these boards, such as planning boards and police commissions, was the presumed desirability of keeping the issue in question "out of politics," and as a result these bodies are not meant to be particularly responsive to public opinion. Not only are the boards themselves not accountable, but their separate existence presents a very confusing picture to the citizen, and the divided jurisdictions that result give both the council and the boards an opportunity to indulge in buck passing.

Fragmented Administration

Problems are also found within the administrative structure of the municipality. Traditionally, there have been serious problems of fragmentation and lack of coordination. Many of the reasons for these problems have already been noted. As municipalities have grown, more and more departments have been established. Functionally specialized, these departments are usually headed by a specialist in that particular discipline, and they tend to be preoccupied with their own area of expertise or specialty. This narrow focus is reinforced by the existence of provincial departments similarly specialized, each of them maintaining close contact with their municipal counterparts. These provincial departments deploy a variety of conditional grant programs to ensure that the municipal departments give high priority to their specialized area. While all of this is understandable, it results in little attention being paid to the overall needs of the municipality.

> SHORTCOMING 4:
> FUNCTIONALLY SPECIALIZED DEPARTMENTS
> NARROW OUTLOOK REINFORCED BY STANDING
> COMMITTEES AND PROVINCIAL COUNTERPARTS

Where municipalities use a standing committee system, it has already been noted that these committees often tend to reinforce a narrow focus on the activities of "their" departments, to the neglect of a broader consideration of overall municipal needs. Even where municipalities succeed in getting their departments to work together, further fragmentation is evident in the existence, as previously noted, of a variety of special purpose bodies, many operating quite independently of council.

C: Modifications to Machinery

Especially in the past couple of decades, many municipalities have modified their governing machinery in an attempt to overcome some of the weaknesses discussed. At first glance the resulting organizational forms seem quite diverse. There have only been two main types of change, however. One has been the introduction of some form of executive committee of council in an attempt to provide stronger political leadership. The other, and more widespread, change has involved the establishment of some form of Chief Administrative Officer to provide leadership and coordination at the staff level. The latter reform is examined first.

Chief Administrative Officers

Chief Administrative Officers (CAOs) are found in Canadian municipalities under a variety of names and with a variety of powers and responsibilities. In essence, this approach involves appointing an individual to lead, coordinate, and direct the administration within the policy framework established by council.

The most common form of CAO is that of the city manager or council manager system that spread into this country from the United States in the early 1900s. The first Canadian city manager was appointed in Westmount in 1913 and the system is still found particularly in Quebec where legislation has authorized municipal councils to appoint a manager since 1922. In contrast, Ontario's Municipal Act did not give municipalities the authority to appoint any type of CAO until a 1970 amendment. While the number of CAO positions has increased markedly since, most are not full-fledged managers but rather weaker forms of co-ordinating officer or expanded clerk-treasurer, as described below.

In the Western provinces, the principal form of CAO has been the commissioner, usually found in a group of three or four operating as a board of commissioners. As described in Chapter 3, the commissioner system, like the council manager system, arose out of the turn of the century reform era and was first established in Edmonton in 1904. Within a decade Regina, Prince Albert, and Saskatoon followed suit. In a number of respects, the commissioner system is comparable to a mul-tiheaded council manager system as can be seen from the examination of the two that follows.

The Council Manager System

As it developed in the United States, this system is predicated on a complete separation of the policy and administrative activities of the municipality. It involves the appointment of a professional administra-tor — the manager — to whom is delegated complete responsibility for administering the programs of the municipality including the supervi-sion and coordination of staff. The council is elected at large and on a nonpartisan basis and directs its attention to its representative role and the formulation of overall policies for the municipality. In the "pure" council manager systems found in the United States, there are not usu-ally any standing committees and therefore not any regular council contact with the administration except through the manager. (See Chart 2.)

• CHART 2 •
COUNCIL-MANAGER SYSTEM

The duties of the manager may be summarized as follows:[15]

1.   To see that all laws and ordinances are enforced.

2.   To exercise control over all departments and in accordance with civil service regulations appoint, supervise, and remove department heads and subordinate employees of the city.

3.   To make such recommendations to the council concerning the affairs of the city as may seem desirable to the manager.

4.   To keep the council advised of the financial conditions and future needs of the city.

5.   To prepare and submit the annual budget to the council.

6.   To prepare and submit to the council such reports as may be required by that body.

7.   To keep the public informed, through reports to the council, regarding the operations of the city government.

Proponents of the council manager system contend that it provides for greatly improved coordination of administrative activities, frees the council from unnecessary detail, and allows councillors to concentrate on their primary role of policy making. While there is considerable potential for improved coordination in the organization of the manager system, its greatest weakness is the premise on which it is based, that it is possible to separate policy and administration in municipal government. To the contrary, it is very difficult to identify in advance whether a particular issue is a routine administrative matter or has political implications. Even if this distinction could be made, it is not desirable to rigidly separate the two activities. In practice, much policy arises out of ongoing administration and the council's complete separation from the administrative activities of the municipality leaves it making policy in a vacuum.

PROS AND CONS OF MANAGER SYSTEM:
IMPROVED COORDINATION
FREES COUNCIL FROM UNNECESSARY DETAIL
POLICY/ADMINISTRATION SEPARATION UNREALISTIC
MANAGER-COUNCIL CLASHES

Moreover, while the system provides for a more effective administrative structure, it does not provide for strong political leadership. Indeed, because of the focus on the manager, he or she is often a more conspicu-

---

[15] From the *City Manager Directory,* quoted in T. J. Plunkett, *Urban Canada and its Government,* Toronto, Macmillan, 1968, p. 38.

ous public figure than the members of council including the mayor. In addition to producing friction and jealousies that frequently result in the dismissal of managers, this situation also leads to managers becoming publicly identified with particular viewpoints and policies. If, as a result, they become embroiled in political controversies, their role as administrative leaders is impaired and they will likely be replaced. One author dryly observes that a manager's departure from work is often the result of illness or fatigue: "The council was sick and tired of him."[16] Thus the successful operation of the council manager system not only requires a manager who does not dominate the council and usurp its policy-making role but also one who does not seem to do so.

The Manager System in Canada   As adapted to Canada, the council manager system has undergone certain modifications that minimize some of the problems noted above and, at the same time, minimize somewhat its strength and coordinating potential. Not surprisingly, these modifications reflect both the different governing principles of the two countries and the differing conditions that prevailed at the time of the system's introduction.

In most Canadian cities in the early years of the twentieth century the need for such an administrative reform seemed less pressing or necessary than in American cities. Corruption and the worst excesses of local party politics were much less evident in Canadian cities, and appointments based on merit were much more prevalent. Moreover, administrative coordination was being achieved informally by utilizing the potential of certain key municipal positions, notably that of clerk and treasurer. Particularly where the two positions were combined in people with leadership skills, their overall knowledge of the municipality's operations and the influence inherent in their responsibilities for preparing agendas, background reports, minutes, by-laws, budgets and financial reports, often made them unofficial chief administrative officers. Some municipalities went further and confirmed the coordinating potential of these positions by formally designating the clerk or treasurer as something more — with positions such as Clerk-Comptroller, Clerk-Treasurer-Administrator, and Clerk-Coordinator the result.

---

[16] Wayne Anderson, Chester A. Newland, and Richard J. Stillman, *The Effective Local Government Manager,* Washington, International City Management Association, 1983, p. 68.

Even where the council manager system was adopted, the Canadian version usually incorporated certain features designed to maintain the significance and prestige of the elected council.[17] First, the Canadian council manager system does not attempt to enforce a complete separation between administration and policy. The council usually has a direct relationship with at least its main department heads as well as the manager — normally accomplished "by the attendance of the department heads at a meeting of a limited number of standing committees of council when matters affecting their particular areas of jurisdiction are under review."[18] Second, the responsibility for the appointment of staff is exercised by council not the manager, although often council only exercises this responsibility after receiving recommendations from the manager.

CANADIAN MANAGER:
POLICY/ADMINISTRATION SEPARATION LESS SEVERE
STANDING COMMITTEES OFTEN RETAINED
LESS POWERFUL POSITION

With such modifications, Young feels that the Canadian version has managed to avoid the fundamental problem of council's complete separation from administration. As he explains, the council in a Canadian council manager system continues to concern itself with administration but "does so from a much broader viewpoint." The advice and recommendations of staff are coordinated by the manager and "it is this opportunity and ability to place such recommendations within the broader perspective of the city's needs as a whole which represents his greatest value to the council in his capacity as policy advisor."[19]

Halifax provides a good example of a Canadian city with a council manager system, since it has experienced this system since 1951 and has carried out a major study of its operations.[20] Confirming the less extreme

---

[17] See Dennis A. Young, "Canadian Local Government Development: Some Aspects of the Commissioner and City Manager Forms of Administration," in Lionel D. Feldman and Michael D. Goldrick (eds.), *Politics and Government of Urban Canada*, Toronto, Methuen, pp. 276–278.

[18] *Ibid.*, p. 277.

[19] *Ibid.*, p. 278.

[20] Halifax Commission on City Government, *Report on the Structure and Processes of Halifax City Government 1982*, Halifax, Institute of Public Affairs, Dalhousie University, 1982.

nature of Canadian versions of the manager system, the commission studying Halifax noted that when the system was introduced it resulted in "neither the abolition of Council's committee system nor any major reorganization of existing boards and commissions".[21] The commission concluded that the system as it had evolved worked reasonably well and should be continued. It noted, however, three main areas of concern. First, the councillors have been required to devote a large amount of time to the details of government because of the absence of any executive body or cabinet to coordinate policy matters. Second, the manager's workload has increased greatly because, in addition to managing and coordinating the day to day activities of the city, he or she must also — in the absence of any real mechanism for coordination at the political level — seek to interact with council to promote consistency and policy coherence.[22] Third, the number of separate special purpose bodies in the local government of Halifax impose additional time demands on both councillors and the manager, raise questions about diffusion of authority and duplication of administrative costs, and questions about policy control and public accountability.

The commission's observations on the link between the structures at the political and administrative level merit further consideration. First, however, let us examine the other main reformed internal structures that have been introduced.

The Commissioner System

The commissioner system has traditionally been found only in Western Canada and except for Winnipeg has been confined to the provinces of Alberta and Saskatchewan. It has long been used in Calgary and was also in use in Edmonton until 1984. The commissioner system has been established, more recently, in Fort McMurray and Medicine Hat. It involves the appointment of a limited number of commissioners[23] who are delegated administrative responsibilities by council. As individuals, these commissioners are charged with supervising and coordinating the activities of the departments under their jurisdiction. In addition, the commissioners

---

[21] *Ibid.*, p. 5.

[22] *Ibid.*, p. 4.

[23] In fact, some cities such as Red Deer, Alberta and Prince Albert and Estevan, Saskatchewan have established a single council-appointed commissioner as described by Plunkett, *op. cit.*, p. 53.

may meet together as a board of commissioners with responsibility for overall management and coordination of the municipality's activities. The head of council is also usually a member of this board.

Taking the example of Calgary,[24] there is a chief commissioner, a commissioner of planning and transportation, a commissioner of finance and administration, and a commissioner of operations — each directly responsible for the supervision of a number of municipal departments. These four commissioners together with the mayor constitute the commission board that is responsible for determining how council's general policy directions are to be carried out through the administrative structure. The commissioners are also resource persons for the five standing committees of council, and actively participate in their discussions. (See Chart 3 for the general structure.)

The commissioner system is similar to a council manager system except in two important respects. The fact that there is more than one commissioner permits a degree of specialization not possible under the manager system where one person must supervise the entire administrative structure no matter how large and complex. Typically, one commissioner is concerned with hard services (such as water and sewerage facilities and roads), another with soft services (such as health and welfare programs and libraries) and a third — if available — with finance and planning. Moreover, the commissioners provide a two level approach to administrative coordination, both as individual commissioners in charge of a group of related departments and as a board of commissioners in charge of the entire administrative structure.

COMMISSIONER SYSTEM:
TWO MAIN DIFFERENCES
FROM MANAGER SYSTEM
SEVERAL COMMISSIONERS
ALLOW SPECIALIZATION
MAY MEET AS BOARD WITH COUNCIL

The second difference from the manager system is the somewhat less marked separation of policy and administration found in the commissioner system. This is particularly reflected in the mayor's membership on the board of commissioners, although this combination has not been

---

[24]   Jack Masson, *Alberta's Local Governments and Their Politics,* Edmonton, University of Alberta Press, 1985, pp. 36–37.

without problems. On the one hand, Plunkett, while acknowledging the delicate relationships involved, endorses this combination on the grounds that the mayor participates:

> in the vital stage when problems are being analyzed, as well as when recommendations are formulated for presentation to the council. Under this arrangement direction and leadership in civic affairs is provided by the city's recognized political leader, supported by the managerial coordination of the appointed city commissioners.[25]

Masson also favours combining these two elements. He describes as retrogressive Calgary's 1968 change that transferred the chairmanship of the commission board from the mayor (who remains an ex-officio member) to the chief commissioner. The more limited role played by the mayor is unfortunate in his view, "since the mayor is the linchpin in the whole system, the bridge between the formulation of policy on council and its administration through the commission board."[26]

· CHART 3 ·
COMMISSIONER SYSTEM

---

[25] Plunkett, *op. cit.*, p. 54.

[26] Masson, *Alberta's Local Governments, op. cit.*, p. 36.

On the other hand, Hickey's study of decision-making processes in Canadian municipalities concluded that the inclusion of the head of council on the board of commissioners is a mistake. In support of this claim, he notes that the mayor was dropped from the board in Vancouver (so was the board dropped, in 1972, when Vancouver appointed a single manager instead). He further cites the examples of Saskatoon and Calgary where the mayors, while still members, have ceased to exercise their powers.[27] Among other disadvantages, Hickey contends that the head of council's presence on the board tends to inhibit the appointed commissioners and overburdens the individual who cannot be effective as leader of council and the community and chief administrative officer as well. Another disadvantage was cited in a consultant's report to Edmonton City Council in 1982.

> It is our view that when the mayor chairs the Commission Board there is ambiguity regarding the nature of recommendations emanating from the board as to whether they are politically or administratively generated and endorsed .... the political and administrative responsibilities and authority are blurred and the authority of the Chief Commissioner to manage and exercise administrative authority is undermined.[28]

This report also concluded that the mayor's chairmanship of the commission board had been a factor in the high level of conflict between council and administration. As previously noted, at the beginning of 1984 Edmonton replaced its commission board with a city manager and established an executive committee of council.

What can be seen as a variation of the commissioner system has been appearing in a number of Ontario cities in recent years. This has involved grouping together related departments and appointing commissioners to oversee the department heads within the groupings. This structure often includes a CAO — who then operates as the equivalent of the chief commissioner. However, in at least some instances, one of the main purposes of the change has apparently been to reduce what was considered an excessively heavy span of control for the CAO.

Overall, the commissioner system appears to have more advantages than disadvantages. The attempt to focus council's attention on policy making and representation and to delegate administrative responsibili-

---

[27] Hickey, *op. cit.*, p. 218.

[28] Norm Duce and Associates Ltd., *Final Report: Review of Organization — Council and Commission Board in the City of Edmonton*, Edmonton, July 8, 1982, p. 2.

ties to the commissioners and subordinate staff is commendable. As previously indicated, where commissioners specialize in major fields of activity such as hard services and soft services, the potential exists for knowledgeable advice to council and the coordination of municipal activities. Where the system involves a board of commissioners operating under a chief commissioner, council can benefit from collective policy advice. Finally, if the heads of council enjoy a good working relationship with the commissioners, especially the chief commissioner, they are better able to act as the chief executive officer of the municipality. In this situation, unlike the council manager system, the link between policy and administrative activities may be retained.

PROS AND CONS OF COMMISSIONER SYSTEM:
COMMISSIONERS SPECIALIZE
COORDINATION IMPROVED
POLICY/ADMINISTRATION LINK BETTER MAINTAINED
BUT, POLICY/ADMINISTRATION LINK MAY BRING CONFLICT
TOO INVOLVED IN DETAIL
COMPLEX STRUCTURE AND REPORTING RELATIONSHIPS

Disadvantages include, in addition to the previously referred to difficulty concerning the head of council, a tendency for commissioners to become too involved in detail in their supervision of departments. Hickey charges that too much of their time and effort goes into directing and controlling and not enough into planning and organizing.[29] In addition, the relationship and lines of communication between the commissioners, the senior staff of the municipality, the council, and the committees of council are far from clear and smoothly operating in every case. For example, the Committee of Review on Winnipeg Unicity noted that there was overlapping of roles between the board of commissioners and the standing committees and questioned whether both elements could be effectively combined in one system.[30]

A different kind of problematic overlap is noted by Lightbody with respect to Edmonton's commissioner system — since replaced by a single manager.[31] He points out that some conflicts are inevitable given the attempt to group departments under three broad functional areas

---

[29] Hickey, *op. cit.,* p. 221.

[30] Committee of Review, *op. cit.,* p. 19.

[31] Lightbody in Magnusson and Sancton, *op. cit.,* pp. 274–275.

headed by the three commissioners and cites, as an example, the fact that land use planning is under public affairs while transportation planning is under utilities and engineering. More serious is his allegation that internal struggles over policy alternatives are almost never allowed to reach the public and that "upwardly mobile civic managers do not upset applecarts in Edmonton."[32] Lightbody goes on to observe that commissioners "have usually been recruited from the world of hard services and, by virtue of their training, have not been overly sympathetic to the direct intrusions of citizen amateurs into civic policy-making."[33] Masson also expresses concern about this lack of citizen involvement.[34]

It is important to bear in mind, therefore, that even under the most efficient commissioner system, the emphasis is on administrative rather than political leadership and any resultant improvements in service delivery do not necessarily enhance the representative role of local government. Indeed, we should remember that these various types of CAO system originated at a time when the representative role was largely ignored in the preoccupation with reducing political influence and improving service delivery.

Executive Committees

Over the years the most persistent method of attempting to deal with these various problems of political leadership has been the establishment of executive committees of council. As had been the case with the establishment of CAO systems, a major impetus was the turn of the century reform movement that emphasized a strong executive along with such measures as smaller councils and at large elections in its concern to make municipal government more efficient and less political. This prompted the introduction of boards of control, a form of executive committee that became quite prominent in Ontario during the first half of the twentieth century. Other forms of executive committee have also been established in a number of large city or metropolitan municipalities in an effort to duplicate a cabinet organization and a semblance of the parliamentary system.

---

[32] *Ibid.*, p. 275.

[33] *Ibid.*

[34] Masson, *Alberta's Local Governments, op. cit.,* p. 38.

Board of Control

The board of control first appeared in Canada in the City of Toronto in 1896, and within a decade it had spread to Winnipeg (1907) and then Montreal (1910). It didn't last long in either of those latter cities, however, and became an exclusively Ontario structure. In fact, it became mandatory for cities over 100 000 population in Ontario, although it could be dispensed with by a two-thirds vote of council if affirmed by the Ontario Municipal Board. In addition, cities and towns over 45 000 and other local municipalities over 100 000 could establish a board of control if approved by a two-thirds vote of council and affirmed by the Municipal Board. Given these statutory provisions, the board of control became a prominent feature of the government system of many of Ontario's largest municipalities — although this is no longer the case as will be noted.

The head of council and two or four (usually) members elected at large constitute the board of control. All are full members of the municipal council, the other members of which are elected by ward. The responsibilities of the board of control include:

1. The preparation of annual estimates.
2. The calling of tenders and awarding of contracts.
3. The supervision of works in progress.
4. The nomination of all heads and subheads of departments and other permanent employees and the suspension or dismissal of department heads.
5. The submission of proposed by-laws to council.
6. Any other duties as assigned by council.

Thus, a number of the most important executive responsibilities are given to the board. These powers are not delegated by council at its discretion but are assigned by statute, and the board is not responsible to council but to its electorate. Indeed, major decisions taken by the board can only be altered or overturned by a two-thirds vote of council. This concentration of power within a special group of councillors may seem a curious arrangement until one recalls the conditions and attitudes at the time the board of control was originally established. Controllers were deliberately given the more important responsibilities because they were elected at large and therefore were expected to be a better calibre of representative than the ward politicians who comprised the rest of the council. It was anticipated that the board of control would provide effective leadership and contribute to a more efficient management of the affairs of the municipality.

In practice, however, the board of control system experienced a number of difficulties and fell into increasing disfavour. The limited number of members involved became increasingly overburdened in attempting to oversee the administrative activities of the municipality. Nor was the board very effective in attempting to coordinate the ever more complex, fragmented administrative structures that evolved. The board's supposed similarity to a cabinet was shown to be very superficial at best. As the cabinet system operates at the provincial and federal levels in Canada, the cabinet is made up of ministers who are the heads of the various departments of government. All ministers are members of the same political party and the twin forces of party loyalty and cabinet solidarity impose a strong collective will on the deliberations of this body. In contrast, the board of control was made up of individuals without necessarily any collective purpose — indeed, it was not uncommon for one or more of the controllers to be eyeing the mayor's job, with resultant infighting.

PROBLEMS WITH BOARD OF CONTROL:
TOO FEW TO OVERSEE MANY DEPARTMENTS
LACKED COHESION
OVERLAPPING JURISDICTION
WITH STANDING COMMITTEES
CONFLICT WITH COUNCIL, ESPECIALLY
PROVISION FOR 2/3 VOTE

An added problem was that many municipalities with boards of control also retained standing committees of council. This arrangement not only reinforced a fragmented departmental outlook inimical to coordination, but also caused conflict between the board of control and the standing committees in terms of the responsibility for supervising administration. The overall complexity of the municipal organization has also been a problem with, typically, a board of control, a council, standing committees, and a variety of special purpose bodies. As a result of this complexity, the decision-making process was often slow, discussion was duplicated, buck passing was common, and the lack of clear lines of authority and responsibility also confused the public and undermined the accountability of the system.

Probably the most serious difficulty was the pronounced and persistent friction between the board of control and the rest of council. In effect, there were two classes of councillor and those considered second class were acutely aware of it. They resented the controllers' argument that election at large had given them (the controllers) a stronger mandate and they resented the special powers given to the controllers. But, most of all the rest of the councillors resented the provision that a two-thirds vote was required to overturn board of control decisions. Since the members of the board had a vote as councillors, there had to be near unanimity among the rest for the necessary votes to be marshalled. Consider, for example, the City of Hamilton as it was structured some years ago. With a council that was composed of a mayor, four controllers and 16 councillors, it was necessary for 15 of the 16 councillors to join together to defeat a recommendation supported by all members of the board of control. Not surprisingly, it was felt that the board of control enjoyed excessive power and that the result was too often a case of "the tail wagging the dog."

Given all of these difficulties, it is not surprising that the board of control system fell into increasing disfavour. A report at the beginning of the 1970s noted that "16 of the 25 councils that are required or authorised to establish the system .... have sought and obtained approval to reject the system."[35] By the time the Robarts Royal Commission on Metropolitan Toronto had reported in 1977, the number of board of control systems had been further reduced to seven. Four of these were in the boroughs of Metropolitan Toronto and the Robarts Commission recommended their abolition — a step that was finally taken at the time of the 1988 municipal elections.[36] Of the remaining three, those in Hamilton and Ottawa have been abolished — leaving London as the only municipality featuring this once so prominent form of executive committee. Moreover, legislation has removed the two-thirds vote provision with respect to the board in London.

Given its virtual extinction, one might wonder why so much attention has been given to the board of control. Part of the reason is that an appreciation of the difficulties faced by this type of executive committee is helpful when considering some of the alternative forms that have been attempted or contemplated. Moreover, some of the other forms, as we will see, are essentially variations of the board of control.

---

[35] Hickey, *op. cit.,* p. 158.

[36] Following a further study, the Report of the Task Force on Representation and Accountability in Metropolitan Toronto, *Analysis and Options for the Government of Metropolitan Toronto,* Toronto, November 1986.

Other Forms of Executive Committee

Apart from the board of control, a variety of other forms of executive committee are found in Canadian municipalities. Some of these are similar to the board of control in having a statutory foundation, including those established in a number of the reformed local government structures. There are also nonstatutory executive committees. By their nature they are much harder to categorize, and often are not even called "executive" committees. However, their purpose is reflected in their membership and their mandate. They are usually composed of those chairing the major standing committees of the municipality together with the head of council. They are responsible for financial, and often personnel, matters, and may also be charged with providing leadership and coordination of municipal activities. The few examples that follow are designed to illustrate the nature of statutory executive committees — apart from the board of control — and their operation.

Montreal is likely the Canadian city with the longest experience with an executive committee, since there are references to such a body as early as the 1850s. Montreal did, as previously mentioned, establish a board of control in 1910, the result of a new charter prompted by councillors endorsing the views of the reform movement of that time. However, charter revisions in 1921 abolished the board of control and provided for an executive committee to be named by council. The mayor was made a voting member of this executive committee but could not assume the chair, a deliberate attempt to curb the power of the mayor.

Montreal's executive committee, which has continued to the present, was authorized to initiate legislation and to supervise the municipal departments, with each member normally assigned a number of specific departments to oversee. Its powers were similar to those of an Ontario board of control, even to the extent of the two-thirds vote provision for council to overturn most major decisions of the committee. However, it has evolved into quite a different, and more powerful, position because of the emergence of a very dominant political party organization within Montreal's council. The Civic Party under the leadership of Jean Drapeau, controlled a majority of the council seats from 1960 until Drapeau's retirement in 1986. The result was that Drapeau's personal choices for membership on the executive committee were ratified by council and the committee could initiate actions with every expectation that they would be supported by council. Moreover, the mayor's exclusion from the executive committee obviously did not detract from his position, since he controlled the voting block he needed through his leadership of the dominant party. Party domination has continued since Drapeau with the election of a large majority of members of the Montreal Citizens' Movement, including Jean Doré as mayor.

An executive committee is also found in the *Montreal Urban Community* established in 1969. In fact, this executive committee, as established, consisted of the City of Montreal's seven member executive plus five suburban representatives, an arrangement that reflected Montreal's dominant position within the new upper tier government. A 1982 revision, however, changed the composition of the executive committee and reduced the city's membership. The executive committee now comprises the chairman and vice-chairman of the council as well as the chairmen and vice-chairmen of its five new standing committees. The council also chooses, by a two-thirds vote, someone from among the other council members to chair the executive committee.[37]

The cities of *Quebec, Hull* and *Laval* established executive committees in the mid-1960s after studies that found that the existing government machinery exhibited weaknesses of excessive council involvement in administrative detail, lack of executive direction, and uncoordinated administration. These executive committees are composed of the mayor (as chairman) and four councillors selected by the mayor. According to Hickey, the system was based on the premise that a candidate for mayor runs as the head of a team of like-minded councillor candidates.[38] The existence of what is, in effect, a local political party provides the strong political leadership previously noted with respect to the City of Montreal.

One of the earliest executive committees in Ontario was established by the new *Municipality of Metropolitan Toronto* in 1954 under the council's general authority to establish "standing and other committees." This committee was given powers almost identical to Ontario's board of control, but unlike the board it was not directly elected. Instead it was composed of the chairman of the metropolitan council, the mayors of the six lower tier municipalities in the system, and seven other specified representatives from the lower tier councils. Therefore, each member of the executive committee was there because of a prior position in the government structure.

---

[37] See Andrew Sancton, "Montreal," in Magnusson and Sancton, *op. cit.,* pp. 80–82.

[38] Hickey, *op. cit.,* p. 199.

The 1977 Robarts Commission recommended that the metropolitan council be given a general power of delegation that would authorize it to elect from its own membership an executive committee and any number of standing committees and to vest them with such responsibilities as council sees fit.[39] No action was taken on this recommendation — as with virtually all of the recommendations of the Robarts Commission — and yet the lack of strong political leadership in the Metropolitan Toronto system must be attributed, at least in part, to the way in which the executive committee has been chosen and the absence of organized political parties on council. Under these past arrangements, the executive committee members have not been responsible to the full metropolitan council for their selection nor could they depend on continuing majority support for their proposals. Indeed, there was not even any certainty that the executive committee members themselves would agree on what needed to be done in particular circumstances. They were individuals with different constituencies, different viewpoints, and different — perhaps competing — ambitions.

Following a Task Force on Representation and Accountability in Metropolitan Toronto[40] changes were finally made in the executive committee at the time of the 1988 municipal elections. As previously recommended by the Robarts Commission, the legislative requirement for an executive committee has now been abolished. It is left to the discretion of the Metropolitan Toronto Council whether or not it establishes such a committee, how it is composed, and what it does.

**POLITICAL PARTIES:
THE KEY ELEMENT FOR
STRONG EXECUTIVE COMMITTEE?**

Winnipeg Unicity in its philosophical base and its actual experiences provides the most striking example of the link between organized political parties and the operation of an executive committee. It will be recalled from Chapter 5 that a major objective of those designing the government machinery of Unicity was the development of a parliamentary model at the local level. A central feature was the provision for an executive policy committee chaired by the head of council and in-

---

[39] *Report of the Royal Commission on Metropolitan Toronto* (John Robarts, Commissioner), Toronto, Queen's Printer, 1977, p. 113.

[40] *Op. cit.,* Chapter 6.

cluding those chairing the three major standing committees established as part of the new structure. From the outset, however, the potential of this arrangement was weakened by the fact that the mayor was directly elected, rather than being chosen from among the councillors as had been proposed in the White Paper that led to the new structure.

A Committee of Review of Unicity reporting in 1976 provided a forceful argument in favour of the parliamentary model and its words bear repeating at some length.

> A functioning municipal parliamentary system would require an executive — a civic equivalent of a cabinet at the provincial or federal level — to which was delegated the responsibility to govern. As in other parliamentary governments, this executive would be continuously responsible to the council and ultimately to the electorate. It should have strong leadership while retaining collective responsibility.
>
> The leadership would have to come from the head of the government .... But in order to be, in truth, the leader of the government, and in a position corresponding to that of a premier in a provincial government, the mayor should have the power to choose the members of the executive group. The group ... should include the chairmen of the standing committees, each of whom would have a civic equivalent of ministerial responsibility.
>
> The two way responsibility vested in the executive council would require not merely political cohesion but, in fact, discipline .... Such discipline must be the discipline of the group, just as responsibility must be shared responsibility, collective responsibility.[41]

Implicit in this approach, of course, was the existence of political parties, although the committee acknowledged that "proposals to promote the development of party politics in local government frequently draw reflex actions of a highly negative sort." The committee felt that it could not legislate the development of a party system but would have to hope for "a full fledged party system to evolve over the course of time, under the influence of the parliamentary characteristics of our model."

The committee's reasoning was lost on the Manitoba government, however, and 1977 amendments to the Unicity legislation further undermined the parliamentary features that had been intended in the original White Paper. Not only was the mayor to remain directly elected, contrary to the recommendations of the Committee of Review, but this position was removed from the executive policy committee — changes which, as previously described, seemed intended to reduce the position of mayor to a largely ceremonial role.

---

[41] Committee of Review, *op. cit.,* p. 57.

Another Committee of Review reported in January 1986,[42] and recommended that a significant amount of the city's powers be delegated to an executive committee composed of six councillors and chaired by the mayor. The members would be nominated by the mayor and elected by council. While no changes have yet been introduced, the initial government response[43] suggests that once again there will be a reluctance to strengthen the mayor's position dramatically. Instead of six members, the government proposes a 12 member Executive Policy Committee. It would be composed of the mayor and his or her appointees — the deputy mayor and the chairmen of the four major standing committees of the city — and a councillor from each of the six community committees as elected annually by the community committee councillors. With the mayor and appointees only comprising half of the membership of this overly large body, his or her position would obviously be weaker than envisaged by the Committee of Review in their recommendations.

Edmonton established an executive committee in 1984, replacing the commissioner system that had prevailed for three-quarters of a century. According to Edmonton's mayor at the time, a major reason for the change was that the commissioners had become too powerful, more powerful than the elected representatives. He also felt that pushing decisions back down to the departmental level, as a result of the abolition of the commissioner system, had led to more imaginative and creative decisions.[44] Described as "the nerve centre of city government," Edmonton's executive committee is directed to prepare the annual budget, call for tenders and award contracts, develop long-range policies, act as policy coordinator between the city manager and the council's standing committees, set the council's agenda, and direct and coordinate the flow of information and business between council, its committees, and the administration.[45]

---

[42] *City of Winnipeg Review Committee Final Report*, Winnipeg, Queen's Printer, 1986.

[43] Minister of Urban Affairs, *Strengthening Local Government in Winnipeg: Proposals for Changes to the City of Winnipeg Act*, Discussion Paper, Winnipeg, February 27, 1987.

[44] "A Better Deal for Cities," (Interview with Mayor Laurence Decore), *City Magazine*, Vol. 8, No. 3 & 4, Fall 1986, p. 31-34.

[45] Jack Masson, *op. cit.*, p. 40.

Summary: Assessing the Modifications

As noted earlier in the chapter, the pressures of growth and change highlighted a number of weaknesses in the internal governing machinery of Canadian municipalities. In particular, concerns were expressed about the need for stronger political leadership and executive direction from within council, a clearer focus of accountability and responsibility within the municipal decision-making process, and greater coordination and integration of municipal programs and activities. To what extent have these problems been overcome by the modifications in municipal machinery described above?

It would appear that the establishment of a chief administrative officer system has the potential to effect improved coordination and integration of municipal programs and activities. This system may help to develop an expanded research and analytical capability and the provision of more comprehensive advice and recommendations to council, although much depends on whether complementary changes are introduced in the management and decision-making process as discussed in later chapters dealing with financial management and human resource management. Designating a chief administrative officer also provides a specific focus of accountability and responsibility for the administrative performance of the municipality.

By itself, however, the establishment of a chief administrative officer system does nothing to strengthen *political* leadership and accountability; to the contrary, as discussed above such a system may even detract from the latter objectives by creating a very bureaucratic system and by undermining the power and public status of the council. In fairness, chief administrative officers may also find themselves drawn into the council's realm of activities to fill the void created by the absence of any form of political executive — and this added role may detract from the fulfillment of their primary responsibilities as was noted with respect to the Halifax experience.

**EXECUTIVE COMMITTEES HAVE BEEN
LESS EFFECTIVE THAN CAO SYSTEMS**

The establishment of an executive committee system has proven to be a less effective structural reform in most instances. Most of these committees have lacked political cohesion and have not had any means, except persuasion, to ensure that their initiatives receive the necessary support of council. The effectiveness of these committees has been dependent upon their method of selection and whether or not they were reinforced in their position and activities by the existence of organized political parties on council. As discussed in the next chapter, even where political parties have captured a majority of the seats on council, they have usually been groups alleging a nonpartisan approach who evaded responsibility for council's performance. Instead of strong political leadership, the result was usually the protection of the interests of this group and accountability was certainly not enhanced. The main exception to this pattern has been in a number of the Quebec municipalities, notably the City of Montreal, where council's domination by a political party has provided the basis for strong leadership. While accountability has also been present, the overwhelming dominance of Mayor Drapeau's regime afforded the public little in the way of alternatives.

The establishment of a stronger executive without an accompanying reform in the administrative structure has also hampered the intended benefits. For example, Hickey notes that while Montreal, at the time of his study, had an executive secretary to link the executive and the department heads, "he has been granted neither the authority nor the staff to exercise essential leadership, coordination and direction among the directors."[46] Since taking power, however, the Montreal Citizens' Movement has created the post of Secretary-General, staffed it with a leading Quebec civil servant, and streamlined the organization of services.[47]

Another problem arises when executive committees are not authorized to delegate any administrative powers to the directors of the departments and thus are overly immersed in administrative detail to the neglect of their responsibility for policy development. In contrast, such cities as Quebec, Hull, and Laval have attempted to overcome this situation through the appointment of chief administrative officers (managers), while also retaining the beneficial features of an executive committee responsible to and supported by the council.

While these observations would suggest that the most effective reforms would involve the establishment of a chief administrative officer system *and* an executive committee system supported by organized political parties, it is important to emphasize that changes in organizational form must be accompanied by changes in the municipality's

---

[46] Hickey, *op. cit.*, p. 197.

[47] *City Magazine,* Vol. 10, No. 2, Winnipeg, 1988, p. 6.

management processes if they are to be really effective. These latter changes may be particularly difficult to implement because of the extent of ingrained habits and traditions — as we saw, for example, with the Unicity experience. However, in later chapters we will examine a number of aspects of an improved management and decision-making process.

DEFICIENCIES:
MODIFICATIONS PREOCCUPIED WITH
SERVICE DELIVERY AND EFFICIENCY
LITTLE EMPHASIS ON CITIZEN ACCESS
AND ACCOUNTABILITY

Another deficiency with the modifications to municipal machinery described above is the fact that their preoccupation with efficiency and improved service delivery has meant insufficient attention to such matters as responsiveness, accountability, and citizen participation. This problem is most obvious with the reforms at the administrative level that inevitably emphasize a more bureaucratic system. In this connection, we may recall not only the Lightbody and Masson reservations concerning the commissioner system, but also the observations in Chapter 5 about the regional government reforms in Ontario.

But even at the council level this problem persists. Many of the reforms at this level have favoured smaller, less unwieldy councils and elections at large to produce councillors with a broader viewpoint. Whatever the merits of these changes with respect to council's efficiency, they do nothing to enhance its representative role. The lack of cohesion within council, because of the absence of organized political parties in most municipalities, has also meant that a focus of accountability is missing.

In the final analysis, the real measure of these various modifications to the municipal machinery is the resultant performance by the municipal governments and the extent to which this performance is in accord with the needs and wishes of their local inhabitants. Indeed, before going any further a closer examination of the extent to which municipalities appear to act in accordance with the wishes of the public — as opposed to the property development industry — is long overdue. Unless the public interest is reflected in council decisions, is not a primary justification for local government missing? Chapter 9 attempts to shed some light on this question.

9 Municipalities, the Public, and the Property Industry

Objectives

1. To explore the historic and continuing relationship between local government and property.
2. To assess the prevalence and impact of citizens' groups and of political parties on the operation of municipalities, through profiles of four large Canadian cities.
3. To examine the arguments for and against the introduction of political parties in municipal government.

Introduction

Any examination of Canadian local government reveals a recurring paradox. On the one hand, municipal institutions are praised as the foundation of democracy, the most accessible, responsive governmental institutions we have. On the other hand, municipal governments are also dismissed as nothing more than the servants of the property industry, compliantly providing the basic services that facilitate the excessive growth and destruction of our cities. As is usually the case, a balanced assessment would appear to lie somewhere between these two extremes, although the undeniable influence of the property industry is reflected in the wording of this chapter's title.

It should be noted that while the term *property industry* will be used as a convenient shortform, this term refers to "the complex of business and professionals involved in real estate and land development. It includes developers, builders, investors, lawyers, realtors, architects, planners, and they are involved in the provision of housing, office space, shops, factories and so on."[1]

Historical Limitations

At the outset, it is important to recognize that, notwithstanding the rhetoric that has surrounded the topic, local governments were never

---

[1] "Corporate City: Definitions and References," in *City Magazine,* Vol. 10, No. 4, Spring 1989.

intended to be instruments of mass democracy. Indeed, Magnusson argues that "by putting great numbers of people under the same authorities and giving exclusive powers of decision to elected or appointed officials, early municipal reformers made sure that democracy would not be government by the masses and so would not be a threat to property."[2] He observes that even such oft-quoted "local democrats" as de Tocqueville and Mill favoured the creation of larger units of local government that made mass participation impracticable.[3]

CONFLICTING PERSPECTIVES:
MUNICIPAL INSTITUTIONS SEEN AS —
BASIS FOR MASS PARTICIPATORY DEMOCRACY
JUDICIAL TRIBUNALS LIKE COURTS OF
QUARTER SESSION FROM WHICH THEY EVOLVED
PUBLIC CORPORATIONS WITH
POWERS GRANTED BY CROWN

At best, it would appear that while the democratic virtues of local government were one motivating factor in the establishment of municipal institutions, there were other — and contradictory — motivations. This viewpoint is well expressed by Kaplan and was previously noted in Chapter 2.[4] He explains that even though reformers emphasized the democratic value of local government, the image of local officials as magistrates — arising from the operation of the justices of the peace and the Courts of Quarter Sessions — was too firmly established to be completely dislodged. In any event, landowners found this latter image reassuring, since it seemed to suggest that the new municipal institutions wouldn't embark on costly local improvements but would wait until specific problems were raised and then deal with them individually. In addition to these perspectives, Kaplan identified a third view that saw local government as a public corporation, deriving its power from a Crown-issued charter. He describes the inconsistency of these three perspectives as follows:

---

[2] Warren Magnusson, "Community Organization and Local Self-Government," in Lionel D. Feldman (ed.), *Politics and Government of Urban Canada*, Toronto, Methuen, 1981, p. 61.

[3] *Ibid.*, pp. 61–65.

[4] See Harold Kaplan, *Reform, Planning, and City Politics: Montreal, Winnipeg, Toronto*, Toronto, University of Toronto Press, 1982, pp. 60–63.

One cannot model local government on both a judicial tribunal and a business corporation. Local government cannot be both an experiment in mass participatory democracy and a corporation created by and for property owners.[5]

As already discussed, the turn of the century reform era emphasized the nonpolitical nature of local government and encouraged such features as fewer, larger wards or preferably at large elections; small councils; the transfer of sensitive or complex matters to separate boards of appointed citizens; and the delegation of complete responsibility for administration to expert staff. Quoting the experience in many American cities, Gutstein contends that at large nonpartisan elections had the effect of discouraging political participation.

> By removing the party label, this reform often took away one clue a voter had to a candidate's policy orientation. Second, by removing ... [the] party's role in city politics, this reform took away the best mobilizing forces for informing and involving the electorate. Third, in placing the responsibility for discovering a candidate's merits squarely on the individual citizen, it greatly raised the time and information costs of participation.[6]

Another important consequence of these reforms was the strengthening of the position and influence of municipal staff at the expense of the much-maligned politicians. Kaplan observes that these new professionals were a significant new force.[7] While the positions were less political in the fact that they were not patronage appointments, the municipal staff were more political in the sense that they believed strongly in the need for new policies and structures in their own program areas and in the open advocacy of these objectives. This bureaucratic level was often more cohesive and influential than the council level and was frequently portrayed as representing the public interest, whereas council "was an irritating roadblock, implanted in the mud of small-minded 'politics', to be legitimately circumvented wherever possible."[8]

---

[5] *Ibid.,* p. 63.

[6] Peter A. Lupsha, "The Politics of Urban Change," *Current History,* December 1968, p. 330, quoted in Donald Gutstein, "Vancouver," in Warren Magnusson and Andrew Sancton (eds.), *City Politics in Canada,* Toronto, University of Toronto Press, 1983, p. 197.

[7] Kaplan, *op. cit.,* p. 205.

[8] *Ibid.,* p. 209.

TURN OF CENTURY REFORMERS:
ATTACKED POLITICAL ROLE OF LOCAL GOVERNMENT
REDUCED AVENUES FOR PUBLIC PARTICIPATION
ELEVATED INFLUENCE OF BUREAUCRATS AND EXPERTS
INCREASED INFLUENCE OF BUSINESS INTERESTS

Politics, of course, was the evil influence under constant attack by the turn of the century reformers. What many of them meant by removing politics from local government, however, was removing the political influence that could now be exercised by growing city populations. In this respect, the reformers were quite undemocratic or anti-democratic. As Plunkett and Betts describe the situation:

> ... their intention was not to try to halt the process of making decisions on public policy at the local level. Their intention, rather, was to exclude various groups from the process.... The reformers were interested in restoring the efficiency and effectiveness of municipal service delivery. At the same time, they were plainly concerned with restricting the influence of the cities' burgeoning population of working people upon the conduct of municipal affairs.[9]

This latter viewpoint reflected the fact that many of the reformers were middle class merchants and businessmen who had little sympathy for the democratic aspects of local government. In their minds, the solution was to run local government more like a business. It is ironic that almost 100 years later there is an intense debate underway about the apparently excessive influence over city government of the business community, and especially the property industry.

Preoccupation with Property

The continuing link between local government and property was reflected historically in the restricted franchise at the local level. In the early years only property owners were allowed the right to vote. Baker's study of St. John's, Newfoundland, for example, notes that the incorporation of the city in 1888 was accompanied by strict property qualifications for both voters and candidates. He describes a number of measures that had the effect of ensuring that it was the merchants, lawyers and shopkeepers who dominated — within the colonial legislature as

---

[9] T. J. Plunkett and G. M. Betts, *The Management of Canadian Urban Government,* Kingston, Queen's University, 1978, p. 27.

well as within the city council.[10] Similarly, Higgins observes that when Halifax was incorporated in 1841, its charter limited the vote to only about 800 people who could meet a property qualification, and restricted candidacy for office to a fraction of that number.[11]

Even when the franchise was gradually extended, property owners for a long time retained certain special voting rights, such as voting on money by-laws. A primary justification for this limitation of the franchise was the argument that local governments were mainly concerned with providing services to property. For this reason, the dominant form of municipal revenues — the tax on real property — was regarded as quite appropriate, as was the limitation of voting rights. This meant, however, that just as the increase in tenant population called into question the limited franchise, so did it cast doubts on the continuing appropriateness of the property tax.

MUNICIPAL FRANCHISE:
HISTORICALLY LIMITED TO PROPERTY OWNERS
JUSTIFIED BECAUSE MAINLY SERVICES TO
PROPERTY AND FINANCED BY PROPERTY TAX
INVALIDATED BY GROWTH OF TENANT POPULATION

Critics of the property tax also contended that many of the newer responsibilities of local government were essentially services to people — such as the growing range of social service programs and recreational and cultural facilities — rather than services to property and that, therefore, the continued dependence on the property tax was inappropriate. One result was that a number of studies of local government seized upon this "services to property versus services to people" distinction as a basis for delineating a new division of provincial and local responsibilities. Given the limited financial resources available to municipalities, primarily from the property tax, it was suggested that local governments should particularly deal with services to property, with the provincial level taking over the responsibility for services to people.

---

[10] M. Baker, "William Gilbert Gosling and the Establishment of Commission Government in St. John's, Newfoundland, 1914," *Urban History Review*, Vol. IX, No. 3, February 1981, pp. 37–39.

[11] Donald J. H. Higgins, *Local and Urban Politics in Canada*, Toronto, Gage, 1986, p. 39.

As discussed in Chapter 5, this approach was followed in a number of the local government reform studies of the postwar period, including the Michener Commission in Manitoba and the Byrne Commission in New Brunswick. A somewhat similar approach was used by the Graham Commission in Nova Scotia, which contended that municipal responsibilities should be divided into two groups: "... local services, which are of primarily local benefit or which might best be provided by municipal government, and general services, which are of more general benefit to the province or which the province might best provide."[12]

As Cameron points out, however, there are two shortcomings with this type of analysis.[13] First, it suggests that municipal responsibilities don't extend beyond the provision of services, however defined, and it therefore ignores the representative role of local government. Second, the specific distinction used is vague and inevitably requires an arbitrary allocation of responsibilities. For example, Cameron finds no evidence to support the Graham Commission's assertion that sidewalks provide a local benefit while education is a general benefit. He suspects that the key distinction is found in the Commission's observation that education is one of the most important and costly of the services provided, and questions whether local government can have any serious role to play in our governmental system if it is to be responsible only "for that which is unimportant or inexpensive."[14] While Cameron's analysis may seem very critical, it properly draws attention to a danger that had become far too evident in the evolution of local government responsibilities.

The possibility of local governments becoming involved in the provision of a wide range of services financed by a variety of sources appears to have been largely undermined by the impact of the Depression, World War II, and rapid postwar growth. When the Depression began, local governments exercised the main responsibility for the limited social service programs then in existence. Up until World War II, municipalities could finance their expenditures on these and other programs from local sales tax and even income tax as well as from the property tax. With the onset of the Depression, however, municipalities could not afford the financial burden of relief payments. Neither could a number of provincial

---

[12] Nova Scotia, *Royal Commission on Education, Public Services and Provincial-Municipal Relations, Report,* Halifax, Queen's Printer, 1974, Vol. II, p. 3:22.

[13] David M. Cameron, "Provincial responsibilities for municipal government," in *Canadian Public Administration,* Summer 1980, pp. 222-235.

[14] *Ibid.,* p. 226.

governments for that matter, and the result was federal government intervention, which has since evolved into the modern welfare state. "Canadian municipalities are now almost totally excluded from this crucial area of government policy."[15]

**MUNICIPAL FOCUS NARROWS:
IMPACT OF DEPRESSION, WWII,
AND POSTWAR GROWTH
RISE OF WELFARE STATE
CENTRALIZATION OF FINANCES
LOCAL LEVEL "SQUEEZED OUT"
OF SOCIAL SERVICES FIELD**

The outbreak of World War II brought about a centralization of finances in Canada that ushered in an era of federal-provincial tax-rental and tax-sharing agreements. As the federal and provincial levels competed for the largest possible share of the major tax fields, local governments were increasingly squeezed out, reverting to their historical dependence upon the property tax. For example, Ontario introduced its first unconditional grant in 1936 when it preempted municipal governments from the income tax field. Access to the corporate tax field was lost just five years later when the various provincial governments entered into a wartime agreement with the federal government that included the "rental" of this field to the federal level.[16] Instead of tax sources, municipalities were offered an increasing number of conditional grants directed to ensuring the provision of services and servicing standards felt to be important to the senior levels of government.

The rapid urbanization of the postwar period further confirmed local government's primary role as that of providing the physical services needed to support the continued growth and expansion of our cities. The primary thrust of federal and provincial policies and financial assistance was clearly in this direction, as evidenced by the lending policies of the Central (now Canada) Mortgage and Housing Corporation, and the grants for road construction and for the provision of water supply and sewage disposal systems. Consistent with this viewpoint is Timothy

---

[15] Andrew Sancton, "Conclusion," in Magnusson and Sancton, *op. cit.,* p. 313.

[16] These examples are from the Association of Municipal Clerks and Treasurers of Ontario, *Municipal Administration Program,* Toronto, 1979, Unit One, Lesson Seven, p. 6.

Colton's observation that Metropolitan Toronto was invented to promote what was presumed to be a common and profound interest in rapid urban growth.[17]

Ultimately, a strong public backlash against this narrow role developed. Increasingly active citizens and citizens' groups became a familiar sight in most Canadian cities in the 1960s, often campaigning for seats on council with the avowed intention of stopping the pro-business/property industry bias of existing administrations. While initial gains seemed impressive, the passage of time provides a better perspective on what has been accomplished, and on the ebbs and flows that seem to characterize such local political activity.

Local Politics in Practice: Profiles of Four Cities

In order to appreciate the developments that have been occurring, brief profiles of political activity in four major Canadian cities over the past two decades are presented. In all instances, there is a mixture of citizen group and political party activity. One also finds, in all four instances, that the gains that the citizen movement appeared to make in the 1960s were largely undermined by developments in recent years. By the end of the 1980s, however, there is again at least some evidence of a resurgence of citizen activism, a reaction against what is perceived as the renewed excesses of the property industry and their council allies. With this long term perspective, one is better able to appreciate the enduring nature of this struggle. Pronouncements about the dominance of either side — citizens' groups or developers — are likely to have very limited application, given the shifting influences that are described below.

I Winnipeg

Political party activity in Winnipeg dates from 1919 when the General Strike of that year polarized the city. A Civic Election Committee was formed by downtown businessmen to endorse, and raise funds for, anti-labour candidates. Through the ensuing years this organization, later known as the Metropolitan Election Committee, then the Greater Winnipeg Election Committee, and finally the Independent Citizen Election

---

[17] Timothy J. Colton, *Big Daddy*, Toronto, University of Toronto Press, 1980, p. 175.

Committee (ICEC) continued to elect a majority of the members of council against the efforts of the Independent Labour Party, the CCF and, most recently, the NDP.

PARTY ACTIVITY:
BEGAN IN 1919
PRO-BUSINESS ICEC DOMINANT FORCE OVER YEARS
NDP LIMITED SUCCESS IN EARLY 1980s

While essentially a pro-business local political party, the ICEC insisted that it was not a party at all and that support for its candidates would prevent parties — especially socialist parties — from bringing their politics and policies into the municipal council chamber. As a result, the ICEC was able to avoid accepting the responsibility for leadership in spite of its dominant numerical position within Winnipeg council over the decades.

The year 1972 was a watershed for Winnipeg, ushering in the new Unicity structure of government. As discussed in Chapter 5, a major objective of the new system was the fulfillment of the representative role of local government and the encouragement of increased public participation through special consultative machinery. Of particular note were the resident advisory committees, consisting of citizen representatives who would liaise with community committees of Unicity councillors and thereby provide direct input into the governance of the municipality.

CITIZEN ACTIVITY:
EMPHASIS OF UNICITY REFORM NOT REALIZED
RESIDENT ADVISORY GROUPS MADE LITTLE IMPACT

As discussed in Chapter 5, the great increase in citizen participation in the decision-making process did not materialize. The resident advisory groups and community committees were hampered from the outset by very vague and limited responsibilities. In 1976, the ICEC-dominated council voted to prohibit the community committees from continuing with the allocation of modest sums to various community groups including the resident advisory groups, leaving the latter financially starved. A further setback occurred in 1977 with the revisions to the Unicity legislation. With the reduction in the size of council and in the number of wards, the resident advisory groups found themselves facing greatly increased areas and populations of approximately 100 000, thereby undermining the close contact and familiarity with local issues that was just about their only strength.

Nor is there likely to be much improvement as a result of the recommendations of the 1986 Report of the City of Winnipeg Act Review Committee. While the report recommended that the community committees be given greater powers respecting local plans and zoning and be given financial resources for expenditures on local services and programs, the government's response to date offers no prospect of funding for the community committees.

The ICEC continued its domination through the first decade of new Unicity government in Winnipeg. By the 1980 municipal election, however, ICEC's veneer of nonpartisanship had worn quite thin, and the NDP scored a breakthrough by capturing seven seats on the Unicity Council, with another nine going to independent candidates and the remaining twelve to ICEC candidates. Shortly before the 1983 election, the ICEC announced that it was disbanding. One analyst interprets this step as a clever ploy rather than a sign of collapse.[18] It removed from the scene a name associated with the past council's record, it put off the need for a consensus among the traditional ICEC candidates until after the election, and it avoided the necessity of providing an alternative to the NDP program.

Whatever the motives underlying the dissolution of the ICEC, the election results were quite disappointing for the NDP. They lost one of their seven seats, and nearly lost two others. The local NDP party was undoubtedly hurt by the controversial attempt by the NDP provincial government of Howard Pawley to entrench French as an official language in Manitoba, especially after this became a local referendum issue. In addition, however, the local party was hurt by its own internal divisions between "old guard" members and newer, more progressive members.

The NDP presence on Unicity council was reduced even further — to just two members — in the 1986 municipal elections. The other 27 members elected were all independents, although the majority of them represented the now-disbanded ICEC. Indeed, one assessment identified 20 of these 27 "independents" as actively involved with the Progressive Conservative or Liberal parties,[19] continuing the domination of the ICEC

---

[18] Dave Hall, "Twisted Tale of Intentions," *City Magazine*, Winnipeg, Vol. 6, No. 3, April 1984, p. 14.

[19] This is the assessment of Jeff Lowe, in "Winnipeg: User-Unfriendly," *City Magazine*, Winnipeg, Spring 1988, p. 9.

type of candidate. According to one observer,[20] the provincial NDP again contributed to the poor showing of the local NDP, this time much more directly. He claimed that the provincial party created confusion for the local party by overruling its decisions, deciding for the local party that it would not run a candidate for mayor, and redirecting key party workers to the elections in Saskatchewan and British Columbia, thereby weakening the local campaign.

II Vancouver

As with the case in Winnipeg, it was the threat of political gains by the left that prompted the establishment of a pro-business party in Vancouver. The year was 1936, and three CCF candidates were elected in the city's first at large municipal election. In response, business interests founded the Non-Partisan Association (NPA), its very name designed to conceal its real status as a local political party.

> **CITIZEN ACTIVITY:**
> **EXPANDED IN 1960s**
> **CONCERNED ABOUT PACE AND**
> **LOCATION OF DEVELOPMENTS**
> **OPPOSED TO EXPRESSWAYS**
> **FORMED NEW PARTIES**

The NPA finally ran into increasingly strong citizen opposition in the 1960s, concerning both the pace and the location of developments. The city's urban renewal initiatives, for example, were typical of the time in that they involved the displacement of large numbers of families. The Strathcona Property Owners' and Tenants' Association was established in 1968, devoted to halting further such projects in its neighbourhood. The following year the federal government announced that it would not provide funds for the urban renewal project in Strathcona unless the residents were involved in the planning process. The result was a working committee comprising government officials and members of the Association, "one of the first instances in Canada of citizens sharing this kind of decision-making with government."[21] As launched in 1972, the re-

---

[20] Kent Gerecke, "Winnipeg Hits Bottom," *City Magazine,* Winnipeg, Vol. 9, No. 1, Winter 1986–87, p. 35.

[21] Donald Gutstein, "Vancouver," in Magnusson and Sancton, *op. cit.,* p. 201.

habilitation plan became a model for other such programs. Rather than expropriating homes, it emphasized repairs and renovations and provided stability for the Strathcona neighbourhood.

Vancouver's various expressway schemes also prompted strong public opposition that led to their rejection on several occasions. The June 1967 release of the Vancouver Transportation Study triggered a prolonged debate. Leo notes that "citizen protest against the expressway system culminated in November in an acrimonious public meeting attended by five hundred citizens. Some thirty organizations and individuals prepared briefs for submission at the meeting."[22] More significantly, new political parties were formed to challenge the NPA and its vision of the city.

An important breakthrough appeared to occur in 1972 with the defeat of the NPA and the election of a municipal government controlled by TEAM (The Electors Action Movement). A coalition of reformers and more conservative business interests, TEAM did make some noteworthy changes.[23] It restructured the bureaucracy, replacing the commissioner system with a single city manager with reduced executive powers, and made some moves to open up city hall to public involvement. Within four years, however, TEAM was badly divided and in the 1978 election the NPA re-emerged as the major party on council.[24]

PARTY ACTIVITY:
BUSINESS INTERESTS FOUNDED NPA IN 1936
LOST GROUND TO OTHER LOCAL PARTIES
AND NDP IN 1970s AND EARLY 1980s
DOMINANT AGAIN AT END OF 1980s

But control of council by right-wing interests faced a new challenge in 1980 when Mike Harcourt, a New Democrat, won the mayoralty and the Committee of Progressive Electors (COPE) elected three councillors. COPE had been formed in 1968 by the Vancouver and District Labour

---

[22] Christopher Leo, *The Politics of Urban Development: Canadian Urban Expressway Disputes,* Monographs on Canadian Urban Government – No. 3, Institute of Public Administration, 1977, p. 46.

[23] Gutstein in Magnusson and Sancton, *op. cit.,* pp. 206–209.

[24] For an analysis of Vancouver's political parties by a founding member of TEAM, see Paul Tennant, "Vancouver City Politics," in Feldman, *op. cit.,* pp. 126–147.

Council with the objective of bringing together labour, ratepayer groups, the NDP, and other interested groups to establish a base to enter municipal politics. The left was still in a minority on the 1980 council, however, and discussions were often acrimonious, with members of the NPA, TEAM, and COPE increasingly polarized. In addition to this constraint on the mayor's initiatives, the Social Credit provincial government continued to protect business interests and obviously had misgivings about the election of an NDP mayor.

Harcourt was returned as mayor in 1982, along with four COPE councillors and two independent NDP councillors. Gutstein refers to this election result as the "first successful challenge to business dominance at the local level in the city's 96 year history."[25] However, there were some difficulties in maintaining a progressive voting block on council, and continuing problems with interference from the Social Credit provincial government. Indeed, one book during this period[26] expressed concern that local autonomy was being threatened by the neo-conservative forces in power provincially and their view that local authorities should not be allowed to follow policies contrary to the market-oriented revival being promoted provincially.

On the surface, the 1984 election results were quite similar to those of 1982. Harcourt was re-elected mayor, along with five progressive members — four of them from COPE. Opposing them were three members from the NPA and two from TEAM. According to Gutstein,[27] the polarization of the city was completed with this election. As he saw it, Vancouver is really two cities: a working class east side city and a middle class west side city — which elect two entirely different councils.

The 1986 election results were quite dramatic, bringing Vancouver's developers back into power at Vancouver's city hall. The NPA captured nine of the eleven seats on council — including its mayoral candidate, developer Gordon Campbell — and eight of nine seats on the School Board. According to Gutstein,[28] Campbell was successful in attracting

[25] Donald Gutstein, "Vancouver: Progressive Majority Impotent," *City Magazine,* Winnipeg, Vol. VI, No. 1, p. 12.

[26] Warren Magnusson, William K. Carroll, Charles Doyle, Monika Langer and R. B. J. Walker (eds.), *The New Reality: The Politics of Restraint in British Columbia,* Vancouver, NewStar Books, 1984.

[27] Donald Gutstein, "Civic Election Wars," in *City Magazine,* Winnipeg, Vol. 7, No. 3, Summer 1985, p. 12.

[28] Donald Gutstein, "Vancouver Voters Swing Right," *City Magazine,* Winnipeg, Vol. 9, No. 1, Winter 1986–87, p. 30. The brief outline that follows is based on the Gutstein article.

the moderate voters in spite of his right wing, pro-development record, especially when the alternative was Harry Rankin of COPE, a long time socialist councillor who was seen by many as quite radical.

Campbell easily won re-election in 1988 and the NPA maintained its majority on council. COPE only managed to increase its representation from two to three, with Harry Rankin regaining his council seat. If Campbell can continue to present a relatively moderate image, he may be difficult to unseat in the near future.

III Montreal

The modern period of local politics in Montreal can be dated from 1914 according to Guy Bourassa.[29] Since that time, we have witnessed a succession of powerful and popular mayors, often gaining re-election. The regimes over which they presided, however, were often corrupt and financially strapped, and the provincial government had to intervene on a number of occasions, notably in 1918 when the province virtually took over the running of the city by appointing a five member administrative commission.[30] Corruption within the city government finally led to a judicial inquiry, prompted by the urgings of the Civic Action League and its offshoot, the Committee for Public Morality. One of the investigators for this inquiry was Jean Drapeau, who became the Civic Action League's successful candidate for mayor in 1954 and the rest, as they say, is history!

> **PARTY ACTIVITY:**
> **DRAPEAU AND CIVIC PARTY HELD**
> **POWER FROM 1960–86**
> **MCM GAINED POWER IN 1986**

Drapeau's first term of office was a difficult one, because the Civic Action League had not gained control over the council itself. After losing the 1957 election, Drapeau disassociated himself from the Civic Action League but managed to attract most of their city councillors to his new

---

[29] Guy Bourassa, "The Political Elite of Montreal: From Aristocracy to Democracy," in Lionel D. Feldman and Michael D. Goldrick, *The Politics and Government of Urban Canada,* Toronto, Methuen, 1976, pp. 146–155.

[30] Andrew Sancton, "Montreal," in Magnusson and Sancton, *op. cit.,* p. 67. The following outline of events leading up to Drapeau's long tenure in office is largely based on Sancton's material.

Civic Party. It was as head of this highly disciplined party that he returned to power as mayor in 1960 — a position he was to hold until his retirement prior to the 1986 election.

By the end of the 1960s, however, there were signs of growing citizen activism in Montreal. Potentially strong opposition to Drapeau first surfaced in 1970 in the form of the Front d'action politique (FRAP), a grouping of trade unions and left-wing nationalist organizations.[31] Whatever prospects this organization had were dashed by the FLQ kidnapping crisis and Drapeau's success in linking FRAP with the outlawed terrorist group and in capitalizing on the public's desire for stability and security.

CITIZEN ACTIVITY:
TRADE UNION AND LEFT-WING NATIONALIST
ORGANIZATIONS PROVIDED EARLY OPPOSITION TO DRAPEAU
JOINED BY MIDDLE CLASS GROUPS CONCERNED ABOUT
PRESERVING NEIGHBOURHOODS AND OPENING UP GOVERNMENT
DEVELOPMENT ISSUES STILL TROUBLING
CITIZENS UNDER MCM REGIME

Over the next several years opposition to Drapeau grew, not only from radicals who deplored his failure to provide sufficient housing and social and recreational services in the poorer sections of the city but also from middle class groups concerned with stopping high-rise development, saving the city's older buildings and neighbourhoods, and forcing a more democratic, open system of government.[32] These opposition forces came together in 1974 to form the Montreal Citizen's Movement (MCM), which made a dramatic impact on the November municipal elections. Drapeau received only 55.1% of the popular vote for mayor — almost a rebuff in relation to his past results — and his Civic Party won only 36 seats on council, with the MCM winning 18 and a group called Democracy Montreal winning another.

The following year the provincial government took over responsibility for the preparations for the 1976 Olympic Games because of the city administration's poor performance. For the first time there was also clear evidence of corruption within the city administration. One might have expected, therefore, that the opposition forces would consolidate their position and prepare for the overthrow of the Drapeau regime in

---

[31] *Ibid.,* p. 73.

[32] *Ibid.*

the 1978 election. Instead, the MCM split apart and was taken over by a group of radical socialists. Their policy orientation alienated the newly elected provincial government of the Parti Québècois which, in any event, was not anxious to tangle with Drapeau and was quite prepared to stay out of city politics if Drapeau would keep his influential voice out of the sovereignty-association debate. A new party, the Municipal Action Group (essentially a front for Federal Liberals) emerged in time for the election, but Drapeau was re-elected easily and his Civic Party won 52 of the 54 seats on council.[33]

The resurrection of the MCM in the early 1980s was largely due to their new leader, Jean Doré.[34] While Drapeau was returned in 1982 and his Civic Party captured 39 of the 57 council seats, popular support was down — almost 18% less with respect to Drapeau. The 1986 election saw a massive victory for the MCM, with only one Civic Party councillor and two independents elected to council. According to Milner, the Doré-led MCM "appeared reasonable and approachable, especially when contrasted with Drapeau's Gaullist style; its hammering at everyday bread and butter issues corresponded more closely to the emerging public mood than Drapeau's seeming preoccupation with grand projects."[35]

In contrast to the autocratic, secretive style long followed by Drapeau, the new administration is characterized by a cautious and consensual approach. Consultation is the watchword. The fact that little of substance has changed in Montreal is, in Milner's view, due less to the style of the new administration than to the nature of power at the municipal level. He points out that even a very activist administration is powerless to act in many spheres of local concern and cites the powers allocated to separate local boards and to the upper tier government of the Montreal Urban Community.

However, Milner also notes that grass roots involvement in the MCM has apparently diminished. Developers and businesspeople have been busy courting the new administration and party activists find little scope for their activities. Their best leaders have become city councillors or political advisors. Milner's assessment of what has happened bears repeating:

---

[33] *Ibid.*, p. 76.

[34] According to Henry Milner, "The Montreal Citizens' Movement, Then and Now," in *Quebec Studies*, No. 6, 1988, on which the following discussion is based.

[35] *Ibid.*, p. 5.

> The syndrome is a classic one: the reformist movement takes power and effectively moves toward the centre of the spectrum, attempting to rule in the name of the electorate as a whole, not merely the party activists, who find their activities largely confined to vindicating such limited actions, raising money and recruiting new members. And with no opposition left in City Hall, the external enemy is gone: there's no one, out there, to fight.[36]

At least for the present, therefore, the main threats to the MCM are probably internal, not external. The party must not sacrifice (or appear to sacrifice) its goals and principles because of its admission to the corridors of power.

IV Toronto

Citizen activism became prominent in Toronto during the 1960s. A well documented example concerned an urban renewal scheme for the Treffan Court area of the city, which proposed the usual demolition of buildings. Citizen opposition led, as in Vancouver, to a new approach in which the affected citizens became involved in the development of the urban renewal plans.[37] More generally, the extent of high-rise commercial redevelopment and apartment construction was threatening middle and upper class neighbourhoods. Opposition to such projects prompted the establishment or revival of ratepayers' and residents' groups, which became increasingly aggressive in their opposition. "In 1968, A Confederation of Residents' and Ratepayers' Associations (CORRA) was established as a co-ordinating agency; it not only linked the middle-class organizations with one another, but brought them into contact with community groups being formed in poorer neighbourhoods."[38] Equally significant was the creation of the Stop Spadina, Save Our City, Coordinating Committee (SSSOCCC).[39]

---

[36] *Ibid.,* p. 8.

[37] An excellent analysis of this episode is found in Graham Fraser, *Fighting Back,* Toronto, Hakkert, 1972.

[38] Warren Magnusson, "Toronto," in Magnusson and Sancton, *op. cit.,* p. 115.

[39] See Higgins, *op. cit.,* pp. 282–287, and Christopher Leo, *The Politics of Urban Development: Canadian Urban Expressway Disputes,* Monographs on Canadian Urban Government, No. 3, Toronto, Institute of Public Administration of Canada, 1977.

CITIZEN ACTIVITY:
GROUPS ESTABLISHED TO PRESERVE
NEIGHBOURHOODS FROM URBAN RENEWAL
AND HIGH-RISE DEVELOPMENTS
OPPOSITION TO SPADINA
RENEWED ACTIVITY IN LATE 1980s
BECAUSE OF RAPID DEVELOPMENT OF AREA

Both inner-city poor who felt ignored and middle class urban conservatives who felt their neighbourhoods threatened agreed that city council had sold out to development interests. In addition to opposing specific development projects, the citizens' movement became influential in the municipal election process. The 1969 election brought a minority of reformers onto city council, and they were quite effective in defining their issues and concerns. The 1972 election appeared to be a breakthrough (just as it had appeared to be in Vancouver) with the election of a majority of reformers on council and a self-proclaimed member of the reform group — in the person of David Crombie — as mayor.

PARTY ACTIVITY:
CROMBIE AND REFORM GROUP GAINED CONTROL IN 1972
SOON SPLIT INTO RADICALS (REFORMERS) AND MODERATES
REFORM COUNCILLORS OFTEN IDENTIFIED WITH NDP
NEW REFORM BLOCK IN 1988, BUT AGAIN NOT COHESIVE

Once elected, however, David Crombie operated as a moderate and, in fact, voted against the reform councillors on many of the major issues facing council.[40] While he was genuinely concerned about the threat to neighbourhoods posed by the excessively pro-growth mentality of previous councils, Crombie was no less committed to private property and private enterprise. Rather, he wanted to find a way of providing continued development without the disruption and dislocation that had accompanied it in the recent past.[41]

The reform group that had appeared to capture control of council in 1972 soon split into moderates and more militant reformers, with the

---

[40] See Jon Caufield, *The Tiny Perfect Mayor,* Toronto, James Lorimer and Company, 1974.

[41] Magnusson in Magnusson and Sancton, *op. cit.,* p. 119.

latter becoming increasingly critical of Crombie's moderate policies. Ironically, while reform councillors continued to be elected throughout the 1970s, one of them — Michael Goldrick — persuasively argues that the election of 1972 was not the beginning but "the zenith of the reform movement."[42] As he explains, the moderates were satisfied that the reform movement would now ensure that neighbourhoods were protected, the automobile would be treated with common sense, and the style of development would be modified — all objectives of the middle class. The hard line reformers elected from working class wards, however, believed that the objective was one of redistributing wealth and power.

> They wanted real, not token, decision-making power shifted to neighbourhoods, not only the style of development controlled but its pace, location and ownership subject to public decision; they challenged private property rights exercised by financial institutions and development corporations and attacked the fortresses of civil service power.[43]

After the 1974 election, six of the more radical reformers established the reform caucus, a disciplined group that attempted to develop alternative policies to those proposed by the moderates and the "Old Guard." While it was successful in expressing the interests of working class people, the reform caucus suffered from a negative, obstructionist image in the eyes of the media and from internal differences, partly based on personality conflicts.

A key figure was John Sewell, undoubtedly the most conspicuous and widely identified member of the reform group, and a community activist who had been earlier associated with a number of the citizen confrontations with city hall.[44] Sewell was a very independent minded politician and, while he had made some unsuccessful attempts to build a reform party around himself, when he ran for mayor in 1978 it was as an independent.[45] After one very controversial term, especially in relation to Sewell's defence of various inner-city minorities and his demands for police reform, he was defeated by Arthur Eggleton, a Liberal with strong

---

[42] Michael Goldrick, "The Anatomy of Urban Reform in Toronto," in *City Magazine,* May-June 1978, p. 36, an article that provides an excellent analysis of the reform group to that point in time.

[43] *Ibid.*

[44] For his personal reflections on these experiences, see John Sewell, *Up Against City Hall,* Toronto, James Lewis and Samuel, 1972.

[45] Magnusson in Magnusson and Sancton, *op. cit.,* p. 123.

ties to the business community. Eggleton has been re-elected throughout the 1980s.

In the meantime, however, reform councillors continued to be elected
to council, although increasingly identified with the NDP. By 1980 they
had nine of the twenty-three seats on council, with all but one of the
victorious candidates having run with offical party backing.[46] The differences between reformers and old guard seemed more muted by the
early 1980s, partly as a result of the policies that had been adopted by
the councils of the time and partly because the economic decline in the
country had reduced the growth pressures.

It was this economic downturn, Frisken claims, that most influenced
the rapid decline in Toronto city council's commitment to restricting the
height and density of downtown buildings.[47] Even John Sewell, during his
one term as mayor, gave high priority to keeping industrial jobs in the
city and attracting new ones. By the mid-1980s, critics referred to a "let's
make a deal" mode of decision making to signify the city's willingness to
allow developers building heights and densities that greatly exceeded
the limits specified in its Central Area Plan.[48] By this time, as well, a building boom was underway in Toronto, highlighted by such major projects
as the new domed stadium and the development of Harbourfront and
railway lands at the south end of the city. Indeed, one observer described the air at city hall as full of "echoes of the 1960s," the heyday of
the developers and their lobbyists.[49] He claimed that city hall was once
again firmly under the control of the development industry, which had
simply acquired a new level of sophistication in its dealings with the
council — a council that was more pro-development than any since the
end of the 1960s.

If the developers were back, so were the citizens' groups — although
perhaps not to the same degree. Frisken states that citizen group activity has been both limited and fragmented since the mid-1970s, posing
little threat to incumbent aldermen or the conservative make-up of council as a whole.[50] Part of the problem, she notes, is that citizens' groups

---

[46] *Ibid.*, p. 122.

[47] Frances Frisken, *City Policy-Making in Theory and Practice: The Case of
Toronto's Downtown Plan*, Local Government Case Study No. 3, London,
University of Western Ontario, 1988, pp. 98–99.

[48] *The Globe and Mail*, May 23, 1984, as quoted in Frisken, p. 81.

[49] Geoffrey York, "The Politics of Influence," *Toronto*, November 1986, p. 50.

[50] Frisken, *op. cit.*, p. 93.

have become very issue-specific, lacking the tendency toward coalition building that characterized political pressure groups in the early 1970s — such as the previously cited examples of CORRA and SSSOCCC. Nonetheless, such groups as the Federation of North York Resident Associations and resident associations in Markham and Vaughan have been quite conspicuous.

Given this background, the results of the 1988 municipal elections in Toronto were quite striking. The voters defeated two pro-development aldermen, voted in a majority of designated reform candidates, and elected reform candidates to fill six of the eight city positions on the Metropolitan Toronto council.[51] More specifically, nine of the seventeen members of Toronto City Council are considered to be the reform group, of which six are NDP members. One of the nine was acclaimed to office, but all others were endorsed by Reform Toronto, a citizens' coalition that was established out of opposition to the pro-development old guard at city hall.

It is noteworthy that a number of other Ontario municipal election results in 1988 appeared to reflect a victory for citizens' groups over pro-development forces. For example, the heads of council in both Richmond Hill and Markham, very rapidly growing areas just north of Toronto, were both defeated after a series of reports about the allegedly excessive influence of the development industry in their municipalities. Cottage owners also used their voting power to elect councillors concerned with the environment and commited to slowing the pace of growth in a number of Ontario's resort areas.[52]

Time will tell, however, how effective and long lasting this renewed citizen power really is. In the case of Toronto, for example, we must remember that the majority group of nine reformers is not really one homogeneous group at all, and does not necessarily share a common vision of what is best for the city. If one recalls the fate of the reform majority that had supposedly captured power at the beginning of the 1970s, one can appreciate the challenge facing this new group.[53]

---

[51] Michael Valpy, "Voters Demonstrate Power of Ballot Box," *Globe and Mail,* November 16, 1988, p. A8.

[52] "Cottagers Pick Slow-Growth Councillors," *Globe and Mail,* November 16, 1988, p. A24.

[53] Indeed, most observers would conclude that it failed its first real test when it could not hold together and reverse the outgoing council's approval of the Bay Adelaide high rise development. See Kent Gerecke, "The New Vocabulary/ The New Toronto," in *City Magazine,* Vol. 10, No. 4, Spring 1989, pp. 24–25.

Local Politics in Practice:
Some General Observations

Based largely on the experiences of the four cities described, some general observations can be made about the nature of local political activity in Canada.

(1) First, there is continuing resistance to overt political party activity at the local level. The word overt should be stressed, since many local elected members are widely known to be associated with one of the provincial or national political party organizations. This type of association is apparently quite acceptable to the voters, but a more negative reaction could be expected if the same individuals were to run locally with a specific party affiliation.

An interesting example of this mind-set is provided by the results of the 1969 municipal elections for the City of Toronto. The Liberal Party, fresh from its 1968 national election victory, was interested in establishing a stronger base in Toronto, partly as a necessary prerequisite to the overthrow of the long-entrenched Progressive Conservative provincial government. The decision to enter a slate of candidates for municipal office was hotly debated, however, and the internal split in the party on this issue resulted in a less than wholehearted effort in the ensuing election.[54] Whatever the reasons, the election results were not heartening for the national parties. The Liberal Party's candidate for mayor, Stephen Clarkson, finished third with fewer than half as many votes as the victorious William Dennison. Significantly, Dennison had refused to run as an NDP candidate even though he was closely associated with the party. Only three candidates of the NDP and two of the Liberal candidates were elected as aldermen.[55]

(2) A second observation is that where we find political parties at the local level, they are not usually branches of the long-established provincial and federal parties but are purely local creations — often in the guise of a non-partisan group whose primary objective is to keep party politics out of local government, especially if it comes in the form of the

---

[54] For an examination of this election campaign by one of the key participants, see Stephen Clarkson, *City Lib,* Toronto, Hakkert, 1972. See also the exchange of views between Clarkson and J. L. Granatstein in Jack K. Masson and James Anderson (eds.), *Emerging Party Politics in Urban Canada,* Toronto, McClelland and Stewart, 1972, pp. 60-67.

[55] Donald J. H. Higgins, *Urban Canada: Its Government and Politics,* Toronto, Macmillan, 1977, p. 239.

NDP. This pattern has already been noted in connection with the rise of the Civic Election Committee in Winnipeg in 1919 and the Non-Partisan Association (NPA) in Vancouver in 1936. In addition, for over two decades after 1934, elections for Edmonton's council "revolved around the slate-making activities of the Citizens' Committee...."[56] This group splintered in 1959 when its leader, William Hawrelak, resigned as mayor after conflict of interest irregularities. While the number of new factions reached the point where local parties really no longer existed, "aldermen sharing a business orientation retained total domination of council."[57]

BRANDON EXAMPLE:
LOCAL ESTABLISHMENT ORGANIZES TO
KEEP OUT (SOCIALIST) PARTY POLITICS

One further example is provided by the experience of Brandon, Manitoba, in which the local establishment successfully resisted an effort by the municipal NDP to elect members to city council.[58] The NDP challenge was mounted after the provincial NDP government elected in 1969 implemented recommendations that introduced a ward system in Brandon. In September 1971 plans were announced for a nominating meeting to choose a slate of NDP candidates in order to "break the domination of council by Conservatives and Liberals."[59] The meeting led to the nomination of a candidate for mayor and candidates for seven of the ten aldermanic positions on council.

The response of the local establishment took a rather familiar form. A Citizens Independent Voters Election Committee (CIVEC) was formed to encourage and support candidates who would be independent of party politics. All of those elected to the executive of CIVEC were active in the Conservative and Liberal parties.[60] By early October CIVEC had endorsed candidates in all ten wards (seven of whom were incumbents) as well as the incumbent mayor. On October 27th there was a 55% voter

---

[56] James Lightbody, "Edmonton," in Magnusson and Sancton, *op. cit.*, p. 261.

[57] *Ibid.*, p. 264.

[58] See Errol Black, "Small City Politics: The Brandon Experience," in *City Magazine*, Winnipeg, Vol. 6, Summer 1984, pp. 28–35, on which the following outline is based.

[59] *Ibid.*, p. 29.

[60] *Ibid.*, p. 31.

turnout, the largest since the Second World War — and it is apparent that many of them turned out in order to support CIVEC. No NDP candidates were elected, and most received very significantly fewer votes than the victorious CIVEC candidates.

In the aftermath of the defeat, a number of explanations were offered for the poor showing of the NDP. These included the rather hurried preparations for entering the municipal election campaign, the overly comprehensive and detailed nature of the election platform, and the lack of credible candidates. Most of all, however, the results were attributed to the effectiveness of CIVEC's campaign against party politics at the local level.

There has been little change since this 1971 election. The local establishment continues to dominate city council, in many instances through representatives who are active in the Conservative and Liberal parties.

(3) A third observation, which follows closely from this second one, is that the NDP — of all the national parties — has shown by far the most persistence and commitment to the introduction of party politics at the local level. As a result, "if other national parties are not to be outflanked in the organization of the core metropolitan areas, the necessary response has to be an electoral challenge."[61]

It is unclear, however, how quickly municipal elections in our major urban areas will become party contests. Even the NDP contests municipal elections only sporadically and selectively. Experience has shown that there is still strong voter resistance to the overt introduction of party politics at the local level. Moreover, the other two national parties have continued to devote their energies to working behind the scenes supporting, and sometimes organizing, local groups of candidates who would oppose the NDP. About the only certainty is that the increase in partisan activity will continue to generate controversy and debate as to its appropriateness.

(4) A fourth observation is that the relative influence of citizens' groups versus development interests seems to wax and wane, depending in large part on the underlying economic conditions. In admittedly oversimplified terms, the experience of the past couple of decades suggests that pro-development forces can prevail for some considerable period until their perceived excesses prompt renewed citizen activism leading to changes on city council. The citizen activism is difficult to sustain, however, and pro-development forces again begin to assert themselves.

---

[61] Lightbody in Masson and Anderson, *op. cit.*, p. 199.

Thus, for example, the so-called citizens' movement of the 1960s appeared largely to disappear during the 1970s. Much of the progress in reducing the influence of the property industry and the business community generally over council operations seemed to have dissipated. Whether in Vancouver, Toronto, Winnipeg or even Montreal, the "gains" of citizens' groups and the election successes of "reform councillors" were not consolidated. Instead, the traditional pro-business councillors regained some of the ascendancy in the first three of these cities, and quickly came to terms with the MCM in Montreal. More recently, however, we see renewed citizen activism, highlighted by the dramatic changes in Toronto's 1988 election results.

(5) Part of the explanation for this waxing and waning of citizen influence can be found in a fifth observation, that reformers upon gaining power tend to moderate their positions and objectives. As Lorimer points out, "the thrust for democratic reforms has been blunted by citizen-oriented politicians once in office. They are inclined to take their own election as an indication that the present political system can work reasonably well...."[62] This pattern was previously noted with respect to the experience of Toronto's city council after the election of reformers in 1972. It is also apparent in Milner's comments, quoted earlier, about MCM's move toward the centre in Montreal.

(6) A sixth point concerns the influence on local political developments of the provincial party in power and its prevailing attitude and philosophy. This point is obvious in one sense, given the all-pervasive nature of provincial controls over local governments. But, over and above that fundamental relationship, local political actors may be reinforced or undermined in their efforts depending on the position taken by the provincial governing party.

Three examples should suffice. Frisken, in discussing the increasingly pro-growth mentality of Toronto's council, stated that "in following this course of action the council majority acted consistently with, and sometimes directly in response to, signals or directives from other governments. Ontario Municipal Board and Ontario Cabinet decisions favoured a more rapid pace of downtown development than was provided for in the Plan...."[63]

---

[62] James Lorimer, "Introduction: The Post-developer Era for Canada's Cities Begins," in *City Magazine Annual 1981,* Toronto, James Lorimer and Company, 1981, p. 9.

[63] Frisken, *op. cit.,* p. 90.

Mention has also been made of the constraints under which Vancouver operated in relation to the provincial Social Credit government after it elected an NDP mayor. More generally, Magnusson and others have warned of the threat to local autonomy in British Columbia because of the provincial government's apparent viewpoint that it should curb local initiatives contrary to its governing philosophy.[64] Problems can also arise even where provincial and local parties share the same philosophy, according to Gerecke's description, above, of the provincial NDP's interference with the election efforts of the local NDP in Winnipeg.

(7) A seventh, and final, observation relates to the effect of the underlying economic conditions on the local political patterns that unfold. Lorimer, for example, contends that it was the downturn in economic activity toward the end of the 1970s, and the resultant reduction in urban growth pressures, which led to more moderation in city hall — not the citizens' movement or the election of reform councils.[65] According to this school of thought, the prominence of developers and the pro-growth mentality only abated because these features were not compatible with the changed economic conditions.

This viewpoint is certainly consistent with what has been witnessed in major urban centres in the face of the rapid expansion of the economy in the second half of the 1980s. In Toronto, in particular, a "let's make a deal" mentality characterized city council's response to the extremely strong growth pressures of the time. To a considerable extent, then, one can expect local political activity to increase and decrease in response to underlying economic performance and growth and development pressure.

At the same time, however, it must be appreciated that local governments themselves are — or could be — major influences on the economic growth and development that occurs. The one essential power that is largely controlled by the local level relates to the regulation of land use. Local governments are also responsible, albeit with substantial funding assistance from the senior levels, for providing many of the basic services that constitute the infrastructure necessary for growth and development to occur.

---

[64] Magnusson et al, "The New Reality," *op. cit.*

[65] *Ibid.*

**TWO VIEWS OF DEVELOPMENT:
INFLUENCES LOCAL POLITICAL
ACTIVITY AND DECISIONS
ALSO INFLUENCED BY LOCAL
POLITICAL DECISIONS
CHALLENGE FOR LOCAL LEVEL —
BE PROACTIVE, NOT REACTIVE**

Local government's continuing preoccupation with property, therefore, can be seen as a two-edged sword. Yes, this preoccupation has
contributed to the view that municipalities are too narrowly focused in
their activities, and that they act too much as servants of the property
industry. On the other hand, the close ties to property give local governments an opportunity to be principal players in shaping the future
growth and development of the major urban centres (and by extension,
the country) if they have the vision and the commitment to set the future
course rather than react to events.

Political Parties in Local
Government: A Closer Look

Much of the preceding discussion about local political activity in our
cities has concerned political parties — their advancement at the local level or their rejection. Parties were also cited earlier, in Chapter 5,
as a potentially key element of a strengthened political executive. It
is time to consider, therefore, what it is about organized political parties that allegedly makes them such an important addition to the municipal organization.

Advantages of Political Parties
in Local Government

Basically, parties perform the same task locally as they do at the senior levels: they organize the council into a governing group and an
opposition group. The creation of a governing majority is significant
because it provides the basis for concerted action. If heads of council
are chosen by council, they would presumably be leading members
of the majority party or group on council and thus would have a
power base to support their leadership. If they in turn choose their

executive committee from this ruling group then the committee has cohesiveness because of the common party affiliation and is somewhat analogous to a federal or provincial cabinet. The creation of a strong executive centred on the mayor is felt to be necessary for decisive action on the increasingly complex issues facing the municipality, especially in large urban areas.

ADVANTAGES:
PROVIDE GOVERNMENT AND OPPOSITION
LEADERSHIP AND FOCUS OF ACCOUNTABILITY
BETTER DEBATE AND VOTING TURNOUT

Organized political parties provide the potential for not only strong leadership but also more effective scrutiny of the municipality's activities through an organized opposition or alternative governing group. As a result there is a group within council pledged to scrutinize and criticize municipal activities, an important role that is normally left to everybody — and nobody. The mayor and executive committee members need to retain the confidence of council since they owe their positions to council, not the electorate. Those who find this situation somehow less democratic might reflect on the fact that this is the same process followed in choosing our heads of government at the senior levels. If it is felt that the head of council must be elected at large, then why do we not choose premiers and prime ministers that way?

In addition, with political parties the operations of council become more understandable and accountable to the public. Since councillors run as a group on the basis of specific programs, there is a greater likelihood that citizens will vote on the basis of substantive issues and policies instead of on the usual basis of selection among personalities. It is also argued that an election campaign organized around opposing parties and alternative approaches generates greater public interest and a higher voting turnout. In part this is because parties can be expected to play their usual roles of aggregating interests, mobilizing public support, and attempting to draw more citizens into the political arena. More importantly, at the end of a term the public can attach responsibility for performance to the governing party since this group had the means to effect change. It is not possible for a ruling party to evade responsibility for action or inaction as individual councillors can and do.

Disadvantages of Political Parties in Local Government

There are, of course, a number of arguments against the introduction of organized political parties at the local level. Chief among these is the assertion that parties would introduce division where none exists or should exist. "There is no political way to build a road," claim proponents of this viewpoint that reflects the lingering notion that local government activities are administrative not political in nature. Yet, if the actual construction of a road is a matter of engineering not politics, the decision on where to locate a particular road is certainly political. The decision on whether the traffic problem in question should be solved through building a road or providing an alternative form of public transit is also clearly political. The decision on whether the scarce financial resources of the municipality should be used on transportation or some other pressing need is again political. Indeed, if the municipal council is concerned with establishing priorities in relation to conflicting public needs and demands, its role must be political. If the council is not to be charged with this task, one may well question the value of a separate level of local government. Since political decisions are an essential element of municipal operations then, they are not brought into the local arena by parties. Rather, parties — for reasons already advanced — may help to make these unavoidable political decisions more systematic and also more accountable to the public.

DISADVANTAGES:
CAUSE UNNECESSARY DIVISION
BRING CORRUPTION
NATIONAL PARTIES WOULD NEGLECT LOCAL ISSUES
LOCAL PARTIES LACK COHESION —
REMOVING BASIS FOR LEADERSHIP
AND ACCOUNTABILITY

At the same time, it must be acknowledged that parties tend to exaggerate differences and to criticize excessively for purely partisan purposes. These traits have been all too evident in the actions of the parties operating at the senior levels of government. Kaplan provides a good example of this excessive polarization in the operation of party politics in the City of Montreal in the postwar period.[66] He notes that the Lique

---

[66] Kaplan, *op. cit.*, p. 380.

d'Action Civique (LAC), the first local party with which Drapeau was associated, found itself opposing a 1956 public housing project that it would otherwise have supported because the project was associated with Quebec Premier Duplessis and the anti-LAC element of council. Similarly, urban renewal reports in 1959 and 1960 were judged by their source rather than their contents, and there were frequent deadlocks that at times paralyzed the administration of the city. Opponents of party politics in local government decry this type of division.

A second major objection to parties is the feeling that they would bring corruption and unsavoury practices into local government. This feeling was undoubtedly strongly influenced by the excesses of party politics and the spoils system in the United States in the period leading up to the turn of the century reform era. Nor were such practices entirely absent from Canadian local government, as illustrated by discussions in Chapter 3. However, it should be remembered that it is people who are potentially corruptible, not that specialized subgroup known as politicians. If there are opportunities for dishonesty and abuse, some people may succumb to the temptation, but they will presumably do so whether they are individual councillors or members of an organized political party.

An important qualification in all of this discussion is the nature of the political parties involved. In particular, the discussion of potential advantages presumes a balanced situation with two or more parties that would alternate in power. If one party is very dominant and controls council for many years, then there is undoubtedly more likelihood of insensitivity to public opinion and other abuses — traits exhibited by the provincial and federal governments in the same situation. Here again, Montreal provides an example from the lengthy regime of Jean Drapeau and his Civic Party. Higgins observes that:

> Indicative of how unprogressive is the City of Montreal is the fact that in the whole month that I was there conducting research, the city council did not meet at all—and there are no real committees of council which could have met, aside from the powerful executive committee, which met only in camera.[67]

Another key consideration is whether the parties involved are local or are branches of the existing provincial and federal parties. In the latter case, the concern is that the parties would likely neglect local issues and

---

[67] Donald J. H. Higgins, "Progressive City Politics and the Citizen Movement: A Status Report," in *City Magazine,* op. cit., p. 93.

become essentially a grass roots organization for the senior level party. There is also the danger that local election results will reflect the popularity or unpopularity of the "parent" parties rather than the positions taken by the parties on local matters. This pattern has been noted in Britain, where many municipal council elections are contested by the national Labour and Conservative parties.

On the other hand, local parties are often short-lived coalitions of local interests that display very little ongoing discipline or concerted action once elected. Indeed, they may more properly be described as "factions" that reappear under a variety of names at election time and attempt to ensure the election of certain types of candidate, but do not exercise disciplined party voting in council.[68] As we have seen, Canada's limited experience with political parties in local government has been very much of the latter category involving factions. The major national and provincial parties have not been actively involved in municipal elections — at least overtly — until fairly recently. The main exceptions were the early CCF efforts to elect councillors in Western cities such as Vancouver and Winnipeg.

WHY LIMITED ACTIVITY AT LOCAL LEVEL BY NATIONAL PARTIES?

A number of reasons have been suggested for this absence of activity by the major parties.[69] Both British and American influences were at work. To the extent that the Canadian system of local government was modelled upon that of the British, it may also have inherited the nonpartisan approach that originally characterized the British system. A more direct influence was doubtless the United States-initiated reform movement at the turn of the century with its strong emphasis on the nonpolitical role of local government. Canadian local government embraced this concept even though it had never had the excesses — especially the party bosses and political machines — that inspired it in the United States.

---

[68] See Harold Kaplan, "Electoral Politics in the Metro Area," in Masson and Anderson, *op. cit.*

[69] See Higgins, *Urban Canada*, op. cit., pp. 236–238, and Lightbody in Masson and Anderson, *op. cit.*, pp. 194–197.

Another factor was simply that the national parties weren't all that interested in contesting municipal elections, seeing little to be gained from such efforts. Consistent with the justification of local government as a training ground, the senior parties did recruit some of their candidates from this level, but they found that they could do so without becoming directly involved. In any event, municipal governments were very much constrained by their legal dependence upon their provincial governments and by the program and funding decisions of both the provincial and federal levels. "Because of the lack of significant independent authority, the sandbox politics of City Hall offered little incentive for organized partisan activity or division."[70]

However, with the pressures of postwar urbanization, the increasing concern about the quality of life and the character of the neighbourhood, the reform of many of our urban governments, and the increasingly politicized nature of urban decision making, "the stakes involved had become worthwhile, and the major parties sensed a growing need for the kind of interest-aggregating expertise that they possessed."[71] A much more practical consideration may have been the fact that "the electoral redistribution preceding the 1968 federal general election, by according the majority urban population an appropriate share of the ridings, has emphatically alerted the politically aware to the impact of the metropolitan vote in the shaping of future federal and provincial governments."[72] It is clear, for example, that a more equitable provincial redistribution contributed to the NDP victory in Manitoba in 1969. The emergence of the NDP as a mass, urban, and substantially working class party has encouraged it to strengthen its organizational base through expanded involvement in municipal elections.

As noted, the NDP has not found it easy to expand its municipal election successes — given the pervasiveness of the nonpolitical tradition and the wariness of the voters about any invasion by the senior parties. Ironically, the result has been that the other senior parties, and the business and property interests that they represent to a considerable extent, have therefore been able to maintain their dominant position on many municipal councils in the guise of independent councillors or of citizen non-partisan groups allegedly opposed to party politics. To some degree then, the issue of party politics at the local level in Canada

---

[70] *Ibid.,* p. 196.

[71] Higgins, Urban Canada, *op. cit.,* p. 237.

[72] Lightbody, in Masson and Anderson, *op. cit.,* pp. 198–199.

involves more than the general advantages and disadvantages outlined above. It represents a more fundamental power struggle about which interests and philosophies should govern our cities.

Summary

To a large extent, this chapter has continued the examination of the local political process and some of the key players in that process, previously discussed in Chapter 7. It began by tracing local government's historic strong links with property and with the business community. It noted the combined impact of the Depression, World War II and rapid postwar urbanization in squeezing local government out of the limited social services responsibilities it had begun to assume and returning it to a preoccupation with property.

Through profiles of four large cities, the chapter has examined Canada's experience with political party and citizen group activity at the local level. While organized political parties offer a number of potential advantages, Canadian voters have shown much more inclination to elect candidates who claimed to be nonpartisan or opposed to the introduction of party politics at the local level. The result has been that the councils of major cities have been dominated by like-minded, pro-business representatives, often active in the Conservative and Liberal parties nationally. While these councillors have had the numerical strength to accomplish many of their objectives of accommodating rapid growth and development, they have managed to avoid responsibility for their actions because of their supposedly independent status.

Citizen activism has tended to wax and wane in response to the growth pressures being experienced and the extent to which particular councils were successful in "managing" this growth in a way that did not threaten established neighbourhoods or values. There is some indication of a cyclical pattern in which citizens mobilize against developers and their council allies, achieve some electoral success, moderate their actions in light of their apparent victory, find themselves facing renewed developer "excesses," and start a new cycle of vigorous action again.

BOOM OR BUST:
CITIZEN ACTIVISM FOLLOWS CYCLICAL PATTERN

The chapter emphasized that local government's close links with the property industry are not without their positive side, at least potentially.

Critics only see the influence wielded over councillors by developers and their allies. What is also important is the influence that councillors can wield through their decisions on the regulation of land use and the provision of infrastructure. Few decisions will be more vital to the future development of Canada's communities and the resultant lifestyle of its citizens. As a result, the local political process will continue to be both relevant and controversial.

10 The Municipal Policy-Making Process

Objectives:

1. *To clarify the nature of policy making and the steps in the municipal policy-making process.*

2. *To outline and assess the rational model of policy making.*

3. *To identify and describe various limitations on policy making in practice.*

4. *To offer suggestions for improvements in municipal policy making.*

Introduction

The preceding three chapters have examined the governing machinery of municipalities and the local political process within which this machinery operates. With this background, attention can now be given to how decisions are made and implemented by municipalities and to the effectiveness of the municipal policy-making process.

As with so many other aspects of local government, municipal policy making is characterized by paradoxes and imprecision. There are striking contrasts between the way in which policies are made in theory and the way the process actually takes place in practice. The roles performed by staff and councillors in the policy-making process also differ from the abstract concepts that are often put forth as ideal. Even the nature of a policy is a matter of some uncertainty, and it seems appropriate to begin by attempting to clarify that term.

Nature of Policy Making

One of the simplest definitions is provided by Morgan, who suggests that public policy is "whatever governments choose to do or not to do".[1] This definition is useful in recognizing that a failure to take action may represent government policy, although such inaction is sometimes the result

---

[1] David R. Morgan, *Managing Urban America,* Belmont, Wadsworth Publishing Company Inc., 1979, p. 69.

of omission or oversight rather than a deliberate decision. To distinguish policy making from decision making, Morgan goes on to suggest that a policy can be viewed as a potential series of decisions that create a more comprehensive set of standards or guidelines dealing with a subject.[2]

It is in this fashion that local governments often make policy, sometimes not even consciously. Over time a council makes a series of decisions about purchasing or personnel matters that may gradually evolve into something approaching a general policy on the subject. One danger, of course, is that such isolated decisions may not be consistent — especially if made over a number of years with a changing representation on council. The preferred alternative is for council to make a conscious decision to establish its position and approach to a particular subject and to adopt this position formally as a council policy. Examples would include a purchasing by-law setting out the purchasing policies and procedures to be followed or a council policy on lot levies or capital imposts to be charged in connection with subdivision developments. Similarly, the adoption of an official plan provides policies on a wide range of planning matters that up to this time had to be decided by council on an ad hoc basis.

Traditionally, the policy-making role of municipal government has received very little attention. In large part, this is because of the almost total preoccupation with the service delivery role of local government. Municipalities existed to administer services as efficiently as possible; they weren't expected to become involved in debating issues or resolving conflict. Such activities smacked of politics and, as Chapter 3 has made clear, the turn of the century reform era had been largely successful in establishing the notion that politics had no place in local government. Chapters 7 and 9 provided further evidence of how politics at the local level has been denied and decried.

In any event, with the extent of provincial supervision and control over municipal governments and the strict legal and financial constraints within which they operated, there was a widespread feeling that municipal councils didn't have sufficient autonomy and discretion to undertake any significant policy making.[3] Municipalities were creatures of the province and, as Chapter 6 pointed out, they were strongly and

---

[2] *Ibid.*

[3] For a good description of the legal limitations on municipal policy making see Stanley M. Makuch, *Canadian Municipal and Planning Law,* Toronto, Carswell, 1983, especially pp. 134–139.

often adversely influenced by ill-considered actions by both the provincial and federal governments. In such circumstances, was it not presumptuous to speak of a policy-making role for local government?

Conflicting Perspectives on Municipal Policy Making

Several factors have combined to alter this perception. Particularly important has been the impact of urbanization in the postwar period. Chapter 9 described how the resulting pressures undermined, and revealed the inappropriatenesss of, the nonpolitical tradition inherited from the turn of the century reform era. Increasingly activist citizens and citizens' groups demanded to know how municipalities made decisions and also insisted that the views and concerns of the affected public must become an integral part of the decision-making process. The general support for such concepts as participatory democracy, the public's right to information, and the desirability of more openness in government all conspired to direct attention to the "democratic nature" of the municipal decision-making process and the extent to which council policies reflected the apparent wishes and needs of the local populace. As already discussed, a major issue was the perceived power of the property industry and resultant narrow focus of many council decisions.

> POLICY-MAKING INFLUENCES:
> POSTWAR "CITIZEN MOVEMENT" DEMANDED
> PARTICIPATORY, RESPONSIVE POLICY PROCESS
> SYSTEMATIC, RATIONAL POLICY PROCESS ALSO SOUGHT
> THESE INFLUENCES IN POTENTIAL CONFLICT

Interest in policy making has also arisen from another completely different set of influences. Faced with ever-growing demands and needs and yet very limited financial and personnel resources, municipalities have become increasingly concerned with methods and techniques for improving their efficiency and effectiveness. There has been greater recognition of the need for improved planning and priority setting, for more rigorous research and analysis, and for the measurement of performance or results to ensure value for the dollar spent. During this same time period, approaches to research, analysis, and policy making were being refined as a result of the advances in science and technology spurred by the space and defence programs of the United States government. More rational, systematic approaches to policy making were developed, often described by the term "policy analysis."[4] Thus, just when local governments were interested in developing a more rigorous policy-making process, a variety of new techiques and approaches appeared to be available.

It is important to recognize that these two sets of influences directing attention to municipal policy making are not easily reconciled and, indeed, even appear to conflict. While they want the policy-making process "improved" and made more rational, most citizens also want it to be open and responsive to their particular views and concerns. They believe that the views of the populace affected by a potential decision are just as valid in the decision-making process as the testimony of technical experts. In addition, while people believe that governments need more research and analysis in relation to policy problems, they also believe that the elected representatives should remain in charge. Representatives should call on the services of experts and analysts but should not abdicate their political functions to them. To use some over-worked terms, there is a widespread feeling that experts should be "on tap, not on top," and a fairly strong attitude of fear and mistrust of "the bureaucracy."

The result as Lindblom points out, is that a deep conflict runs through common attitudes toward policy making.[5]

> On the one hand, people want policy to be informed and well analyzed. On the other hand, they want policy making to be democratic, hence necessarily political .... On the one hand they want policy making to be scientific; on the other they want it to remain in the world of politics.

For local governments, this conflict represents the tension between their two basic administrative and representative roles, to which frequent reference has been made. But the conflict is made more complex by the fact that even those who want local governments to be more democratic, to pay more attention to their representative role, often think that they don't want local governments to be political — thanks again to the distorted legacy of the reform movement. As has

---

[4] See Kenneth L. Kraemer, *Policy Analysis in Local Government,* Washington, International City Management Association, 1973. A brief outline of the main quantitative and non-quantitative techniques of policy analysis is found in Association of Municipal Clerks and Treasurers of Ontario, *Municipal Administration Program,* Toronto, 1987, Unit Four, Lesson Three, Appendix.

[5] Charles E. Lindblom, *The Policy Making Process,* Englewood Cliffs, Prentice-Hall Inc., 1980, p. 12.

been argued in Chapter 7, however, one must recognize that municipal councils make (and should make) political decisions. They don't
necessarily follow the recommendations made by their staff; nor do
they necessarily follow the apparent wishes of local citizens. Instead,
councils consider these factors as well as their own beliefs, values,
and judgment, and make what they feel are appropriate decisions in
the circumstances.

In an attempt to simplify the examination of this obviously complex
and contradictory topic, this chapter provides two quite contrasting
versions of municipal policy making. First, it outlines policy making as it
might idealistically occur if undertaken as a totally rational process.
Second, it describes policy making in the real world, with its practical
constraints and limitations. This second perspective will be to some
extent a review and summary of limitations discussed earlier in the text.
While the initial version will be naive and unrealistic and the latter version will exaggerate the obstacles to systematic policy making, the
combined perspectives should give a reasonably balanced picture of the
nature and potential of municipal policy making.

Policy Making in Theory

Much has been written about what is termed the rational-comprehensive
or classical approach to policy making. This approach is the way management textbooks say that decisions should be made. One such text[6]
suggests that a logical series of steps are involved, such as the following:

1. Recognizing the problem.
2. Agreeing on facts and overall objectives.
3. Identifying alternative solutions, analyzing alternatives, and
assessing the consequences flowing from each.
4. Choosing.
5. Implementing and evaluating.

If such an idealized process did exist in a mythical municipality, it
might take the following form:[7]

(1) The issues requiring a response from the municipal council are
correctly identified and are dealt with in the proper sequence. This task

[6]   Morgan, *op. cit.,* p. 98.

[7]   What follows is partly based on Association of Municipal Clerks and
Treasurers, *op. cit.,* Unit Four, Lesson Three, pp. 62–63.

is facilitated by the existence of overall (corporate) objectives that provide a framework for the consideration of more specific issues.

(2) Each issue is subjected to thorough policy analysis. As Kraemer describes this step, the process of analysis involves three interrelated activities — perception, design, and evaluation.[8] The perception stage is concerned with the clarification of the issue, the determination of the limits of the inquiry, and the identification of objectives in a way that helps to highlight alternatives. The design stage identifies existing alternatives, develops new alternatives, and gathers information for the comparison of these alternatives. The final, evaluation stage examines the alternatives for feasibility and compares them in terms of their benefit and cost.

(3) After careful consideration of all of this information, the "best" alternative is selected and a decision is made.

(4) The decision is communicated to the appropriate personnel within the organization who proceed to implement it accordingly.

(5) The implementation stage is subjected to careful evaluation and analysis to determine the effectiveness of the decision, policy, or program in practice and, where necessary, to introduce modifications.

In this imaginary municipality, councillors and staff have quite clearly defined roles that are distinct and yet complementary. The task of issue identification is primarily carried out by councillors who, as elected, responsible representatives, possess a clear understanding of the "public interest" and are able to determine how best to serve it. The staff of the municipality have both the time and the expertise to undertake in-depth research and analysis into all of the alternative courses of action that must be considered. The councillors are then responsible for weighing the alternatives studied and are able to determine the one that is "best" from both a technical viewpoint and in terms of the perceived public interest.

Council's decision is then communicated clearly to an administrative structure that is organized in a manner that provides for prompt, thorough implementation of the decision. Mechanisms exist to ensure that council's decision is implemented as intended and to monitor and assess the consequences of that implementation. Various forms of performance measurement and analysis provide councillors with information that can be used to modify or refine the decision and the implementing process where necessary.

---

[8]   Kraemer, *op. cit.*, p. 30.

Policy Making in Practice

While our mythical municipality is in many ways most impressive, in practice decisions are not made in such a neat, sequential order. The policy-making process is more fluid, the internal stages are less distinct, and the whole process is definitely not as tidy and rational as suggested above.

CONSTRAINTS:
WEAKNESSES IN STRUCTURE AND INTERNAL ORGANIZATION
INFLUENCES FROM EXTERNAL ENVIRONMENT
NONELECTED SOURCES OF POWER AND INFLUENCE

A number of the constraints on policy making in the real world are related to previously discussed limitations and weaknesses in the structure and internal organization of municipalities, and these will be briefly summarized first. Another set of influences stem from the external environment, the changing socio-economic context in which municipalities exercise their policy-making powers. A third category might be termed "nonelected sources of power and influence,"[9] which for our purposes will be used to describe not only the external pressures highlighted in studies of community power, but also internal, bureaucratic pressures.

Structural Limitations

The very fragmented structure of local government in Canada has been frequently noted. There are too many municipalities, many with small or inappropriate boundaries, and this fragmented pattern is particularly evident in major urban areas — although it has been improved somewhat by the previously described local government reforms. Further fragmentation arises because of the extent to which the responsibilities of local government are vested, not in the council, but in a variety of special purpose bodies operating with considerable independence. Consider, for example, the difficulty in developing social service policies in Ontario local government when relevant responsibilities may be exer-

---

[9]   This terminology is used by Frances Frisken in *City Policy-Making in Theory and Practice: The Case of Toronto's Downtown Plan,* Local Government Case Study No. 3, London, University of Western Ontario, 1988, p. 4.

cised by such bodies as the lower and upper tier municipal councils, childrens' aid societies, homes for the aged, housing authorities, health units, and boards of education.

Even without this fragmentation, of course, there would still be very little scope for municipal policy setting in the social services field because of the dominant position in that field of the provincial and federal governments. Indeed, the most pervasive jurisdictional limitation is undoubtedly the inferior constitutional position of local governments, the fact that they can only operate in the manner specifically provided for by their provincial government. The significance of this legal arrangement and the impact on local government of the activities of the senior levels of government were examined in Chapter 6.

Also previously discussed (in Chapters 4 and 8) were various limitations on policy making inherent in the internal structure and operation of municipalities. Briefly, these limitations relate to such matters as the lack of strong leadership and executive direction, the lack of much in the way of long term planning and priority setting, and the absence of a focus of responsibility and accountability within council.

The Socio-Economic Context

Much of the reason that the policy-making process does not unfold as described in the rational model is because it takes place in the real world, where it is subject to numerous external influences. The very significant impact of urbanization and industrialization, for example, has been discussed in Chapter 4. As economic and social conditions change, so too does the emphasis of municipal policy making. Masson offers the example of Spruce Grove, a community on the outskirts of Edmonton.[10] Over the past couple of decades it has become a dormitory suburb, with many young families attracted by its cheaper housing. Its population doubled between 1966 and 1970 and its per capita expenditure for recreation and community services went from $2.47 to $13.43. This substantial policy shift occurred because the younger population increased the demand for recreation.

Another common example is provided by various rural municipalities within commuting distance of cities. The public's desire for open space, and especially for waterfront properties, has led to very strong develop-

---

[10] Jack Masson, *Alberta's Local Governments and Their Politics,* Edmonton, University of Alberta Press, 1985, p. 137.

ment pressures on those rural municipalities with attractive land for residential development and has posed major policy challenges for those municipalities in attempting to reconcile this growth with the preservation of the beauty of their natural features.

The aging of Canada's population presents quite a different challenge for municipal policy makers, especially for some places that have become attractive as retirement communities. In these municipalities, other policy initiatives and shifts will be necessary.

A major policy issue affecting both urban and rural municipalities concerns the development of waste management guidelines and the selection of future waste management sites. While debate rages about the relative merits of various waste disposal alternatives, and while studies and public hearings drag on interminably, our ability to dispose of the waste that we create moves closer and closer to a crisis situation. There is no better example of the NIMBY syndrome (not in my back yard), and yet with little land available in Canada's major urban centres, the search for sites inevitably involves the surrounding less developed areas.

Specifically economic influences on municipal policy making are singled out by both neo-classical (public choice) and neo-marxist analysts, as already outlined briefly in Chapter 7. Frisken's study of Toronto's Downtown Plan clearly illustrates the economic influences on municipal policy making. Indeed, she notes that "the event most clearly associated with a rapid decline in council's interest in restricting the height and density of downtown buildings was the economic slowdown that began in the mid-1970s and culminated in severe recession in the early 1980s."[11] At the same time, however, she rejects a doctrine of economic determinism that allows for no variation in the way municipal governments act under similar circumstances. The fact is that municipalities are also influenced by a variety of other factors, some of them already outlined. Indeed, Frisken notes that Toronto's pro-growth approach during the period under study was consistent with, and sometimes directly in response to, signals or directives from the provincial government[12] — which is a reminder of the influence of the senior levels, previously discussed. Since the senior levels of government are also strongly influenced by developers and the business community generally, however, the economic impact on policy making is still very much in evidence.

---

[11] Frisken, *op. cit.*, pp. 98-99.

[12] *Ibid.*, pp. 90–91.

Nonelected Sources of Power and Influence

To this point, the discussion has concerned factors that may influence the way in which *the council* makes policy decisions. One must also take into account, however, the outside forces that influence those formally charged with making decisions. There have been numerous studies designed to measure who actually wields power in a particular community. American studies of this nature have traditionally revealed two main viewpoints. One is the power elite concept originally propounded in Floyd Hunter's study of Atlanta.[13] Largely on the basis of interviews with people holding formal positions of power and with those reputedly influential, he concluded that policy making in Atlanta was the preserve of a fairly small group of people prominent in the business community and on close personal terms with those public officials nominally in charge.

WHO WIELDS POWER?
POWER ELITE VIEW
PLURALIST VIEW

The other main viewpoint is the pluralistic concept found in Robert Dahl's study of New Haven.[14] He examined a number of specific issues to determine who exercised influence, but concluded that no single elite dominated. Instead, numerous individuals and groups had some influence, which they might exert depending on the issue involved. An attempt to synthesize the findings of both pluralists and elitists is provided in Paul Peterson's ambitious *City Limits*.[15] Based on a review of the experiences in such cities as New Haven and Baltimore, however, Stone finds several problems with Peterson's approach and concludes that "when all of his cards are put on the table, Peterson is very much the pluralist, largely reiterating the argument of Robert Dahl in *Who Governs?*"[16]

Perhaps surprisingly, the first major study of community power in Canada concluded that if there was a dominant elite it was composed of the elected and appointed municipal officials. Harold Kaplan, studying the operations of Metropolitan Toronto, found that:

---

[13] Floyd Hunter, *Community Power Structure,* New York, Anchor Books, 1963.

[14] Robert Dahl, *Who Governs?,* New Haven, Yale University Press, 1961.

[15] Paul E. Peterson, *City Limits,* Chicago, University of Chicago Press, 1981.

[16] Clarence N. Stone and Heywood T. Sanders (eds.), *The Politics of Urban Development,* Lawrence, University Press of Kansas, 1987, p. 165.

The creation, agitation and resolution of issues occurred within the formal institutions of government. Interaction among public officials was far more significant for the outcome of issues than interaction between officials and private actors.[17]

However, Kaplan was examining an upper tier government, while many of the issues that would directly affect community groups were handled by constituent lower tier municipalities. If his study were expanded to include these lower tier units or repeated since the reorganization of January 1, 1967 gave Metropolitan Toronto more powers, much more outside involvement would likely be evident. As Chapter 9 pointed out, citizens' groups and reform councillors became much more prominent in Toronto in the 1970s.

One of these reform councillors, subsequently Mayor of Toronto, was John Sewell, who assessed the decision-making process quite differently. Admittedly, he was writing about the City of Toronto not Metro, and his political autobiography was hardly a scholarly analysis of the Kaplan variety.[18] Sewell emphasized the intimate links between councillors and the development industry. From his experience, councillors did represent and speak for outside interests — those of the developer — and power was concentrated outside the formal institutions. This viewpoint was echoed by a number of other writers during this period, notably Lorimer and Gutstein.[19]

Extensive studies of city politics in seven major Canadian cities at the beginning of the 1980s generally confirmed the prominence of business interests and the extent to which debates over development versus the quality of life have dominated the urban political scene. Whether expressed as boosters versus cutters or production interests versus consumption interests, these forces have remained the focal point of debate and political differences.[20] At the same time, however, these studies also suggested that the business domination was moderating. Sancton con-

---

[17] Harold Kaplan, *Urban Political Systems: A Functional Analysis of Metropolitan Toronto,* New York, Columbia University Press, 1967, p. 157.

[18] John Sewell, *Up Against City Hall,* Toronto, James Lewis and Samuel, 1972.

[19] See James Lorimer, *The Real World of City Politics,* Toronto, James Lewis and Samuel, 1970, *A Citizen's Guide to City Politics,* Toronto, James Lewis and Samuel, 1972, and *The Developers,* Toronto, James Lorimer and Co., 1980. See also Donald Gutstein, *Vancouver Ltd.,* Toronto, James Lorimer and Co., 1975, a portrayal of Vancouver as a company town dominated by one powerful interest, the C.P.R.

[20] See Warren Magnusson and Andrew Sancton (eds.), *City Politics in Canada,* Toronto, University of Toronto Press, 1983, especially the concluding chapter.

cluded that "the political representatives of the property industry no longer control the municipal councils of the country's major cities" and that "in most Canadian cities local politics is now genuinely competitive.[21] As discussed in Chapter 9, however, it appears that the property industry has regained at least some of its position of dominance in the past few years.

In addition to the external political influences that have been discussed above, policy making is also influenced by internal or bureaucratic politics. Its significance is emphasized by two American observers examining the limitations of analysis:

> The definition of issues and the data needed to develop rational policy choices are produced by organizational units whose goals, history, and inner workings colour their outputs. Analysis is not something apart from these organizational processes; it is intertwined with and affected by them.[22]

They further note that it is widely recognized that "the resourcefulness and influence of particular advocates carry weight beyond the measure of the objective merits of the arguments which they advance."[23] It must be appreciated then, that a decision made on the basis of internal analysis and recommendations is not necessarily shielded from politics and therefore purer and more objective; instead it may simply reflect the outcome of bureaucratic politics.

BUREAUCRATIC INFLUENCE:
STAFF INFLUENCE STRONG SINCE
TURN OF CENTURY REFORM PERIOD
AUGMENTED BY CENTRALIZED STRUCTURES
CREATED IN LOCAL GOVERNMENT REFORMS

In the Canadian context, the status and potential influence of municipal civil servants have been pronounced ever since the turn of the century reform era and its emphasis on the importance of professional administration as opposed to politics. As already discussed, Kaplan has described the new professional of that era as an important new force in local government.[24]

---

[21] *Ibid.*, p. 297.

[22] Richard S. Rosenblom and John R. Russell, *New Tools for Urban Management*, Boston, Harvard University Press, 1971, p. 229.

[23] *Ibid.*, p. 230.

[24] Harold Kaplan, *Reform, Planning and City Politics: Montreal, Winnipeg, Toronto,* Toronto, University of Toronto Press, 1982, p. 205.

As described earlier, notably in Chapter 5, the postwar municipal reforms attempted in several of the provinces served to create a more bureaucratic form of government in many instances. The development of more centralized administrative structures, particularly with the establishment of chief administrative officer systems, also served to increase the influence of the bureaucracy, especially since parallel efforts to restructure the council with some form of executive committee were rarely as successful. Masson, for example, reviews the internal organizational reforms attempted in Alberta and concludes that the professional management premise (that the provision of public services should be non-political and non-controversial) has been given preference over the political accountability premise (which recognizes that different segments of the citizenry will be differentially advantaged and disadvantaged by any policy, and that local government decisions are therefore political).[25]

It should be apparent, therefore, that attempts to shield the policy-making process from politics or what might be regarded as undesirable outside influences may only result in a different set of political viewpoints — those of the bureaucracy — having even greater influence. As previously noted, the municipal staff have usually been less than enthusiastic about citizen views or demands for greater involvement. An interesting variation is noted by Susan Fish, who explains that the apparent support for the citizen participation movement exhibited by planners in Metropolitan Toronto was largely a means of building up their own power base for their internal struggles with line departments and some elements of council.[26]

Given all of the above-noted limitations on policy making in practice, it is apparent a different description of the policy-making process is needed than that provided by the rational model. Two such alternative descriptions are provided below.

Policy Making as Muddling Through

Charles Lindblom argues that our problem-solving capacity is too limited to encompass all of the options and potential outcomes that might arise, that there is usually insufficient information to assess accurately

---

[25] Masson, *op. cit.,* pp. 47 and 23.

[26] Susan A. Fish, "Winning the Battle and Losing the War in the Fight to Improve Municipal Policy Making," in Lionel D. Feldman and Michael D. Goldrick (eds.), *Politics and Government of Urban Canada,* Toronto, Methuen, 1976, pp. 181–183.

all options, that comprehensive analysis is both too time-consuming and too expensive, and that facts and values cannot be neatly separated as required by the rational approach.[27] Moreover, he points out that decision makers, recognizing these realities, look for simpler approaches to problem solving. Rather than attempting to identify every possible course of action, they consider those few alternatives that represent only small or incremental changes from existing policies. Lindblom has therefore developed an alternative policy-making approach that he calls incrementalism or the science of muddling through.

However inglorious this approach may sound, Lindblom's observations are certainly closer to reality, and he points out that there is little evidence to suggest that organizations that utilize a rational comprehensive approach to policy making produce consistently better decisions (however one might measure "better"). In addition to the obvious reduction in the workload for those involved in policy analysis, Lindblom offers several advantages of incrementalism. Decisions that are a major departure from existing policy may be quite unpredictable in their consequences, and errors that may result are easier to correct when decisions are successive and limited. Also, incremental decisions are likely to be more acceptable politically than are the far-reaching changes that might result from the rational model of policy making. To his critics, Lindblom asserts that "the piecemealing, remedial incrementalist... may not look like an heroic figure. He is nevertheless a shrewd, resourceful problem-solver who is wrestling bravely with a universe that he is wise enough to know is too big for him."[28]

The Penny Arcade Model of Policy Making

One of the most vivid descriptions of the way in which policy making actually occurs is provided by Yates, who uses a metaphor based on three familiar games found in most penny arcades.[29]

---

[27] Charles E. Lindblom, *The Intelligence of Democracy*, New York, The Free Press, 1965, pp. 138–143. The discussion of Lindblom that follows is largely based on Morgan, *op. cit.*, pp. 100–102.

[28] Charles E. Lindblom, *The Policy Making Process*, Englewood Cliffs, Prentice-Hall Inc., 1968, p. 27.

[29] Douglas Yates, *The Ungovernable City*, Cambridge, M.I.T. Press, 1977. (Presumably an enterprising academic will update this metaphor in line with our brave new world of video games and give rise to a new school of policy making.)

First, Yates points out that the process of determining the problems that require the attention of the municipal policy maker is rather like being in a shooting gallery.

Like the urban policy maker the shooting gallery player has far more targets than he can possibly hit, and they keep popping up in different places or revolving around and around in front of him.[30]

The player is continually reacting to a new target (problem) and is conscious of the fact that firing at any one target (dealing with any one problem) means letting most of the others go by until the next time. Given the need to react quickly and to deal with such a variety of targets, the player is likely to rely on reflexes more than any considered plan of action.

PENNY ARCADE MODEL:
SHOOTING GALLERY OF PROBLEM SELECTION
SLOT MACHINE OF RANDOM POLICY VARIABLES
PIN BALL MACHINE OF POLICY IMPLEMENTATION

Second, Yates compares the municipal policy maker's ability to predict and control the kinds of decisions he must make with that of someone operating a slot machine. By this he means that the policy-making characteristics of a particular problem can vary just as randomly as the apples, oranges, and cherries that appear in various combinations on a slot machine. "Urban policy making variables include the nature of the problem, the issue context, the stage of decision, the configuration of participants, the institutional setting, and the government function involved."[31] The policy maker does not know what kind of problem he will be dealing with from one moment to the next, or which of his available policy responses or procedures is likely to be relevant or useful. He may need to negotiate, appeal to the senior levels of government, enforce an existing policy more thoroughly, set up an interdepartmental task force, provide new channels for citizen input — or a wide variety of other possible approaches. The policy maker who relies on one or two standard responses or develops a standard approach to decision making will be responding inappropriately much of the time.

Finally, Yates views the process of policy implementation as similar to the operations of a pinball machine.

---

[30] *Ibid.,* p. 91.

[31] *Ibid.,* pp. 91–92.

> Given the central policy maker's weak control over his own administration, street-level bureaucrats, and higher level governments, decisions once taken are likely to bounce around from decision point to decision point.[32]

In other words, even when a policy decision is made by the municipality, it may be knocked off course by both predictable and unforeseen obstacles by the time it reaches the street level. If this happens, the implemented policy may well give rise to a new set of problems that enter the shooting gallery of agenda setting all over again.

> To that extent urban policy making will become a continuous process in which a particular problem receives brief, often frantic, attention; some kind of decision is made, which bounces around in the implementation process; and then the problem pops up again in a new or slightly altered form.[33]

Examples of such a pattern are fairly common.[34] A stricter enforcement of property standards may lead to housing abandonment and/or rent increases that create new problems of housing shortages for low income residents. A police department moves to car patrols to increase coverage and then faces demands that the police officers go back on the beat to provide greater visibility and responsiveness. Planning policies call for the infilling of existing hamlets so as to prevent strip development in rural areas and then the concentration of septic tanks and wells bring health problems that necessitate the provision of expensive water and sewer systems. The policy-making process is rarely simple and straightforward.

Obviously, Yates' portrayal of policy making in the penny arcade provides a marked contrast with the rational model outlined as a starting point for discussion. It may exaggerate somewhat the random, unpredictable nature of policy making, and it is based on the experiences of large urban areas. But it does highlight the idealistic nature of the rational model that assumes that answers can be found for any policy problems if enough intelligence is brought to bear on them.

The real world of policy making doesn't work that way.[35] Policy makers cannot carefully select their problems and then analyze them with great thoroughness and detachment. They face a constant barrage of

---

[32] *Ibid.*, p. 93.

[33] *Ibid.*

[34] See Association of Municipal Clerks and Treasurers, *op. cit.*, Unit Four, Lesson Three, p. 66.

[35] See Yates, *op. cit.*, pp. 94–97.

new and changing problems and service demands. It is not possible to stop the policy-making process, "freeze" a particular problem, and then dissect it in clinical fashion. In addition, municipal policy makers deal with problems that may not be clearly understood or that generate conflicting political pressures. Rather than undertaking thorough research and analysis — as suggested by the rational model — the response may be to grope for a plausible remedy and hope that it works better than previous attempts.

In any event, often the issues involved do not call for analytical solutions as much as subjective assessments and political bargaining. The rational model also ignores the rapidity with which municipal policy problems may change. "To abstract and analyze a problem in a meticulous, detached way may be to lose track of the problem and wind up fighting yesterday's battles."[36] Finally, even if the "right" decision is made, implementing it is often not easy because of the fragmentation of the local government structure. Given all of these considerations, Yates dismisses the rational model of policy making as "a greenhouse conception that cannot thrive in the harsh climate of urban politics.[37]

Summary: Improving Policy Making

The foregoing discussion has moved a long way from the idealized policy-making process outlined toward the beginning of the chapter. Inevitably, these attempts to provide a more realistic picture of how and in what context municipal decisions are made may appear quite discouraging. However, the limitations that have been noted are not a reason to give up on a municipal policy-making role. Rather, it can be argued that precisely because their operations are so closely circumscribed and so vulnerable to outside influences, municipalities must attempt to identify quite specifically what objectives they hope to accomplish and then must ensure that their scarce financial and personnel resources are allocated accordingly.

Such actions will not make them immune from these influences. Nor is it desirable that they be immune from a number of the influences that have been described, if local government is to take into account local views and concerns. But at least the effort to identify objectives will allow a municipality to pursue its interests in a more concerted,

---

[36] *Ibid.*, pp. 96–97.
[37] *Ibid.*, p. 96.

effective fashion. Therefore, this chapter concludes with a few suggestions for strengthening the policy-making process at the municipal level. Inevitably, these suggestions lead back to some elements of the rational model previously described. But at least one can now consider these elements more realistically, in light of all of the limitations that have been examined.

Who Does What in Policy Making?

From a very practical point of view, one of the problems with municipal policy making is that the key players involved — the councillors and staff — may not fully appreciate the numerous stages involved in the policy-making process and/or may not be appropriately participating in these stages.

The results of council-staff training sessions in various provinces suggest that two aspects of the policy-making process merit special attention. Councillors tend to be too little involved in policy initiation, reacting instead to proposals initiated by staff or to community pressures. At the same time, councillors (and staff, for that matter) tend to be too little involved in policy review — a stage that is overlooked or ignored in too many cases. Both of these matters are addressed in the comments and suggestions that follow.

> **THE CRITICAL LINK:**
> **COUNCIL-STAFF ROLES IN POLICY MAKING**

The authors' experience reveals that most municipalities would benefit from a frank exchange between councillors and senior staff as to what they perceive as the various stages in the municipal policy-making process and *to what extent* and *in what ways* each believe that they should be involved in these policy-making stages. Too often the roles and relationships reflect historical patterns or the influence of dominant personalities rather than any deliberate, conscious choice by the key personnel involved.

Where Are We Going (Trying to Go)?

For reasons already advanced, the municipality needs a clearer focus and sense of direction than is usually evident. Rather than merely reacting to day to day pressures, municipal personnel need to set out some long term goals and objectives that can provide a framework within which the daily decisions can be made more systematically. In the past, various structural reforms have been attempted to provide a more central focus — in particular, the establishment of some form of executive committee and/or chief administrative officer system. However, changes in machinery alone may accomplish little unless accompanied by improvements in the overall management process. Ironically, many municipalities have a variety of long term plans and objectives scattered among such documents as official plans, capital works programs, roads needs studies, master plans for recreation, economic analyses, and social planning studies. What is needed is the drawing together of the implications of these various long term policies and projections into a statement of overall objectives for the municipality. The increased attention now being paid to strategic planning may be a recognition of this need.

Plunkett and Betts suggest the need for what they term a policy planning process, comprising the following elements:[38]

1. The identification by the local government of certain needs, present and foreseen, in its environment;

2. The establishment of objectives in relation to the identified needs — that is, the extent to which the organization will plan to meet those needs; and

3. The consideration of alternative ways of achieving the objectives that have been determined.

As already indicated, councillors should be much more involved in this process of determining objectives and priorities. Rather than reacting to events, councillors need to become more proactive, attempting to discern the kind of future community desired by the inhabitants and working — albeit within various limitations — to achieve it.

Determining which alternative will be most effective in fulfilling a particular objective demands more research and analysis than has been customarily attempted by local governments and reveals the shortcomings of their traditional information base. The following questions are typical of the information needed to decide among alternative courses of action.[39]

1. What activities are currently being undertaken?

2. What do they cost?

3. How effective are they?

---

[38] T. J. Plunkett and G. M. Betts, *The Management of Canadian Urban Government,* Kingston, Queen's University, 1978, p. 236.

[39] Based on *ibid.,* p. 237.

4. How do they contribute to the securing of the objectives established?

5. Would a change of emphasis in the allocation of resources among different activities or programmes be more effective in achieving the objectives established?

As discussed in the next chapter, such information is not readily available from the traditional budget and accounting systems and, as a result, a variety of other approaches to budgeting and financial management have been introduced.

Thus far, the emphasis has been on greater attention to the determination of priorities and the analysis of methods of fulfilling these priorities. Important questions have also been raised about how these priorities will be determined, and about the key role of councillors in setting the policy agenda. One must also consider how the views and concerns of the local citizenry will be incorporated into the policy process. Also to be considered is how the policy advisory role of staff is to be carried out, and what provisions can be made to ensure that staff experts are "on tap, not on top" — to repeat a previous concern.

Any efforts to improve policy making must also deal with the inevitability of a political dimension to this process. Political decisions are not only inevitable, but desirable and, indeed, essential in a democratic, accountable system of government. "To charge an elected leader with political motivation is to accuse him of doing precisely what he was elected to do."[40] As Masson points out, "any attempt to take politics out of government invariably ends up eroding democratic principles."[41]

Are We Getting Where We Want To Go?

Some further suggestions for improving policy making are needed. Even with a more systematic selection of alternatives and determination of policies, the policy-making process will not be effective unless equal attention is given to the implementation of the policies that have been adopted. This presupposes an organizational structure with an appropriate allocation of responsibilities to qualified personnel and mechanisms for ensuring the coordination of their activities. It also requires the establishment of performance standards and processes for monitoring and evaluating the activities of the administration to determine that

---

[40] Theodore Sorenson, *Leadership in Transition*, undated address.

[41] Masson, *op. cit.*, p. 33.

policies have been implemented efficiently and effectively. It calls for a fundamental shift in emphasis to the *results* of expenditures and the *consequences* of policy decisions.

In this context Plunkett and Betts refer to the concept of administrative general management and the responsibility to ensure that:[42]

1.   the organizational structure is adequate to respond effectively to the requirements of the policy planning process;

2.   the financial resources allocated are utilized to acquire the necessary equipment, supplies and personnel and to develop and employ productively the personnel;

3.   the departments and other organizational components are integrated and directed toward the corporate objectives rather than those of functional self interest.

Here again, a review of the roles and involvement of councillors and staff can be very beneficial. In many municipalities there has been a tendency for councillors to be too involved in policy implementation, often to the extent of "second-guessing" their staff or interfering with the staff in their day to day activities. On the other hand, in many of these municipalities neither councillors nor staff have given sufficient attention to what might be considered the final stage of the policy-making process — policy review. This stage involves an examination of the effectiveness of policy implementation and of the extent to which the policy, as implemented, succeeded in dealing with the problems or concerns that prompted its introduction. It also extends to a consideration of whether or not what transpired was cost-effective, was providing value for the dollar spent.

The following two chapters should provide further insights into the municipal management process — as it traditionally operates and as it should operate — through an examination of the two key elements of financial management and human resource management.

---

[42]   *Ibid.,* pp. 253–254.

11 *Financial Management*

Objectives:

1. To review the nature and general implications of the financial dilemma facing local governments.

2. To examine the limitations of the traditional budget process.

3. To identify alternative approaches to budgeting, their general nature, and their potential benefits and shortcomings.

4. To delineate the basic elements in a system of financial management.

Introduction

Central to the operations of local government — and just about any other organization — is money, or the lack thereof. As discussed, there is a serious fiscal imbalance at the local level in Canada. That is to say, the expenditures of local governments greatly exceed the revenue sources directly available to them. Explanations for this development have been given in earlier chapters, but the basic problem is that local governments have acquired major new expenditures because of the impact of urbanization and yet are still limited to one main source of revenue, the historic tax on real property.

> ### FINANCIAL PROBLEMS ARE
> ### MANAGERIAL AS WELL AS FISCAL

As Sharpe explains the situation, local governments have been unable to limit the range of their responsibilities and yet it is the senior governments that have the bulk of the growth taxes that expand fastest when the economy grows.[1] The result is that "prosperity gives the national government the affluence and local governments the effluents."[2] As discussed in Chapter 6, the financial plight of local governments has been accentuated in recent years by the tendency for various

---

[1] L. J. Sharpe (ed.), *The Local Fiscal Crisis in Western Europe, Myths and Realities,* London, Sage Publications, 1981, p. 7.

[2] Walter Heller, quoted in *ibid.*

provincial governments to attempt to ease their own financial difficulties by transferring more responsibilities (and costs) to the local level, while simultaneously reducing the rate of increase of provincial transfer payments.

It is important to recognize, however, that the apparent financial problems of local government aren't just fiscal, they are also managerial. The provision of unlimited additional funds — admittedly an unlikely prospect — is not the answer. Indeed, one only has to look at the experience of the federal and provincial governments whose relatively unlimited revenue sources have led them to increasingly large, apparently irreversible budget deficits. While more money is always attractive, what is needed even more is for local governments to demonstrate that they are making the best possible use of their existing scarce resources.

Local governments (all governments) must learn to "manage with less."[3] Gone are the days when one could anticipate an ever-growing financial pie from which to allocate expenditure choices. Instead, new programs can only be launched if old ones are discontinued or reduced. Tough decisions must be made — tough, political decisions. The new reality also means consideration of a number of different approaches to the operation of local government.[4] For example, the privatization movement popularized by Margaret Thatcher can be expected to receive increasing attention at the local level.[5] Volunteerism, once associated primarily with the recreational field, will become more and more necessary. With proper training and support, volunteers can perform various duties on a par with permanent employees. Self-help will receive more emphasis. In other words, citizens will be encouraged to do for themselves what they have come to expect from local government.

---

[3]   See Ivan Robinson, "Managing Retrenchment in a Public Service Organization," in *Canadian Public Administration,* Vol. 28, No. 4, Winter 1985, pp. 513–530, for a discussion of the approach used by an Alberta public body faced with the downturn in that province's economy in the early 1980s. Cynthia Hardy, "Fighting Cutbacks: Some Issues for Public Sector Administrators," in *Canadian Public Administration,* Vol. 28, No. 4, Winter 1985, pp. 531–549, explores the "other side of the coin," by examining strategies used by four public sector organizations to resist cutbacks.

[4]   The suggestions that follow are based on Elizabeth K. Kellar (ed.), *Managing with Less: A Book of Readings,* Washington, International City Management Association, 1979, pp. 2–7.

[5]   For a discussion of the reasons for the current popularity of privatization, the techniques involved, and the implications of this concept, see Lionel Ouellet, "La Privatisation: Un Instrument de Management Public?" in *Canadian*

While the transition will not be easy, one of the greatest benefits could be to give people a greater sense of control of their own lives. Difficult questions will have to be asked about how high a standard of service can be afforded and what price can be justified for further reducing the risks that citizens face. How much increase in police costs is acceptable for a one percent decrease in the risk of loss of property? Can we afford to ensure that no public facility is inaccessible to handicapped persons, and how quickly can this be achieved?

OPTIONS FOR MANAGING WITH LESS:
PRIVATIZATION
INCREASED VOLUNTEERISM
SELF-HELP
REVIEW EXPECTATIONS OF WHAT IS ATTAINABLE

Notwithstanding the importance of these broader considerations, the focus of this chapter is on the more specifically financial aspects. If municipalities are to demonstrate that they are making the best possible use of their existing resources, they need to give more attention to the priorities that are reflected in their expenditure decisions and they need to examine the results of those expenditures in an attempt to ensure value for the dollar spent.

Yet such considerations have received far too little attention in municipal financial activities. The traditional emphasis, reinforced by provincial requirements, has been on accountability and control in the use of public funds. There has been a preoccupation with ensuring that money was spent legally, but little concern with whether it was also spent wisely. A further limitation was found in the fact that the various financial activities of the municipality were usually carried out as separate, discrete tasks, rather than being integrated into an overall system of financial management.

These limitations of the traditional approach become more evident if we examine the current budget process — the one financial activity carried out in all municipalities regardless of size and sophistication, the

---

Public Administration, Vol. 30, No. 4, Winter 1987, pp. 566–584. See also James C. McDavid and Gregory K., Schick, "Privatization Versus Union-Management Cooperation: The Effects of Competition on Service Efficiency in Municipalities," in *Canadian Public Administration*, Vol. 30, No. 3, Fall 1987, pp. 472–488, in which the authors conclude that public producers of municipal services can provide an alternative to privatization if exposed to competition.

one with the greatest potential for contributing to overall financial management, and the one most obviously constrained by a variety of external and self-imposed restrictions.

Traditional Budget Process

The current budget is usually viewed very narrowly as an annual exercise carried out in the spring for the purpose of determining the mill rates to be levied. While this is one important facet, the budget has at least two other major purposes — it is, or should be, a statement of municipal priorities and policies, and it is, or can be, an important tool of financial management and control. Because of the controversial nature of the property tax, however, and the critical media coverage that accompanies any tax increase, councillors are understandably preoccupied with mill rates to the virtual exclusion of other important aspects of the budget exercise.

PURPOSES OF BUDGET:
POLICY STATEMENT
INSTRUMENT FOR FINANCIAL CONTROL
BASIS FOR TAXES

Still on the revenue side of the budget, transfer payments from the senior levels of government constitute a second major source of funds, which for some years now have rivalled the portion generated by the property tax. The fact that most of these grants are conditional imposes a constraint on council's budget deliberations. The grants are offered provided that the money is spent on a specified purpose and usually on condition that the municipality contribute its specified share. Since the provincial government's portion of these shared cost programs is usually between 50% and 80%, municipalities are strongly tempted to participate. While these grants reflect the views of the senior governments as to what are the most important areas of local government activity, local councils and their citizens may have different views. Therefore, to the extent that the municipality opts for these shared cost programs, its expenditures may reflect provincial rather than local priorities. Moreover, the provincial grants are scarcely the bargain that they are often seen to be since there is only one set of taxpayers in Canada regardless of the level of government!

Further constraints are evident if we turn to the expenditure side of the budget. It is surprising to discover the small portion of its own expenditures that the council actually controls. At the outset there are certain financial obligations that the council is legally required to meet. These include debt charges arising from long term borrowing and the funds requested by certain special purpose bodies that operate independently of council. The best (or worst) examples of the latter are the financial demands of the boards of education — although the financing of elementary and secondary education has become primarily a provincial responsibility in New Brunswick and Quebec.

EXPENDITURE CONSTRAINTS:
DEBT CHARGES
OUTSIDE BOARDS
SHARED COST PROGRAMS
EXISTING SERVICE COMMITMENTS

The municipality's contribution to various shared cost programs may also account for a substantial portion of the expenditures. Yet, as described above, the sizeable provincial grant money offered makes these programs difficult to resist. For example, because of the heavy provincial subsidies available, rural municipalities are influenced to allocate as much as half of their budget to roads. Indeed, Siegel argues that the local responsibility for roads in Ontario has effectively been taken over by the provincial government because of the conditional grant system and the role played by professional engineers at the provincial and municipal levels.[6]

Even expenditures on services that are not part of a shared cost program and are not required at a provincially determined standard are difficult to control. This is because once a service is established there is public resistance to any action that would remove it or even significantly reduce it — a fact of life well known by those councils that have, for example, attempted to limit expenditures by reducing their snow removal activities. Expenditure reductions may also be resisted quite effectively by municipal staff, who often imply that there is a strong public demand for certain services or service levels, as a way of maintaining or expanding levels of activity.

---

[6] David Siegel, *Provincial-Municipal Relations in Ontario: A Case Study of Roads,* a paper presented at the Annual Meeting of the Canadian Political Science Association, Montreal, June 2–4, 1980.

With the extent of inflation in the past decade, significantly increased expenditures are often necessary just to provide the same range and level of service as was offered the previous year. Insufficient effort has been devoted to educating the public (and the media) about the unrealistic nature of their demands for tax relief *and* continuing high standards of service. Overall, councillors usually find that only a small portion of the budget, probably about 10%, is "free" to spend as they might wish.

Obviously it would be desirable to remove or reduce these financial constraints. Such approaches as more unconditional financial assistance or the removal of education expenditures from the local level have been previously mentioned. Changes are likely to be slow and modest, however, and it is important that the budget process concentrate on priority setting so that the council can take maximum advantage of whatever limited freedom of choice it does have. But in most municipalities the way in which the budget is prepared and the kinds of information provided during that process, far from facilitating the establishment of priorities, serve to perpetuate existing spending patterns.

Shortcomings of Traditional Budget Preparation

The traditional budget is prepared "from the bottom up," in that the process is initiated by a request from the treasurer to the various departments for an estimate of their spending requirements.[7] The department heads are responsible for the preparation of their department's spending needs, starting with an examination of the actual expenditures of the previous year and building upon them. Thus, there is a tendency to accept the level and general distribution of departmental expenditures as given, as a base from which to build. This perspective is reinforced by the inclination of department heads to preserve the status quo and, if possible, to enlarge their department's budget, activities, and importance in the municipal organization.

When completed, the various departmental estimates may be reviewed by the treasurer for any obvious instances of duplication or omission. They are then forwarded to the appropriate standing commit-

---

[7]   It is difficult to generalize because of the variety of municipal organizations, but for illustration let us use what is probably still the most common structure involving a standing committee system but no chief administrative officer. Even where CAO systems have been established, there is often a failure to introduce complementary changes in basic management processes, and the budget process may still follow the path to be outlined herein.

tees for examination. The basic responsibility of the committee is to ensure that the expenditure requirements proposed for the particular department reflect the policies laid down by council. However, the committee is considering these estimates in isolation, without regard to the overall expenditure and revenue projections for the municipality, and there is a tendency for committee members to support the needs of "their" department rather than attempting to take a broad view of the overall needs of the municipality.

"BOTTOM-UP"
BUDGET PROCESS

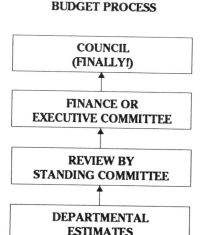

Following examination by committee, the departmental estimates, together with the other expenditure claims on the municipality, are combined, the nontax revenues expected are calculated, and the implications for the mill rate projected. In other words, a draft budget is prepared and the process enters the critical stage. This draft budget is examined by a finance or executive committee where such exist or by the full council. In either event the crunch is on! For the first time councillors become aware of the mill rate implications of the various expenditure requests that they had only examined in isolation up to this time. In most cases the increase in taxes is felt to be excessive and reductions in expenditure are required. The basis for these reductions varies but it is rarely as rational as it should be. It is still common to order a percentage decrease across the board, which appears equitable but takes no account of the varying importance of different programs and services. Moreover, this approach serves to penalize department heads who have submitted a "rock-bottom" budget and encourages those who had the foresight to "pad the budget" against just such an eventuality! Alternatively, the cutbacks may be the result of an elaborate set of political tradeoffs and/or a judicious balancing that avoids neglecting any particular area of the municipality. Another possibility is that those department and committee heads with the strongest voices and political clout will save their estimates at the expense of other departments.

None of these approaches is particularly satisfactory and each reflects the fact that council does not have information that would allow it to make a more intelligent choice among competing claims for funds.[8] These claims constitute the fragmented demands of specific departments and local boards and do not readily indicate what overall activities or objectives are being fulfilled as a result. A major limitation is the line-item format of the traditional budget. This is the oldest and simplest budgetary format and emphasizes the input of resources for particular objects of expenditure such as salaries and wages, materials and supplies, and financial expenses (interest and debt charges). This type of budget is straightforward, relatively easy to prepare and administer, and is easily understood by administrators, council, and the public. It usually reflects the municipality's accounting system, and therefore facilitates a close link between the two for control purposes. But, this line-item format gives little attention to the objectives to be accomplished as a result of the expenditures incurred.

LINE-ITEM BUDGET:
SIMPLE AND STRAIGHTFORWARD
FACILITATES CONTROL
IGNORES *RESULTS* OF EXPENDITURES

An example should help to illustrate these limitations. Consider a situation in which a council wishes to reduce the estimates of its parks department. It can examine the categories of the budget allocated to

---

[8]   The elaboration of this point is generally based on Association of Municipal Clerks and Treasurers of Ontario, *Municipal Administration Program*, UNIT Three, Lesson Three.

salaries, supplies, travel, and other inputs and can look for significant variations from the pattern of previous years. It can compare this budget breakdown with that of other departments in the municipality or with the parks departments of comparable municipalities. While such exercises may be of some value, there are several important questions that council can't easily answer with the traditional budget and the financial information normally associated with it, including:

1.   What is the total municipal expenditure on parks? (Some expenditure on parks may be found in other department or board estimates.)

2.   What specific park facilities does the municipality get for its expenditure and to what extent are these facilities utilized?

3.   Which existing park programs or facilities are most expendable because of costly operation and/or limited fulfillment of public needs or demands?

4.   Which proposed park projects are most justified on the basis of some form of cost/benefit analysis?

As Plunkett and Betts point out, the traditional budget is focused on what is required to maintain the existing service delivery system and to control the funds that have been allocated for various functional purposes. As a result, if a municipality does attempt to develop a more rigorous process for determining priorities, "the decision-makers are then confronted with the fact that the information provided through the conventional budgetary process is of little value in assessing alternative courses of action." If they are to decide which alternatives, if any, are available, "the decision-makers need to know more about what is actually being achieved in the way of meeting public needs."[9]

Knight also describes these shortcomings in the traditional budget process and adds several others.[10] In addition to inadequate information and the absence of choices, he observes that the traditional budget format can contribute to inequities in resource allocations. The documentation does not usually distinguish the request for funds that is cost-effective from the one that is not, and the former will be more adversely affected by a reduction in the allocation than the operation in which judicious "padding" has been provided. Knight also points out

[9]   T. J. Plunkett and G. M. Betts, *The Management of Canadian Urban Government,* Kingston, Queen's University, 1978, p. 240.

[10]   Henry C. Knight, *The Zero-Budgeting Process: A Practical Guide to Evaluation, Implementation and Use,* Hamilton, Society of Management Accountants, 1979, pp. 9–10.

that the traditional budget process is often carried out in relative isolation from other aspects of management with which it is (or ought to be) closely interrelated.

> Setting objectives, reviewing methods and procedures, planning activities, improving productivity and budgeting often take place at different times. It is as though a decision on the resources to be allocated could be separated from a consideration of these other matters.[11]

Instead, these activities should be properly integrated so that resource requirements are only authorized after a demonstration of effective performance and reasonable productivity.

A final problem is that many involved in the traditional budget process are unhappy with it. Those responsible for the preparation stage are frustrated when cutbacks are made without any apparant regard for the probable impact on the operating programs. At the same time, those responsible for deciding on the funding allocations are frustrated by the need to make decisions without sufficient information regarding the consequences for the organization.

Alternative Approaches to Budgeting

In light of the above-noted limitations, there has been a growing recognition that the budget process in the municipality needs to be improved in at least two main respects.[12] It should start with some delineation of the goals and objectives desired by council so that conflicting expenditure claims can be assessed within this framework. Without such "top-down" directives, the budget will remain incremental because of the "bottom-up" method of preparation. Second, the budget process needs to be extended to incorporate some analysis of existing programs and activities to demonstrate that such activities are not only consistent with municipal objectives but are being performed effectively.

IMPROVEMENTS NEEDED:
INITIAL PRIORITY SETTING
FOLLOWTHROUGH TO MEASURE RESULTS

---

[11] *Ibid.,* p. 10.

[12] The discussion that follows is partly based on Association of Municipal Clerks and Treasurers, *op. cit.,* Lesson Three.

Over the past several decades, a number of alternative budgeting systems have been introduced in both the public and private sectors. While all of them have introduced useful new approaches, there has been a tendency to oversell their advantages and to minimize the problems associated with implementing them. As a result, we have gone through a cycle in which each new budgeting system was heralded as a panacea and then abandoned after a few years as disillusionment set in. As can be seen from even the brief outline that follows, however, each of these systems introduced important new approaches or shifted the focus of the budgeting in appropriate new directions.

Performance Budgeting

Introduced in the United States at the beginning of the 1950s, performance budgeting differed from the traditional line-item budget in the emphasis placed on accountability and achievement. It focused on the delivery of services and work activities and attempted to measure the relationship between the input of resources and the output of services. Accordingly, the performance budget concentrated on the measurement of quantitative data concerning units of work performed for services rendered. Criteria such as the number of tons of refuse collected, dollars per ton of asphalt laid, or number of welfare recipients processed were performance measures that could be used for increasing or decreasing the staffing and related operating expenses that a particular unit received to meet its responsibilities.

PERFORMANCE BUDGETING:
MEASURES WORK PERFORMED
ACCOUNTABILITY FOR RESULTS
BUT, ELABORATE COST ACCOUNTING REQUIRED

Performance budgeting was considered to be an improvement over line-item budgeting in allowing for tighter control over expenditures by the elected representatives and in promoting a sense of responsibility and concern for achievement on the part of administrators.[13] It also

---

[13] This assessment of performance budgeting is based on V. N. MacDonald and P. J. Lawton, *Improving Management Performance,* Local Government Management Project, Toronto, Ministry of Treasury, Economics and Intergovernmental Affairs, November 1977, pp. 32–33.

served as a useful communications tool, helping to improve relations with interested citizens' groups and others concerned with how municipal funds were being spent and what was being accomplished as a result.

A major problem with performance budgeting, however, has been the need for an elaborate cost accounting system to support it. Critics have argued that without such an accounting system related to managerial responsibility, performance budgeting lacks depth and completeness and accuracy in performance feedback. A further criticism has been that the cost accounting system creates excessive amounts of data, tailored to a few people, used by even fewer, and requiring too much manpower to produce. There have also been difficulties in defining costs, quantities, and work units. It should be emphasized, however, that even though performance budgeting as a system has lost popularity over the years, the concepts behind it have been retained, refined, and incorporated into other systems. Indeed, as will be seen later in the chapter, the concept of *performance measurement* is today one of the key ingredients in any discussion of improving financial management.

Program Budgeting and PPBS

Even though performance budgeting was useful in directing attention to the results of particular expenditures, policy makers still sought improvements in the information and analysis available to them for making expenditure decisions. Program budgeting represented an attempt to measure the total cost of a specific function or activity comprising a program regardless of the number of departments or agencies that might be involved in executing the program. It was concerned with examining global functions such as protection to persons and property (which could encompass fire and police protection, emergency measures, building inspection, licensing, by-law enforcement, and animal control) or transportation services (public transit, airport transportation, traffic control, street lighting, major arterial roads, local streets, and parking). Within the defined program structure, objectives were then established for each program, function, and activity.

While the traditional budget is spending unit oriented, the program budget is not interested in who administers the activity but in what is the objective of the activity. While the traditional budget emphasizes control, the program budget emphasizes the rational determination of priorities in relation to defined goals. Rather than being prepared from the bottom up, the program budget is prepared from the top down in that it should start with a definition of the overall goals and objectives of the municipality. Within this framework, proposed expenditures are related to programs that contribute to the attainment of the overall goals.

> **PROGRAM BUDGETING AND PPBS:**
> **RATIONAL METHOD OF PRIORITY SETTING**
> **MULTI-YEAR PERSPECTIVE**
> **PROBLEMS DEFINING GOALS AND QUANTIFYING ALTERNATIVES**
> **REQUIRES EXTENSIVE ANALYTICAL CAPACITY**

A major emphasis of program budgeting is the identification of alternative programs and the measurement of their relative effectiveness in meeting the municipality's objectives. Such analytical tools as cost-benefit analysis are applied to help select the most effective alternative. To the extent that government activities can be quantified, this approach provides a rational method of selecting priorities. Budget reductions would not follow any of the procedures described above under the traditional budget but are made with respect to the projects least fulfilling the objectives defined by the municipality. Expenditures are not justified on departmental lines or on the basis of the previous year's budget but in relation to their contribution to the objectives. In short, program budgeting attempts to replace "the pernicious practice of incremental budgeting, under which the budget allocation process does not involve a review of the basic structure of programs but primarily consists in making decisions about how much the existing program is to be increased or, much less frequently, decreased."[14]

The program budgeting approach has been most effective when combined with the multi-year and more comprehensive perspective of the planning-programming-budgeting-system (PPBS). The first major application of the latter was in the United States Department of Defence in 1961. The PPBS is designed to help managers attain the objectives of the organization through a better selection of alternatives for the allocation of resources.[15] Its purpose is to develop and present information in a way that gives the full implications — costs and benefits — of each of the alternatives being considered. It represents a further attempt to

---

[14] Charles L. Schultze, *The Politics and Economics of Public Spending,* Washington, The Brookings Institution, 1968, p. 19.

[15] The description that follows is based on MacDonald and Lawton, *op. cit.,* pp. 33–37.

make decision making more systematic, by trying to minimize the amount of fragmented, incremental, and last minute planning and budgeting occurring in government organizations.

PPBS has been described as follows:

PLANNING: assessing the community needs, setting objectives and choosing the means of attaining them from among available alternatives.

PROGRAMMING: organizing and controlling specific courses of action in relation to the objectives they service and presenting them in a performance and resource use plan over a period of years.

BUDGETING: translating planning and programming decisions into specific financial plans for a relatively short period of time (one year).

SYSTEM: integrating, checking, and reviewing all planning, programming, and budgeting decisions within a consistent framework of general management.[16]

It can be seen that the PPBS approach greatly expands the scope of municipal budgeting from the simple financial control role of the line-item budget. It incorporates features from both performance and program budgeting and adds a multi-year perspective (usually three to five years) and a more sophisticated analysis of alternatives, drawing on the fields of economics, mathematics, computer science, and operations research.

PARKS AND PAPERCLIPS:
COMPARISON OF BUDGETING SYSTEMS

Henry distinguishes these various budgeting systems by considering how they would deal with two items — paperclips and parks.[17] The *traditional budget* is concerned with inputs and it would indicate the cost of a year's supply of paperclips or a year's program of park maintenance. With the shift to outputs inherent in the *performance budget,* we would direct attention to how many papers will be clipped by the paperclips

---

[16] *Ibid.,* p. 34, which in turn is quoting Department of Director General, Greater London Council, *Some Questions and Answers on the Greater London Council's Planning, Programming, Budgeting System,* London, Greater London Council, April 1972, p. 8.

[17] Nicholas Henry, *Public Administration and Public Affairs,* Englewood Cliffs, Prentice-Hall Inc., 1975, pp. 160–166.

and how many people will visit the parks. *Program budgeting and PPBS* are concerned not only with inputs and outputs but with effects and alternatives. Does paperclipping material facilitate the goals of our organization or should staples be used instead? How do we measure the benefit of the parks for those who visit them?

In practice, program budgeting and PPBS have not worked as well as this outline would suggest. A major problem is defining the goals of the municipality and attempting to quantify the alternative methods of achieving these goals. In the public sector many goals are rather nebulous, especially when they are concerned with prevention rather than affirmative action. For example, how does one compute the value of crime prevention or protection from disease, and yet without such quantification how can cost-benefit analysis be applied?[18] Local governments have traditionally lacked the analytical capabilities required to carry out detailed cost-benefit analyses of alternative programs. Critics have argued that it is unrealistic to expect that a system that was only partially successful in a huge analysis-oriented agency like the U.S. Defence Department could be implemented at the local government level.

A more fundamental problem has been the failure to recognize the extent to which program budgeting and PPBS require a complete change in the operations of the municipality and the roles of elected and appointed personnel. They represent not just a different way of classifying figures but a completely different approach to decision making. PPBS seeks to identify and remove overlapping and redundant activities, to expose the inefficient or ineffective use of resources, and to highlight the long range cost implications of proposals with relatively low initial expenses. While these objectives are commendable, they appear threatening to all but the most secure managers and, not surprisingly, attempts to introduce PPBS have sparked considerable resistance. Compounding the problem is the fact that some organizations have moved too quickly and others have acted without an adequate commitment to, and understanding of, the process on the part of administrators and elected representatives. The result has been lack of success, disillusionment, and abandonment or modification of the system in a number of instances. However, a number of U.S. and British municipalities made considerable use of this system, and more modest initiatives were also undertaken in

---

[18] For an example of a successful exercise in municipal goal setting, see J. R. Nininger, V. N. MacDonald, and G. Y. McDiarmid, *Goals for Dallas 'A'* and *Goals for Dallas 'B'*, Local Government Management Project, Toronto, Ministry of Treasury, Economics and Intergovernmental Affairs, May 1975.

such Canadian municipalities as Calgary, Edmonton, Ottawa, and London.[19] But as the 1970s progressed, PPBS gave way to yet another new budgetary system.

NEW BUDGETARY SYSTEMS MEAN:
NEW APPROACHES TO *DECISION MAKING*
NOT JUST CHANGES IN FIGURES, BUT IN *FUNDAMENTALS*

Zero Base Budgeting (ZBB)

ZBB has replaced PPBS as the most fashionable form of budgeting system, although it has now been around long enough for the predictable disillusionment to have begun.[20] It was developed by Peter Pyhrr for the U.S. electronics firm Texas Instruments at the end of the 1960s and achieved widespread prominence when it was implemented by Jimmy Carter while Governor of Georgia and then adopted as one of his policy commitments during his successful 1976 presidential election campaign.

The basic concept of ZBB is simple and consists of the simultaneous organization-wide examination of all programs. Under this system each program must compete for funding authorization on the basis of its cost-benefit value compared with all of the other programs of the municipality. "Through an extensive system of review and prioritization, obsolete programs which have continued through inertia or by design, or programs which should no longer be continued at the same level, are highlighted and either cut from the budget or cut back as required."[21] ZBB is, therefore, similar to some other fiscal ap-

---

[19]   See J. R. Nininger, V. N. MacDonald, and G. Y. McDiarmid, *Developments in the Management of Local Government,* Local Government Management Project, Toronto, Ministry of Treasury, Economics and Intergovernmental Affairs, 1975, which not only highlights Canadian municipal experience with PPBS but also includes a useful bibliography on this and other topics concerning local government management.

[20]   For a detailed examination of this topic see Knight, *op. cit.* Other references include the Ontario Ministry of Intergovernmental Affairs, *Zero Base Budgeting,* Financial Procedures Bulletin 4, Toronto, May 1979 and MacDonald and Lawton, *op. cit.,* pp. 37–38, on which this section is largely based.

[21]   *Ibid.,* p. 37.

proaches in attempting to link the internal financial resource allocation system to program management, with the important difference that there is no incremental portion of the budget. Under ZBB, "programs have no history — only a possible future."[22]

There are several key steps in the ZBB process,[23] beginning with the identification of decision units, which are activities or groups of activities for which a single manager has the responsibility for performance. Such a decision unit might be a traditional cost centre like a water treatment plant, a group of people like non-uniform staff in the fire department, or a particular service like tax billing. The necessary common feature is that there must be a measurable output resulting from the resources committed to the decision unit in the budget year. Especially when this system is first introduced, the municipality's accounting system may inhibit the identification of decision units below the departmental level.

STEPS IN ZBB:
IDENTIFY DECISION UNITS
MINIMUM SPENDING LEVEL
ALTERNATIVE DECISION
PACKAGES FOR EACH UNIT
RANKING OF PACKAGES

Step two involves the determination of a minimum level of spending for each decision unit — the level of effort below which the activity cannot be continued. Managers are then responsible for developing decision packages for each of the decision units. A decision package is a form or document that describes one way of performing the activity in question. The manager would develop a number of service improvement alternatives above the previously defined minimum and would highlight the resulting costs and benefits. All of the decision packages from all of the managers are then grouped in order of decreasing benefit in relation to the municipality's objectives. The identified merits of all activities in all departments are weighed one against another, and where funds are insufficient to cover all items, those with a lower priority rating are dropped from consideration.

---

[22] *Ibid.*

[23] The outline that follows is based on Ministry of Intergovernmental Affairs, ZBB Bulletin, *op. cit.*

ZBB has been utilized by a number of Canadian municipalities, including Hamilton, Regina, Ottawa, and Thunder Bay.[24] One difficulty is the amount of time needed to develop and implement ZBB, particularly for those organizations that do not already have clearly defined objectives for their programs. Another problem is the tendency for managers to take a very short term perspective. "Since long range programs have no immediate pay-off and consequently do not look especially valuable when weighed against a shorter term, higher priority program, there is a tendency to let long term programs drop or to stress the short range objectives of programs in general."[25] Critics also point to the difficulty of maintaining a non-threatening atmosphere, since ZBB is seen as a method of exposing "cushioned" budget areas.

On the other hand, supporters of ZBB cite a number of advantages. They claim that, when properly used, the system forces managers to identify feasible alternative ways of providing programs and thus to display creativity and initiative. In addition, those managers closest to the implementation of programs are given more influence in identifying areas for budget cuts or increases. It is also contended that ZBB increases managerial awareness of the cost per unit of output, and increases the participation of both top and middle management in financial decision making.

Kernaghan and Siegel explain that ZBB, like PPBS before it, is a product of its times. They describe PPBS as "a budgetary system for a dynamic, expanding government. It evaluates new programs and helps determine which to implement immediately and which must be put off until next year."[26] While PPBS points the way to new programs, ZBB shows where to make cuts. As such, it is an obvious system for an age of fiscal restraint. These and the other budgeting systems outlined, however, are ideal types in that they are seldom seen applied in pure form. More common is "a hybrid system which borrows the particular parts most suited to a particular environment and produces a new form of budgeting process."[27]

---

[24] For example, see City of Thunder Bay, *1980 Budget Manual,* Chief Administrative Officer's Department, July 1979, which incorporates a ZBB process.

[25] MacDonald and Lawton, *op. cit.,* p. 37.

[26] Kenneth Kernaghan and David Siegel, *Public Administration in Canada,* Toronto, Methuen, 1987, p. 533.

[27] *Ibid.,* p. 534.

When considering ZBB in relation to the municipal sector, it is recognized that local governments, by their nature, provide a number of mandatory programs such as the continued operation of a basic road network. To streamline the process, it might be appropriate at the outset, therefore, to designate certain programs as being automatically above the cut-off line, rather than wasting time in justifying an obviously necessary program. Alternatively, the ZBB approach might be used periodically, perhaps every two or three years. The general benefits of the system can still be obtained at frequent intervals without the heavy time demands of annual usage. Kernaghan and Siegel indicate that a variation of ZBB is practised in a number of municipalities in which, for each program, the manager is required to estimate the effects on the program — in terms of the level of service — if it were to operate at three different levels of funding: the same budget as last year (adjusted by inflation and population served), and, for example, 80% and 120% of last year's funding. "This provides decision makers with a significant amount of knowledge which they can use in deciding on funding levels."[28]

Potential of Budgetary Reform

Each of the alternative budgeting systems introduced over the past few decades has brought improvements over the traditional line-item budget. Unfortunately, each new system has also been oversold, and there has been a tendency to search for the one perfect system that meets all of our financial management needs. There is no such panacea, and each of the alternative systems appears to emphasize certain features to the relative neglect of others.

Thus, ZBB focuses on the importance of a rational priority setting exercise to determine the items to be included in the budget, but it doesn't appear to give much attention to measuring the results of the expenditures undertaken. This latter focus was found in performance budgeting, of course, but it neglected the initial determination of priorities. Program budgeting represents a somewhat broader approach that attempts to relate proposed expenditures to defined programs and then to the overall goals and objectives of the municipality. PPBS involves the most comprehensive approach and the one that seems to recognize most fully that budgeting is an integral part of an ongoing management

---

[28] *Ibid.*, p. 530.

process — but it is also viewed as the most complex and difficult to implement of the various approaches. A brief comparative summary of the main budgeting alternatives is found in Figure 1 below.

• FIGURE 1 •
COMPARISON OF BUDGETING SYSTEMS

Features	Line-Item	Performance	Program	ZBB
Focus	Object of expenditure	Unit cost	Program	Decision package
Timeframe	Annual	Annual	Multi-year	Annual (some longer)
Prepared	Bottom-up	Bottom-up	Top-Down	Bottom-up & top-down
Measure	Not over-spending	Minimize unit cost	Maximize program performance	Maximize program performance
Decision-making style	Incremental	Incremental	Rational	Rational
Weak points	Emphasize status quo	No comparisons across programs	High cost Dubious technique	High cost Dubious technique Morale problems

*Source: Modified from Kernaghan and Siegel, **Public Administration in Canada,** Toronto, Methuen, 1987, p. 524.*

The Budget as a Political Process

Whatever budget system is used, moreover, it is important to look beyond its rational design to the political context within which it must be made operational. The budget process and content will be influenced by not only the predilections of the elected representatives but also the pressures generated by various groups and individuals in the community. Notwithstanding the alleged advantages of a long term perspective, political reality will dictate a short term and constituent-oriented response.[29] Budgetary systems that attempt to be totally rational

---

[29] J. Richard Aronson and Eli Schwartz (eds.) *Management Policies in Local Government Finance,* Washington, D.C., International City Management Association, 1975, p. 66.

often fail by ignoring these political realities. Under a ZBB system, for example, it is easy to waste considerable paperwork and time rationalizing programs that must be continued for political and other reasons. Similarly, Adie and Thomas, in explaining the very limited success in attempting to implement PPBS, note the incompatibility of its logical-rational nature with a budget process that is inherently political and hence incremental.[30]

CAUTION:
BUDGETARY SYSTEM MUST OPERATE IN REAL WORLD

Drucker points out other forms of political reality in explaining the psychology of government institutions.[31] He notes that to persons within a budget organization, "performance" is the ability to maintain or increase one's budget and "results" is obtaining a larger budget. Therefore, efficiency and cost control, however much they may be espoused, are not considered virtues by those in the organization. To achieve results with a smaller budget or fewer staff is not desirable and might actually endanger the institution. Similarly, not to spend every penny in the budget is to signal to those who must approve the budget that it can be cut in the subsequent year. The practical reality is that the normal processes of government decision making do more to encourage spending and aggrandizement of the organization than cost-effectiveness or savings.

Meltsner and Wildavsky display a realistic insight into the limited possibilities of budgetary reform when they conclude that:[32]

> ... no proposal to change city budgeting will be acceptable that makes the budget appreciably less useful for control and cutting purposes; that calls for a large increase in personnel; that requires a high degree of analytical talent to make it work; or that depends upon the existence of, or the likelihood of obtaining, good data relevant to the actual decision.

---

[30] Robert Adie and Paul Thomas, *Canadian Public Administration: Problematic Perspectives,* Scarborough, Prentice-Hall Canada Inc., 1987, p. 268.

[31] Peter F. Drucker, *Management: Tasks, Responsibilities, Practices,* New York, Harper and Row, 1974, p. 142.

[32] Arnold Meltsner and Aaron Wildavsky, "Leave City Budgeting Alone: A Survey, Case Study and Recommendations for Reform," in John P. Crecine (ed.) *Financing the Metropolis,* Beverly Hills, Sage, 1970, p. 348.

As a result, they suggest limited reforms including the implementation of performance budgeting on a selective basis where there is a known relationship between costs and the unit of work measured, and the use of program analysis rather than full fledged program budgeting.

The best hope would appear to be a more systematic approach to budgeting that gives greater attention to the initial determination of spending priorities and the subsequent measurement of results. It is also important to integrate the budgeting exercise with the other financial activities of the municipality as part of an overall system of financial management. Thus, the budget needs to be seen not only as a financial document that determines taxation levels, but also as a statement of municipal policies and priorities and as a management tool for overseeing, coordinating, and assessing the administrative activities of the municipality. The accounting system must generate information that can help to measure the effectiveness of municipal spending activities in addition to its traditional emphasis on safeguarding the use of public funds and ensuring legal compliance. The information generated by the accounting system must be provided to council and senior staff in a form that will facilitate their task of monitoring and, where necessary, redirecting the municipality's programs and priorities.

Toward A Financial Management System

The main elements of a financial management system can be developed from the budget process if the breadth of the latter is recognized and fully exploited. The budget process should be seen as continuous and it involves at least four significant stages as illustrated below:

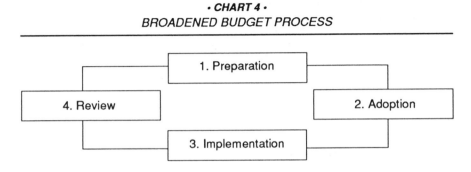

• CHART 4 •
BROADENED BUDGET PROCESS

The preparation of the budget provides an opportunity for council to review and assess existing policies and programs in relation to the overall objectives of the municipality. It is at this stage that council gives some top-down direction to those responsible for the compilation of the budget. In doing so, council takes into account any information and analysis that helps to identify the municipality's long term goals and commitments. For example, the implications of such documents as the official plan and the capital works program would be carefully considered.[33]

The adoption of the budget identifies the amount of expenditure to be financed from municipal taxation that year. This aspect usually receives far too much attention and is often treated as if it were the whole budget exercise. More importantly, however, the adoption of the budget signifies that council has authorized the expenditure of specified amounts of money for specified purposes for the coming year. The budget is, therefore, a control document that can be used, in conjunction with the accounting system, to monitor the spending activities of the municipality.

The implementation stage of the budget process is where this monitoring occurs. Through an internal audit or pre-audit, management control is exercised by ensuring that funds aren't expended except as authorized by council — whether as part of the previously adopted budget or as extraordinary items that have received separate approval. Periodic reports assist council in overseeing the spending activities and identifying unusual patterns or instances of likely overspending. Reports are also needed on the revenue picture for the preceding year and the effectiveness of existing policies and procedures concerning revenue collection and handling. Increasingly, attention is also being directed to reports and analyses that help council to measure the effectiveness of expenditures.

PERFORMANCE MEASUREMENT:
EFFICIENCY AND EFFECTIVENESS
DOING THINGS RIGHT AND DOING RIGHT THINGS

This latter concept of *performance measurement* has been receiving growing emphasis as financial restraint requires all governments to demonstrate that their operations are cost-effective. In simplest terms,

---

[33] The latter connection is particularly important and yet municipalities often fail to examine the full consequences of their capital expenditure decisions or the implications for their future current budgets. See Garnet Gaven and Richard J. Long, "Capital budget decision-making processes in Canadian urban municipalities" in *Canadian Public Administration*, Winter 1981, pp. 634–640.

performance measurement can be defined as the quantitative determination of the efficiency and effectiveness of municipal services.[34] While efficiency is concerned with minimizing the resources used to produce a given output, effectiveness provides an important balance by directing attention to whether the organization is achieving its goals and objectives. For example, while the efficiency of a building inspection operation would be measured on the basis of man-hours per inspection, effectiveness measures would include such aspects as the accuracy rate of inspections, the percentage of violations corrected, and the percentage of court judgments favouring the municipality. Similarly, fire fighting efficiency would be reflected in such measures as cost per alarm and cost per fire, but to determine the effectiveness of the service we would need to consider such aspects as the number of casualties per fire, the dollar loss per fire, the average response time, and the average time to control fires.[35]

Obviously, the effectiveness of this implementation stage of the budget process depends on the nature of the accounting and reporting system that is maintained by the municipality and on the extent to which council receives information that helps it to measure the effectiveness of the expenditures that are occurring.

The review stage completes the budget process and leads back into the first stage again. While review should be continuous as part of the implementation of the budget, the fiscal year-end provides an appropriate time to assess the causes of over- or under-expenditure during the year and, more importantly, to review the efficiency and effectiveness of expenditures. The insights gained from the review stage can then be carried forward to the preparation of the following year's budget as part of the ongoing process.

While the external post-audit carried out by a municipal auditor each year is likely to broaden because of the increased emphasis at all levels of government on comprehensive or "value for money" auditing, it is suggested that municipalities should also be conducting their own internal management audit to review their operations for the preceding year and to make improvements where possible. The municipal perspective is important because many activities do not lend themselves easily to productivity measurements. For example, an outside auditor might look

---

[34] For a good introduction to this topic, complete with examples, see Ontario Ministry of Municipal Affairs and Housing, *Performance Measurement for Municipalities,* Toronto, 1981.

[35] These examples are from *ibid.,* pp. 23–25.

at the cost of committee and council meetings, compare the time spent with the decisions reached, and make the assumption that the costs are inappropriate. What can be missed in the evaluation is the importance to our democratic system of people coming together, sharing ideas, and generally engaging in the difficult process of decision making.[36]

Summary

Any discussion of municipal government will inevitably extend to a consideration of the so-called municipal financial dilemma. The financial difficulties facing municipal government should not be minimized. Obviously it would be helpful if municipalities enjoyed more unconditional grants, additional local revenue sources, or even a property tax system based on a better assessment process than is found in a number of the provinces. It would also be preferable if municipalities were better able to resist expenditure burdens caused by actions of the senior levels of government. Under the circumstances, however, the best approach for municipalities is to make the wisest use of the scarce financial resources available to them. While no one budgeting system is a panacea, most municipalities would benefit from a broadened approach to budgeting that served to direct greater attention to the initial determination of priorities and the subsequent measurement of results.

---

[36] Example provided by Donald Smeltzer, Letter of April 24, 1989. See also Sharon Sutherland, "The Politics of Audit," in *Canadian Public Administration,* Toronto, Vol. 29, No. 1, Spring 1986, pp. 118–146, for some well argued concerns about the increased authority of the federal Auditor-General to "second-guess" the decisions of federal politicians. Her comments have considerable validity for the municipal level, should the concept of comprehensive auditing be introduced there.

12 *The Management of People*

Objectives:

1. To illustrate the breadth and changing nature of the concept of management.
2. To describe the general scope of human resource management, and its increasing importance in municipal operations.
3. To elaborate the steps involved in the acquisition and development of municipal personnel.
4. To establish an effective approach to performance appraisal of employees.

Introduction

Notwithstanding all of the factors discussed in the preceding chapters, ultimately it is people who make the difference. "People — not laws, charters, computer systems, or organizational structures — determine the quality of government performance."[1] This statement should come as no surprise. It has already been noted that local governments must operate under severe constraints, including fundamental legal and financial limitations. Their imminent demise has been predicted more than once. The fact that local governments have survived, and even displayed an impressive resiliency at times, is to a large extent a tribute to the elected and appointed personnel who have served over the years at the local level.

But today more than ever, there is a need for improved performance from those responsible for managing the muncipality. First and foremost, the management task itself needs greater recognition. Traditionally, the emphasis in municipal operations was placed on the delivery of a variety of specific services. Technical skills were, therefore, particularly valued — as in the turn of the century reform era's glorification of the expert. Now, especially in larger municipalities, there is a growing recognition of the greatly changed context of local government.

---

[1] Brian W. Rapp and Frank M. Patitucci, *Managing Local Government for Improved Performance,* Boulder, Westview Press, 1977, p. 35.

Changing Nature of Municipal Management

Municipal managers today face an accelerating range of demands. They must help the council respond to these demands knowing that financial resources are quite inadequate and that there are conflicting public views about desirable courses of action. They will be expected "to demonstrate an awareness of existing demands and expectations and an ability to anticipate future concerns."[2] Today's municipal managers can expect their activities to include more brokering among interests in the community, more negotiating among conflicting interests.[3]

In addition to these pressures, municipal managers must also manage their staff effectively in the context of a strong and growing union movement. At a time of financial restraint and periodic legislated limits on salary increases, they must find ways of motivating staff and increasing their productivity. They must develop their team-building skills to counteract the fragmented and narrow perspectives that commonly characterize the municipal organization. They must operate in a tangled web of intergovernmental relations, seeking the provincial and federal programs that are beneficial to the municipality and trying to minimize the impact of those that are not. In short, the municipal manager must operate within severe constraints in a complex, rapidly changing environment.

One reflection of these new conditions is the enhanced policy advisory role of staff. They will now be expected to provide more information and to assemble it in a form that is intelligible for the decision makers.

...this will require the administrator to analyse it in order to draw out its significance. More importantly, the administrator will be expected to extend his analysis of information about particular issues to the point where alternative courses of action are examined and their possible consequences indicated.[4]

---

[2] Anne B. McAllister, *An Approach to Manpower Planning and Management Development in Canadian Municipal Government,* Toronto, Institute of Public Administration, 1979, p. 37.

[3] This point is made frequently in Wayne F. Anderson et al, *The Effective Local Government Manager,* Washington, D.C., International City Management Association, 1983.

[4] T. J. Plunkett and G. M. Betts, *The Management of Canadian Urban Government,* Kingston, Queen's University, 1978, p. 172.

In addition to their traditional technical skills, therefore, the administators or managers who advise on policy require analytical ability, conceptual skills, political sensitivity, foresight, and the ability to think imaginatively and creatively.

SKILLS OF MANAGER:
ANTICIPATING FUTURE CONCERNS
BROKERING AMONG INTERESTS
ANALYTICAL ABILITY
IMAGINATION AND CREATIVITY
COACH AND COUNSELLOR

Human relations skills are also increasingly important in local government managers. This requirement is partly a function of the increased size of municipalities and their staff. Plunkett has estimated that for every 1 000 of population added to a municipality at least ten more employees must be added.[5] With more and larger departments, it is obviously important that managers be effective in directing and supervising subordinates and in coordinating the activities of increasingly complex organizations. There has also been a growing recognition of the potential of motivating subordinates, developing their abilities, and thereby improving the work capacity and productivity of the municipality. These activities are seen as especially important in the present restraint period when we are expected to do more with less and when job satisfaction for employees has to be provided by more than just the size of the salary increase.

Traditional, "top-down" management styles are seldom very effective in these changed circumstances. A much-quoted study of successful organizations has concluded that managers need to be coaches, counsellors and "nurturers of champions."[6] The same study popularized the term MBWA, "Management by Walking Around," and provided evidence that successful managers practised this technique. They didn't stay in their offices reviewing reports and procedural manuals; they spent their time "on the floor." They listened to their employees, talked to them about the organization's core values (fundamental objectives), and tried

---

[5] T. J. Plunkett, *Training and Qualifications of Senior Municipal Administrators,* paper presented to the 32nd Annual Conference of the Canadian Federation of Mayors and Municipalities, Ottawa, June 1969.

[6] Thomas J. Peters and Robert H. Waterman Jr., *In Search of Excellence,* New York, Warner Books, 1982.

to remove obstacles to successful achievement of those values. These successful managers encouraged innovation and experimentation, and they tolerated mistakes provided that something was learned from the experience. Above all, they had an abiding faith in their employees, and were prepared to give them ample discretion as to how they carried out their duties — consistent with the core values of the organization.[7]

However impressive these newer approaches to management may be, the reality is that most municipalities have been slow to recognize and practice even the basic functions of management. A well documented example of this problem was Ontario's *Local Government Management Project* (LGMP) of the 1970s, a pilot project intended to introduce a system of goals and objectives in four large urban municipalities, one a regional government. Even with these relatively sophisticated municipal systems, the project encountered difficulties because administrators had little understanding of management. It is stated, for example, that:

> When a management improvement project encounters managers who do not regard themselves as managers, who have not considered the various aspects of a managerial role, and yet who supervise an area of responsibility containing hundreds or even thousands of people, it is evident that the management improvement process needs to begin at a very basic level.[8]

According to the LGMP findings:

> Many managers needed basic training to gain an understanding and appreciation of the content of a manager's job. They needed some help with delegation, they needed help in giving staff and employees feedback and direction, in helping them to fill useful organizational roles....[9]

That these findings are not atypical is evident from a later Canada-wide study by Anne McAllister, which observed that "there has been relatively little recognition of the critical importance of human resources or of the pressing need to manage, anticipate and plan for the growth of the municipal service."[10] She explained that rarely had significant

---

[7] See *ibid.*, and also Thomas Peters and Nancy Austin, *A Passion for Excellence,* New York, Random House, 1985, for an elaboration of these points.

[8] V. N. MacDonald and P. J. Lawton, *The LGMP Experience Phase II: The Implementation of Organizational Change in Local Government,* Toronto, Ministry of Treasury, Economics and Intergovernmental Affairs, May 1978, p. 53.

[9] *Ibid.*

[10] McAllister, *op. cit.,* p. 13.

responsibility for management development been assigned to a senior official or an identifiable department. Moreover, she found that senior managers and administrators often showed a disregard for personnel policies and activities and that "personnel departments may be relegated to a low status by having to report through another department such as finance or by being attached to a city manager's office in a staff capacity."[11]

One indication of the potentially serious consequences of this neglect for management development was documented in a detailed Ontario study entitled *Managers for Local Government*.[12] It forecast that between 700 and 900 new managers would be required in Ontario municipalities before the end of the 1980s, and yet found little indication that consideration had been given as to where these managers would be found. Almost half of the municipalities surveyed had no response to the question of how they would fill their additional management needs. But 45 percent of the respondents did state that their successor would be found in another municipality — perhaps an indication that they had more confidence in the staff development activities of other municipalities than in their own!

There has been a gradual improvement in the intervening years. Educational institutions and municipal associations in a number of provinces have expanded their offerings of educational and professional training courses and materials. Municipalities have shown some increased commitment to the professional development of their staff. Nonetheless, a recent Ontario survey[13] found that three-quarters (74%) of the municipal staff responding to the survey felt that they needed more education and training in order to achieve their career objectives or even to remain proficient in their present position. Yet, the same survey found that two-thirds of municipalities do not have written education and training policies for their staff.

---

[11] *Ibid.,* p. 14.

[12] Ministry of Treasury, Economics and Intergovernmental Affairs, *Managers for Local Government,* (a study carried out by David Michener), especially "Report 3: The Data Base," 1976 and "Discussion Paper 5: Education, Training, Development," Spring, 1977. The three reports and five discussion papers arising out of this study provide a wealth of information about needs and resources in education for municipal management.

[13] Decima Research, *A Survey Among Senior Non-elected Municipal Officials and Councillors for the Ministry of Municipal Affairs,* April 1988.

Traditional Hiring and Promotion Practices

A number of the shortcomings in municipal management can be traced to traditional hiring and promotion practices. Staff acquisitions have tended to occur on an ad hoc basis and to perpetuate established structures and job qualifications rather than to anticipate the changing needs of the municipality. Individuals have usually been hired for their technical competence in relation to the provision of a specific service or program. Successful performance of their duties, reinforced by seniority, normally results in the promotion of such individuals into more senior management positions. But there appears to be insufficient appreciation of the fact that technical skills become less important with each step up the hierarchy, while other, quite different skills will be increasingly demanded.

As Plunkett and Betts point out, a skilled tradesman is faced with an entirely different set of problems when promoted to superintendent of the municipal workshops, with forty skilled tradesmen in eight different trades.[14] He no longer performs as the machinest he was, but must now be concerned with scheduling and directing the work force and a variety of personnel and budgetary duties. But in appointing him to the position, did anyone bother to ascertain whether he possessed the requisite skills or was any attempt made to provide him with an opportunity to attain them? A similar situation arises when a professional employee such as an engineer moves into a management position. While the engineer may have spent her first few years utilizing her professional skills in designing and supervising works construction projects, her progression up the ladder makes these skills less and less relevant, while her ability to handle planning, budgeting, and personnel matters becomes paramount.[15]

One result of this pattern is that many individuals in municipal management may feel uncomfortable with their responsibilities and may tend to concentrate on the functional aspects of the work for which they are responsible. For example, an accountant who becomes Director of Finance may feel unable to cope with the new demands of his job and may direct attention to the accounting activities with which he is familiar.

---

[14] Plunkett and Betts, *op. cit.,* p. 256.

[15] *Ibid.,* pp. 255–257.

> Responsible for a department of 40 to 50 employees, of which four are
> professional accountants, he may choose to spend much of his working
> day with a calculator checking routine accounting operations.[16]

We should probably update this scenario by referring to a micro-computer rather than a calculator (and a female Director as much as a male), but the problem remains the same. What must be recognized, however, is that while such individuals are neglecting their management roles, they derive satisfaction from doing something for which they were trained and with which they are familiar.

McAllister offers some explanations for the shortcomings of the traditional approach by outlining a number of constraints on management development activities.[17] Several relate to what might be termed the uncertain political environment of local government. Since manpower planning and development efforts require a long term commitment, this is often difficult to obtain from councillors who are more interested in short term results. Moreover, a change in council can result in an existing program being modified or abandoned before its effects can be felt. Unexpected decisions by the federal or provincial governments can upset the plans of a municipality and leave it with the wrong number or type of staff for its changed circumstances. The limited financial base of municipal governments is another major constraint. It not only inhibits the hiring of new staff, but also has a detrimental effect on the proportion of the municipal budgets devoted to staff training and development — activities that are often considered "luxuries" or at least "non-essentials."

THE CASE FOR TRAINING AND DEVELOPMENT — EVEN IF THE EMPLOYEE LEAVES

This lingering attitude on the part of some councillors must be strongly resisted. There is no better investment that the municipality can make than the money it spends on developing its employees. The standard excuse for inaction is that the municipality doesn't want to "waste" money training an employee who will just leave in a couple of years anyway. To this rationale, there are at least three rebuttals. First, this argument is very short-sighted in ignoring the fact that wherever the better qualified employee may go, he or she helps to strengthen the

---

[16] *Ibid.,* p. 257.

[17] McAllister, *op. cit.,* Chapter Four.

calibre of the overall municipal civil service — a necessary step if the local level is to gain greater operating freedom from the provincial level. In other words, municipalities should view their expenditures on staff training and development as an investment in the whole system of local government, not just an investment in their own municipal operations. Second, since municipalities continually "raid" each other when hiring new staff, wouldn't they like to count on the fact that the other municipalities from whom they are hiring have invested in staff training and development? Third, and most to the point, isn't it vastly preferable to have a qualified, well motivated individual for even a couple of years than to retain staff who have received no encouragement to stay current or to develop their skills and abilities? Some long time municipal staff have 20 years of experience, and some only have one year of experience, twenty times.

Municipalities must broaden their perspective to a concern for the overall management of their activities. Earlier chapters have indicated the need for council to provide a clearer sense of leadership and direction through the establishment of overall goals and objectives and an improved priority setting process. More specifically, in the context of this chapter, council should be concerned with providing an environment conducive to the recruitment, development, and retention of professional managerial staff.

> This would include the establishment of policy guidelines within which management can pursue development programs and activities, the approval of adequate budgetary allotments, and the extension of strong moral and political support to those senior administrators and managers who are responsible for designing, implementing and assessing management development activities.[18]

From Management of Personnel to Personnel Management

Discussions thus far have suggested that the changing needs of municipal management can best be met by municipalities giving greater attention to the kinds of employees they hire and how they are trained, developed, and deployed subsequently. At this point, therefore, the focus of the chapter shifts from management generally to personnel management, or human resource management as it is increasingly

---

[18] McAllister, *op. cit.,* p. 62.

termed. Even this subject, however, is much too broad to allow any overall examination.[19] The primary concern is the acquisition and development of municipal staff. Since these activities take place within an increasingly unionized environment, a brief explanation of the municipal collective bargaining process is provided first.[20]

Municipal Collective Bargaining

In simplest terms, collective bargaining involves negotiations between representatives of labour and management to achieve a written agreement, binding on both parties, covering the terms and conditions of employment. While this process, with its competing weapons of strike and lockout, has long been the basis for labour-management relations in the private sector, its introduction to the public sector came much later. Senior levels of government resisted the concept, largely on the grounds that collective bargaining would compromise the sovereignty of parliament (the Queen does not negotiate) and that strikes were incompatible with the essential nature of many government services. With the notable exception of Saskatchewan, where a CCF government included its employees in the coverage of its general labour legislation from as early as 1944, all other provinces and the federal government rejected collective bargaining until the mid-1960s. By 1975, however, virtually all public sector employees had legally been given the right to engage in collective bargaining.

It is ironic that, notwithstanding the reservations that provincial governments had felt about allowing collective bargaining for their employees, they showed no such hesitation when it came to the local government level. Nor did they feel the need for a separate piece of legislation. "By and large municipal governments simply were included in the definition of 'employer' and members of the municipal service considered as 'employees' under the general labour legislation en-

---

[19]   The personnel management lesson of the Association of Municipal Clerks and Treasurers of Ontario *Municipal Administration Program,* for example, lists as personnel management activities: personnel planning, recruitment, job descriptions, classification system, wages and salaries, fringe benefits, working conditions, labour relations, collective bargaining, appointments, orientation, training, counselling, performance appraisal, staff motivation and development, promotion, transfer, discipline, dismissal, administration of collective agreements and grievance procedures. Unit Four, Lesson Seven, p. 168.

[20]   The outline that follows is partly based on *ibid.,* pp. 169–170.

acted in each province."[21] The main exception has been the provision, in virtually all provinces, for modified collective bargaining procedures for police and firefighters. A primary objective for both groups has been to require membership in a separate bargaining unit consisting only of police or firefighters. There has also been an attempt to provide for the settlement of deadlocks through compulsory arbitration rather than strikes and lockouts, although this was more successful in the case of police than firefighters.

In addition to police and firefighters, two other bargaining units commonly found in all but the smallest municipalities are "outside workers" and "inside workers." Most of these units are represented by the Canadian Union of Public Employees (CUPE), the largest union in Canada.

Constraints on Collective Agreements

The rapid spread of unions throughout the municipal public service has had important implications for the matters under review in this chapter. On the one hand, collective agreements have unquestionably improved salaries and benefits for municipal staff generally, and provided protection from potentially arbitrary actions by management. Because individuals performing managerial tasks are often part of a bargaining unit, however, collective agreements can also be seen as restricting the flexibility of management development programs. Most collective agreements contain provisions concerning promotional procedures, job competitions, job classifications, provision of training and development opportunities, and compensation — and these provisions therefore apply equally to management as well as non-management personnel. "As a result, the flexibility and freedom that is desirable when designing and implementing management development activities is sharply curtailed."[22] As McAllister explains:

> It becomes very difficult to tailor a sequence of development activities for one or two particularly qualified individuals without offering the same opportunities to all personnel at the same level or in the same job area. Exceptional cases cannot easily be treated as such without risking a labour complaint or grievance.[23]

---

[21] T. J. Plunkett, "Municipal Collective Bargaining" in *Collective Bargaining in the Public Service,* Toronto, Institute of Public Administration, 1973, p. 2.

[22] McAllister, *op. cit.,* p. 53.

[23] *Ibid.,* pp. 53–54.

Other personnel practices such as those associated with the posting of vacancies, the nature of competitions, and job appeals may also restrict management development efforts. Senior members are not free to move staff around from position to position as a means of broadening their experience. Moreover, the ability of management to control the selection process in identifying and encouraging key personnel is handicapped somewhat by preferences related to seniority, internal candidates, point systems, and other measures. "While the application of objective criteria is merited to a considerable degree, an element of intuition, subjective judgment and management discretion is also required when assessing personnel."[24]

According to Plunkett and Betts, municipalities have been slow to recognize the implications of the expansion of trade union activity beyond the traditional blue and white collar occupations. Increasingly professions such as engineers, planners, teachers, and nurses have obtained certification as bargaining units. In addition to the normal concern about wages and other economic benefits, these professionals often demand more input into policy planning and decision making, especially with respect to the quality of the services provided by their own professional disciplines. The result has been a growing invasion of what was once regarded as the sacrosanct area of management rights. In response, municipalities must assert their need "to have a primary voice in the determination of program goals, organizational structure, financing, work methods, and the recruiting, selection, promotion and discharge of staff."[25]

The Acquisition and Development of Staff

These activities are singled out for special attention because they are felt to be not only the essential aspects of the personnel management function but also the key to the improved performance of management generally. These activities are important to all municipalities, regardless of their size or organizational structure. They involve all staff, not just personnel specialists. It is only through careful acquisition and subsequent development of municipal staff that one can give the appropriate emphasis to human resources cited at the beginning of

---

[24] *Ibid.*, p. 54.

[25] Plunkett and Betts, *op. cit.*, p. 284.

this chapter. The fact that, as has been seen, these activities have traditionally not been well handled is an added reason for singling them out for special consideration.

Personnel Planning

As previously mentioned, most hiring decisions have been made in isolation rather than in the context of a long term comprehensive analysis of the municipality's personnel needs, both quantitative and qualitative. Yet there is a growing recognition that municipalities now require quite different staff resources than those previously employed to handle routine administration and service delivery functions. Especially in large cities, the increasing attention given to policy planning has underlined:

> ...the urgent need for the establishment of a support staff capacity to measure performance, to review programme effectiveness, to analyze and predict the impact of demographic, social, economic and fiscal trends and to develop rational alternatives which will assist in the control and direction of urban and regional growth....[26]

As a result, the recruitment of staff should take place within a framework of personnel planning defined as "the process by which an organization ensures that it has the right number of people and the right kind of people, at the right places, at the right time, doing things for which they are economically most useful."[27]

The need for personnel planning is obvious in large municipalities with significant numbers of staff being hired, retiring, receiving promotions, and taking other employment. But it might be thought that this activity is not necessary in small municipalities with few employees and limited growth potential. Such is not the case, however. Since even the addition of one employee may represent a substantial cost increase for a small municipality, forward planning of staff requirements is highly desirable.[28]

---

[26] Plunkett and Betts, *op. cit.*, pp. 275–276.

[27] Thomas J. Patten, *Manpower Planning and the Development of Human Resources,* New York, John Wiley and Sons, 1982, p. 14.

[28] For a detailed guide, see L. Suzanne Park and Marilyn Melville, *Human Resource Planning and Training Needs Analysis,* Oshawa, Ontario Municipal Management Institute, 1983.

More important is the need to consider the changing demands facing the municipality and the resultant implications for the knowledge and skills required by the staff. In many small municipalities, it has been common for the clerk or clerk-treasurer to serve for decades and this has meant an inevitable tendency for traditional attitudes and practices to become firmly entrenched. If a small municipality experiences rapid growth, personnel planning becomes even more important. Too often the facet of municipal operations that lags most in a situation of sudden growth is the deployment of the staff. Generally, the approach is simply to add more staff of the conventional type without considering qualitative changes that have occurred and that call for new kinds of staff. For example, the municipality's departmental structure may expand until serious fragmentation exists before any thought is given to the appointment of a coordinating officer. Even more rare, traditionally, has been the employment of staff with research and long term planning ability. It has been difficult to receive budgetary approval for such positions even though closer examination might reveal existing, approved positions that no longer appear to serve any real purpose in relation to the objectives of the municipality.

PERSONNEL PLANNING:
PERSONNEL NEEDS
AVAILABLE SUPPLY
IDENTIFICATION OF GAP
POTENTIAL OF TRAINING
NEED FOR RECRUITMENT

The two main components of personnel planning are the forecast of personnel needs and the determination of the supply of personnel. The first task is quite difficult. There are obvious limitations to a simple projection of historical patterns, but any other estimates are usually little more than educated guesses. Potentially helpful information may be found in various long term policy documents of the municipality, such as a financial plan, official plan, and capital budget, but all too often their implications are not adequately considered. Insight into future staff needs should also be found in any long term goals and objectives that the municipality may have developed.

The first step in determining the supply of personnel involves the preparation of a detailed inventory of the municipality's existing staff, based on information that is largely available from job descriptions and employee personnel records. This record should extend to information on rates of turnover and absenteeism, age distribution, dates of retirement, attrition rates, and related matters. From this inventory, the municipality can then estimate how many staff of various kinds are likely to be available to meet estimated future needs.

Plunkett and Betts point out that if this data is stored in appropriate computerized programs, its ready accessibility can allow other useful analyses.[29] The impact on future budgets of wage scale changes proposed during negotiations can be easily determined for example. The costs for the employment of part-time staff can be compared to the payment of overtime rates to full time staff to cover peak workload situations. "Make or buy" decisions for special tasks such as printing, architectural, or engineering services can be assessed when the integrated costs of wages, fringe benefits, support staff, etc., are available by function as well as by department.

The main purpose of the inventory, however, is the identification of the gap between need and supply — that is, the determination of the number and types of staff who will be required at various intervals in the future and will not apparently be available from the municipality's own staff resources. Once this personnel gap is known, the municipality must then consider to what extent existing employees could be trained and developed to meet some of the future needs. The remainder will presumably have to be filled by recruitment.

Recruitment

Assuming that a municipality is engaged in at least some elementary personnel planning, then the recruitment of a new employee will not commence until the following kinds of questions have been asked:[30]

1. To whom does this position report?
2. What is its main purpose?
3. What specific tasks must be performed to achieve that purpose?
4. What special skills, training, and education does a person need to perform those tasks?

---

[29] Plunkett and Betts, *op. cit.*, p. 279.

[30] Ministry of Intergovernmental Affairs, *Recruiting — II: The Right Person for the Job*, Bulletin No. 27, Toronto, June 1979, pp. 2–3.

5. Does the person need prior experience and, if so, of what kind and duration?
6. What personal qualities should the person possess?
7. What salary range should be offered for this position?

Such questions may seem unnecessary or redundant where there is an existing job description for the position under consideration. But it is important not to accept the status quo too readily. An existing job description may be deficient or outdated in certain aspects. There may even need to be changes in the position and its reporting relationships that necessitate some internal reorganization. A careful review of the matter by the manager responsible and the personnel specialist (where the latter exists) can help to ensure that positions that are filled will meet the future needs of the municipality.

The increasing attention being given to employment equity and to various types of affirmative action programs may also have a major impact on the recruitment process. Employment equity has been described as offering assistance to members of disadvantaged groups to have fair access to jobs. "Its goal is to achieve a balanced representation of: qualified members from all groups, in all occupations, and at all organizational levels."[31] This definition indicates that the concept of employment equity is much broader than, but includes, the pay equity activities also underway in municipalities in provinces such as Ontario. Because of the growing commitment to employment equity, the recruitment process must be very sensitive to any form of discriminatory biases or emphasis. More than that, recruitment may have to give primary attention to certain targeted groups (which have been subject to past discrimination) in the case of some affirmative action initiatives.

Another important early consideration is whether recruitment should take place from within or whether the position should be advertised outside. Obviously, if the position in question is part of the bargaining unit and must be filled on the basis of seniority, then only if there are no suitable internal applicants can outsiders be recruited. Even where this limitation does not exist, however, recruitment from within may be favoured, partly because of the apparent savings in time and money, and because experience in the particular municipality is considered an asset. Such "promotions" are felt to motivate existing employees by providing for career advancement.

---

[31] Ministry of Municipal Affairs, *Employment Equity,* Municipal Personnel Management, Unit 2, Toronto, 1988, p. 2.

It must be emphasized, however, that recruitment from within very definitely limits the municipality's choice. Much depends on how well the municipality has developed its existing staff through varied responsibilities and support for education and training — but, as previously indicated, staff development has not traditionally received much attention in Canadian municipalities. It is suggested that even if a particular employee is favoured, both the employee and the municipality are likely to feel better if that preference holds up against the challenge of outside competition. Therefore, in most circumstances it is felt that vacancies should be advertised outside of as well as within the municipality, subject to any collective agreement limitations.

The recruitment process itself includes the following steps: [32]
1.   Writing the job advertisement;
2.   Placing it in appropriate publications;
3.   Examining the applications and selecting those to be interviewed;
4.   Determining a "short list" of three or four candidates for final consideration; and
5.   Making the selection and confirming through a letter of appointment.

Before the process begins, there should be a specific assignment of responsibility for the various tasks and a budget allocation to cover the estimated costs. Particularly important to determine is the extent of council's involvement, although it should be mainly concerned with positions that report to it directly, and with the establishment of hiring procedures to be followed by staff in all other instances. The services of an outside personnel consultant may also be desirable where a senior staff position is being filled.

JOB AD:
WHAT IT *CAN'T* SAY
WHAT IT SHOULD SAY
WHERE IT SHOULD BE

The job advertisement deserves more careful attention than it typically receives, both in its format and content and in where it is placed.[33] Careful attention must also be given to what *cannot* be included in the

---

[32]   Ministry of Intergovernmental Affairs, *Recruitment — III: Advertising*, Bulletin No. 28, Toronto, July 1979.

[33]   For examples of ads that exhibit both good and bad features see *ibid.*

ad because of human rights legislation and, more recently, the Charter of Rights and Freedoms. If the municipality is to obtain the best possible candidate, the ad must "sell" the job by presenting it (and the municipality) in an interesting and challenging fashion. The ad must also describe the requirements of the position in such a way that only appropriate candidates apply. The objective is not to generate the most applications possible; this result only complicates the later task of determining a short list for interviewing. Rather, the objective of the ad is to attract appropriate numbers of the right kind of candidates. However well worded, the ad can only be effective if it is placed in publications where it is likely to attract the attention of these candidates — and with sufficient lead time to give them adequate time to respond.

The screening of applications is the next important step. It must be done thoroughly and yet promptly enough to avoid losing good candidates. If those handling the recruitment have given prior consideration to the kind of candidate desired, by posing the types of questions previously listed, they will obviously be better able to assess the applications and arrive at a short list for interviewing.

Interviews are critical to the recruitment process. They should be appreciated as a two-way exchange that gives the municipality enough information and insight to assess whether or not the applicant is best suited for the position and also gives the applicant an opportunity to make judgments about the job opening and the municipality. By its very nature, the process tends to be imprecise and subjective. It is desirable to use trained professional interviewers if they are familiar with the job and organization in question. Structuring the interview helps to ensure that it covers all the areas considered relevant and that comparable information is obtained from all interviewed. A number of interviewers may also be used, either in the same interview or in a series. Any other assessments that are available should also be considered along with the interview. Reference checks are important, although it should be borne in mind that there is a tendency for those contacted for a reference to hedge their comments, especially if the contact is by telephone.

Once an applicant has been selected, council's approval must be sought if it has not been directly involved in the process. The successful applicant's acceptance must then be obtained, and the other candidates notified of the decision. It is also suggested that the successful candidate receive a letter of appointment confirming the terms and conditions that were agreed to in previous discussions and outlining any special arrangements such as municipal contribution to relocation expenses and probationary period of employment.

These approaches to personnel planning and recruitment should produce effective hiring practices, but the real measure is the on the job performance of the employee. Recruitment should be appreciated as but one element in a broader process of human resource management that includes the ongoing assessment of employee performance and the development of employees to their full potential. As previously indicated, such employee evaluation and development is also important if future manpower needs are to be met, at least in part, from the existing staff complement of the municipality.

Staff Evaluation and Development

There is no way that employees will learn all of the knowledge and skill needed to be effective managers by completing certain courses or work assignments before entering the municipal service. Nor will they acquire the necessary skill and knowledge automatically on the job, especially if, as is typical, that experience includes long years of internship within the hierarchy. The latter is likely to encourage the observance of traditional practices and approaches that become familiar and comfortable even though there is a strong need for municipal managers to be innovative and imaginative in the discharge of their duties. One of the best ways to avoid inertia is to expose managers to education and training programs on a continuous basis as part of their career development.

Staff Training

Staff training activities can take many forms. Orientation programs are quite helpful for new staff — and for new councillors as well. They provide an introduction to the municipality, its major policies and procedures and its organizational structure, and can help newcomers to understand their roles and how they relate to the overall activities of the corporation.

On the job training may relate to the operation of specific equipment, the acquisition of specific skills, or more general training in the operation of local government and in administration. The training is available from suppliers of equipment, from seminars and workshops offered by government departments and educational institutions, and from a number of training courses offered by professional associations including several in the municipal field. There has been a growing emphasis on broader management topics such as objective setting, leadership styles, and human relations and communications skills. Particularly through the use of outside consultants, training activities have extended to such aspects as team building and a number of related activities often referred to as organizational development.[34]

TRAINING AND DEVELOPMENT ACTIVITIES:
ORIENTATION PROGRAM
ON THE JOB TRAINING
INTERNSHIPS TO DEVELOP GENERAL MANAGERS
JOB ROTATIONS AND EXCHANGES
SABBATICALS

Administrative trainee programs have been used in a number of provinces to develop staff who can advance to senior management positions within the municipality. The trainees are recruited from the private sector or, more commonly, from appropriate university and college programs, and are moved through several municipal departments while working on administrative tasks. The objective is to produce generalists with a broad background of experience. Ontario, for example, has had a two-year internship program of this sort for a number of years.

Some of the same benefits are obtained through job rotations. Within a municipality, for example, individuals can be systematically moved through several departments so as to broaden their perspective. This approach may be related to a planned promotion or it may simply be intended to develop potential future managers. Intermunicipal exchanges of staff, while still far too rare, may be very beneficial. Individuals may gain new responsibilities that simply weren't available in their own municipalities and, in any event, will experience a fresh perspective on a variety of activities.

One other technique is the granting of sabbaticals or educational leave. Granted to only the most senior management personnel until recently, this opportunity is now being extended to middle management personnel with demonstrated potential.

Overall, however, staff training and development activities in municipal government are still far too limited. Moreover, almost all staff education and training activities are carried out in isolation, without any comprehensive approach that identifies the real needs of the staff or evaluates the effectiveness of the training that they do receive. Council

---

[34] For a discussion of this concept and examples of its application, see David Morgan, *Managing Urban America,* Belmont, Wadsworth Publishing Company Inc. 1979, pp. 196–201.

and senior management need to ensure that a climate exists in the municipality that will promote and encourage ongoing training and professional development. Employees quickly become frustrated and disillusioned if they return from conferences or seminars and find that their organization is unwilling to listen to new ideas and approaches. The potential benefit of much training activity is also lost if the new skill or knowledge is not demanded back in the workplace. Part of the answer is to integrate staff training efforts with performance appraisals, as discussed below.

A policy on education and training should be established in every municipality.[35] Its central component should be a strong commitment to the importance of education and training for municipal staff *and* councillors. If this commitment is to have any practical meaning, the policy must include a specific budget allocation, however modest. The costs of seminars and courses related to an employee's duties, present or potential, should normally be paid in full by the municipality. Time off with pay should also be provided where necessary, if it is at all feasible.[36]

An inventory of educational and training courses available to the employee should be compiled by the municipality, employees should be encouraged to pursue such courses, and their achievements should be recognized by the municipality.

Performance Appraisal

In simplest terms, this activity involves an examination and assessment of the employee's performance at regular intervals. However, it can be undertaken for a variety of purposes, including: [37]

1. To provide feedback on performance to employees, supervisors and other managers.

2. To establish information for employee guidance, development, and training aimed at improved performance.

---

[35] See Ontario Municipal Management Institute, *Preparing a Training and Development Policy: A Guide for Municipalities,* Oshawa, 1982. For a sample policy statement on staff training, see Ministry of Municipal Affairs, *Personnel Operations for Smaller Ontario Municipalities,* Toronto, 1984, pp. 105–106.

[36] For a discussion of one approach to determining the relative responsibility of employer and employee with respect to training costs, see Patrick Doyle and C. Richard Tindal, "Professional Development: Who Pays?" in *Training and Development Journal,* Alexandria, May 1986.

[37] Winston W. Crouch (ed.), *Local Government Personnel Administration,* Washington D.C., International City Management Association, 1976, pp. 264–265.

3. To identify employees with potential for promotion, transfer or special projects.

4. To establish reference data for personnel decisions, such as compensation and position classification review.

5. To clarify or to develop mutual goals, objectives, and evaluation criteria.

While this list is impressive, "of all managerial activities, performance appraisal of subordinates is more often done poorly, or even defaulted upon, than any other activity."[38] Part of the explanation is that performance appraisal systems can be intended to serve so many different purposes that they end up serving none very well. Different members of an organization may have quite contrasting views as to the purpose of their appraisal system.

Further confusion arises from the varied methods that exist for conducting employee evaluations. The *traditional* approach, which seems to be still the most widely used, involves assessing employee performances against a number of criteria. While this approach sounds systematic and consistent, the criteria used tend to involve personality traits such as initiative, leadership skills, dependability, and ability to get along with others. The result is that the evaluation process becomes quite subjective and is almost always influenced by the supervisor's feelings about the subordinate. It is quite likely that many managers feel uncomfortable about performance appraisals partly because they are dubious about the basis of their assessments, and because they would prefer to avoid the inevitably stressful discussions that arise if critical comments must be made.

METHODS OF APPRAISAL:
TRADITIONAL
OBJECTIVES

The *objectives* approach to performance evaluation is widely considered to be the best method, but it presupposes certain activities on the part of the municipality. Specifically, if the municipality has identified overall corporate goals and objectives, then within this framework departmental objectives can be established that, in turn, lead to the elaboration of more specific individual objectives for the employees. Where such objectives are jointly developed, employees are likely to feel moti-

---

[38] T. J. Stevens, *The Business of Government,* Toronto, McGraw-Hill Ryerson, 1978, p. 142.

vated by their participation in the determination of their activities. Both they and their supervisors will have a tangible basis for approaching the next evaluation since their performance will presumably be measured in relation to the achievement of these objectives. Moreover, staff training activities will now have a focus, since they can be directed to enhancing employee ability to accomplish these objectives.

This approach undoubtedly appears idealistic. Few municipalities have developed overall corporate objectives, and it is even more rare for the objective setting to be extended through the various levels of the organization. The tightly circumscribed legal framework within which municipalities must operate doesn't leave much scope for employees to define their own work objectives. For example, an employee who is a statutory officer would obviously have to include the statutory duties in any list of objectives. The whole concept may seem far too sophisticated for small and rural municipalities but, as was discussed in connection with personnel planning, it may be especially beneficial in just such instances. Because of the rudimentary nature of the personnel function and the informal manner in which operations are conducted, there is often not even a job description for the employee of the small municipality. As a result, there is not even the most elementary basis for assessing performance. Yet such joint discussions often provide the best opportunity for council and staff to examine ways in which they can better serve each other and improve the operating procedures and practices of the municipality. Performance appraisal will have performed a valuable service if it clarifies what is expected of the employee and provides an opportunity for regular, frank discussions with the employer.

Effective Evaluations: Some Key Steps

Whatever evaluation method is used, there are a few key steps that can help to make the process more effective for all those involved. *First,* it is important that employees know in advance the basis on which their performance will be measured. If this basis is established after discussions between the employee and the supervisor, then the understanding and commitment of both parties is better assured. The basis for assessing performance should be measurable. Both the employee and the supervisor should know how they will determine whether or not the agreed upon objectives or standards or work activities have been fulfilled.

Second, managers should make themselves available for meetings and discussions throughout the evaluation period. This regular contact allows for adjustments if circumstances change. The ongoing discussions also ensure that both supervisor and subordinate have a mutual understanding of how matters are progressing — making the eventual evaluation meeting much more of an anti-climax (and much less stressful accordingly).

Third, evaluations could be undertaken as a joint exercise, in which employees are asked to assess themselves. They are usually at least as demanding and critical as their supervisors would have been. This approach may be especially appropriate for those supervisors who are reluctant to undertake evaluations of subordinates with whom they don't have close contact on a day-to-day basis.

Fourth, during an evaluation meeting, performance problems must be faced, not avoided or glossed over. The objective of the discussion should be to help the employee overcome weaknesses or deficiencies. Part of the response may be the provision of training for the employee, and the expected results of that training should then be identified and built into the next evaluation process. On the other hand, if unsatisfactory performance continues and necessitates dismissal of an employee, the existence of previous evaluations that identified problems and attempted to solve them is one of the municipality's main protections against any wrongful dismissal suits that may be launched.[39]

Fifth, and perhaps most important, the actual evaluation meeting should not dwell on past performance — good or bad — but should focus on the future and what will be accomplished in the next time period. It should always conclude with an action plan setting out what has been agreed upon as the desired achievements during the next period, how these achievements will be realized, and how that realization will be measured.[40]

It is the responsibility of council to ensure that an effective performance appraisal system is established and followed. In addition, council

---

[39] For some guidance on this topic, which has become of increasing concern to municipalities, see Ministry of Municipal Affairs, *Avoiding Wrongful Dismissal: A Guide to Employer and Employee Rights,* Municipal Personnel Management, Unit No. 1, Toronto, 1988.

[40] For an excellent collection of writings about performance appraisal, see Christine S. Becker (ed.), *Performance Evaluation: An Essential Management Tool,* Practical Management Series, Washington D.C., International City Management Association, 1988.

should undertake the evaluation of those senior staff who report directly to it. These staff should, in turn, evaluate their subordinates, down through the organization.

Summary: From Personnel Management to Management of Personnel

As we examine these various personnel topics, it becomes increasingly evident that personnel management activities are likely to be most effective if integrated into the overall management process within the municipality. How can one decide what staff are needed or evaluate their performance without some idea of what the municipality is trying to accomplish? Otherwise, the result is the same limited perspective previously discussed (in Chapter 11) in connection with the municipal budget process. In other words, if viewed narrowly, personnel management is concerned with the acquisition of resources — in this case human resources instead of financial or physical resources —to deliver services. As with the traditional approach to budgeting, this emphasis is on inputs instead of outputs. Too little attention is given to whether these human resources are being deployed as effectively as they could be, and to the underlying question of the numbers and kind of staff who will be needed to achieve the objectives of the municipality.

In part, these problems arise because of the tendency to view human resource management as a separate activity carried out by a personnel department in relative isolation from the other activities of the municipality. It is ironic that after efforts in the first couple of decades after World War II to establish personnel departments in municipal government, we are now seeking ways to overcome the notion that personnel management is solely the responsibility of the personnel department. While this department obviously has certain specific duties to perform, the responsibility for personnel management should pervade the management level. In the words of one standard text, personnel management "is a part of the general management function and is a central, pervasive subsystem of all organizations."[41] Peter Drucker, as usual, summarizes the situation even more succinctly and memorably — "To depend on the personnel

---

[41] Wendell L. French, *The Personnel Management Process,* Boston, Houghton Mifflin Company, 1978, p. 9.

department to do management development is basically a misunderstanding. A marriage counselor can help with a marriage, but it's your job."[42]

In concluding this, the final chapter devoted to municipal policy making and management, the underlying unity of these activities becomes increasingly clear. If a municipality can identify overall goals and objectives, then it is better able to analyze specific spending alternatives and to determine its budget priorities, and it is better able to assess staff performance and to determine the appropriate combination of individual and departmental objectives that will best contribute to the overall objectives of the corporation. For most municipalities, this means a need to broaden their management activities to give greater attention to the initial determination of their priorities and the subsequent measurement of performance and results.

---

[42] John J. Tarrant, *Drucker: The Man Who Invented the Corporate Society,* London, Barrie and Jenkins Ltd., 1976, p. 260.

13   Retrospect and Prospect

Objectives:

1. To review the historical developments that help to explain the present system of local government.
2. To assess the present system, its problems and potential.
3. To speculate on the future prospects for local goverment in Canada.

Introduction

In the introductory chapter to this text, it was argued that the problems presently facing the local government system in Canada can be better understood and assessed when viewed in relation to the historical evolution and adaptation of that system. This concluding chapter, therefore, has two main purposes, as its title indicates. It attempts to look back over the local government system as it has evolved and been discussed in this text and to discern any significant lessons to be learned. It also attempts to look ahead, to consider the major challenges that will face local government in the next two decades and to suggest how it is likely to respond to these challenges in light of its past experiences.

The Record of the Past:
Plus Ça Change, Plus C'est La Même Chose

In reviewing the evolution of Canadian local government one is struck by certain recurring themes and the underlying similarity of early and more recent developments. This is evident, for example, in both the impact of urbanization and the nature of the responses and reforms introduced as a result of it, as outlined below.

The Recurring Impact of Urbanization

While it has been customary to view the effect of urbanization on local government as a fairly recent, post World War II phenomenon, it is clear that the urbanization of the early 1800s strongly influenced the establishment of municipal institutions in Central Canada. The increased service demands that resulted could not be handled by assigning still more responsibilities to the already overburdened justices of the peace. That fact coupled with the incessant demands of the Loyalists for local self-government led to the provision of the first elected councils in the form of boards of police. Initially, these new governing arrangements were only authorized in a few urban centres where servicing problems were particularly acute.

The second major wave of urbanization in Canada toward the end of the nineteenth century again significantly affected the local government system. In this case, the growth pressures and attendant service demands strained the existing machinery of government and called into question the efficiency and competence of many city administrations. The reformers of that era denounced politics (defined very narrowly and negatively) as the cause of the difficulties and sought to elevate the position and power of the expert as their solution. They encouraged the establishment of various special purpose bodies to provide services at arm's length from council. It is now clear, as Chapter 3 points out, that many of these reformers were not really eradicating politics but attempting to substitute their version of what the priorities of the city should be. Nonetheless because of their efforts there has been a persistent, still lingering notion that local government is only concerned with administration, with the efficient delivery of services, and not with politics. In addition to this erroneous and inappropriate governing philosophy, the reformers left us with a municipal administrative structure fragmented by the existence of numerous separate special purpose bodies, especially in Ontario.

The third wave of urbanization began at the end of World War II and its influence is still very much felt. The rate of urbanization moderated in the 1970s — the first decade in Canadian history to record a faster growth rate for rural areas than for urban areas — but picked up again in the 1980s. As indicated in Chapter 4, Canada's 25 census metropolitan areas increased their populations by 5.9% between 1981 and 1986, growing almost 50% faster than the national average. The Toronto, Montreal and Vancouver CMAs together contained 30.5% of Canada's population in 1986, with the central cities in all three areas experiencing a resurgence of growth.[1]

As in the previous two instances, the resultant growth pressures were reflected in increased service demands that overtaxed — literally as well as figuratively — the existing system. The growth pressures also generated passionate debate about the way future development should occur, and led to a number of confrontations between citizens' groups and city

---

[1] All figures from Statistics Canada.

hall. During this period, municipal reforms were introduced in a number of the provinces, not only with respect to municipal boundaries and responsibilities but also internal organization and machinery. As indicated below, however, most of these reforms did not really represent a break with the past.

Municipal Reforms: Nothing New Under the Sun?

Most examinations of Canadian local government have suggested that the system was fairly static from its historical origins until the reform initiatives of recent decades. To the contrary, local government has gone through a number of periods of change and adaptation — displaying considerable versatility and resiliency in the process. Not only are the recent local government reforms not the first to be introduced, but neither are they particularly innovative in approach or emphasis.

For example, while the establishment of regional, district, or metropolitan governments in several provinces has received considerable attention, these units have, in most instances, approximated the two-tier county system of government found in Ontario and Quebec since the mid-nineteenth century. In addition, these units have often been introduced after long experience with one or more metropolitan special purpose bodies that helped to demonstrate the need for area-wide government. Several examples of this pattern were noted in Chapter 5, with regional boards dealing with such services as water supply and drainage found in the Vancouver area from the early years of this century, the Montreal Metropolitan Commission dating from 1920, and Winnipeg's Metropolitan Planning Commission established in 1943 and credited with helping to shape the area-wide thinking ultimately ushered in the Unicity reforms. Moreover, further examples of this pattern seem likely. As Chapter 5 noted, the as yet unsuccessful initiatives to establish a regional government in St. John's, Newfoundland are building on the existence, since 1963, of the St. John's Metropolitan Area Board; while the existence of several inter-municipal boards embracing the Halifax and Dartmouth areas of Nova Scotia is cited as providing a possible foundation for a future metropolitan government.

INFLUENCE OF THE PAST:
REGIONAL GOVERNMENTS BASED ON OLD COUNTY GOVERNMENTS
EXECUTIVE COMMITTEE AND CAO SYSTEMS CAME
FROM TURN OF CENTURY REFORM ERA

There is even an interesting historical parallel in the way in which some of these new structures were introduced. Chapter 5 notes that the 1950s saw an ad hoc, crisis management approach to reform with the introduction of metropolitan governments in three of Canada's four largest urban centres, but not broader, more comprehensive approaches to the strengthening of the overall local government systems. Similarly, Ontario's regional government program of the 1960s was specifically introduced on an ad hoc basis in which areas with the greatest need (essentially, with the strongest growth pressures) would be reformed first. This piecemeal approach to resolving servicing needs was also evident over a century earlier with the provision of boards of police in selected urban centres in Upper Canada. Nor is metropolitan reform a new idea as evidenced by the fact that Wickett had a plan for a Toronto metropolitan government as early as 1913.[2]

A similar pattern exists with respect to internal reforms. While there has been a growing emphasis on the establishment of chief administrative officers and, to a lesser extent, executive committees, these concepts are not new. Indeed, the basic form of both of these structures can be traced to the turn of the century reform era and the introduction of the board of control and city manager systems. Even the recent preoccupation with introducing the parliamentary model in local government, notably with respect to Winnipeg Unicity and the Graham Commission recommendations on Nova Scotia, cannot be considered a completely new development. A central feature of this approach, the selection of the head of council by and from among the members of council, was found in municipal government over a century ago and is still the practice in choosing the county warden. Another key feature, the organization of the council along party lines, has also occurred in some municipalities well into the past, although the concept has admittedly been slow to take hold in any widespread fashion. Over 100 years ago, for example, there were complaints in Ontario about the extent to which party politics "are wormed into municipal elections."[3] None of these parallels is intended to deny the importance of the modifications or refinements that have been instituted with a number of the recent reforms in governing machinery, but to draw attention to the underlying similarity of problems and responses over time.

---

[2] John C. Weaver, *Shaping the Canadian City: Essays on Urban Politics and Policy, 1890–1920*, Monographs on Canadian Urban Government, No. 1, Institute of Public Administration, 1977, p. 66.

[3] J. M. McEvoy, *The Ontario Township*, Toronto, Warwick & Sons, 1889, p. 27.

There appears to be, however, one significant departure from past trends that should be noted. Attention has been shifting from the form of local government to the process of governing. In other words, there has been a growing appreciation that structural reforms — changes in boundaries or in the internal organization of a municipality — may not bring much improvement if traditional practices and procedures continue to prevail. Accordingly, more emphasis is now being given to the management process itself — the way in which a municipality makes and implements decisions — and techniques that can be introduced to produce more efficient and effective operations. Many of these techniques have been adapted from the private sector, and examples of them were noted in the preceding three chapters, especially in connection with the discussion of more rational, systematic approaches to policy making. Not only are these techniques and management concepts relatively new, but historically these matters received very little attention as compared to the possible benefits to be gained from changes in the structure and form of local government.

Assessment of the Present Local Government System

Notwithstanding the legacy of the past, a major concern is how well does the present system of local government in Canada function. At the outset, we must be careful to distinguish the actual performance of the system from its alleged virtues. According to its defenders, who seem to become especially staunch at any mention of change or reform, local government is the foundation of our democratic system; it is accessible, aware of local conditions and needs, and responsive to these needs. Through their elected council, inhabitants of a particular area are able to determine the range and magnitude of services that they desire. These and other arguments, as outlined earlier, make local government sound very attractive.

PRESENT PICTURE:
REPRESENTATIVE ROLE NEGLECTED
ADMINISTRATIVE ROLE DEFICIENT

Unfortunately, local government in practice presents a very different picture. In spite of the supposed democratic attributes of local government, its representative role appears to be largely ignored. Most citizens regard local government, if they consider it at all, as strictly a vehicle for service delivery. However, even this administrative role of local government is severely constrained by legal and financial limitations and provincially imposed and induced priorities. As a result, council has very little flexibility to respond to local priorities even if these are articulated and even if the council genuinely wishes to respond to them. A closer examination of these representative and administrative roles should help to clarify the present state of local government.

The Neglected Representative Role

While the tendency to view local government narrowly as only a vehicle for service delivery may be regrettable, it is by no means a new development. Indeed, we have noted that our romantic notion of local government being wrestled from an unwilling central authority only after a long and bitter struggle is hardly in accord with the historic facts. While such a struggle did take place in Ontario, in most other provinces the attitude of the populace toward the granting of local government ranged from apathy to strenuous opposition. The arbitrary action of the central authority was in forcing municipal institutions on a resistant public! Even in Ontario, it was not only the urging of the United Empire Loyalists but the inability of the justices of the peace to assume additional administrative burdens that prompted the British government to provide the initial forms of local government. As Kaplan has pointed out, local governments weren't simply established as models in direct democracy. They were also seen as public corporations limited to the powers contained in their charters, and as tribunals dispensing justice and resolving grievances.[4] The inconsistencies inherent in these original premises were noted in Chapter 2.

Developments since have done little to emphasize local government's representative role and some have strongly undermined it. Particularly significant in this latter connection was the impact of the turn of the century reform movement. As discussed in Chapter 3 the reformers were so preoccupied with taking politics out of local government that they virtually disavowed the representative role. Throughout much of the twentieth century, efforts to adapt local government to the pressures of growth and change again seemed preoccupied with the administrative

---

[4]   Harold Kaplan, *Reform, Planning and City Politics: Montreal, Winnipeg and Toronto,* Toronto, University of Toronto Press, 1982, pp. 60–63.

role to the neglect of the representative aspect. For example, with many municipalities facing bankruptcy during the Depression of the 1930s, the general response was a combination of increased provincial financial assistance and increased provincial supervision and control of local spending decisions. While the independence and discretionary power of local government was obviously undermined in the process, guaranteeing financial solvency and the capacity to maintain the provision of services were seen as higher priorities.

The narrow preoccupation with the administrative role of local government is also reflected in the emphasis of most of the local government reform efforts in the various provinces. As described in Chapter 5, the reforms concentrated on improving the efficiency of local government in providing services by transferring powers to a strengthened upper tier unit and/or consolidating many of the smaller municipalities. A number of the changes in the internal organization of reformed municipalities have also been concerned with improving the management and administration of local services. The main exceptions have been Winnipeg Unicity, the proposed reforms in Nova Scotia, and some recent local government reviews in Ontario, where attention has been directed to making municipal government more representative and responsible and not just more efficient administratively.

Perhaps inevitably a reaction set in and the 1960s in particular saw increasingly active citizens and citizens' groups demanding a greater say in municipal decisions. To a considerable extent this so-called citizens' movement did serve to remind local government of its representative role; yet its contribution should not be exaggerated. The citizens' groups varied greatly in their interests, approach, and longevity. Many were single issue groups, usually organized to oppose some development that was regarded as undesirable, and frequently dissolving once the particular issue was resolved. In addition, however pious their proclamations of public interest, many of these groups were primarily concerned with protecting the (propertied) interests of their membership. Indeed, one observer of residents' and ratepayers' associations asserts that they have "usually acted in response to specific decisions that they did not like, sought to divert the impact of that decision, conceded that they were acting in self-interest and made no claim to speak for the public interest."[5]

---

[5]   Harold Kaplan, *Urban Political Systems: A Functional Analysis of Metropolitan Toronto,* New York, Columbia University Press, 1967, p. 168.

Another limiting factor is that many of the citizens' groups lacked the resources to undertake necessary research, analyze municipal proposals, and offer alternatives. They were especially disadvantaged compared to the "corporate groups" described in Chapter 7, bodies such as the Urban Development Institute and the Housing and Urban Development Association of Canada that had extensive financial resources and technical information to present the views of the development industry.

As Chapter 9 indicates, the activities of these citizens' groups appear to wax and wane depending on the extent of growth pressure being experienced and the perception of the way in which local government is dealing with this pressure and with the property industry in particular. As a result, the citizen group contribution to a broadened awareness of the representative role of local government tends to vary considerably with the particular groups involved and with the times.

WHY LIMITED REPRESENTATIVE ROLE?
NOT EMPHASIZED BY TURN OF CENTURY
OR POST WWII REFORM EFFORTS
NOT ENCOURAGED BY LOCAL GOVERNMENT
STRUCTURE, PROCEDURES, OR ELECTION PROCESSES

Presumably one of the factors limiting the attention directed to the representative role is that this role can mean a number of different things, depending on how one defines it. Do we want council to represent equally all of the different areas of the municipality? Such a concern might suggest the universal use of ward elections, whatever their imperfections. Do we want each councillor to represent approximately the same number of people? While representation by population might appear to be a basic tenet of a democratic system, it would require us to re-think the composition of the councils of many of our indirectly elected upper tier governments in Canada. Do we want the councillors to represent faithfully the views of their electorate? Those who hold to the view that the elected representatives should faithfully mirror the views of the electorate rather than exercising any independent judgment might want to see greater use of plebiscites and referrenda, although these devices have been used more extensively in Canadian local government than is commonly realized, some 168 times for example in the decade 1955 to 1965.[6]

---

[6]   See J. Patrick Boyer, *Lawmaking by the People, Referendums and Plebiscites in Canada,* Toronto, Butterworths, 1982, and the articles by Boyer in *Municipal World,* St. Thomas, June and July 1983.

Local government's representative role is also measured by the ballot box and the extent to which the public exercises its municipal franchise. As discussed in Chapter 7, however, this form of public participation is quite disappointing, with acclamations to council fairly widespread and voting turnout low.

There is no consensus as to why this is the case. At one time the municipal franchise might well have been a factor with its restrictive property qualifications. In recent decades, however, there has been a general movement toward a broadening of the franchise. At present, the three main qualifications to be a voter are age and citizenship, together with residency or ownership of land in the municipality in question. The voting age has been lowered to 19 or 18 in most provinces, in line with lowered voting age requirements in provincial and federal elections. Still, as Chapter 9 pointed out, a number of factors have combined to generate an overly narrow focus on property matters thereby limiting the ability of local governments to attract public interest and involvement.

Voter interest is almost certainly affected adversely by the nature of the municipal election campaign. With few exceptions, the campaign is devoid of issues or clear policy choices. Since there is usually no governing group within council it is very difficult for the electorate to assign responsibility for the action or inaction of the sitting council. Without such a governing group, candidates for office are reluctant to offer specific promises that they may not be able to fulfil. The result is that the election becomes largely a personality contest, one in which the incumbents are likely to be favoured if only because of the lengthy list of names and multiple ballots facing the voter.

Other limiting factors are inherent in the structure of local government. It is argued that voter turnout and citizen interest generally may be inhibited by the fact that traditional municipal boundaries do not coincide with the community of interest of today's population. Particularly in the urban areas of Canada, people may ignore municipal boundaries in their pursuit of employment, leisure activities, and various specialized services. Where municipal boundaries divide obvious communities of interest it is felt that the municipal governments involved will appear to have little relevance for their inhabitants.

Another structural factor is the existence of a number of special purpose bodies operating largely independently of council. As previously discussed, these boards erode the power of council, inhibit coordination, and cloud and weaken the focus of accountability in local government. It is felt that citizens see the council as lacking in power because of these boards and are therefore less inclined to vote or, for that matter, to stand for office. Paradoxically, many of these boards appear to have been established by the provincial governments because of a lack of confidence in the municipal council. We are faced, therefore, with a chicken-egg argument. We need higher voter turnouts and an improved calibre of councillor if the municipal council is to receive more power vis-à-vis the boards and the provincial government. Yet until councils receive this additional power will they be able to attract the necessary citizen involvement through voting and candidacy?

The way in which municipal governments operate in many instances may discourage public interest and involvement. Mention has previously been made of the general tendency toward secrecy and particularly the attempt to avoid airing controversial matters in public. It should be appreciated, however, that the local level is still more open in its deliberations than the senior levels of government. The fact that most staff advice to council is presented in public meetings is particularly significant, affording the interested public an opportunity to observe the background to, and influences affecting, a decision in a way that is not normally possible at the provincial and federal levels.

Even so, specific municipal operating procedures and practices often discourage citizen interest and participation. In this context it is common to criticize the large municipality with its big bureaucracy and its formal procedures and requirements. Citizens or groups with concerns to express may only appear before council after giving appropriate advance notice and making the agenda, or they may be diverted to a standing committee to present their case. By contrast, the small municipality where most citizens know their councillors personally and can attend any council meeting and be heard has long been praised as the most responsive and democratic. But, when such small municipalities find themselves attempting to complete their regular agenda after midnight because of a stream of unexpected delegations earlier in the evening, one has to ask if the democratic rights of the inhabitants at large are being neglected because of the attention given to a few? In addition, how accessible is the government of the small municipality if the clerk-treasurer works at home or at best operates from an office on only a part-time basis? How accessible is it if there are few formal records, if by-laws are not indexed, and few public documents are readily available? Clearly, the small municipality may, in its own way (and perhaps quite unintentionally), discourage meaningful citizen involvement just as much as the more publicized or stereotyped bureaucratic regimes.

Another closely related factor is the availability of information about council activities and the adequacy of what might best be termed the municipality's public relations efforts. The media must accept considerable responsibility for the lack of information about, and understanding of, local government, as explained in Chapter 7. But the fact remains that most municipalities appear to give far too little attention to the need to inform the public about their activities. Quite often the only documents produced are those required by provincial regulation and their format is usually not too informative for the ordinary citizen. A prime example is the audited financial statement, which provides a great deal of data desired by the provincial government and useful for comparative purposes, and yet is virtually incomprehensible to the general public and, one suspects, to many councillors. Newsletters or other publications explaining municipal programs, discussing policy alternatives, outlining how the municipal tax dollar is spent, or otherwise informing the public are insufficiently used, although developments in this direction are encouraging.

For a balanced assessment, the representative role of local government must be considered in relation to its administrative role, since council's performance is largely judged on the basis of the nature and level of services provided for its inhabitants. Yet for all of the attention that it has received over the years, this administrative role of local government is also poorly filled.

The Deficient Administrative Role

It is not only disturbing but rather surprising to discover that local government's administrative role is deficient, since most of the services that determine whether or not our day to day living is pleasant or unbearable are provided largely by the local level. As illustrated in Chapter 1, if the typical city government somehow disappeared, the city's inhabitants would find themselves without such vital services as fresh water, waste disposal, police and fire protection, roads, public transit, and a wide variety of social and health programs. The point can hardly be made more forcefully than in Sir Ernest Simon's statement that "the City Council's services mean the difference between savagery and civilization."[7] Yet the local level is by far the most neglected of all three levels of government in terms of the financial and personnel resources available to it.

---

[7]   Quoted in Harold J. Laski, W. Ivor Jennings, and William A. Robson (eds.), *A Century of Municipal Progress 1835–1935*, London, Allen and Unwin, 1935, p. 11.

> ### WHY LIMITED ADMINISTRATIVE ROLE?
> ### SUBORDINATE CONSTITUTIONAL POSITION
> ### INSUFFICIENT RESOURCES
> ### UNWILLINGNESS OF COUNCILS
> ### (AND THEIR ELECTORATES)
> ### TO MAKE NECESSARY CHANGES

In large part, of course, this neglect results from the subordinate constitutional position of local government. Municipalities can only be as strong and effective as their provincial governments are prepared to make them. However, the problem is not that simple, nor the blame that easily assigned. The municipalities themselves must accept a good deal of the responsibility for their unfortunate state because they have often been unwilling to make or to accept necessary changes that would improve their operations. The fact that most citizens have little understanding of local government or appreciation of its present limitations and tend to resist strenuously any changes has also been a limiting factor. Unless provincial governments are prepared to wield their constitutional power with respect to local government quite arbitrarily and without regard for the political consequences, local government is likely to be changed and strengthened only if there is some basis of popular support for these actions. In the absence of this support we find such approaches as British Columbia's "strategy of gentle imposition" of reforms and Ontario's resort to renaming regional governments as restructured counties. One may decry these tactics and may criticize the limitations of the reforms introduced, as was done in Chapter 5, but it is probably unrealistic to expect much change without a major improvement in the public's understanding of, and attitude toward, local government reform. Indeed, after the major but distinctly limited reform initiatives of the 1960s and early 1970s, only a few ad hoc reforms have been considered since.

Looking specifically at the inadequacy of local government finance, a complicating factor has been the federal nature of Canada. With both the federal and provincial governments seeking to maximize their constitutionally guaranteed sources of revenue to meet their growing expenditure needs, local governments have been virtually squeezed out and find themselves still relying on the historical property tax as their main source of funds. Given this situation, they have had to rely on transfer payments from the senior levels, the vast majority of these conditional in nature. The result is that "local governments in Canada, to a considerable extent, are really acting as agents, spending provincial funds on provincially designated activities."[8]

It is difficult to visualize any major improvement in the municipal financial position except as part of a more comprehensive tri-level adjustment. Underlying such an adjustment would need to be a redefinition of our priorities as a nation. What do we really want our various levels of government to do on our behalf? Which level or levels of government best fulfil these objectives? If, as is possible and desirable, such an exercise identifies the local level as important in meeting the aspirations for government of the Canadian people, then a new allocation of resources and a new emphasis becomes necessary. A change in the tax structure would be required so that most of the nation's wealth is not siphoned off for use by the senior levels of government. The important point in this discussion is the recognition that municipal financial problems cannot be examined in isolation from the broader government system. "Urban fiscal problems constitute just one aspect of the basic public finance question of designing the national fiscal system that will best achieve the objectives of society as a whole."[9]

If the potential revenues of the local level should not be drawn away to the senior levels, neither should its personnel resources. This comment applies particularly to elected personnel. Appointed staff are free to pursue their career ambitions and to that end may aspire to a position with one of the senior levels of government. The gradual improvement in salaries and fringe benefits at the local level and the increased inter-municipal mobility of staff should, however, help to offset this loss upward. The situation concerning elected representatives is more intangible and difficult to resolve. There is a tendency for successful and effective local politicians to seek election as provincial and federal members. Higgins found that this stepping-stone relationship appeared to be on the decline with respect to members of the House of Commons, but that an increasing proportion of members of provincial legislatures had had prior experience as local politicians.[10] This link may be strengthened further if the national political parties intensify their efforts to run local candidates on a party slate.

---

[8]   Richard M. Bird and N. Enid Slack, *Urban Public Finance in Canada*, Toronto, Butterworth, 1983, p. 112.

[9]   *Ibid.*, p. 115.

[10]   Donald J. H. Higgins, *Local and Urban Politics in Canada*, Toronto, Gage, 1986, pp. 390–391.

However, the basic concern here is not with the actual numbers involved but the underlying, perhaps unspoken, assumption that having proven themselves, councillors should now go on to bigger and better things. This attitude reflects one of the theoretical justifications of local government, that it is a training school for democracy wherein the politician learns the rules of the game and then "graduates" to a higher level. It is this notion that provincial and national political activities are more important that must be combatted. "We miss the essence of democracy if we think of it mainly as something practised by statesmen in a distant capital and forget that it consists of an attitude of mind towards, and a method of dealing with, all the stresses and strains of living together in a society."[11] Therefore, if our reordering of government priorities indicates that the local level is important, then it is natural and desirable that many of our ablest politicians should pursue their careers at that level. Far from encouraging these politicians to seek higher office, we should indicate that such a move would be looked upon with disfavour. As Allan O'Brien has noted, "In trade union circles you are often considered a traitor if the boss promotes you out of the union. It's time that notion got abroad at the municipal level."[12]

The local government system today has been weakened by a prolonged period of centralization. Most analysts decry the steady shift of greater responsibility and control to the senior levels of government, largely through the use of conditional grant programs. One variation, which is not really a departure from this pattern, has been the action of some provinces in "divesting administrative responsibility for certain 'unwanted programs' to the local level but retaining policy control" — a shift that is likely to make local governments even more "the adminstrative peons of provincial policy-makers."[13] As a result of these developments, Plunkett and Graham conclude that "local governments are adhering to their role as agents of provincial interest to the detriment of their role as interpretors of the local scene."[14] Bird and Slack reach at least as pessimistic a conclusion when they note that "many municipalities have been virtually downgraded so to speak, to field offices of the

---

[11]　J. A. Corry and J. E. Hodgetts, *Democratic Government and Politics,* Toronto, University of Toronto Press, 1959, p. 623.

[12]　Allan O'Brien, "Local Government Priorities for the Eighties," in *Canadian Public Administration,* Spring 1976, p. 111.

[13]　T. J. Plunkett and Katherine A. Graham, "Whither Municipal Government," in *Canadian Public Administration,* Winter 1982, p. 616.

[14]　*Ibid.,* p. 614.

provinces — branches with troublesome delusions of autonomy, but 'fortunately' without sufficient control over their own fate to mount any real opposition to the provincial governments...."[15]

Prospects for the Future:
Local Government in the Year 2000

Our assessment of the present system of local government in Canada has concluded on a somewhat negative note. As indicated, Canadian local governments are not effectively fulfilling either of their basic representative or administrative roles. They remain weak even after more than two decades of reform initiatives. Moreover, many of the improvements that are desirable are resisted by a public suspicious of change and determined to retain the familiar — even though most citizens are anything but familiar with the nature and operations of their municipal governments.

Having reviewed the lessons of history and the potential of the present system, it is now time to consider the prospects for the future. When the first edition of this text was being prepared in the late 1970s, it seemed safe to speculate about local government in the year 2000 — a time yet far in the future. It is a more sobering proposition to tackle this question now, realizing that this edition will presumably be in use just a few short years before that date.

To some observers in the not-too-distant past, the question has not been what form local government will take in the year 2000 but whether there will still be local governments at that time. One of the most widely quoted documents of the 1970s was a statement from FCM that forecast "the decline and fall of municipal government as we know it in Canada in five years."[16] It is felt, however, that the difficulties facing local government are sometimes exaggerated or over-dramatized. The current problems, however serious they seem, must be kept in perspective, and in this context the historical background provided earlier in the text is particularly helpful.

Admittedly, we have serious servicing problems today, but are they any worse, relatively, than those of previous periods? Consider the situation in the Toronto area in the early 1950s "with both of the local

---

[15] Bird and Slack, *op. cit.*, p. 116.

[16] Canadian Federation of Mayors and Municipalities (now Federation of Canadian Municipalities), *Puppets on a Shoestring*, Ottawa, April 28, 1976, unpaginated).

rivers — the Humber and the Don — fast turning into open sewers, and with North York, alone, struggling with the burden of some 20,000 septic tanks."[17] What about the sewer overflow into Fort William's water supply in the winter of 1905–1906 and the approximately 800 typhoid cases that resulted? As Chapter 3 makes clear, the turn of the century period witnessed urban problems relating to such issues as housing, health, and transportation that seemed at the time at least as serious as the problems of today.

PROBLEMS IN PERSPECTIVE:
SERVICING STRAINS NOT NEW
FINANCIAL DIFFICULTIES
FROM EARLIEST TIMES
CONSTITUTIONAL GUARANTEE
NOT NECESSARILY BENEFICIAL

It is also helpful to examine the current financial crisis of local government in this historical perspective. One finds, for example, that local governments have always suffered from what was felt to be inadequate funding. Even the earliest forms of elected local government such as the district councils in Central Canada in the 1840s had "paltry sums for the needs of large districts ... a rather important factor in the backward condition of the country for so many years."[18] It is also clear that the property tax has always been unpopular. Notwithstanding all of the fanfare about Proposition 13 and the taxpayer revolt, current feelings seem mild compared to the newspaper editorial of 1843, which explained that a proposal to establish municipalities and introduce the property tax "would have cut loose that many-headed monster, Direct Taxation and its Myrmidon, the Tax-Gatherer, into the happy home of every poor man throughout the land."[19] Chapter 6 has made it clear that the property tax has been unfairly maligned over the years. It is neither as regressive nor as burdensome as has been argued by its critics.

---

[17] F. Smallwood, *Metro Toronto: A Decade Later*, Toronto, Bureau of Municipal Research, 1963, p. 10.

[18] Adam Shortt and Arthur G. Doughty (gen. eds.), *Canada and Its Provinces: A History of the Canadian People and Their Institutions*, Toronto, Glasglow, Brook, and Company, 1914, Vol. XVIII, p. 437.

[19] H. J. Whalen, *The Development of Local Government in New Brunswick*, Fredericton, University of New Brunswick, 1963, pp. 20–21.

There is also little hard evidence to support the notion that we have a municipal financial crisis because local spending is excessive or is out of control. Most municipal governments have turned in an admirable performance in holding the line on spending during the restraint period of recent years. While total expenditures have gone up considerably (as is true of government at all levels), is this necessarily undesirable in light of the valuable services provided? Sharpe puts this issue in the proper perspective by comparing local government expenditures with other items on which we spend equal or larger sums. While his figures are for Britain, his conclusion would certainly apply generally to Canada as well.

> ...although the local government bill is not small, it provides education, public health, social services, highways, libraries, fire, police, refuse collection and a whole range of other public services which most people need and demand, at a total cost that is no larger than the amount we collectively spend on such things as wine and beer, cigarettes, eye shadow, tennis rackets and a flutter on the horses.[20]

Looking ahead, it is likely that the property tax will not only remain but play an increasingly important role as a source of municipal revenues — partly because of the revenue squeeze now being experienced by municipalities. Kitchen has demonstrated that this tax field has not been exploited as much as it could be, and could have generated some $3 billion in 1980 if utilized to the extent that it had been in 1968.[21] One can expect the expanded use of the miscellaneous local revenue sources to continue as well, especially with respect to user fees. There does not appear to be as much likelihood of municipalities gaining access to significant new tax sources. Over the years provincial governments have shown little willingness to share what they regard as their limited tax fields with municipalities, and they are even less likely to feel generous in their present mood of restraint.

In any event, even if the provincial governments should have a change of heart, there are few eligible taxes that lend themselves to administration within the very small areas encompassed by most municipalities. Auld, for example, has illustrated the difficulties that could arise with a municipal personal income tax or with municipal responsibility for such

---

[20] L. J. Sharpe (ed.), *The Local Fiscal Crisis in Western Europe, Myths and Realities,* London, Sage Publications, 1981, p. 224.

[21] Harry Kitchen, *Local Government Finance in Canada,* Toronto, Canadian Tax Foundation, 1984, Chapter 15 and especially pp. 398–399.

location-specific taxes as those on corporations or retail sales.[22] Kitchen also considers the possibilities for such alternative tax sources, and also finds problems and difficulties.[23] He notes that a local income tax system in which tax bases and rates differed from area to area would have a negative impact on the primary objectives of equity and efficiency. "Piggybacking" onto an existing provincial tax base through the application of a surtax would significantly lower collection and administration costs without creating inequities and distortions. "Piggybacking," however, would be essentially a form of revenue sharing and would provide very little in the way of local autonomy, accountability, or responsibility. Kitchen comes to a similar conclusion with respect to a possible municipal sales tax — that it would be cheaper and cause fewer distortions to "piggyback" onto an existing provincial sales tax. Here again, however, the arrangement would operate more like an unconditional grant, than an additional taxing power that municipalities would exercise at their discretion and be held accountable for by the electorate.

What about the concerns about local government's very weak position within the Canadian federal system? It may be recalled that for at least a few years in the 1970s the efforts of the federal Ministry of State for Urban Affairs to encourage tri-level consultative mechanisms for dealing with the needs of urban Canada offered the possibility of an enhanced status for local governments. The prospect of the patriation of the Canadian constitution appeared to offer a second opportunity that municipalities hoped to use to obtain at least some basic constitutional declaration of their existence and rights.[24]

But provincial resistance, among other factors, led to the demise of the Ministry of State for Urban Affairs in 1979 as discussed in Chapter 6. Even more significant, when the new Constitution Act came into effect in 1982 municipalities were not explicitly mentioned in it except for the references contained in the 1867 British North America Act, which were incorporated into the new act. Noting the short-lived nature of tri-level

---

[22] D. A. L. Auld, "Fiscal Dimensions of Provincial-Local Relations in Ontario," in *Intergovernmental Relations,* Toronto, Economic Council of Canada, 1977, pp. 137–148.

[23] Kitchen, *op. cit.,* pp. 404–405.

[24] See, for example, Federation of Canadian Municipalities, *Municipal Government in a New Canadian Federal System, Report of the Task Force on Constitutional Reform,* Ottawa, F.C.M., 1980.

consultations and the continuing centralization by provincial governments, Doerr concludes that "the municipal voice has not been silenced but it has been toned down on the national scene."[25]

On the other hand, Jacques L'Heureux argues persuasively against any constitutional amendment that would provide a guarantee of municipal institutions. Quite apart from the fact that the provincial legislative assemblies would never agree, in his view, to the loss of power implied in such a guarantee, L'Heureux contends that such an amendment would not be desirable.[26] He claims that protection of municipalities by the Constitution would achieve the very opposite.

> It would favour direct federal intervention and direct dealings between the federal government and the municipalities. The resulting division of powers would be even more complicated and a matter of contention. Given the difficulties the federal government and our ten provinces have now in reaching agreement, it is easy to imagine what would happen if the more than 4,600 Canadian municipalities were added![27]

Instead, L'Heureux suggests that it would be more realistic to protect municipal interests by way of provincial constitutions. Cameron also came to this conclusion, arguing that since the division of powers between provincial and local government promotes such values and liberty and equality, then this division should be recognized and protected, but within provincial constitutions.[28]

> Municipalities have no place in a federal constitution, at least not beyond the present references which consign them to provincial jurisdiction. Any further reference could only serve to remove decisions about the provincial-municipal division of power to extra-provincial constitutional processes. Any direct participation by municipalities in the federal-provincial constitutional process could only occur at the price of their becoming special interest groups.[29]

---

[25] Audrey Doerr, "Public Administration: Federalism and Intergovernmental Relations," in *Canadian Public Administration,* Winter 1982, p. 571.

[26] Jacques L'Heureux, "Municipalities and the Division of Power," in Richard Simeon, Research Coordinator, *Intergovernmental Relations,* Vol. 63, Royal Commission on the Economic Union and Development Prospects for Canada, Toronto, University of Toronto Press, 1985, pp. 200–201.

[27] Ibid., p. 201.

[28] David M. Cameron, "Provincial Responsibilities for Municipal Government," in *Canadian Public Administration,* Summer, 1980, pp. 222–235.

[29] *Ibid.,* p. 235.

To protect municipalities, L'Heureux suggests including in the provincial constitutions such principles as the existence of autonomous municipalities governing local affairs, the election of municipal councillors, and the possession by municipalities of independent sources of revenue sufficient to allow them to perform their obligations. The right of a municipality to act by itself in the absence of legislation to the contrary, as well as its right to delegate its powers, might also be included, along with a limitation on the review of municipal by-laws by the courts.[30]

While it is a considerably simpler legal process to add a statement protecting municipalities to constitutions of individual provinces, such action would still require the compliance of the provincial governments involved. As has been seen, however, provincial governments have shown little appreciation for municipalities as a separate level of government, often treating them instead as a means to an end, a set of institutions through which the province must work in order to achieve provincial objectives.

This provincial attitude is well illustrated by the actions taken by several provinces, as described in Chapter 6, in meeting their fiscal restraint objectives by reducing transfer payments to municipalities and/or shifting expenditure burdens to them. In so doing, the provinces seem to regard municipal government as merely an extension of their operations. "The approach appears to be that where across the board expenditure reductions are required as part of the fiscal restraint exercise, transfers to municipalities need not be treated any differently than any other expenditure."[31] The rebuttal to this point of view, from New Brunswick municipalities, is well worth repeating:

> The reality is, however, that municipal government is much more than just another program or interest group demanding its share of a shrinking pie. Notwithstanding its constitutional position as a creature of the Province, municipal government is precisely what the name suggests; another distinct and legitimate level of government. Comprised of representatives directly elected by the people, funded to a greater and greater extent by direct taxation, empowered to independently legislate within a clearly defined mandate, and directly

---

[30] L'Heureux, *op. cit.*, p. 202.

[31] Brief to the Policy and Priorities Committee of the Government of New Brunswick, *Re The Unconditional Grant to Municipalities and Related Matters*, Provincial-Municipal Council, Inc., October 11, 1988, p. 2–3.

accountable to those who are taxed and serviced, municipal governments exist as a legitimate co-equal of the other two levels of
government in Canada. Thus the unilateral decision by the Province
not to honour the full financial transfer agreement made with municipalities is *more than merely another program cut; it is nothing less
than the abrogation of a genuine intergovernmental commitment*
(emphasis added).[32]

CENTRAL ISSUE:
LOCAL GOVERNMENT AS
SEPARATE LEVEL OF GOVERNMENT
NOT JUST AGENT OF PROVINCIAL GOVERNMENT

This would appear to be the crux of the matter. Municipalities need
to be treated as a separate level of government, serving separate and
legitimate purposes, not just as agents of the provincial government.
Expressing this concept within provincial constitutions would be a relatively easy matter. Getting provincial authorities to appreciate this concept, to incorporate it into their constitutions, and to honour and live
by it, is quite another matter.

Whatever the constitutional and legal arrangements, however, futur-
ists claim that we are moving into an era of decentralization. Toffler
was one of the earliest, and certainly most widely quoted, to predict
this change.[33] Naisbitt pursued the concept much further, and offered
a number of examples relating to local government.[34] In his view, the
key to decentralization of political power is local action. He argues that
local political power is not delegated from the senior levels down
through the hierarchy of governments; rather it stems from initiatives
taken by lower level governments in the absence of a top-down solution. He goes on to point out that:

> Power that is bestowed from the top down can be withdrawn if the
> donor's priorities change. Successful initiatives hammered out at the
> local level have staying power. Local solutions are resistant to top-
> down intervention and become models for others still grappling with
> the problems.[35]

---

32 *Ibid.*

33 Alvin Toffler, *Future Shock,* New York, Random House, 1970.

34 John Naisbitt, *Megatrends,* New York, Warner Books, 1982.

35 *Ibid.,* p. 121.

> **FUTURE PROSPECTS:**
> **AGE OF DECENTRALIZATION,**
> **FAVOURING LOCAL GOVERNMENT**
> **VITAL ROLE OF REGULATING AND SERVICING PROPERTY**
> **POSSIBLE EXPANSION OF SOCIAL SERVICE ROLE**

The Federation of Canadian Municipalities has argued that this process of decentralization is underway in Canada. In a brief to the MacDonald Commission, the Federation noted that the prolonged centralization of power had prompted many commentators in the 1960s to predict a "withering away" of local government, but that this has definitely not happened.

> On the contrary, starting in the late 60s and early 70s, struggles over environmental quality and a host of community planning and other quality-of-life issues have found their main outlet at the local level since it is here that the majority of these issues are regulated.... Today people once again value towns and cities sufficiently to commit themselves to making them better places in which to work, live and play.[36]

The brief goes on to state:

> We seem, in effect, to be coming full circle; from a time when locally-based institutions bore responsibility for all aspects of daily life, to one in which the capacity to fulfill this role has been eroded and therefore largely removed to other orders of government, to one in which people are again viewing local government and institutions as the most direct and accessible outlets for their most pressing concerns.[37]

In order for this rather optimistic future to be realized, however, it will be necessary for local governments to be responsible for activities that are felt by the public to be sufficiently important and vital so as to warrant their interest and participation. As Chapter 9 outlined, local governments have traditionally been preoccupied with providing services to property. While this focus is narrow, it is at least the source of lively interest and considerable controversy — especially over the extent to which councils have been serving the interests of the property industry. Indeed, it was a growing concern about how our cities were being developed that triggered much of the citizens' movement of the 1960s. Local governments may have been unpopular during this period, but at least

---

[36] Federation of Canadian Municipalities, *Brief to the Royal Commission on the Economic Union and Development Prospects for Canada,* October 1983, p. 17.

[37] *Ibid.,* p. 140.

they attracted attention! They were recognized as bodies making decisions of vital interest to the local populace. The slowdown of urban growth in the late 1970s and early 1980s, while easing some of the pressures and concerns previously discussed, also threatened to remove a primary cause of local dynamism. As Chapter 9 indicates, however, the second half of the 1980s witnessed a strong revival of citizen interest in how our cities were growing and in the continuing influence of the property development industry. It seems safe to predict that as long as municipalities retain their responsibilities in connection with the regulation and servicing of land, they will remain institutions attracting strong, albeit sporadic, citizen interest.

How much of a future role local governments play in relation to the servicing of people (as opposed to land) depends, to a considerable extent, on how they respond to the significant changes underway in the age composition of the Canadian population. Between 1976 and 2026 the percentage of the population under 18 years of age will decline sharply while the proportion of the population over 65 years will increase.[38] One study suggests that since local government expenditures have been oriented toward the young rather than the elderly (for whom the federal government incurs the bulk of the expenditures), this shift in demographics could ease somewhat the financial pressures on the local level, notably for schooling.[39] This study also notes, however, that a larger retirement group will exert more political influence and seek higher expenditures for services to the aged in areas such as recreation and culture, public transit, and housing for seniors.[40] A projected increase in the number of single-parent families will expand the demand for child-care centres. All of these new expenditures are unlikely to be as large as the potential savings from the decrease in the school age population.[41] As a result, municipalities may have an opportunity to take some new initiatives in the social services field, to round out what has been perceived as an overly narrow focus on property, and to do so at a time when reductions in other expenditure commitments (especially education) make this initiative financially feasible.

---

[38] Statistics Canada, *Population Projections for Canada and the Provinces, 1976–2000*, Occasional Publication 91-520, Ottawa, 1981.

[39] Harry Kitchen and Melville McMillan, "Local Government and Canadian Federalism," in Simeon, *op. cit.*, p. 233.

[40] *Ibid.*, p. 234.

[41] *Ibid.*

Given all of these considerations, what is the most likely future prospect for local governments in Canada? It is felt that many of the prognostications about local government exaggerate its problems and overlook its long record of survival and adaptability. However, while local government is unlikely to collapse before the end of this century, neither is it likely to undergo a radical restructuring and emerge as a new much stronger system. This lack of major improvement will not be because we are unaware of what needs to be done: indeed, many of the necessary changes are obvious from previous discussions in this text. However, it must be said, that the provincial governments are not necessarily in favour of fundamental reforms that would significantly strengthen local government. A stronger, more independent local government system might pursue different priorities than those felt to be appropriate by the provincial governments and might provide an overly forceful challenge to the authority of the provincial level.

Another barrier to effective reform rests with local governments themselves. As Cameron has noted, "there is clearly a great deal that needs to be changed in relation to the organization, boundaries, responsibilities and resources of municipalities .... and we must surely marvel at the capacity of municipalities to resist most of these changes."[42] Just as a chain is only as strong as its weakest link, so the systems of local government in the various provinces of Canada are only as strong as the weakest municipalities among them.

> **FUTURE DEPENDS ON LOCAL GOVERNMENTS:**
> **OPPORTUNITIES ARE THERE**
> **TIME FOR NEW INITIATIVES,**
> **WILLINGNESS TO CHANGE**
> **SUPPORT AND UNDERSTANDING**
> **OF PUBLIC IMPORTANT**

Local governments need to take greater control of their destinies. Too often they have accepted reform only when sufficiently threatened or bribed, rather than seeking it out as their key to survival. This does not refer only or primarily to highly visible changes in boundaries and jurisdictions; it also refers to a myriad of internal, but equally important, changes in operating practices and procedures — many of which have been touched on in the chapters in Part B.

---

[42] Cameron, *op. cit.,* p. 235.

Yet another barrier to reform of local government is the attitude of the general public. It is characterized by widespread apathy tempered by occasional outbursts of vigorous resistance when changes are proposed. There is a strong tendency for citizens to regard reforms as undesirable and somehow destructive of local autonomy, even though precious little autonomy is to be found in the present system.

Between now and the year 2000, the system of local government is most likely to continue as it has in the past — wracked by recurring crises, never completely collapsing but never becoming much stronger or more independent either. It will adapt as much as it needs to survive, or perhaps it would be more accurate to suggest that the provincial governments will shore it up enough to keep it functioning.

There is, however, another more positive scenario. It has been demonstrated that opportunities now exist for local governments to enhance their roles and relevance. They will continue to be vitally important because of their activities with respect to the regulation and servicing of property. They can take the initiative in developing programs and services that will be needed by the aging population of this country. They can also improve somewhat their fiscal autonomy through greater use of both the property tax and miscellaneous revenues — even if this "improvement" is being forced upon them by the restraint policies of the senior governments. They can take steps to improve their priority setting and their management of resources — both financial and personnel.

These changes are more likely to occur if there is a better understanding by the public of the nature and limitations of the present system and the potential of a reformed, strengthened local government system. It is hoped that this text has made a modest contribution toward generating that required understanding.

Bibliography

What follows is not a comprehensive bibliography but a list of a number of selected readings through which the reader may follow up the subjects dealt with in this text.

Adie, Robert and Paul Thomas, *Canadian Public Administration: Problematic Perspectives,* Scarborough, Prentice-Hall Canada Inc., 1987.

Advisory Commission on Intergovernmental Relations, *A Look to the North: Canadian Regional Experience,* Washington, D. C., 1974.

Advisory Committee on Municipal Elections to the Minister of Municipal Affairs, *Issues and Options: An Interim Report on Municipal Elections in Ontario,* 1986.

Anderson, Wayne, Chester A. Newland and Richard J. Stillman, *The Effective Local Government Manager,* Washington, International City Management Association, 1983.

Antoft, Kell (ed.), *A Guide to Local Government in Nova Scotia,* Halifax, Institute of Public Affairs, Dalhousie University, 1985.

Armstrong, C. and H. V. Nelles, *The Revenge of the Methodist Bicycle Company: Sunday Streetcars and Municipal Reform in Toronto, 1888-1897,* Toronto, Peter Martin, 1977.

Armstrong, J. L., "Retrenchment at City Hall," in *Canadian Public Administration,* Winter 1986.

Aronson, J. Richard and Eli Schwartz (eds.), *Management Policies in Local Government Finance,* Washington, International City Management Association, 1987.

Axworthy, L. and James M. Gillies, *The City: Canada's Prospects, Canada's Problems,* Toronto, Butterworths, 1973.

Banfield, Edward C., *The Unheavenly City,* Boston, Little, Brown and Company, 1968.

Barbour, George et al, *Excellence in Local Government Management,* Washington, International City Management Association, 1985.

Beck, J. M., *The Government of Nova Scotia,* Toronto, University of Toronto Press, 1957.

Becker, Christine (ed.), *Performance Evaluation: An Essential Management Tool,* Practical Management Series, Washington, International City Management Association, 1988.

Bernard, Andre, Jacques Leveille, and Guy Lord, *Profile: Calgary, The Political and Administrative Structures of the Metropolitan Region of Calgary,* Ottawa, Ministry of State for Urban Affairs (MSUA), 1975.

_____, *Profile: Edmonton, The Political and Administrative Structures of the Metropolitan Region of Edmonton*, Ottawa, MSUA, 1974.

_____, *Profile: Halifax-Dartmouth, The Political and Administrative Structures of the Metropolitan Region of Halifax-Dartmouth*, Ottawa, MSUA, 1974.

_____, *Profile: Hamilton-Wentworth, The Political and Administrative Structures of the Metropolitan Region of Hamilton-Wentworth*, Ottawa, MSUA, 1975.

_____, *Profile: Montreal, The Political and Administrative Structures of the Metropolitan Region of Montreal*, Ottawa, MSUA, 1974.

_____, *Profile: Ottawa-Hull, The Political and Administrative Structures of the Metropolitan Region of Ottawa-Hull*, Ottawa, MSUA, 1974.

_____, *Profile: Quebec, The Political and Administrative Structures of the Metropolitan Region of Quebec*, Ottawa, MSUA, 1975.

_____, *Profile: Toronto, The Political and Administrative Structures of the Metropolitan Region of Toronto*, Ottawa, MSUA, 1975.

_____, *Profile: Vancouver, The Political and Administrative Structures of the Metropolitan Region of Vancouver*, Ottawa, MSUA, 1975.

_____, *Profile: Winnipeg, The Political and Administrative Structures of the Metropolitan Region of Winnipeg*, Ottawa, MSUA, 1975.

Bettison, David G., J. Kenward and L. Taylor, *Urban Affairs in Alberta*, Edmonton, University of Alberta Press, 1975.

Bird, R. M. and N. E. Slack, *Residential Property Tax Relief in Ontario*, Toronto, Ontario Economic Council and University of Toronto Press, 1978.

_____, *Urban Public Finance in Canada*, Toronto, Butterworths, 1983.

Bish, Robert L., *Local Government in British Columbia*, Richmond, Union of British Columbia Municipalities in cooperation with the University of Victoria, 1987.

_____ and Vincent Ostrom, *Understanding Urban Government: Metropolitan Reform Reconsidered*, Washington, American Enterprise Institute for Public Policy Research, 1973.

Black, E. R., *Politics and the News: The Political Functions of the Mass Media*, Toronto, Butterworths, 1982.

Boadway, Robin W. and Harry M. Kitchen, *Canadian Tax Policy*, Toronto, Canadian Tax Foundation, 1980.

Bourne, Larry S. (ed.), *Internal Structure of the City*, Toronto, Oxford University Press, 1971.

Boyer, J. Patrick, *Lawmaking by the People, Referendums and Plebiscites in Canada*, Toronto, Butterworths, 1982.

Brittain, Horace L., *Local Government in Canada*, Toronto, Ryerson Press, 1951.

Bureau of Municipal Research, *Citizen Participation in Metro Toronto: Climate for Cooperation*, Toronto, 1975.

_____, *Reorganizing Local Government: A Brief Look at Four Provinces*, Toronto, 1972.

_____, *The Metro Politician: A Profile*, Toronto, June 1963.

_____, "The News Media and Local Government," *Civic Affairs*, Toronto, August 1976.

_____, "Cost Saving Innovations in Canadian Local Government," *Civic Affairs*, September 1979.

_____, *Providing Municipal Services: Methods, Costs and Trade-offs*, 1981.

Busson, Terry and Philip Coulter (eds.), *Policy Evaluation for Local Government*, Westport, Greenwood Press, 1988.

Cameron, David M. "Provincial responsibilities for municipal government," *Canadian Public Administration*, Summer 1980.

_____, "Urban Policy," in G. Bruce Doern and V. Seymour Wilson (eds.), *Issues in Canadian Public Policy*, Toronto, Macmillan, 1974.

Cameron, John R., *Provincial-Municipal Relations in the Maritime Provinces*, Fredericton, Maritime Union Study, 1970.

Canadian Federation of Mayors and Municipalities, *Puppets on a Shoestring*, Ottawa, April 28, 1976.

Canadian Tax Foundation, *Provincial and Municipal Finances*, Toronto, biennial.

Carver, H., *Cities in the Suburbs*, Toronto, University of Toronto Press, 1962.

_____, *Compassionate Landscape*, Toronto, University of Toronto Press, 1975.

Caufield, Jon, *The Tiny Perfect Mayor*, Toronto, James Lorimer and Co., 1974.

Chartered Institute of Public Finance and Accountancy, *Programme Budget: Concept and Application*, London, 1969.

_____, *Programme Budgeting: The Approach*, London, 1971.

Chekki, Dan and Roger T. Towes, *Organized Interest Groups and The Urban Policy Process*, Report no. 9, Winnipeg, Institute of Urban Studies, University of Winnipeg, 1985.

City Magazine Annual 1981, Toronto, James Lorimer and Company, 1981.

Clarkson, Stephen, *City Lib*, Toronto, Hakkert, 1972.

Cook, Gail C. A. and Lionel D. Feldman, "Approaches to Local Government Reform in Canada: The Case of Winnipeg," *Canadian Tax Journal*, May-June 1971.

Colton, Timothy J., *Big Daddy*, Toronto, University of Toronto Press, 1980.

Crawford, K. G., *Canadian Municipal Government*, Toronto, University of Toronto Press, 1954.

Crouch, Winston W. (ed.), *Local Government Personnel Administration*, Washington, International City Management Association, 1976.

Cullingworth, J. Barry, *Urban and Regional Planning in Canada*, New Brunswick, Transaction Books, 1987.

Cutt, James and Richard Ritter, *Public Non-Profit Budgeting: The Evolution and Application of Zero-Base Budgeting*, Toronto, Institute of Public Administration, 1984.

Dahl, R. A., *Who Governs? Democracy and Power in an American City*, New Haven, Yale University Press, 1961.

Dente, Bruno and Francesco Kjellberg (eds.), *The Dynamics of Institutional Change: Local Government Reorganization in Western Democracies*, Newbury Park, Sage Publications, Inc., 1988.

Department of Municipal Affairs and Environment, *Review of New Brunswick's Unconditional Grant to Municipalities*, Fredericton, February 1986.

Dickerson, M.O, S. Brabek and J. T. Woods (eds.), *Problems of Change in Urban Government*, Waterloo, Wilfred Laurier Press, 1980.

Doerr, Audrey, "Public Administration: Federalism and Intergovernmental Relations," in *Canadian Public Administration*, Winter 1982.

Downs, Bryan T., "The Management of Fiscal Stress by Municipal Governments in British Columbia," in Michael Fitzgerald and William Lyons (eds.), *Research in Urban Policy*, Greenwich, Jai Press, 1987.

Dupre, J. Stefan, *Intergovernmental Finance in Ontario: A Provincial-Local Perspective*, Toronto, Queen's Printer, 1968.

Economic Council of Canada, *Fourth Annual Review*, Ottawa, Queen's Printer, 1967.

d'Entremont, Harley and Patrick Robardet, "More reform in New Brunswick: rural municipalities," *Canadian Public Administration*, Fall, 1977.

Eden, Lorraine, "Provincial-Municipal Equalization in the Maritime Provinces," in *Canadian Public Administration*, Winter 1987.

Eulau, H., "The Legislator as Representative: Representative Roles," in J. Wahlke et al (eds.), *The Legislative System*, New York, John Wiley and Sons, 1962.

Federation of Canadian Municipalities, *Municipal Government in a New Canadian Federal System, Report of the Task Force on Constitutional Reform*, Ottawa, F.C.M., 1980.

_____, *Management and Planning Capabilities in Small Communities,* Ottawa, 1982.

_____, *Brief to the Royal Commission on the Economic Union and Development Prospects for Canada,* October 1983.

Feldman, Lionel D., *Ontario 1945-1973: The Municipal Dynamic,* Toronto, Ontario Economic Council, 1974.

_____, "Tribunals, Politics and the Public Interest: The Edmonton Annexation Case, A Response," in *Canadian Public Policy,* Spring 1982.

_____ (ed.), *Politics and Government of Urban Canada,* Toronto, Methuen, 1981.

_____ and Katherine Graham, *Bargaining for Cities,* Toronto, Butterworths, 1979.

Finnis, Frederick, *Property Assessment in Canada,* Toronto, Canadian Tax Foundation, 1979.

Fraser, Graham, *Fighting Back,* Toronto, Hakkert, 1972.

French, Wendell L., *The Personnel Management Process,* Boston, Houghton Mifflin Company, 1978.

Frisken, Frances, *City Policy-Making in Theory and Practice: The Case of Toronto's Downtown Plan,* Local Government Case Study No. 3, London, University of Western Ontario, 1988.

_____, "Canadian Cities and the American Example: A Prologue to Urban Policy Analysis," in *Canadian Public Administration,* Fall 1986.

Gaven, Garnet and Richard J. Long, "Capital budget decision-making processes in Canadian urban municipalities," *Canadian Public Administration,* Winter 1981.

Gertler, L. O., *Regional Planning in Canada,* Montreal, Harvest House Ltd., 1972.

_____ and R. W. Crowley, *Changing Canadian Cities: The Next 25 Years,* Toronto, McClelland and Stewart Limited, 1977.

Goldrick, Michael, "The anatomy of urban reform in Toronto," *City Magazine,* May-June 1978.

Goldsmith, Michael, *Politics, Planning and the City,* London, Hutchinson, 1980.

Goodman, J. S., *The Dynamics of Urban Government and Politics,* New York, Macmillan, 1980.

Gottdiener, M., *The Decline of Urban Politics: Political Theory and the Crisis of the Local State,* Newbury Park, Sage Publications, 1987.

Granatstein, J. L., *Marlborough Marathon,* Toronto, Hakkert and James Lewis and Samuel, 1971.

Gunlicks, Arthur B. (ed.), *Local Government Reform and Reorganization: An International Perspective,* London, Kennikat Press, 1981.

Gutstein, Donald, "The Developers' TEAM: Vancouver's 'reform' party in power," *City Magazine,* December 1974-January 1975.

_____, *Vancouver Ltd.,* Toronto, James Lorimer and Co., 1975.

Gyford, John, *Local Politics in Britain,* London, Croom Helm Ltd., 1976.

Halifax Commission on City Government, *Report on the Structure and Processes of Halifax City Government 1982,* Halifax, Institute of Public Affairs, Dalhousie University, 1982.

Hanson, Eric, *Local Government in Alberta,* Toronto, McClelland and Stewart Limited, 1956.

Hardy, Cynthia, "Fighting Cutbacks: Some Issues for Public Sector Administrators," in *Canadian Public Administration,* Winter 1985.

Hickey, Paul, *Decision Making Processes in Ontario's Local Governments,* Toronto, Ministry of Treasury, Economics and Intergovernmental Affairs, 1973.

Higgins, Donald J. H., *Urban Canada: Its Government and Politics,* Toronto, Macmillan, 1977.

_____, *Local and Urban Politics in Canada,* Toronto, Gage, 1986.

Higgins, Benjamin, *The Rise and Fall of Montreal: A Case Study of Urban Growth, Regional Economic Expansion and National Development,* Moncton, Canadian Institute for Research on Regional Development, 1986.

Hobson, Paul A. R., *The Economic Effects of the Property Tax: A Survey,* Ottawa, Economic Council of Canada, 1987.

Hodge, Gerald, *Planning Canadian Communities,* Toronto, Methuen, 1986.

Inuit Committee on National Issues, *Completing Canada: Inuit Approaches to Self-Government,* Kingston, Institute of Intergovernmental Affairs, Queen's University, 1987.

Ircha, Michael C., "The Crisis of Central-Local Government Relations: The British Experience," in *Canadian Public Administration,* Spring 1986.

Jacek, Henry J., "Regional Government and Development: Administrative Efficiency versus Local Democracy," in Donald C. MacDonald (ed.), *The Government and Politics of Ontario,* Toronto, Nelson, 1985.

Jones, George and John Stewart, *The Case for Local Government,* Winchester, Allen & Unwin Inc., 1984.

Joyce, J. G. and H. A. Hosse, *Civic Parties in Canada,* Ottawa, Canadian Federation of Mayors and Municipalities, 1970.

Kaplan, Harold, *The Regional City,* Toronto, Canadian Broadcasting Corporation, 1965.

_____, *Urban Political Systems: A Functional Analysis of Metro Toronto,* New York, Columbia University Press, 1967.

_____, *Reform, Planning and City Politics: Montreal, Winnipeg, Toronto*, Toronto, University of Toronto Press, 1982.

Kay, B.J., "Voting Patterns in a Non-partisan Legislature: A Study of Toronto City Council," *Canadian Journal of Political Science*, June 1971.

_____, "Urban Decision-Making and the Legislative Environment: Toronto City Council Re-examined," Canadian Journal of Political Science, September 1982.

Kellar, Elizabeth K. (ed.), *Managing with Less: A Book of Readings*, Washington, International City Management Association, 1979.

Kernaghan, W. D. K. (ed.), *Public Administration in Canada: Selected Readings*, Toronto, Methuen, 1982.

_____ and David Siegel, *Public Administration in Canada*, Toronto, Methuen, 1987.

Kitchen, Harry M., *Local Government Finance in Canada*, Toronto, Canadian Tax Foundation, 1985.

_____, *Local Government Enterprise in Canada*, Ottawa, Economic Council of Canada, 1986.

_____, *The Role for Local Governments in Economic Development*, Toronto, Ontario Economic Council, 1986.

_____ and Melville McMillan, "Local Government and Canadian Federalism," in Richard Simeon, Research Coordinator, *Intergovernmental Relations*, Vol. 63, Royal Commission on the Economic Union and Development Prospects for Canada, Toronto, University of Toronto Press, 1985.

Knight, Henry C., *The Zero-Budgeting Process: A Practical Guide to Evaluation, Implementation and Use*, Hamilton, Society of Management Accountants, 1979.

Kraemer, Kenneth L., *Policy Analysis in Local Government*, Washington, International City Management Association, 1973.

Krause, Robert and Trevor Price, "The Impact of Financial Restraint on the Provision of Municipal Services in Canada," in *Planning and Administration*, 23, 1980, pp. 252–268.

Krueger, Ralph R., "The Provincial-Municipal Revolution in New Brunswick," *Canadian Public Administration*, Spring 1970.

L'Heureux, Jacques, "Municipalities and the Division of Power," in Richard Simeon, Research Coordinator, *Intergovernmental Relations*, Vol. 63, Royal Commission on the Economic Union and Development Prospects for Canada, Toronto, University of Toronto Press, 1985.

Landon, Fred, *Western Ontario and the American Frontier*, Toronto, McClelland and Stewart Limited, 1967.

Lapointe, Jean-Louis, "La Reforme de la Fiscalité Municipale au Quebec," *Canadian Public Administration,* Summer 1980.

Leach, Richard, *Whatever Happened to Urban Policy? A Comparative Study of Urban Policy in Australia, Canada and the United States,* Research Monograph no. 40, Canberra, Australian National University, 1985.

Lennox and Addington County Study. *Reports* (C. R. Tindal, Commissioner), Toronto, Ministry of Treasury, Economics and Intergovernmental Affairs, 1977.

Leo, Christopher, *The Politics of Urban Development: Canadian Urban Expressway Disputes,* Monographs on Canadian Urban Government, no. 3, Toronto, Institute of Public Administration, 1977.

_____, *Strong Government, Weak Government: Classifying Municipal Structural Change,* Research and Working Paper no. 23, Winnipeg, Institute of Urban Studies, University of Winnipeg, 1986.

Leonard, Jean-Francois and Jacques Leveillee, *Montreal After Drapeau,* Montreal, Black Rose Books, 1987.

Lightbody, James, "With Whom the Tolls Dwell: The Great Edmonton Telephone Dispute, 1984-1987," in *Canadian Public Administration,* Spring 1989.

_____, "The Rise of Party Politics in Canadian Local Elections," *Journal of Canadian Studies,* February 1971.

_____, "The Reform of a Metropolitan Government: The Case of Winnipeg," in *Canadian Public Policy,* Autumn 1978.

Lindblom, Charles E., *The Intelligence of Democracy,* New York, The Free Press, 1965.

_____, *The Policy Making Process,* Englewood Cliffs, Prentice-Hall Inc., 1980.

Lithwick, N. H., *Urban Canada, Problems and Prospects,* Ottawa, Central Mortgage and Housing Corporation, 1970.

_____, and Gilles Paquet (eds.) *Urban Studies: A Canadian Perspective,* Toronto, Methuen, 1968.

Lorimer, James, *A Citizen's Guide to City Politics,* Toronto, James Lewis and Samuel, 1972.

_____, *The Real World of City Politics,* Toronto, James Lewis and Samuel, 1970.

_____, *The Developers,* Toronto, James Lewis and Samuel, 1978.

_____ and Carolyn MacGregor (eds.), *After the Developers,* Toronto, James Lorimer and Company, 1981.

_____, and E. Ross (eds.), *The City Book: The Planning and Politics of Canada's Cities,* Toronto, James Lorimer and Company, 1976.

Loughlin, Martin, David Gelfand et al, *Half a Century of Municipal Decline, 1935-1985,* London, George Allen & Unwin, 1986.

MacDonald, Donald C. (ed.), *The Government and Politics of Ontario,* Toronto, Nelson, 1985.

Makuch, Stanley M., *Canadian Municipal and Planning Law,* Toronto, Carswell, 1983.

Magnusson, Warren, "The New Neighbourhood Democracy: Anglo-American Experience in Historical Perspective", in L. J. Sharpe (ed.), *Decentralist Trends in Western Democracies,* London, Sage Publications, 1979.

_____, "Community Organization and Local Self Government" in Lionel D. Feldman (ed.), *Politics and Government of Urban Canada: Selected Readings,* Toronto, Methuen, 1981.

_____, "Metropolitan Reform in the Capitalist City," in *Canadian Journal of Political Science,* September 1981, pp. 557–585.

_____, "The Local State in Canada: Theoretical Perspectives," *Canadian Public Administration,* Winter 1985, pp. 575–599.

_____ and Andrew Sancton (eds.), *City Politics in Canada,* Toronto, University of Toronto Press, 1983.

_____ and William K. Carroll, Charles Doyle, Monika Langer and R. B. J. Walker (eds.) *The New Reality: The Politics of Restraint in British Columbia,* Vancouver, NewStar Books, 1984.

Manitoba, Government of, *Proposals for Urban Reorganization in the Greater Winnipeg Area* (White Paper), Winnipeg, Queen's Printer, 1970.

Manitoba Royal Commission on Local Government Organization and Finance, Winnipeg, Queen's Printer, 1964.

Marshall, A. H., *Financial Management in Local Government,* London, George Allen and Unwin Ltd., 1974.

Masson, Jack, *Alberta's Local Governments and Their Politics,* Edmonton, University of Alberta Press, 1985.

_____, "Decision-Making Patterns and Floating Coalitions in an Urban City Council," *Canadian Journal of Political Science,* March 1975.

_____ and James D. Anderson (eds.), *Emerging Party Politics in Canada,* Toronto, McClelland and Stewart Limited, 1972.

Matzer, John Jr., *Creative Personnel Practices: New Ideas for Local Government,* Washington, International City Management Association, 1984.

McAllister, Anne B., *An Approach to Manpower Planning and Management Development in Canadian Municipal Government,* Toronto, Institute of Public Administration, 1979.

McDavid, James, "Part-time Firefighters in Canadian Municipalities: Cost and Effectiveness Comparisons," in *Canadian Public Administration*, Fall 1986.

_____ and Gregory K. Schlick, "Privatization Versus Union-Management Cooperation: The Effects of Competition on Service Efficiency in Municipalities," in *Canadian Public Administration*, Fall 1987, pp. 472–488.

McEvoy, John M., *The Ontario Township*, University of Toronto, Political Studies, 1st series no. 1, 1889.

McIver, J. M., "Survey of the City Manager Plan in Canada," *Canadian Public Administration*, Fall, 1960.

Meng, Ronald and W. Irwin Gillespie, "The Regressivity of Property Taxes in Canada: Another Look," in *Canadian Tax Journal*, November-December 1986, pp. 1417–1430.

Merriman, David, *The Control of Municipal Budgets: Toward the Effective Design of Tax and Expenditure Limitations*, Westport, Greenwood Press, 1987.

Miles, Simon R.(ed.), *Metropolitan Problems*, Toronto, Methuen, 1970.

Milner, Henry, "The Montreal Citizens' Movement: Then and Now," Hanover, *Quebec Studies*, No. 6, 1988.

_____, *The Long Road to Reform: Restructuring Public Education in Quebec*, Kingston and Montreal, McGill-Queen's University Press, 1986.

Minister of Urban Affairs, *Strengthening Local Government in Winnipeg: Proposals for Changes to the City of Winnipeg Act*, Discussion Paper, Winnipeg, February 27, 1987.

Ministry of Municipal Affairs, *Personnel Operations for Smaller Ontario Municipalities*, Toronto, 1984.

_____, Report of the Advisory Committee on County Government, *Patterns for the Future*, Toronto, 1987.

_____, Report of the Consultative Committee to the Minister of Municipal Affairs, *County Government in Ontario*, Toronto, January 1989.

_____, *Avoiding Wrongful Dismissal: A Guide to Employer and Employee Rights*, Toronto, April 1988.

_____, *Employment Equity*, Toronto, October 1988.

Ministry of Municipal Affairs and Housing, *Performance Measurement for Municipalities*, Toronto, 1981.

Ministry of Treasury, Economics and Intergovernmental Affairs, *Managers for Local Government* (three reports, five discussion papers), Toronto, 1976–1977.

Morgan, David R., *Managing Urban America*, Belmont, Wadsworth Publishing Company Inc., 1979.

Municipal Submission to the first National Tri-Level Conference, *Policies, Programs, and Finance*, Ottawa, 1972.

Municipality of Metropolitan Toronto, *The Crumbling Financial Partnership*, Toronto, March 1989.

Munro, W. B., *American Influences on Canadian Government*, Toronto, Macmillan, 1929.

Nader, George A., *Cities of Canada Volume 1, Theoretical, Historical and Planning Perspectives*, Toronto, Macmillan, 1975.

Naisbitt, John, *Megatrends*, New York, Warner Books, 1982.

Niagara Region Study Review Commission, 1975-1977. Report (W. L. Archer, Commissioner), Toronto, Ministry of Treasury, Economics and Intergovernmental Affairs, March, 1977.

Niagara Region Review Commission. Report and Recommendations (Harry Kitchen, Commissioner), Toronto, Ministry of Municipal Affairs, 1989.

Nininger, J. R., V. N. MacDonald and G. Y. McDiarmid, *Developments in the Management of Local Government* (Local Government Management Project), Toronto, Ministry of Treasury, Economics and Intergovernmental Affairs, 1975.

Nowlan, David and Nadine Nowlan, *The Bad Trip*, Toronto, New Press/House of Anansi, 1970.

O'Brien, Allan, "Local Government Priorities for the Eighties," in *Canadian Public Administration*, Spring 1976.

_____, "The Ministry of State for Urban Affairs: A Municipal Perspective," in *The Canadian Journal of Regional Science*, Halifax, Spring 1982.

_____, "Holding Pattern: A Look at the Provincial-Municipal Relationship," in Donald C. MacDonald (ed.), *Government and Politics of Ontario*, Toronto, Nelson, 1985.

Ontario Economic Council, *Government Reform in Ontario*, Toronto, 1969.

_____, *Municipal Reform: A Proposal for the Future*, Toronto, 1971.

_____, *Municipal Fiscal Reform in Ontario: Property Taxes and Provincial Grants* (by John Bossons, Michael Denny and Enid Slack), Toronto, 1981.

Ontario Municipal Management Institute, *Preparing a Training and Development Policy: A Guide for Municipalities*, Oshawa, 1982.

Ottawa-Carleton Review Commission. Report (H. B. Mayo, Commissioner), Toronto, Ministry of Treasury, Economics and Intergovernmental Affairs, 1976.

Ottawa-Carleton Regional Review, (David Bartlett, Chairman), *Phase I Report: Accountability and Representation* and *Phase II Report: Functions and Finances*, Toronto, Ministry of Municipal Affairs, 1989.

Ouellet, Lionel, "La Privatisation: Un Instrument de Management Public?" in *Canadian Public Administration,* Winter 1987, pp. 566–584.

Park, L. Suzanne and Marilyn Melville, *Human Resource Planning and Training Needs Analysis,* Oshawa, Ontario Municipal Management Institute, 1983.

Patten, Thomas H., *Manpower Planning and the Development of Human Resources,* New York, John Wiley and Sons, 1982.

Persky, S., *The House That Jack Built: Mayor Jack Volrich and Vancouver City Politics,* Vancouver, Newstar Books, 1980.

Peters, Evelyn J., *Aboriginal Self-Government Arrangements in Canada,* Background Paper 15, Kingston, Institute of Intergovernmental Affairs, Queen's University, 1987.

Peters, Thomas J. and Robert H. Waterman Jr., *In Search of Excellence,* New York, Warner Books, 1982.

_____ and Nancy Austin, *A Passion for Excellence,* New York, Random House, 1985.

Peterson, Paul E., *City Limits,* Chicago, University of Chicago Press, 1981.

Plunkett, T. J., *Urban Canada and its Government,* Toronto, Macmillan, 1968.

_____, *The Financial Structure and the Decision Making Process of Canadian Municipal Government,* Ottawa, Central Mortgage and Housing Corporation, 1972.

_____, "Municipal Collective Bargaining," in *Collective Bargaining in the Public Service,* Toronto, Institute of Public Administration, 1973.

_____ and G. M. Betts, *The Management of Canadian Urban Government,* Kingston, Queen's University, 1978.

_____ and Meyer Brownstone, *Metropolitan Winnipeg: Politics and Reform of Local Government,* Berkeley, University of California Press, 1983.

_____ and Katherine Graham, "Whither Municipal Government," *Canadian Public Administration,* Winter 1982.

_____ and James Lightbody, "Tribunals, Politics and the Public Interest: The Edmonton Annexation Case," in *Canadian Public Policy,* Spring 1982.

_____ and W. Hooson, "Municipal Structure and Services: Graham Commission," *Canadian Public Policy,* Summer 1975.

Poole, Robert W. Jr., *Cutting Back City Hall,* New York, University Books, 1980.

Powell, Alan (ed.), *The City: Attacking Modern Myths,* Toronto, McClelland and Stewart Limited, 1972.

Price, Trevor (ed.), *Regional Government in Ontario,* Windsor, University of Windsor Press, 1971.

Provincial-Municipal Council, Inc., Brief to the Policy and Priorities Committee of the Government of New Brunswick, *Re The Unconditional Grant to Municipalities and Related Matters,* Fredericton, October 11, 1988.

Rae, J.E., *Parties and Power: An Analysis of Winnipeg City Council, 1919-1975,* Appendix IV of the Report of the Manitoba Committee of Review of the City of Winnipeg Act, 1976.

Rapp, Brian W. and Frank M. Patitucci, *Managing Local Government for Improved Performance,* Boulder, Westview Press, 1977.

Regional District Survey Committee, *Summary Report of the Regional District Survey Committee,* Victoria, Queen's Printer, 1986.

Report by the Task Force on Representation and Accountability in Metropolitan Toronto, *Analysis and Options for the Government of Metropolitan Toronto,* November 1986.

Report of the Municipal Study Commission (Parizeau Report), Montreal, Union of Quebec Municipalities, December 1986.

Report of the Special Representative (Drury Report), *Constitutional Development in the Northwest Territories,* Ottawa, 1980.

Report prepared by the British Columbia Ministry of Municipal Affairs, Recreation and Culture and the Union of B.C. Municipalities, *Financing Local Government,* September 1988.

Richardson, Boyce, *The Future of Canadian Cities,* Toronto, New Press, 1972.

Ridler, Neil B., "PPB: Its Relevance to Financially Constrained Municipalities," *Canadian Public Administration,* Summer, 1976.

_____, "Fiscal Constraints and the Growth of User Fees Among Canadian Municipalities," in *Canadian Public Administration,* Fall 1984.

Robinson, A. J., *Economic Evaluation of Municipal Expenditures: PPB,* Canadian Tax Papers, no. 52, Toronto, Canadian Tax Foundation, 1971.

Robinson, Ivan, "Managing Retrenchment in a Public Service Organization," in *Canadian Public Administration,* Winter 1985, pp. 513–530.

Rogers, Ian MacF., *Canadian Law of Planning and Zoning,* Toronto, Carswell Co. Ltd., 1973.

Rosemblom, Richard S. and John R. Russell, *New Tools for Urban Management,* Boston, Harvard University Press, 1971.

Roussopoulos, Dimitri (ed.), *The City and Radical Social Change,* Montreal, Black Rose Books Ltd., 1982.

Rowat, Donald P. *The Canadian Municipal System,* Toronto, McClelland and Stewart Limited, 1969.

_____, *Your Local Government,* Toronto, Macmillan, 1975.

_____, *International Handbook on Local Government Reorganization,* Westport, Greenwood Press, 1980.

Royal Commission on Education, Public Services, and Provincial-Municipal Relations in Nova Scotia. Report (John Graham, Commissioner), Halifax, Queen's Printer, 1974.

Royal Commission on Metropolitan Toronto. Report (H. Carl Goldenberg, Commissioner), Toronto, Queen's Printer, 1965.

Royal Commission on Metropolitan Toronto. Report (John Robarts, Commissioner), Toronto, Queen's Printer, June 1977.

Royal Commission on Municipal Government in Newfoundland and Labrador. Report (H. Whalen, Commissioner), St. John's, Queen's Printer, 1974.

Rutherford, Paul (ed.), *Saving the Canadian City: The First Phase 1880-1920,* Toronto, University of Toronto Press, 1974.

Rutter, Laurence, *The Essential Community: Local Government in the Year 2000,* Washington, International City Management Association, 1980.

Sancton, Andrew, "Montreal's Metropolitan Government," Hanover, *Quebec Studies,* No. 6, 1988.

Scanlon, J., "Board of Control: Its Merits and Defects," *Canadian Public Administration,* Fall 1960.

Sewell, John, *Up Against City Hall,* Toronto, James Lewis and Samuel, 1972.

Sharpe, L. J. (ed.), *The Local Fiscal Crisis in Western Europe, Myths and Realities,* London, Sage Publications, 1981.

_____, "Failure of Local Government Modernization in Britain," *Canadian Public Administration,* Spring 1981.

Shortt, Adam, *Municipal Government in Ontario, An Historical Sketch,* Toronto, University of Toronto Studies, History and Economics, vol. II, no. 2, undated.

_____ and Arthur G. Doughty (eds.), *Canada and its Provinces: A History of the Canadian People and Their Institutions,* Toronto, Glasgow, Brook and Company, 1914.

Siegel, David, "Provincial-municipal relations in Canada: An Overview," *Canadian Public Administration,* Summer 1980.

Siegel, Gilbert B.(ed.), *Human Resource Management in Public Organizations,* Los Angeles, University Publications, 1972.

Singer, Edwin J. and John Ramsden, *Human Resources: Obtaining Results from People at Work,* London, McGraw Hill (U.K.) Ltd., 1972.

Smith, Patrick J., "Regional Governance in British Columbia," in *Planning and Administration,* 13, 1986, pp. 7–20.

_____, "Open Government: Recent Policy Options and Applications in Canada," in *Planning and Administration*, 11, 1984, pp. 54–62.

Smither, Michael, *Municipal Conflict of Interest*, St. Thomas, Municipal World Inc., 1983.

Spelt, Jacob, *Urban Development in South-Central Ontario*, Toronto, McClelland and Stewart Limited, 1972.

Stein, David Lewis, *Toronto for Sale: The Destruction of a City*, Toronto, New Press, 1972.

Stelter, Gilbert A. and Alan F. Artibise (eds.), *The Canadian City: Essays in Urban History*, Toronto, McClelland and Stewart Limited, 1977.

_____, *Power and Place: Canadian Urban Development in the North American City*, Vancouver, University of British Columbia Press, 1986.

Stevens, T. J., *The Business of Government*, Toronto, McGraw-Hill Ryerson, 1978.

Stewart, J. D., *The Responsive Local Authority*, London, Charles Knight and Co. Ltd., 1974.

Stone, Clarence N. and Heywood T. Sanders (eds.), *The Politics of Urban Development*, Lawrence, University Press of Kansas, 1987.

Task Force on Housing and Urban Development. Report. Ottawa, Queen's Printer, 1969.

Task Force on Nonincorporated Areas in New Brunswick. Report, Fredericton, Queen's Printer, 1976.

Tennant, Paul, "Vancouver Civic Politics, 1929-1980," in *B. C. Studies*, no. 46, 1980, pp. 3–27.

_____ and David Zirnhelt, "Metropolitan Government in Vancouver: the strategy of gentle imposition," *Canadian Public Administration*, Spring 1973.

Tindal, C. R. "Regional Development in Ontario," *Canadian Public Administration*, Spring 1973.

_____, *Structural Changes in Local Government: Government for Urban Regions*, Monographs on Canadian Urban Government, no. 2, Toronto, Institute of Public Administration of Canada, 1977.

_____, *Municipal Councillor's Course*, Kingston, CENTRE FOR GOVERNMENT EDUCATION AND TRAINING, St. Lawrence College, 1989.

_____ and Patrick Doyle, "Professional Development: Who Pays," in *Training and Development Journal*, Alexandria, May 1986.

Tri-Level Task Force on Public Finance. Report (3 volumes), Toronto, Queen's Printer, 1976.

Walisser, Brian, *Understanding Regional District Planning: A Primer*, Victoria, Ministry of Municipal Affairs, June 1987.

Weaver, John C., *Shaping the Canadian City: Essays on Urban Politics and Policy, 1890-1920,* Monographs on Canadian Urban Government, no. 1, Toronto, Institute of Public Administration of Canada, 1977.

Weller, G. R., "Local Government in the Canadian provincial north," *Canadian Public Administration,* Spring 1981.

Whalen, H. J., *The Development of Local Government in New Brunswick,* Fredericton, 1963.

Wichern, Phil H., *Evaluating Winnipeg's Unicity: Citizen Participation and Resident Advisory Groups,* Research and Working Paper no. 11, Winnipeg, Institute of Urban Studies, University of Winnipeg, 1984.

_____, *Evaluating Winnipeg's Unicity: The City of Winnipeg Act Review Committee, 1984-1986,* Research and Working Paper no. 26, Winnipeg, Institute of Urban Studies, University of Winnipeg, 1986.

Yates, Douglas, *The Ungovernable City,* Cambridge, M.I.T. Press, 1977.

Index

STUDENT REPLY CARD

In order to improve future editions, we are seeking your comments on *Local Government in Canada,* Third Edition, by Tindal and Tindal.

After you have read this text, please answer the following questions and return this form via Business Reply Mail. *Thanks in advance for your feedback!*

1. Name of your college or university: _____

2. Major program of study: _____

3. Your instructor for this course: _____

4. Are there any sections of this text which were not assigned as course reading? If so, please specify those chapters or portions:

FOLD HERE

CUT HERE

5. How would you rate the overall accessibility of the content? Please feel free to comment on reading level, writing style, terminology, layout and design features, and such learning aids as chapter objectives, summaries, and appendices.

6. What did you like *best* about this book?

7. What did you like *least?*

If you would like to say more, we'd love to hear from you. Please write to us at the address shown on the reverse of this card.

- CUT HERE -

- FOLD HERE -

**BUSINESS
REPLY MAIL**

No Postage Stamp
Necessary If Mailed
in Canada

Postage will be paid by

Attn: Sponsoring Editor, Political Science

The College Division
McGraw-Hill Ryerson Limited
330 Progress Avenue
Scarborough, Ontario
M1P 9Z9

TAPE SHUT